THE ROAD TO SELF-RULE

THE ROAD TO SELF-RULE

*

A Study in Colonial Evolution

by

W. M. MACMILLAN

FABER AND FABER

24 Russell Square

London

First published in mcmlix
by Faber and Faber Limited
24 Russell Square London W.C.1
Second inpression mcmlx
Printed in Great Britain by
Latimer Trend & Co Ltd Plymouth

CONTENTS

*

	Postscript	*page* 7
	Introductory	9
1.	The First Colonial Frontier	28
2.	Empire as a Moral Responsibility	44
3.	The Road to Colonial Self-Government	62
4.	The West Indies	79
5.	The Rule of Law at the Cape of Good Hope	95
6.	The Great South African Schism	119
7.	New Things into Africa	140
8.	'Take up the White Man's burden'	166
9.	Between Two Worlds	186
10.	The Post-War Decade	210
11.	New Patterns in East and Central Africa	233
12.	The Black Man's Burden	256
	Bibliography	276
	Index	285

MAPS

Early American Expansion	*page* 41
Africa, with inset showing the 'Cape Fish' River frontier	104–5

POSTSCRIPT

*

To the debt of gratitude owing to many former guides and hosts I have to add that due for help received on a trip made, after the MS. of this book had gone to the publishers, through much of South, Central and East Africa. My latest mentors will appreciate that at this late stage I could hope only to check what I had already written, not to enlarge on the significance of much spectacular new development they helped me to see and to assess. They can be assured, however, that the text as it now appears has gained in accuracy and in clarity from emendations made in the light of this fresh experience.

I am also expressly indebted for helpful criticism to Mr. E. T. Williams, Warden of Rhodes House, and to Dr. A. F. Madden of Nuffield College, both of whom, of their goodness, made time to 'vet' my crabbed MS. Another busy friend, Dr. T. P. Soper of Queen Elizabeth house, very kindly compiled the Bibliography. In the actual work of writing (and by mischance this was much protracted) I had my wife's expert help: and the long labour never quite exhausted the patience of a long-suffering family.

W.M.M.

St. Andrews, Fife
July 1959

Introductory

OF COLONIES, THEIR FRONTIERS AND PEOPLES

*

This study in colonial evolution directs attention to the neglected history of the less mature peoples of the British Empire: the removal of the weakness manifestly still hindering these from standing firmly alone in the modern world calls for a clear appreciation of the roots from which they spring, of how their old ways of life were affected by coming under outside authority, and of the road they have travelled so far. Before the First World War, and for a good many years after it, these peoples and their ultimate place even in any scheme of Empire were almost entirely left aside; thus South Africans, who had reasons for pondering the future of their 'natives', took their cue from North America, were content to believe that their own history marked the 'triumph of civilization over savagery', and left the future to look after itself. Colonial history (so far as the universities touched it at all) had for its major theme that other evolutionary process which carried the European overseas plantations through their early formative struggles, by way of responsible government to Dominion status and, at last, to sovereign independence. The Empire histories of those days faltered at one point—the motif of self-government running through this story was never quite harmonized with the idea of imperial unity which seemed to be justified or even required by the expansion of beneficent British rule in India. In the end the pursuit of unity gave way to the Commonwealth ideal; but when the status debate was dying away the rights or wrongs of the dependent peoples of the Empire became a major issue, and a focus even of world politics. Just because the Dominions had so long cbeen the entre of colonial history it made for confusion to call this new issue the 'colonial question'; the blanket term was overworked. Colonial rule, in its modern form, originated in North America; Americans accordingly, living on in their eighteenth century, were foremost among those who ascribed all the discontents of colonially-ruled peoples to their being held down by repression in the same state of dependence Americans threw off so long ago. Yet when the stronger, predominantly white colonies were moving fast towards self-government a new, authoritarian but not unsuccessful Crown Colony system had come into being to meet the needs of other communities which were manifestly then incapable of conducting all their own affairs. Confusingly, the stronger and the weaker of these, certain new 'protectorates', scattered forts and trading posts managed by the Colonial Office—all alike were still termed *colonies*, their institutions and their varied 'problems' *colonial.*

The need for a book to bring the essentials of the 'colonial question' into better perspective was borne in upon me when, after a spell away from any university, in 1947 I returned to direct what were now specifically known as 'colonial studies'—for seven years at St. Andrews, and in one final year at the new University College of the West Indies. To meet the new situation, colonial administration—governmental practice, that is to say, in the non-self-governing colonies—had become a special study. But undergraduates, and others, I found, could make little of even the straight history till the position of the dependent peoples was clarified and their story disentangled from that of the Dominions by which it had so long been overlaid. In the lecture room, and when it came to writing it down, it seemed expedient to make use of some acquired personal experience of life in the dependencies; I had found opportunity to visit, usually more than once, all the British African colonies except Somaliland, besides Belgian and Portuguese territory, also the principal West Indian islands; between the wars, and till after 1950, about half my time was spent overseas. Having thus had occasion to confer closely with a great many of the people with intimate experience of colonial affairs, both in the field and at the British end, I have perhaps written of some events from the angle of one who lived through them. Of its very nature, the subject calls in fact for individual treatment. Any study in evolution must be basically historical, and I had never been led to embark upon it had I not served a severe historical apprenticeship working closely for several years on a mass of original evidence bearing on the early clash between white and black in southern Africa. But the scenes of that conflict were at my door and it was natural to go and examine these and, with them, the social conditions for which the earlier conflict was partly responsible. I then came to see that the colonial field of study is a border-land no one of the social sciences can claim for its own. It is partly that the historical records of young societies are inevitably incomplete: their evidence needs to be checked and supplemented by the technique of observation which has become the special instrument of sociology. The conditions ruling in African areas made me sharply aware, too, that economics and physical geography may operate in loosely-knit societies with a naked force which is checked by the well-established institutions of stronger communities—such crude influences played a decisive part in the early struggles of the makers even of America and the Dominions.

For such reasons I have confined this study—except for a preliminary glance at America, which set a bad example—to the affairs of those peoples of African stock of whose lands I have some first-hand experience. These are, after all, far the largest group in the British world and it is improbable, I think, that anything from elsewhere can seriously affect the main outlines. India and other Eastern countries have at any rate always had special status; famous ancient cities remained the centres of cultures which the cosmic religions made not so much national as international in character. In Europe the East was immemorially regarded at once with fear and with respect; a long line of conquerors, from Xerxes to Tamerlane, made 'oriental despotism' a byword. But the East was also the acknowledged cradle of civilization. The prime object of the geographical discoveries which opened the Colonial Age was to develop a traditional trade by opening a sea passage to India. The effort succeeded; yet a mere handful of Europeans sufficed to man the trading posts, without radically altering the channels in which the daily life of the unchanging East continued to flow. Here and there new Western rulers displaced orientals and established empires of their own; but even this made little fundamental change in the pattern of society. The Portuguese indeed, the pioneers of all this maritime activity, were themselves exhausted by their effort.

The points now at issue in the colonial world were first posed only when European seamen burst in upon the hitherto unknown lands and peoples of America and Africa, where there were no older foundations to build on. In those days the strong everywhere ruled the weak without questions asked. Even when our grandfathers had learnt to respect the rights of man, they still confidently assumed that the uncivilized must, in good time, accept civilized standards as they themselves interpreted these; yet, from their time, a battle came to turn more and more, and at last almost exclusively, on the dealings of 'advanced' with 'backward' peoples—those the earlier generation simply but too complacently classified as 'civilized' and 'uncivilized' respectively. The fifteenth-century seamen who first faced the hazards of the open Atlantic were even disappointed at the outcome; the revelation of the true dimensions of Africa left the promoters of the voyages positively dismayed that this vast, profitless mass so much obstructed their quest after the riches of the East. The almost incredulous astonishment caused by the discovery of America made way only gradually for some sense of what would now be called its great 'possibilities'.

The Spanish were first in the American field and their success powerfully influenced others to follow. For the luck held which gave them this prize at their first maritime venture and they found there 'wealth', in what was then universally agreed to be its ultimate form, some gold, and almost unlimited silver. Faced by the 'inflation' that resulted from this sudden expansion of the money supply, the Spanish showed, in the words of Professor R. H. Tawney, 'an incapacity for economic affairs which was almost inspired'! But English historians have made the mistake of writing of the Spanish Empire as if, for this reason, it was, like Mr. Boffin's Rome, never anything but 'declining and falling'. Having no precedent to guide them in their dealings with their strange new world, the Spanish took the short way of treating its lands and peoples as an extension of metropolitan Spain—there were never Spanish *colonies*. In about half a century they had dug themselves in on the 'Spanish Main', the continental mainland, the best of it highland country well out of reach of English and other rivals who spent so much time contending for a holding in the tropical West Indies, or waiting to pounce on the treasure fleets. This great domain at once added two major crops, maize and potatoes, to the world's food supplies, besides at least cocoa and vanilla; it was incidentally the source from which tobacco was introduced, and Peruvian bark, or quinine, an indispensable aid to enterprise in the more unmitigated tropics; the rest of the world can better appreciate the quality of the typical Spanish sphere—the Andean highlands of Ecuador or Colombia, the uplands also of Costa Rica or Guatemala—now that all have heard of and many know the climatic attractions of the far less naturally rich Kenya African Highlands. It was the weakness of the Spanish economy that the wealth more readily accruing from the exploitation of minerals made them neglect agricultural development. But even this was possible only because the native Indians not only worked, even perforce, on the mines, but helped to maintain the food supply: the grant of quasi-feudal *encomienda* put much productive land under men who were political superiors rather than exploiting landlords; even the older Indian economy remained here and there in some sort of being. The social results may be dubious. At Roman law Indians were *personae* and legal discrimination was avoided; yet the universally used terms for class gradations are, significantly, of Spanish origin—creole, mestizo, mulatto, quadroon; the state of debt-slavery, too, or *peonage*, near-serfdom, is an almost peculiarly Spanish-American phenomenon. The evidence suggests, at best, a strong caste-system.

The weaknesses of the Spanish system have been emphasized to the extent of blinding many in our day to the positive side of an achievement which stands at any rate as unique. Sixteenth- or seventeenth-century contemporaries made no such mistake and sought, rather, to emulate their predecessors. Even greater ultimate success was achieved by the English in America; but precisely because it was won in such a completely different way the outcome for the dependent peoples they encountered was fully worse. The predominance of Spain in the early American days left their rivals no alternative but to win their bread by the sweat of their own brows, as real *colonists*. Sir Humphrey Gilbert and Sir Walter Raleigh were preaching and even seeking to practise the virtues of colonization in Elizabethan days; and when at last Virginia began to be settled, after the long Spanish war, its site was pitched as near as anyone dared venture to the sphere of Spanish influence. Corn indeed grew there readily once the colonists themselves had cleared the land and planted it; but there was none of the gold and silver they wanted to stimulate their economy; tobacco was a useful but much less remunerative substitute. It may be that the piecemeal conquest of the wilderness now demanded was a task more suited to the Anglo-Saxon than to the Spanish genius; earlier, about 1539, de Soto, one of the foremost of Spanish adventurers, wandered for some four years in the Mississippi valley—only to retire at last, beaten by the intractability of land that was later to become no mean part of the United States; some of his contemporaries philosophically drew the conclusion that Providence had set limits to the New Spain. Presently the supply of English colonists dried up; the new Poor Law eased the pressure of 'sturdy beggars', and the newer 'mercantilist' economics taught the desirability of conserving population at home. At last religious quarrels supervened to provide a nucleus of the best possible colonists, men and women resolved to make their homes and enjoy freedom in new lands; hence New England.

About the same time the hope of directly emulating Spain revived for a moment: Raleigh's last expedition took him to Guiana, the Spanish Main indeed, convinced that the Orinoco hid a gold-mine—el Dorado. When this failed, interest turned (possibly with Bacon's Essay, *Of Plantations*, 1625, for guidance) to the West Indies; St. Kitts was 'settled' in 1624, Barbados in 1626, Antigua, Montserrat and Nevis before 1632. By 1640 Barbados, originally uninhabited, had reached a peak of prosperity as a colony of as many (it was claimed) as 18,000 tobacco-growing small farmers. That very year sugar-cane was introduced by a Dutch agent from Brazil. The gains might be greater, but capital costs, and the risks of this fickle crop, quickly put the small farmer out of action. The work of producing sugar was also both greedy and wasteful of labour and the planters were soon looking for more workers. This brought Africa at last into the picture as the source of slave-labour; by 1664 Charles II's African Company had come into possession of Cape Coast Castle and were making it the main British centre of the slave-trade. With slave-labour as its long unchallenged basis the sugar industry grew to great but always narrowly based prosperity; Professor Richard Pares in his account of the Pinney family describes the atmosphere of Nevis when Azariah Pinney began there in the 1680s as still like that of 'an expiring gold-rush'. But by this time very many of the original small farmers had moved away to reinforce the temperate colonies of North America. Here success always depended on the colonists' own work getting them sufficiently established to pave the way for others. We know that one party vanished from Virginia leaving no trace; in 1610 a first 'starving time' in that colony reduced the 500 souls it counted in the summer of 1609 to a bare 60: in the more inclement New England only some 50 of the 100 who sailed in the *Mayflower* survived the first winter. It has significance of another kind that in 1622 Indian bands fell on the Virginian outposts and massacred more than 300 colonists; the resulting confusion brought another famine and by 1624 the total white population was still no more than 1,100. By 1634 they were 5,000; survival was ensured and the total had grown by 1666 to around 40,000. It is the measure of the weight of this modest total that New Zealand became self-governing with a population of only 32,000; and a bare 30,000 whites could clearly make their presence strongly felt in modern Kenya. All in all, by their own effort, in spite of neglect tempered by only a little 'interference' from home, the North American colonies throve marvellously, or at any rate, like Topsy they just 'grow'd'.

The question we have to ask is how the indigenous peoples fared; the Indians, having some agriculture, were no mere nomads: the 3 million square miles of the United States may well have supported, originally, 3 or 4 or even 5 millions of them. The standard histories are unhelpful, telling only of the piecemeal occupation of what had been Indian land, and of occasional wars; these last indicate fierce and prolonged resistance. From first to last (so very unlike the histories of African colonies), the books have never a word on any 'native labour problem'—and yet a great deal must always turn on how any nation's work is done. The southern states used slave labour and were economically preponderant for two centuries; all that time the Indians of the non-slave-owning states clearly contributed little or nothing to what became at last the spectacular development of these states' resources. From the very first, these work-shy Indians, having only limited skill, had few superfluities to stimulate trade (it was later that furs came into fashionable demand), and it was because the Indians could not supply even food that colonial beginnings were so often catastrophic. Thus it was in the inglorious but very human pursuit of gainful trade that European governments originally favoured transplantations to the wide open spaces that seemed to invite the development the Indians neglected. The hardships the hopeful pioneers had there to face bore heavily on them and, when the Indians proved not only unhelpful but actively hostile, they commonly took the law into their own hands and carried war into this enemy's camp. Yet organized conquest was no part of the programme either of governments or of the trading interests; governments (as we shall see) frequently incurred the displeasure of colonists by their efforts to curb their costly expansive habits.

Late in time modern Americans have stated the case for the pioneer colonists. In a famous essay, F. J. Turner, greatly furthering our understanding of his country's past, and of all colonial history, brought to its interpretation the illuminating concept of the *moving frontier*. The American frontier, in this view, is not to be thought of as a closely administered chain of forts, still less as a line of customs barriers, and never as a line drawn on a map. It was an expanse of territory, the wide, constantly shifting scene of the doings of pioneers who lived from hand to mouth—hunters first, then traders, ranchers, farmers—all paving the way for a succession of more intensive farmers, finally of industrialists and, with these, railways and all the paraphernalia, all the amenities of civilized life. Till 1890 (a date buttressed by the census) such pioneers were constantly receding from effectual central control, yet their activities were also constantly reacting on the centre's ideas of law-making. The 'frontier' was, admittedly, sometimes lawless; but it was also the great leveller of unjust class distinctions—the hard nursery, in short, of the sturdy individualism that makes American democracy what it is. The accepted picture is of a brave new world in its heroic age.

It is unfortunate for the just appreciation of other peoples' colonial experience that the palmiest days of the American frontier came only after the Revolution. The deduction is much too simple that later success owed all to the change in the form of government. In colonial times the coastal strip east of the mountains, to which the immigrants were for the most part content or constrained to confine themselves, was 'frontier' enough. There was little the authorities could do to stop them going further if they wished; that they feebly tried to check expansion is to their credit. Pent in and depending wholly on themselves, the early colonists had to dig, but the abundance they produced attracted newcomers who produced more, both food and goods in ever greater variety. None of the other transplantations had such a solid foundation to build on. Yet North America's advantages were already unique; no land was so free of natural impediments to enterprise—malaria, locusts, tsetse flies; none attracted a tithe of the capital investment that fertilized the Western States, none had room for a fraction of the immigrants who made good Americans, and were to make America. Another American, Professor W. P. Webb, building a little too much on his own country's success story, has propounded the theory that the colonial world, spread all over the Seven Seas, was to Europe what its own West was to the U.S.A., the perennial source of the wealth that gave it the boon of an 'expanding' economy, which endured for more than four centuries.

This so-called 'Great Frontier' was at any rate not all of a piece; thus, the Cape of Good Hope was founded barely 30 years later than New England; but by 1776, when the 13 American colonies had a settled population of some 2½ millions, the total at the Cape, spread over an area of comparable size, was barely 30,000; the white population of the whole of South Africa, in spite of its supremely healthy climate, reached the 2½ million total only about 1950. It was the very making of North America that its colonizers were obliged, as they were, to dig in on the coast; the states of the seaboard, solidly agricultural, and economically self-reliant enough to be independent of Europe, made an incomparable base for a broad continental advance, when the time came for that adventure. America, the first and greatest of the transplantations, thus led that expansion of Europe which was the outstanding achievement of the Colonial Age, the Age of Western Europe. Many lesser sisters grew more slowly to become, like her, powerful stays of Western values in all parts of the world, yet independent sovereign states in their own right. Their story inevitably came to take up far the greater part of the 'colonial' chapters of the history text-books: their people equally naturally took to themselves, and to their own glorification, the teaching of the American-born 'frontier' theory.

By an extraordinary omission the American version takes no account of the American Indians; it is the original Turner essay which says no more than that the 'frontier' was, among so many other things, 'the meeting place between savagery and civilization'. The Indians, it is true, contributed almost nothing material to American development; but it harmonizes ill with civilized principles to assume that because they so bitterly resisted European occupation of their land, they could only be crushed—the 'frontier' theory as originally stated was no more than a recapitulation of the working rule that established itself in the older America, and long prevailed, with little modification, in other parts. It was not without great provocation given that the rule was arrived at: there was unquestionably ample room for new-comers; something could be said even for the view that new methods and an infusion of new blood were necessary if those in possession (who could not be expected to see this) were to survive. The European record too has its credit side. The new-comers were not only better equipped technically but morally stronger; seamen, traders, planters, administrators, missionaries—they were often only a handful, and most of them ordinary folk; but their influence was out of all proportion to their number and many of their antagonists recognized this quality. Their influence, too, was of the Greek rather than the Roman variety. Particularly when administrators had the help of Christian missionaries (and the classical list significantly includes no *missionaries*' 'frontier'), European influence owed less to military force than to religion and law: the British tradition (as we shall see) insisted always on the necessity of *law* and order. This legal qualification of the old rule is especially clear in the tropical lands which were as a rule affected only later; in earlier days the strange, new tropical environment was such that few Europeans dared face its physical and nervous strain; their interests were long represented in Africa chiefly by a very few scattered, more or less fortified, trading posts. It was impossible that so large a proportion of the world's peoples should remain, indefinitely, shut in upon themselves. But the meeting of the races, when it came, caused friction even where there was no land-grabbing; there is no doubt that an actual sense of helplessness made many of the indigenous rulers enter into submissive, defensive alliance with a European *protector*. The *colonial* relationship became an accepted part of the world order and by the end of the nineteenth century most of the world's new lands had become subject to the then unquestioned authority of some European power. So long as, like the original American Indians, these peoples were as they were, the colonial system of *law* and order served much of its purpose. It is no longer adequate now that many of their individuals are, in the fullest sense, 'civilized' men and women, and a great many 'advancing' fast on this road; but stress will continue so long as a still larger proportion remain much as they always were.

In the beginning the newly discovered lands had it in common that their people had grown up in isolation, even from one another; having no common pool of knowledge from which to draw they were utterly inexperienced; from sheer ignorance their lands, whatever their potential, were only feebly exploited, totally 'undeveloped'. It was as and when the discoverers came to see how little the indigenous peoples made of their opportunities that Europeans were tempted to try their hand, as they never needed to in the actively trading eastern countries; it is commonplace that even the United States began from *zero*. The pioneers of European enterprise, being themselves in no position to 'stand alone', had for a long time no alternative to accepting a colonial status; the original inhabitants, for their part, drifted gradually into a state, rather, of colonial *dependence*; the very 'unlikeness' of the two parties gave them little common ground on which to base any more positive agreement. The history of the indigenous peoples is unrecorded, but the sheer struggle for survival against the undefeated, often very stubborn physical environment continued to dominate—above all in the tropics where the issue is chiefly joined in our day. These peoples varied too much for the outcome to be uniform even, for example, in Africa where widespread Bantu languages suggest a common origin. Mere 'primitiveness' (such as we all started from) is still not unusual: Colonel van der Post, who thinks it needless for archaeologists to go digging to discover how people lived in the Bronze Age, has seen Bushmen practising rites as described in Homer—and, let it be added, even in the vexed modern Africa there is still to be heard, as nowhere else, the most truly Homeric laughter! The smaller local units learnt at least to stand closely together; where want was so familiar it was much that the 'extended' family, the clan, the tribe constituted almost a welfare state. At any higher level, succession feuds and inter-tribal raids made for a state of continuous unrest that little helped inter-racial co-operation when this became necessary. An egalitarian democracy is sometimes postulated, but the few relatively organized states were despotically ruled; in the stronger and richer groups, even today, a small highly privileged class will have many rightless dependants, relics of those reduced by former conquest. Some tribes and whole regions have suffered retrogression; in the once prosperous, cattle-keeping kingdom of Karagwe, which Livingstone and Stanley knew, the cattle have been wiped out by an invasion of the tsetse *rhodesiensis*, the sleeping-sickness fly; the once dreaded Masai have likewise dwindled since a great rinderpest epidemic that swept through Africa in the 1890s killed off their cattle. In face of such catastrophes tribal society may well have been less static than is sometimes supposed; the attitude of the people is evidently still swayed, under any stress, by folk memories no outsider can hope to appreciate fully. But the climate of opinion, there can be no doubt, was most unfavourable to progress or development of any kind; originality, or initiative by individuals, could only be frowned on as threatening the precariously established *status quo*. The traditional institutions clearly did nothing to accustom the people to orderly social change.

Drastic change has at last overtaken these ill-prepared peoples, and still more is strongly demanded by some of themselves. The existence of so many wholly modern men among them is proof enough of latent natural ability; and yet the great majority live and think much as they always did. At the same time centuries of unusually rapid change in the bigger world, above all in the West, may, if anything, have widened the gulf that originally separated the 'advanced' from the 'backward' peoples. Early observers were ordinarily impressed by any considerable towns they saw, like African Benin. Though in Asia no less than in Europe a great, learned literature preserved the human heritage and in Europe was still expanding it, illiteracy was general even in Europe and caused no remark. The universal religions, to which mental activity was largely due, never reached the newer world; Islam came nearest, but penetrated little south of the Equator and touched America and the South Pacific not at all; failing such help these peoples were ruled by animistic beliefs and were left without inspiration, almost without hope. The early travellers also made surprisingly little remark on the generally low state of health. My own serious introduction to life in the tropics followed hard on some close examination of the crowded and impoverished 'Native Reserves' of South Africa. The first impression was stimulating—instead of overcrowding there was ample space, and after a monotony of maize or millet tropical nature seemed even bountiful—the next and more lasting was of much poverty and more human wretchedness, of widespread sickness and debility. In much of the tropics nature may be bountiful, but only when crops are carefully nursed. The native agriculture yields little surplus and anything extra deteriorates and is lost between one harvest and the next; the months immediately before harvest are known even yet, all over Africa, as 'hunger months'. These months are also the time of the early rains, the planting season; but the rains favour the breeding of pests and bring the highest incidence of infection just when the people are most ill-nourished and least resistant. It is an imperfectly exploded myth that tropical peoples are not subject to malaria. Even if in a suppressed form, malaria persists almost throughout these lands where, in addition, sleeping-sickness may be prevalent, plague and smallpox endemic, much other disease, and infections, like hookworm, almost universal. The evidence is that because of the high infantile mortality the total population was stagnant, if not actually declining, till missions, and the colonial services, began at last the promotion of elementary sanitation and hygiene. The boon of uncontaminated water-supplies has been hitherto almost unknown: a senior medical officer who had long experience of India expressed the opinion early in his first war-time tour of service in West Africa that its notorious 'climate' was then still so exacting largely for want of the man-provided amenities. Work like that of this officer, pushed forward as imperatively necessary to safeguard the health of troops and airmen then required on that coast, was the means of speeding the cleansing at least of its larger towns; but 'the bush' remains almost as it was and, with it, the everyday life of the mass of the people.

Since these people can get help and learn only from the knowledge and example of the better established outside world the study of the sequel to the Discoveries calls for calmer realism than it always gets: to speak of the *impact* of the West makes them too much the helpless victims of a blow from without. The starting point is, rather, the chain reaction set up by the tragic sequence of ill-health, precarious food supplies and more continuous ill-health; these social facts are also potent factors in all this history. In the beginning European incomers were themselves under a strain little helpful to 'race relations' and inclined to put their neighbours beyond the pale as (in the Dutch word) *skepsels*, creatures of a lower order. To this day the major causes of strain, and of the typically *colonial* situation that arises, are the poor equipment, the lower standards, and the incapacity of the weaker peoples for sharing fully in the grand adventure of rebuilding their societies and countries. The strain is most obvious where the 'backward' people are a section, as the North American Indians once were, or even a majority, as in South Africa, of an independent self-governing state. But everywhere the essential 'colonial question' is, as Carlyle might have said, a 'condition-of-the-people' question.

At every stage, therefore, in the unfolding of colonial history this basic human factor must be kept in the forefront, and above all in the very latest phases. Till our own day the essentials of the situation changed so little and so slowly that the existence of colonies and the peculiarities of the colonial status passed without question. So lately as 1920 the framers of the Covenant of the League of Nations could do no better than pronounce the weaker peoples a Sacred Trust of Civilization. Since then, and especially since the political upheavals precipitated by the Second World War, representatives of the colonial peoples have for the first time become fully conscious of themselves as political beings, thus making a change at once possible and inevitable. When, however, the colonial question came to be formulated under this new influence it was in exclusively political terms that took no account of the 'backwardness' of the majority of the colonial peoples, of the very thing that kept them in a state of dependence; without more ado they must be set the morally exacting responsibility of taking their place in the world as independent, self-supporting states. But not even leaders of their own can build efficiently except on sound foundations, and without fuller preparation to fit their people to play an equal part in the bigger world. The emergence among them of modern men with political instincts and ambitions is itself largely due to the influence of this outside world. Very recent scientific and technological advances, not their own, have both speeded up the economic development of the colonies and shown the possibility of further advances at a speed undreamt of at any earlier time. Sir Ronald Ross's identification about 1900 of the anopheles mosquito as the vector of malaria was revolutionary; this and the demonstration in the Panama Canal Zone and by Sir Malcolm Watson and others in Malaya that this fell disease can be checked, did more than anything else to open up the tropical lands to exploitation on a bigger scale than ever before. The expansion of the United States was perhaps not much remarked, being almost *sui generis*; but by the time of the First World War Canada and other 'colonies' so called were visibly 'growing up'. Before another generation had passed the sporadic application of technological skill had visibly also increased the productivity of humbler colonies. Such economic development did something to answer one incidental question: by improving the revenues, greater productivity provided the means of meeting the high cost of work for the necessary physical rehabilitation and mental re-equipment of the backward communities.

It then began at last to dawn on those concerned that the weaker colonies must ultimately follow the same road as the stronger Dominions whose agricultural and trading pioneers steadily opened up the country, and by their production stimulated the growth of industries to supply ever-growing needs. The peculiar difficulties of the tropical countries called for special measures: agricultural expansion had to proceed on land already fully occupied by cultivators closely wedded to indifferent and archaic agricultural methods. Trade and industry were the more essential, but handicapped by lack of transport; where production was so deficient there was less need of roads, and there were none: steamers were actually carried in sections for hundreds of miles to be placed in service on inland African lakes; in the 1890s deep-level mining could be started up in Ashanti only when the necessary gear had been carried through miles of forest by African porters. The ultimate answer must be capital investment, on a large or even very large scale. One instance among many was the spectacular effort that went to the opening of the Copper Belt in Northern Rhodesia. As I saw this area in 1929 it was raw and very sparsely peopled 'bush', tsetse-infested, normally dry, but unhealthy, and 1,500 miles distant from any seaport by way of a single-track railway line. There was everything to be provided; even labour had to be imported. When I next saw it in 1952 the Copper Belt had four producing mines, besides several in development, and at least four large and exceptionally well-appointed garden cities, all within 100 miles of each other. Roads had been cut through the bush, swamps drained, pure water laid on, and light and power. Only after this shafts were sunk and processing plant installed and production could begin. The purely preliminary outlay amounted to some £25 millions, and much of this went, not directly to mining, but in the effort to remedy the raw conditions, all in seven or eight years, and make efficient mining possible. The great financial risk taken was here unusually quickly and handsomely rewarded; but the new services, certainly good, are only of the kind considered essential to civilized life anywhere in Europe or Africa, the very desirable amenities only such as are expected and demanded by the citizens of any modern community.

The political awakening of the colonial world is to be seen against a background of rapid and inevitable social change. The results are only more dramatically obvious when set moving by the irruption of highly capitalized industry; the difference is of degree rather than of substance. In earlier times the pressure of hard-working, essentially peaceable European farmers brought about more colonial wars than any other single cause. In the desultory and prolonged struggle with pioneer farmers many even of the displaced people became familiar with Europeans and their ways, and in those slow-moving days the example and the schooling provided by missionaries, and the activities of traders, gave appreciable numbers of them the opportunity of growing slowly into new ways. The effects of large-scale capitalist enterprise are more widely felt and demonstrated, but also more superficially. Mining, for example, being located usually in sparsely inhabited localities, attracted migrant labourers who acquired some knowledge, and a taste for new things. The bigger modern enterprises are themselves so new that they make the defects and deficiencies of the older order more apparent, thus helping to spread a vague discontent and still vaguer aspiration. Capital expenditure put money into circulation and expanding revenues helped to strengthen and improve the schools system, thus also swelling the numbers of the educated minority and providing much to fire their ambitions. Such men no longer accept it that so long as their people supply enterprise with abundant labour progress is as inevitable as the sunrise. When, however, it comes to rebuilding and running the State by themselves, they too have yet to reckon with the factor I have called the 'newness' of their lands and the now bewildered confusion of the great mass of their own people.

The growing but still relatively small groups of educated men, full of new ideas, are now the operative factor throughout the colonial world; adopting the American idiom, we may say they constitute an *emergents*' 'frontier'. Much inevitably depended on satisfying these men's reasonable ambition to serve their own lands and people. The British authorities, unlike the French, failed to appreciate the importance of such *évolues*. The British practice was to rely, rather, on ruling chiefs. In spite of this usage, and of Miss Mary Kingsley's vivid advocacy in the 1890s, it was almost common ground that institutions based on barbaric customs were worthless and doomed to inevitable decay. At last, in the period of disillusionment that followed the breakdown of the liberal order in the First World War, the institutions of primitive peoples were rediscovered as 'cultures'. A highly original teacher, the late Professor Bronislav Malinowski, returned from a long sojourn among the primitive Trobriand islanders to lay great emphasis on 'function'; a people's environment, so he taught, imposes a pattern, each particular custom being evolved in response to some stimulus from outside—some need of security or survival, of climate or geography—all the parts are closely interdependent and a break at any one point is liable to impair the unity and harmony of the whole. The study of primitive cultures, taken up with enthusiasm by many of Malinowski's pupils, added richly to knowledge and understanding especially of the African peoples and their institutions but, concentrating on the need to preserve delicately balanced 'functions', this school took fright at the 'emergents' as the spear-head of 'Westernizing', therefore dangerously disturbing 'culture contacts'. In the same critical years between the wars economic activity was slowly increasing, and secondary education markedly so; but just when 'emergents' were grasping eagerly at new opportunities opening to them, the influence of the academic world was thrown strongly on the side of those bent on applying the brakes to (inevitable) political change. There was still some chance in the pre-war days of re-laying the foundations and preparing the way for orderly progress. But there was no 'training on the job' for those who alone had some capacity for running their societies on the modern lines they wanted or the times demanded. Instead, the Colonial Office took the lead of the functionalists and set itself to build strictly on existing tribal institutions, using chiefs and tribal councillors, but virtually excluding the ambitious new men from any proper part in directing their countries' destinies. The experiment in indirect rule, as it came to be called (p. 201), was an attempt to pave the way for self-rule; failing to make allies of those who shared this aim its promoters drove them into opposition. The modern approach to the 'colonial question' and the stormy debate it occasions are only the natural sequel to that tale of an opportunity missed.

The recoil was sharpest in some West African colonies where many of the well educated, already sitting loose to tribal authority, were little disposed to accept as a forward move a policy that promised to rivet on them the control of tribal chiefs they looked on as backward reactionaries. Thanks both to teachers and to government practice some appreciation of the accepted political principles of liberalism was almost general in British colonies. Like their teachers, earlier pupils had been content to think of progress as inevitable, never doubting, however, that their day was coming. It is a tribute to the equity of colonial rule that political calm reigned for so long. But when the output of secondary schools began to intensify the competition for suitable occupation, the growing literate class seemed to see their rulers closing doors against them rather than providing opportunities for their talent. Their thwarted ambitions turned them very naturally to political action. The essential novelty of the modern situation is this substitution of political opposition for such overt physical resistance as was once the only resort of any who felt aggrieved. In earlier days missionaries, or sympathizers and critics in Britain itself, were always ready to press grievances on the Colonial Office, but in the new phase these no longer had the field to themselves. Colonial politicians were not long in finding other allies, amongst them non-colonial peoples who had grievances of their own against the Western colonial powers. The crisis came, by the chances of history, at a moment when all the peoples of the world were being thrown together as never before. Two unforeseeable world wars greatly speeded a process that was not unheralded; in Edwardian

Oxford many years ago an after-dinner speech of Mr. Rudyard Kipling's offended my youthful optimism, and yet his reiteration of its theme stamped it on my memory: the modern world of mechanized travel he saw as a 'shrinking ball', and it troubled him that its diverse peoples faced the test of living in ever closer, almost alarming proximity to one another.

It is thus a second novel feature of the modern crisis in colonial affairs that local details are fought out before a world audience on principles not always relevant, and usually negative. The indirect rulers may have tried to play Hamlet without the Prince, but their aims were positive, and enthusiastically constructive. The solid farming nucleus of pioneers on the American 'frontier' worked hard for crystal-clear, limited aims. Their successors of this 'emergents' frontier', few of them practical farmers, were inexperienced politicians, and set themselves wide, ill-defined objectives. The first that occurred was the over-simple remedy of ending the colonial rule that had brought them so far on their way. Those of their own people least touched by Western influences may actually have furthest still to go, but 'anti-colonialism' (not immediately so named) fitted well into the framework of the 'advanced' political thought of the day. Long ago, when Disraeli's overseas policy seemed to his critics to be inspired by a dangerous passion for aggrandisement, a leading opponent labelled it *imperialism*. For a time, at least in the '90s, many who felt a mission to redeem the backward lands were proud to be called 'imperialists'; but the critics returned to the charge, triumphantly, when they felt able to point to the South African war as the inevitable outcome of the unholy alliance of the imperialists with greedy mining magnates. J. A. Hobson's book, *Imperialism*, stood as the English classic on this theme even when supplemented, about 1915, by a pronouncement from Lenin. Karl Marx's broodings on the plight of the Western proletariat took no account whatever of the colonial field; but Lenin now made *imperialism* the desperate, expansive phase of capitalism in the search for markets, and the prelude to its promised downfall. Colonial 'emergents', when they began to campaign, much later, were one and all pupils of the West, demanding freedom and self-government. But any agitation causing strain and confusion in the outposts of the Western world promises to hasten the collapse of capitalism, and the devoted apostles of communism are always standing by in the wings, to prompt the actors with denunciations of the evils of capitalism and to recruit disciples to lead the newer peoples by the quicker alternative communist road.

The completely negative anti-colonial approach owed much to the sympathy of Americans—who would seem to have forgotten how the United States 'solved its colonial problem' by getting rid of it altogether. The specific 'anti-colonialist' lead came rather from the East, in particular from India, the greatest of the West's political pupils. After 1920 when Gandhi came to lead the Indian Congress Independence Campaign the Mahatma—well knowing his Englishman!—shrewdly appealed to his conscience, putting him morally on the defensive; knowing well, too, the strength gained from basing politics on morals, he first, and Mr. Nehru after him, missed no opportunity of universalizing the principles of independence, thus staking for India a rival claim to the moral leadership of world opinion long exercised by Western Europe: that peoples all over the world should be deprived by British imperial rule of their natural right to govern themselves was, they claimed, a stark infringement of the liberal principles Britain claimed to stand for. An unknown political genius having identified this precise manifestation of imperialism as *colonialism*, Indians took the lead in another campaign to enlist world opinion in the fight against it. It is an irony of this situation that the imperialism thus doubly denounced is directly derived from traditional Indian practice. British rule in India was never colonial, still less was India thought of as a colony. Queen Victoria, as *Empress* of India, was by no means the first (though nearly the last) foreigner to assume the Indian imperial crown; the Indian Empire then came to be administered by a very small bureaucracy of British officials directing old-established institutions that continued to be manned throughout by Indian personnel; the India Office and the British Indian Services ranked far above any of their colonial counterparts. Early British Indian administrators, having much efficient Indian help, were contemplating Indian self-government long before this was even dreamt of as a possibility for the newer dependencies. The civil servants of later days, the great I.C.S., became perhaps too much enmeshed in the routine of government to think far ahead. But by the time the ambitions of colonial 'emergents' took their strongly political turn—in a world of 'contacts' even more complex and continuous than they were when Kipling sounded his alarm—these had the almost precipitate support of 'progressive' British opinion for the view that self-government is the natural destiny of all dependent peoples.

In the newest phase the constructive guidance of history must not go by the board. Complacent and aloof, high and mighty imperial or colonial rulers may have betrayed an attitude reflected, with less excuse, by stay-at-home imperial historians who treat the history of their own country as an imperial saga to which India contributes a major glory, and the story of the humbler colonies, and of their 'acquisition', a minor embellishment; but the colonial relationship was a sometimes blundering, yet not always ineffective attempt to meet the situation of peoples who were cut off both from the wisdom of the East and the skills of the West. The development of these lands and of their peoples will not be furthered by other teachers who belittle the ascendancy Europe long enjoyed as a triumph of amoral technology—as if the best technology could be other than the product of plain living and high thinking, and of a disciplined capacity for taking pains. Western leadership was not only tolerated; its moral basis was genuinely appreciated, as was the great contribution it made, the greatest in history, to man's battle with natural forces, and to the conquest of his environment. The Western civilization in which alone technology throve is itself a slow growth, deeply rooted in a Greek, Hebrew, Roman and above all a Christian past. The world's peoples must not be taught to think that the fruits so many covet have come without effort, and are to be had for the taking.

Chapter 1

THE FIRST COLONIAL FRONTIER

*

The clash of American colonists with their Indian neighbours dominated the situation on what history must see as the first essentially *colonial* 'frontier'. The Negro slaves of the south were in no way involved, but American beginnings are the indispensable background to all the later African story. Here for the first time the growing ascendancy of mere 'frontier law' was challenged. The crisis in the relations of the colonies with the parent state was directly precipitated by the attempt of British rulers to order the frontier, to subject it to law and, at the climax, to organize the colonists for its defence. In spite, moreover, of this effort being a total failure, the tradition and the forms of British colonial administration in North America long persisted almost unchanged. A just appreciation of our modern 'colonial question' demands first a just apprehension of the early course of events in this early America and, above all, of the circumstances attending the emergence of these greatest of colonies from their pupildom.

By the time of the Revolution, American society, basically English, had become decidedly more cosmopolitan. George Washington's dealings with English relatives, and Thackeray's tobacco-planting 'Virginians' are evidence from fact and fiction that many leading families preserved their links with England; but the incorporation of New York and its neighbours in 1667 brought in a foreign element, and Quaker Pennsylvania welcomed all comers. Population increased, perhaps especially in this middle group of colonies; there was a steady growth of non-slave-owning small farmers even in Virginia, the nucleus of the frontiersmen of the near future. If the New England group were still predominantly English, its people were also among the most politically active and independent. Their original Independency (Congregationalism) made the church meeting a school of democracy, and the church was also sometimes a fort—against the strong Indian tribes who were their near neighbours. Extensive plantations like those of the south and intensive small-scale agriculture being equally impossible in their northern climate, the road to fortune led outwards: hunting, trapping and lumbering drew many to the wilds, the sea many others to fishing, soon to shipbuilding and shipping. New Englanders accordingly became carriers and traders, the pioneers presently of an important traffic with the West Indies. The activities of the northern seaports long far exceeded those even of New York, and 'Yankee' ships and skippers made their way all over the world. The varied interests of these colonists made it hard for them to unite, but it was harder still for the central authority to impose unity on them.

For the century and a half of British rule the home country's interest was no more than to derive all possible advantage by having all colonial trade conducted, as strictly as possible, on mercantilist principles. It is thus a fair measure of the place of colonies in the scheme of things that in Adam Smith's classical analysis of 'The Mercantile System' in *The Wealth of Nations*, published in 1776, he gave 'colonies' only the seventh of the nine chapters in Book IV. The coming or going of no very great number of ships was all there was to judge by of the value of the trading connection; the West Indies were held in rather higher esteem at home because, unlike the American colonies, having few of their own, they kept British ships employed. If the home country was unhelpful it at any rate did little to hinder the colonies' growth. Those of the North American type clearly brought little direct profit. The original Virginia Company, for example, was soon wound up without making obvious English fortunes; the Crown took over; but the chief asset, as Adam Smith and others knew, was the land, and this went cheaply to those on the spot who were able to take and work it; little wonder there was dismay in the city at the surrender in 1667 of the captured Spice Island, Pularoon, for which the *quid pro quo* was an obscure portion of America that included Delaware, New Jersey and New Amsterdam—otherwise New York! Mercantilist law, however, sanctioned free intercolonial trade and, since the navy protected the ships of New England, the colonists continued to take the King's government for granted so long as they were free to go on producing more goods for their own ships to carry. After the Toleration Act, the English nonconformists, who were strongly entrenched in the City of London, were increasingly jealous of these trading and industrial activities. But America, they assumed, was not yet strong enough to dispense with British protection; the Spanish in the early stages and the French later were dangerous neighbours to undefended colonies inclining to any undue independence.

The question comes to be what the King's government of and in the colonies really amounted to; and the answer is not to be inferred from any mere catalogue of its officers and institutions. The Board of Trade, for example, and the Privy Council behind it, might and did at times decree for the colonies in the King's name; but the execution of decrees necessarily depended on the strength and influence of the King's representatives and his agents on the spot, and in North America popular assemblies were the recognized law-makers within their own territory. These assemblies' rights were expressly circumscribed or regulated, for instance by the Acts of Trade; but it was always a matter of some delicacy to override the local legislature—and that even before the famous leading case of *Campbell* v. *Hall* laid it down in 1774 that only the sovereign British Parliament had authority to set aside or overrule the legislation of a duly constituted colonial assembly.

The Governor too was bound to act always by due process of law. Another famous judgment, *Fabrigas* v. *Mostyn*, decided on the eve of the Revolution in 1774, and also by Lord Mansfield, defined and limited the governor's autocracy. This Fabrigas, beyond doubt a 'seditious and turbulent' person, was deported by Governor Mostyn from Minorca to save the peace of the island; but, so this judgment ruled:

> 'to lay down that a governor, acting by virtue of letters patent under the great seal, . . . is accountable only to God and his conscience—and to maintain here that every governor in every place can act absolutely—is a doctrine not to be maintained.'

The alternative principle, the Rule of Law, which prevails, makes rulers and ruled alike answerable to the same courts. In America, moreover, as in British colonies elsewhere, the courts consistently maintained this basic principle which even revolutionary Americans (those who were enfranchised) stood by firmly, for themselves at any rate. For the rest, it is hard to see how better British rulers could have acted in eighteenth-century conditions than by doing as British administration has normally done and leaving its subjects to it. The pattern of British colonial administration was set, in fact, by practice in America; its record, whether in America or anywhere else, may warrant the charge that the home power has in the past done too little for its colonial dependants, but it gives few grounds indeed for alleging excessive government activity of any kind.

Throughout its life trade advantage was accepted to be the sole purpose and justification of the First or 'Mercantilist' British Empire, but the mercantile object was never to restrict trade, only to direct it into the most favourable channels. This mercantile theory was in essence an early form of economic nationalism. Many of my own teachers, brought up on the Whig historians by free-trader fathers and grandfathers, explained the doctrine as at best a sort of measles that Britain in her maturity had completely out-grown. The newer generation, having experienced the insecurity bred of two world wars, are thoroughly inured to the regulation and control by the state of every sort of activity; the effort needed today is, rather, to realize the very limited scope and authority of any premercantile state: two secretaries of state sufficed in Great Britain, even in the late eighteenth century, for virtually all except financial and legal business; few of the great modern departments of state existed even in skeleton to provide the administrative machinery for any nation-wide activity. The characteristic measures used to further the desired 'favourable national balance of trade' include the manipulation of bounties and drawbacks or the restrictive Navigation Laws; but their notoriety distracts too much from the teaching of the German economist, Gustav Schmoller, that the essence of mercantilism was its state-building, its effect in modifying the local and provincial basis of the older economy, and so, in allowing the organs of national government to develop. The mercantilist approach, however ill conceived, was in its day the attempt of those most immediately concerned to make the best of the opportunities opening in a wider world. In practice, the trade laws, which if not bad in themselves, bore especially hardly on the non-tropical American colonies, helped to bring the whole system into disrepute and to final collapse; but this was due to weak and capricious administration, and the annoyance and contempt it bred, rather than to the rigours of penal enforcement. Even had the law and respect for the rule of law allowed, active repression of American or any other British colonies would have been virtually impossible. The Governor, it is true, was also commander-in-chief but his 'command' was normally, and rarely more than, a local militia.

The Governor's civil staff is accordingly a better measure of his real power to impose his will, or that of his sovereign. Direct British-born appointees in any one colony, then and much later, were rarely as many as half a dozen in the most senior posts. Where, as in America, the standard of education allowed, all but this handful would be drawn, if only for reasons of economy, from local talent—unlikely material for the machinery that would be required to enforce an unpopular policy. The officers effectively under the Governor's personal control were chiefly those of his household, secretaries or A.D.C.s. There was as yet no salaried civil service, only a variety of 'placemen'—Lady Ann Barnard describes a wrangle as to whether one such place at the Cape was in the 'gift' of the Treasury or of the Admiralty—and everywhere the Governor's authority had to reckon with that of these powerful departments. It was rarely the Governor who enjoyed such gifts of patronage, and often it was the King himself. Many appointments were 'gifted' by royal letters patent to sinecure holders who left it to local deputies to collect the fees recognized as due for the services of the particular office. Having such poor local help, from a staff he did not control, the Governor was more likely to have to satisfy occasional bursts of inquisitiveness from Crown auditors than to be able to draw any subvention from the Treasury at home. It was the accepted doctrine that he must 'make do' on such acknowledged Crown dues as the 'customs' (hence so named) and appeal for any more he needed to the local assembly.

The local Parliament (the first is said to have 'broken out' in Virginia as early as 1619) had of course something less than responsible self-government as this came to be understood later, but its financial rights were unquestioned; and even its limited control over the executive reflected the governmental ideas of the Stuart age in which it originated rather than a conscious design to keep the colonies under restraint. Sidney and Beatrice Webb once laid their fingers on some lines of *Hudibras* as a faithful, nearly contemporary picture of the English prototype of this American local government: its scope or range was no more than—

> *. . . to impeach a broken hedge*
> *And pigs unringed at Vis.Franc. Pledge:*
> *Discover thieves, bawds and recusants*
> *Priests, witches, eves-droppers and nusance;*
> *Tell who did play at games unlawful.*
> *And who fill'd pots of ale but half-full.*

The business of local authorities was to care for everyday needs—to maintain general law and order, to protect property against petty crimes and misdemeanours, to check the use of fraudulent weights and measures. Action was occasionally political in scope (as with 'recusants'); this would be at the instance of the central authority and orders, it may be guessed, would be strictly or laxly interpreted as local sentiment in these matters dictated. The most modern function in the list is 'nusance' —if this may be stretched to cover a rudimentary regard for public health when the offence was sufficiently blatant! The prime function of the elected representatives, where government responsibilities were so limited, inevitably came to be to curb extravagance; there was little for them to do except to keep down the rates—or, on the higher level, to resist all government demands for more taxation—like the Mother of

Parliaments herself. It was again Sidney Webb I once heard liken no less a national hero than John Hampden to the 'Indignant Ratepayer' who lifts up his voice in the local newspapers! Governments faced in a period of steady inflation by such equally steady and unrelenting opposition to direct taxation were, for this if for no other reason, very ready to lend an ear to mercantilist teaching. Trade was one function a government could hope to influence by indirect measures—whatever served to increase the total national wealth would automatically improve the 'customs' about which Parliament made less debate. Battle was very quickly joined when the trade imposts of the 1760s, though inspired as it happened by national aims, were alleged to infringe the sovereign principle, 'no taxation without representation'. Long before this crisis the colonists had come to hold the purse strings and, notoriously, they kept these so tight that their own zeal for economy left no colonial governor in any position to show administrative initiative or indulge in government activity of any kind.

It was in these conditions that the forms and institutions of colonial government first took shape. Those of colonial America became traditional and can be be pictured from the fashion of British colonial administration in the Crown Colonies of much later times. 'The Government' tended to be the Governor, and its standing in the country to depend first of all on his personality, but also on how far his chosen councillors, official and unofficial, were able to prove themselves something more than a Government House coterie; often enough Governor and Council were at perpetual feud with the Assembly (though in truth not often with general public opinion). The nineteenth century soon reduced the evil of 'placemen', but so long as the do-nothing *laissez-faire* theory dominated economic and political thinking the functions of the state were limited; so long as law and order (services whose usefulness can be under-rated) came first, if not also last, there was no particular reason, certainly no urge, to make radical changes in the traditional forms of colonial government. Still the Governor's principal—almost his only—administrative assistant was a secretary—*the* Colonial Secretary: all public business reached the Governor, 'H.E.', through this one 'C.S.'. The demand for direct government services of many kinds first became marked only in the years between the world wars. It was only then that the centrally recruited 'unified' Colonial Service, pride of our own generation, at last provided the personnel needed to give the 'Government' some effective representation in every district of a colony: this service dated only from 1932, a significantly long time after its famous Indian prototype, the I.C.S. The ever-growing burden of public services, and the consequent multiplication of departments and sub-departments, then began to make the colonial 'Secretariat' notorious everywhere as a 'bottle--neck', till at last the political strains and stresses of the Second World War precipitated an almost frantic rush of really new constitution-making. Thus mercantilist teaching, or even the trade laws it produced, must not be made to carry any exclusive responsibility for the rupture between Britain and America. The revolutionary outcome was due, rather, to the set habit that resists the adaptation of established ways and institutions to new ideas and new needs—the time-lag of history. The mercantilists, it is true, for all their national planning, failed to give the dependencies their due place in the national system. But these dependencies were thirteen small, disunited fragments, not one community; many of them were almost more cut off from one another than from Britain. Certainly the home authorities were alone in a position to see them as the whole their common outlook and physical proximity made them. It was actually H.M.G.'s fateful last-minute attempt to get the colonies to stand and act together that 'upset the apple cart'. Not superior wisdom, not necessarily even considerateness and goodwill, but hard administrative experience made the Secretary of State's advisers sharply aware in the end that matters concerning and affecting all could never be effectively dealt with by thirteen governments. Ironically enough it was this late-born concern for national interests, far more than mercantilist pin-pricks, which provoked the crisis, incidentally making Americans aware, as they had never been before, of the iniquities of the Acts that so long governed and regulated their trade.

The train was clearly laid years before for the explosion conventionally dated from the Stamp Act of 1765. The trade laws continued to be accepted, almost to the last, as part of the established order, but legislation had been taking a turn for the worse. The jealous protection of markets for expanding British industries moved the manufacturing interests to press several dangerous measures on Parliament: an Act of 1719 struck at an indigenous industry for the making of beaver hats (then the height of fashion); the Molasses Act of 1733 laid crippling (but never fully effective) duties on a profitable American trade with the French West Indies; 1750 saw one of several attempts to choke an incipient iron industry. Whether or not it was because these and other laws were easily evaded they drew no serious direct attack. Yet by the middle of this century there was tinder about to catch any live spark. Natural colonial expansion was creating new interests that were increasingly *American*—and times were changing. Social links with England, though still close, were being counterbalanced by the growing cosmopolitanism of the population. New-comers included many easily-roused political malcontents, for example from Ireland. Above all, the predominance of the settled planter class in Virginia and elsewhere was now being challenged by the rapid rise of a less stable body of frontier farmers who had no such reliable export crop. Pioneers were now approaching the first natural mountain barrier; the frontiers were even getting dangerously crowded. The British connection, none the less, safely survived the Seven Years War; stimulated by the leadership of Pitt the colonists joined, even with enthusiasm, to overcome the French challenge to their interests both in Canada and in the frontier region of the Mississippi. But it was about this time that more than one foreign observer prophesied a complete break the moment the conquest of Canada freed the Americans from the fear of their French neighbours; and so it was soon to prove. The crisis began to develop immediately after the Peace of Paris which ended the war in 1763; but it was far from being a simple *post hoc ergo propter hoc*. The Peace only brought the simmering frontier question to an issue.

Conventional accounts of what went before the quarrel broke out commonly make this frontier question appear as no more than the danger threatening from France and the French. Hard-fought wars dimmed but had not yet ended French ascendancy in Europe; in America the previous peace of 1748 positively stimulated this great power's efforts to realize the design of penning up the British colonies behind a French line established from Canada, by way of the Ohio and the Mississippi, to New Orleans. The British authorities thus had manifest reason for wishing to rouse the colonists to defend their own interests more effectively and unitedly than they had done in the past. Common cause against the French was natural, had that been all; but the frontier was also and even more particularly the country of the Indians. From the first, therefore, British and colonial views of the interests to be served were significantly different. The Indians were in the first place a physical menace to the peace and personal security of the colonists. A long century of experience had proved them a people who might acknowledge the ties of *kinship* but had not yet learnt the necessity of extending social ties to include *neighbours*. The frontier was beyond a doubt a place where murder lurked and colonists went in grim danger. The British authorities, on the other hand, insensible of the physical insecurity, were true to type and saw the Indians in the first place as a potential market; the fur trade was important, and to the end of the chapter there were imperfectly grounded hopes that their country would be preserved to them and become an expanding outlet for British goods. The colonists, or such of them as were interested in land development, saw the Indian gardens and hunting grounds most imperfectly used and much to be desired to make farms for themselves. A small but highly influential 'pressure group' arose, as time went on, who saw the land-hunger of the frontiersmen as a heaven-sent opportunity for profitable deals in real estate. Responsible administrative officials, however, were aware from the very beginning, or were made aware by those who knew, that pressure on the Indian hunting grounds was bound to be detrimental to trade, and in itself dangerously disturbing. An Irishman who had trading interests, and had clearly also a 'way' with these people—he was well known later as Sir William Johnson—was one of those who gave timely warning that the French were turning the situation to their own advantage by putting it about that they were a handful, interested only in trade. War being imminent, said the French, the Indians would be wise to join them in pushing back the oncoming rush of land-hungry 'English'.

The British Government could not but try to 'do something about it'. Instructions drafted in London in September 1753 called for a meeting of representatives from the colonies most directly concerned, for the significantly limited purpose of making an agreement with the Iroquois Indians. It was local initiative, apparently, that went one better and made this an occasion to consider the broader question of colonial unity. The widely representative Congress of Albany which met in June 1754 adopted unanimously a motion declaring union to be absolutely necessary, and appointed a committee to draft a suitable plan. The Congress's findings, while rather vague and general about the desirability of unified control of Indian affairs, accepted the need for united defence; at this stage, too, they certainly appeared to contemplate the colonies paying some share of the cost. The Congress proposals were probably more advanced, constitutionally, than the Home Government was looking for, but its good intentions were never put to the test. The Government was well aware that union could not be imposed from above and without, and referred the proposals to the assemblies of the individual colonies—and that was the end of them. As the fathers of the Constitution were to discover in the 1780s, the particularism of the units was obstinate. At this earlier date the dangers facing the colonies were even more immediate; but there was always a British Government to look to. The view prevailed that it was the concern and the bounden duty of the Mother Country to defend its own possessions, to bear this burden, and above all to meet the cost. The promising Congress of Albany finally came to nothing.

It was this failure that drove the Home Government itself to take what immediate action it thought possible. There being no other authority empowered and willing to do so it felt obliged at last to take the responsibility on its own shoulders. It was very soon to suffer the consequences. No American anticipated Cecil Rhodes's saying in the very similar South African circumstances of the next century: 'We want to get rid of the Imperial Factor in this question and deal with it ourselves.' They may have disliked the Imperial Factor but they were not prepared to deal with it themselves. Local jealousies and rivalries prevented the harmonious co-operation which the frontier situation called for in America, as it did later in South Africa. The Home Government got and gets more than its share of blame for the calamitous *dénouement* in either country.

The British move followed quickly, in 1755. Before the actual outbreak of war General Braddock was appointed Commander-in-Chief and Commissary-General for Indians. This unfortunate officer is chiefly known to history by reason of Braddock's 'Disaster'. That same year he was killed when a force under his leadership was cut up near Fort Duquesne—where also George Washington fought as a junior officer. The unitary North American command in fact made Braddock a supra-colonial officer; so also were the two superintendents of Indian affairs (one of them Sir William Johnson) who took over from the provincial officers hitherto in charge. The British Administration, thus reinforced, now made its one sustained effort to establish order on the Indian front. In 1756, by Johnson's insistence, the Governors of the frontier colonies were forbidden to grant lands or make settlements which might infringe Indian rights or hurt their interests. In spite of this, frontier pressure continued; even in time of war Johnson had to move again: in 1761 the watershed between the Atlantic Ocean and the Gulf of Mexico was proclaimed the outside limit of colonial expansion. At the end of the war two years later a general Proclamation made a bid to formulate an enlightened frontier policy for North America as a whole including the newly-acquired province of Canada. As mercantile policy demanded, traders must be allowed to move freely but they must now be officially licensed and give security for good behaviour. As for the newer and larger issue, there was no attempt to do the impossible and stop expansion—the important Ohio valley, for example, was to be settled by the Virginians; but further acquisitions were now to be in strict accordance with the rules: bargains were to be valid only if made at a public meeting with Indian representatives in the presence of the Governor, private deals being expressly prohibited. It was also proposed that 'a large tract of land round the Great Lakes' be set aside and closed against grants or settlement. The designation of this tract as an Indian 'reservation', or 'reserve', is the first appearance of a term that was to become very familiar later in Africa, but in this crucial instance there was never even an approximate delimitation of the 'tract', let alone a survey. No responsible authority existed to examine and confirm extensive colonial claims beyond the Appalachian 'divide', or even to contest them effectively; the forts were always maintained in some sort, but the times and conditions were highly unfavourable for innovation and experiment in frontier administration.

Hopeless though these paper rules and regulations may have been, the gesture does credit to the goodwill and zeal of the British administrators on the spot and, also, those at the Board of Trade in London who took a large part in drafting them. A new and distinctive expression of the spirit of the great English legal tradition was now developing, an attempt to ensure that all done in the name of the law be done decently and in order. The British Civil Service was thus early beginning to take its distinctive colour; Sir Lewis Namier has noted the rise at this time of a class of 'professional administrators'. Humanitarian sentiment came as yet very little into account: hard if not bitter experience ruled, and considerations of common prudence, even of parsimony; continuous frontier strains and stresses must lead to future disorders and mounting expenditure. Only law and order, buttressed by a strong, equitable system of government, gave any hope even of a steady and expanding Indian trade. Official attempts to impose such order were unfortunately bound to appear to pay too much heed to Indian rights in land, and not enough to colonists' claims to share in its development; they also took too little account of the lively sense of wrong felt by colonists who had suffered violence at Indian hands. Regulations could in any event be enforced only with the co-operation of these colonists and of anything up to thirteen governments, to say nothing of the Indians themselves. It still baffles the best administration to harmonize within one society the interests of such diverse peoples as the American colonists and the Indian tribes. This first attempt to regulate the affairs of a frontier remained no more than a gesture: but it stands as a challenge. Law and order are two important elements played down or altogether missing in the American theory of the frontier. The practice that won the day there was often heroic, but it was a disorderly, every-man-for-himself way of it, and essentially lawless. Little more was heard of a policy of national security based on law.

That very year, 1763, confirming the fears of the administration, the unreston the frontier burst into flame. The so-called conspiracy of Pontiac set a major Indian war blazing for nearly three years from the far northwest, by Detroit, to the borders of Virginia. It came at an unlucky moment. The British Government was burdened with war debts and hoping rather for an easing of expense. The French 'menace' was removed but now a formidable Indian war had to be fought, largely by British troops. The divided colonies were still not prepared to shoulder their share of the responsibility even for their own defence. The quarrel with the French was perhaps a British quarrel; the French being gone, their security was so far enhanced and the onus unmistakably on the colonists; their steady pressure had at last provoked this violent Indian reaction. The privileges of the thirteen stood persistently in the way of united action and only the Home Parliament had the constitutional right to legislate for the colonies as a whole. It may be that services rendered by the colonists against the French might have warranted excusing them from further burdens if the French war had really been the end; but now it was certain that the call on British troops and funds for the defence of the frontier must continue indefinitely. It was, therefore, all too likely that political pressure would drive the Home Government to exercise its authority, in disregard of colonial opinion, as best it might.

The American colonies had really outgrown the old colonial 'system'. Expectant, perhaps, and not without a lively sense of services due to them from the King's Government, they were no longer dependent on the Mother Country. Any obligation they felt was fully discharged by the profits, real or supposed, of British control of the colonial trade. The very fact that there was this outside help to call on positively inhibited them from combining for national purposes of their own. In the language of a later day the colonies were over-ripe for 'constitutional advance'; but no Colonial Office held a watching brief, none so much as thought of a Royal Commission to investigate and report—there was no Earl of Durham in sight and constitutional change was out of fashion—the legacy of the Glorious Revolution was to be defended as a perfect whole and stood unquestioned. Adam Smith had not yet written and in the colonial world itself the powerful West Indian interest continued to cling to the old order: mercantile principles and laws brought clear advantages to producers at least in the southern colonies. The existing system was strongly rooted.

So it came about that when the expense of frontier defence was seen to be an indefinite commitment and George Grenville set out to find revenue to pay for it, he turned to the existing trade laws. All that seemed necessary was to get them more effectively administered, to block the notorious loop-holes, and raise the bulk of the new revenue from this old source. The famous stamp duty was only an after-thought, a make-weight to cover a small short-fall. An unfortunate chapter of recent history lay behind this move. Many American colonists had 'done their bit' in the war; but it was notorious that many others had done well for themselves by large-scale trading with the French—giving comfort to the King's enemies, who were also their own. In the financial stress which followed the war some in high places at home were ready to believe the worst of such charges. Grenville's measures were therefore almost welcomed as right and proper; the trade code being law, many said in effect, let it be enforced against such law-breakers. For all its notoriety, the Stamp Act itself did little more than suggest the winning slogan: 'No taxation without representation'. More immediately, the continued presence of British troops in the colonies constituted a 'standing army' and, in terms of the Bill of Rights, this could only be legalized by applying the annual Mutiny Act. A rather forlorn attempt followed to fasten the responsibility where it belonged by using the 'quartering' provisions of the Act to make each colony separately answerable at least for the keep of some of its own defenders. It was this that in 1766 provoked New York to the first overt act of resistance. Upper New York was in those days the very key to the Indian frontier, but New Yorkers were no readier than other colonists to fall in with British plans for ordering their frontier—or, it would seem, even less ready—if that meant paying for its defence.

Meantime the pressure on the transmontane frontier went unchecked. American frontiersmen, like so many of their successors in later African Colonies, looked on this novel British concern for Indian rights and interests as a sentimental foible: the imperial power was bound to take some responsibility for all actions of the population, but colonists at grips with Indians or, later, with African tribesmen saw the restraints put on their own remedies as no more than their rulers' effort to avoid being committed to trouble and expense. The frontiersmen's view manifestly commanded the wide public support without which governmental restrictions on free enterprise were futile—it is on record that so representative a citizen as George Washington had an interest in a frontier land company. Much more than the Ohio Valley was effectively occupied in the remaining few years of British rule and, when that

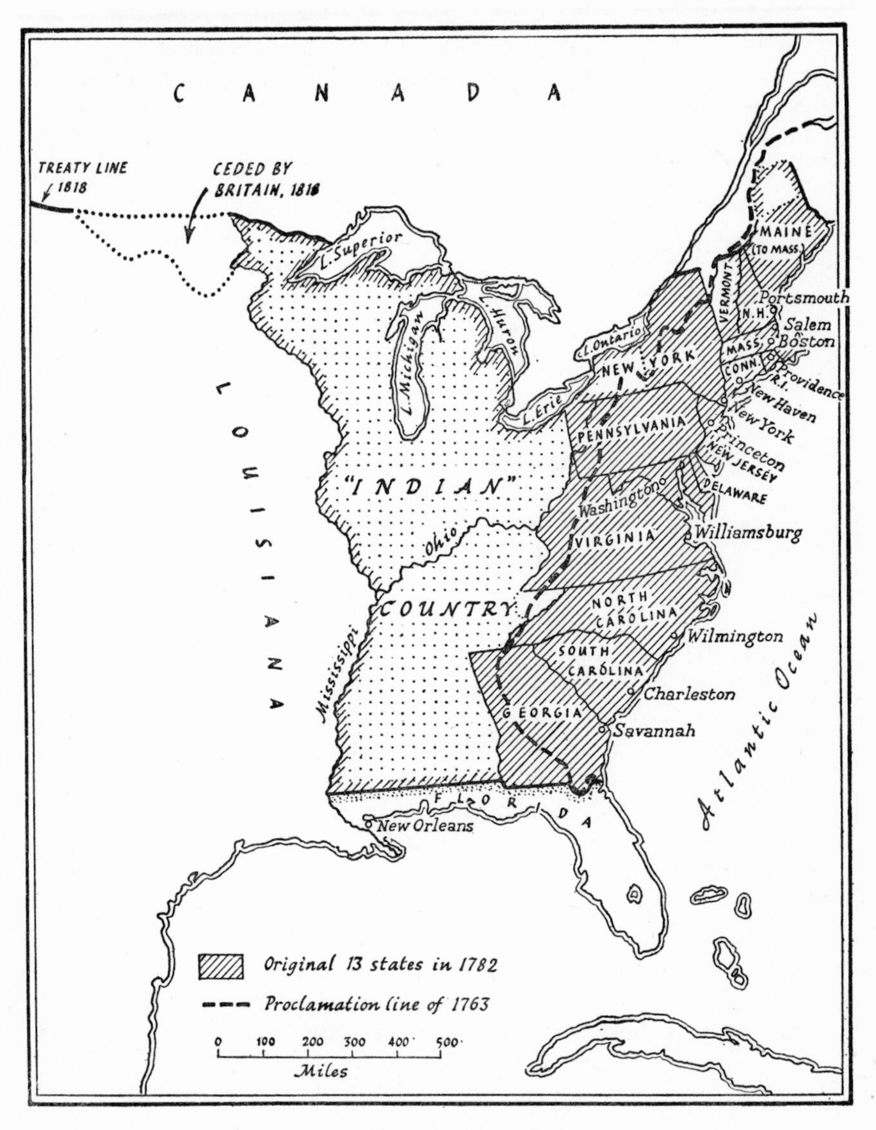
CANADA
TREATY LINE 1818
CEDED BY BRITAIN, 1818
L. Superior
L. Michigan
Huron
L. Ontario
L. Erie
LOUISIANA
"INDIAN"
COUNTRY
Ohio
Mississippi
MAINE (TO MASS.)
VERMONT
N.H.
Portsmouth
Salem
Boston
MASS.
CONN.
R.I.
Providence
New Haven
NEW YORK
New York
Princeton
NEW JERSEY
DELAWARE
PENNSYLVANIA
Washington
VIRGINIA
Williamsburg
NORTH CAROLINA
Wilmington
SOUTH CAROLINA
Charleston
GEORGIA
Savannah
FLORIDA
New Orleans
Atlantic Ocean
Original 13 states in 1782
Proclamation line of 1763
0 100 200 300 400 500
Miles

Early American Expansion

rule ended in 1783 the British withdrew from more of the disputed Indian territory than military necessity strictly required. Lord Sheffield, the Minister concerned, quickly gauged the strength of American feeling; wanting not merely peace but 'amity', he deliberately chose to avoid the risk of further disputes and dropped the British claim to land in the undeveloped north-west, including much that in the days of the French had clearly been wholly in the Canadian sphere of influence. In 1814 the British peace-makers were similarly restrained; this time they abandoned a cherished project of setting up a neutral N.W. Indian state, thus finally waiving all responsibility for the protection of what were still appreciable Indian interests in those parts.

It was now that the practice of the American ex-colonies became 'colonialist'. A bid was made by ambitious interests in some of the coastal states to extend their own state borders even to the Pacific, but this failed; by 1786 the legal, if rather nominal, responsibility for the general control of the West had passed to Congress. It was then under Federal auspices that the famous experiment proceeded which allowed western communities to establish themselves as new States, within the Union, as soon as their numbers warranted. The one weakness in this admirable plan was that it left the Indians out in the cold, with no place even as second-class citizens. The Federal Government stood completely aside, leaving them to be dealt with by frontier 'law'; the long and sometimes gory game of 'Cowboys and Indians' was played by the frontiersmen themselves without either help or hindrance from any higher authority. It is a great matter that the vast resources and the expanding economy of the United States made room in the end for all. Many Indians were 'assimilated' in one way or another; so many died of disease in those pre-medical days, or poisoned themselves with rum, that it was as if 'drink and the devil had done for the rest'. Those who survive and call themselves Indians are not half a million in all. The United States at all events escaped the embarrassment of the modern 'plural societies', except so far as the quickened conscience of a later day was left a legacy of questions to be answered about the rights and status of the Negroes of the former slave states. In conventional histories of the U.S.A. references to the American Indians are too slight to affect the impression that this was always almost exclusively a white man's country—as a glance at the index (s.v. *Indians*) to the United States, Vol. VII, of the *Cambridge Modern History* will show. Only the colonialist suzerain made one vain effort to substitute administrative order for the tragic disorder which marred the glorious freedom of the American 'frontier'.

It is one clear lesson of the American Revolution that when issue is joined on the political level between the ruler and the ruled of any colony, at any rate when the politicians effectively dominate colonial opinion, colonial rule and even orderly administration become impossible. The long American war was futile; piece-meal reconquest was out of the question, and in any but a police state always will be. The real responsibility passed inexorably on to the shoulders of the actual political masters of the situation, and so it always must. That this simple deduction has become clear only in our own day is largely because the British rulers chiefly involved were at such infinite pains to avoid having to face any recurrence of the American situation. But if the lessons of the American crisis have gone to waste, its ghosts have haunted all the rest of the colonial story. In particular, rather than provoke other politicians to raise the old slogan, 'no taxation without representation', British Governments have consistently under-taxed even the less impoverished colonies, choosing rather to sit back and do nothing. All these colonies needed well-directed expenditure far more than North America; but even before they became a world power the mere existence of the United States was standing warrant for governmental inaction; economic development, it seemed evident, even if it was less purposeful than the modern world demands, is best left to free 'frontier' enterprise. In weaker new lands, as in America itself, the weak were allowed, almost remorselessly, to go to the wall, whatever their race or colour. *Laissez-faire* principles, like the law of nature, ruled the battle to the strong. It took long and much more varied experience of the raw conditions of the new countries to win the colonies any special consideration, let alone to bring a real change—of heart or of the mental approach that prevailed in North America.

Chapter 2

EMPIRE AS A MORAL RESPONSIBILITY

*

The bid made by British officials to establish order on the American frontier must be seen in its context; it was a failure, but it witnesses, too, that the acts of Britons in distant parts were coming under observation and no longer passed over with complacency as evidence only of the national capacity for glorious adventure. The influences that inspired attempts to stabilize the American frontier, if not the persons who planned it, were behind the Quebec Act of 1774; this measure sought to conciliate Britain's new French subjects by recognizing not only their French law but their Roman Catholic religion; such a departure from precedent was resented by many Americans but it went through, their disapproval wrecking only the companion project of establishing an Indian 'reservation'. Next, following hard on the end of the American War, the East India Company was brought under the direct control of the Crown by Pitt's India Act of 1784. Miss L. S. Sutherland's study of the Company's history, confirming Sir Lewis Namier's finding on the influence of the new class of 'professional administrators' now arisen, concludes that this Act expressed 'their belief that an orderly and reputable government was a practical necessity'. Here, moreover, moral as well as purely administrative considerations entered: when the Company took over the duty, or the privilege, of collecting the Moghul Emperor's taxes it was untrammelled by any tradition associating taxation and representation, but its agents soon discovered and attacked abuses that struck at the very root of good government; even Macaulay makes handsome acknowledgment of Warren Hastings's 'capacity for administration'. It now became common ground that the Crown's ultimate responsibility for good government could not be devolved on a merchant company—thence the India Act.

The emergence of the doctrine of 'trusteeship' as the working rule of Empire must not be ante-dated—the highly dramatized impeachment of Hastings was a political manœuvre—but even so early, new influences were working strongly to sharpen the sense of responsibility felt in England for the consequences of overseas Englishmen's doings. Edmund Burke was not alone in seeing India as a 'trust'. The enlightenment of the eighteenth century was itself one factor; the sentimental cult of the noble savage was academic—'advanced' writers like Thomas Paine were oblivious of American Indians, or of Africans, slave or free —but there was a widening of interests and the study of mankind stimulated the rise of utilitarianism, and the spread, before the century was out, of humanitarian feeling. 'Evangelicalism', a middle-class variant of the more popular Methodist Revival, was another factor; and the first fruit of Evangelical religion was the enthusiasm which in the 1790s inspired the Protestant foreign mission movement; this direct and wholly new assertion of the moral obligations arising from dealings with 'backward' peoples was to make the next years momentous in the history of the colonies. The British Parliament was not untouched by these new influences: even the unreformed House of Commons, fully conscious of its own revolutionary origins, was neither illiberal nor 'imperialist'; in the best Whig tradition it sponsored enlightened legislation like the India Act, and, bowing to the sheer weight of argument, Parliament also sacrificed important financial interests and enacted the Abolition of the Slave-Trade in 1807. About the same time, whether or not it was a deliberate reform or due to mere pressure of business, a separate Colonial Department of State at last began to take shape and to win more attention for colonial business: Earl Bathurst's long innings as Secretary of State, 1812–27, made for continuity; and in 1812 Sir James Stephen, a famous civil servant (incidentally a devout Evangelical), joined the office as legal adviser and began a career that made him Counsel in 1825 and Permanent Under-Secretary from 1836–47. In the sphere of economics, the effect of the American Revolution was to rule out of court the cruder assertions of the mercantilist doctrine of Empire as a direct source of profit. The lesson deduced from that experience was that colonial responsibilities, being evidently fraught with embarrassing risks, are to be avoided. Trade, however, was the nation's livelihood, expanding industries made new markets more essential than ever, and traders' rights and persons must be protected. The rule came to be to rely on diplomatic action: functioning governments must be fully recognized, and themselves persuaded to guarantee traders' rights and persons. This deduction remained as an abiding influence: it clearly dominated the minds of British statesmen even in the 'imperialist' 1890s (p. 161), as it has American opinion to this day. But British allegiance to the rule inevitably wavered under the pressure of such hard facts as have latterly forced even American governments to admit exceptions. The exploitation of the material wealth of their own continent was long more than sufficient to keep the energy of Americans fully occupied at home, British enterprise, on the other hand, was of necessity for ever seeking markets and new outlets all over the world. None of the remaining 'new' lands proved so absorbingly satisfying as America, and diplomacy was often left, as a recent writer has put it, 'to scrape the bottom of the barrel' and operate in that wide and difficult field where the local rulers are at once unreliable and ineffective.

All in all, active British opinion was philosophical about the death of its 'First Empire', but most Empire historians, as if dazed by that blow, leave the birthday of the Second indeterminate, hardly even noting how its essential character was changed and renewed. The term Empire occurs quite sporadically before the days of the Queen Empress of India, but, long before that, it was common doctrine that imperial responsibilities are to be undertaken only from a high sense of duty, as a *mission.* It was in this spirit that the Royal Navy, having emerged supreme from the Napoleonic Wars, sometimes took on itself to function in what later experience suggests was often a useful part, as an international police force. British colonial responsibilities were at any rate never in abeyance; even in 1783 the highly prized West Indies remained (and why they were prized or what came of them is central to this study). In the long struggle with France a breach with America at one time sharply involved Canada. But that war was, almost above all, a contest for the control of the seas, and victory brought a notable addition to the number of British dependencies, and incidentally to the potential sources of disturbance for those with awakened consciences. No one doubted the new acquisitions to be lawful spoils of war and they also fitted into the established pattern of British trade much more closely than might appear from their world-wide distribution; Trinidad, Demerara and Berbice, for example, rounded off and strengthened the old holdings in the Caribbean. Most of the other acquisitions facilitated further expansion in a field already partly opened by earlier, very practical and by no means theoretical 'mercantilist' activity; in particular a new 'opening of the seas'. Almost before the ink was dry on the Treaty of Paris which ended the Seven Years War, in 1764, Captain John Byron had been deputed to explore between the Cape and the Falkland Islands, to continue thence into the Pacific, and to seek a passage home by way of Hudson Bay. The initiative was the Admiralty's and—so strong is the continuity—the language in which Byron's orders were couched derived from Sir Francis Drake; the working alliance between the state and the trading interest was now only more explicitly 'mercantilist'. Substantial progress came only when the call and the opportunity provided the man for the work; it can be said of Captain James Cook as I once heard General Smuts say of Livingstone, 'he not merely travelled but he saw everything; he missed nothing'. In three great voyages, beginning in 1768 and ended by his death in Hawaii in 1779, he mapped the Pacific as far as the Antarctic ice barriers, putting Australia and New Zealand on the map; *Terra Australis* ceased to be only a legend. These voyages were distinguished from earlier ventures by the modern concern for scientific knowledge. Sailing on the *Endeavour*, a young man named Joseph Banks won his spurs as an observer and collector, paving the way for important later work through the Royal Society. Sir Joseph, as Banks became, long survived Cook and greatly helped to perpetuate what these voyages had well begun. Banks has even been called the 'Father of Australia' for the backing he gave to the occupation of 'Botany Bay', later of Port Philip, on the very favourably situated south-eastern coast he and Cook discovered. Australian beginnings were very modest. Long sea voyages were still too arduous to be undertaken without any hope of rewarding trade and, till after the war, willing emigrants were few. Australia was 'saved' for future development only by making it a penal settlement for transported convicts.

Yet the purposeful work begun by Cook and Banks never quite languished. The West Indies were not forgotten: the famous voyage of the *Bounty* in 1788 was undertaken in an attempt to improve their food supply by transplanting the breadfruit tree from Tahiti. In 1795 the Admiralty set up a hydrographical department to systematize the charting of the trade routes and of the seas in general; it was in the course of a survey of the little-known East African Coast that Captain Owen first showed the British flag at Zanzibar in 1823, and after this Owen and Dr. John Philip were pressing the Cape Government to occupy Delagoa Bay as a check on slave-trading. The accumulation of colonial possessions was certainly no necessary part of the programme, but trade was still something of a 'cold' war and the knowledge gained earlier was turned to account, indirectly but decisively, in the political settlement after the Napoleonic wars. It was a concern of the commercial interests to improve and strengthen the British hold on the great trade routes and this was realized largely at the expense of the Dutch who found themselves on the French side; when it came to making peace the merchant influence secured that the Cape, then chiefly of strategic importance, was retained—it was 'purchased' in 1814—as well as Ceylon, which was a more desirable prize in those days. Java and Sumatra, held for a time, were restored to the Dutch, but Sir Stamford Raffles at once set about laying the foundations of a new base for the Far Eastern trade on a hitherto neglected islet, Singapore. France, temporarily out of the running, surrendered Mauritius, in the Indian Ocean, and Britain now stood, unchallengeably, first among the colonial powers. This Empire is said to have been won in a fit of absence of mind, but the sub-conscious was assuredly not inactive.

Having survived the loss of its principal colonies of settlement, the Empire was almost immediately called on to face the essentially harder task of securing the status of subjects less well able to speak for themselves—in the first instance the slaves of the West Indies. In terms of mercantile theory these colonies long stood as a model. Throughout the eighteenth century they were apparently at such a zenith of prosperity that even the administrative reformers were content to let well alone. The promoters of Captain Cook's voyages could not fail to note the contrast between the long profitless voyage East Indiamen had to make round the Cape and the famous West Indian 'triangle': trade goods carried outward to West Africa secured slaves for the notorious 'middle passage' to the islands, whence there were possible side trips to fetch food or lumber from North America before turning homeward with freights of sugar and other products in ready demand, for consumption at home or for re-export; thus three relatively short runs might each of them yield its separate profit; it is understandable that more ships cleared British ports for the West Indies than for North America. But if more West Indian than North American money circulated in Britain few drew the appropriate inference that gains made in the northern colonies were quickly reinvested locally; it was an obvious lesson missed that those colonies grew in strength just because both production and consumption were steadily expanding. To the end of the chapter much West Indian cash went to pay for the food they failed to grow for themselves. Yet a strong body of opinion thought ill of the treaty-makers who after the Seven Years War chose to keep Canada rather than Guadeloupe—this was, perhaps, taking the cue from the elder Pitt who silenced critics in an earlier debate by first hissing and then roaring at them the one word 'Sugar!' As the years passed British consumers sometimes murmured because sugar was in short supply and dear; merchants and manufacturers were very willing to look for alternative sources. But as late as 1798 the younger Pitt testified that four-fifths of British overseas investment was in the West Indies, where Empire was so highly rated that even Napoleon ventured important forces at a critical moment in an effort to quell a Haitian rebellion and hold St. Domingue. Yet even in Pitt's last days the assault had begun on the slave-trade: in the fifty years following the Peace of Versailles a crusade ran virtually the whole of its meteor-like course and achieved the overthrow, in British territory, of the institution of slavery on which the always brittle prosperity of the West Indies chiefly depended. It is a measure of the importance of the West Indies in this context that their share was £16,589,000 of a total of £20 million voted to owners in 1833 as compensation for the loss of property in slaves; Jamaica alone had 312,000 of them, and the British West Indies a total of 670,000.

This huge dependent labour force suggests why sugar was so often said to be king in the West Indies. Great aqueducts, mostly in ruins but a few of them functioning, still bear witness to the preliminary work of irrigation commonly required. Clearing, draining and tilling the fields, planting, tending, cutting the cane and carting the 'crop' to the mill were still only a beginning; the manufacturing process was a highly skilled operation and, after milling, the highly profitable by-product, rum, was won by distilling the uncrystallized molasses left over. Even then, besides care and maintenance (often also of a windmill), there was more heavy carting to be done, or loading on barges which carried the finished product to the ships. The innumerable decayed sea ports of the West Indies bear witness to the active life of long ago. The detailed ordering of so much work by slave labour demanded the most systematic organization—free labour fends for itself after working hours, but slaves were the care and responsibility of their owners and masters all the time. This great mass, 670,000 slaves, together with dependants young and old, were housed and clothed and fed and doctored, and the industry could not afford to let these cares be merely perfunctory; it is of great social and political significance that the slave labour force, involving the planters as it did in heavy and continuous outlay for its keep, was also their chief capital asset; the mills of those days were simple; sugar technology had far to go to produce the monster central mills that are the major capital investment of the modern industry.

The production of finished sugar was also a prolonged operation; the crop took a year or more to mature and three or four months to 'process', its transport and marketing many months more. While waiting, perhaps two years, for his own remuneration, the producer was at continuous expense for his own and his overseers' keep, for outlay on the fields and the plant and, always, on the slave community. Slavery and slave labour were the base on which the industry rested, but there was much more to it; both in the islands and beyond ships plied constantly in its service; the African slave trade grew to its eighteenth-century dimensions as a mighty subsidiary. The financing of so much activity was a business in its own right. For purely financial reasons, as well as by the rubs of a difficult calling, individual planters were constantly failing and, as bankrupt estates fell into ruin and came on the market, other planters on the upgrade would seize their chance of adding to their own acreage. In either case loan money was in constant demand, whether to bolster up declining estates by accommodating their owners, or to provide new owners with the means of reconditioning the many fields gone to ruin by mismanagement and neglect. The rate of interest was so high (10 per cent and 12 per cent to the end of the chapter), that there was little inducement for creditors to press their debtors and be left to function as absentee owners of cumbered estates; payments of interest, while they lasted, were probably often the only repayment of capital confidently hoped for. The standing of the West India 'interest' in London and Bristol was obviously high. It becomes intelligible only in the light of its members' position as representatives of 'financial houses' which were then among the greatest of their kind.

The sugar industry, in short, *was* the West Indies of that day, but the powerful controlling interests and their orientation were British. And the plural is appropriate, for they were more than one; the famous West India Committee ('est. *circa* A.D. 1750', as its monthly *Circular* long proclaimed) represented principally the sugar 'factors', firms which acted as bankers and wholesale suppliers as well as purchasers of sugar from the plantations. But there were also brokers, refiners and distillers, as well as the slave-traders—and this latter section sometimes went its own way; in the Seven Years War it used the opportunity of a four years' British occupation of Guadeloupe to furnish that island with some 60,000 slaves, contributing materially to the competition—later sharply felt—of sugar from the more nearly virgin soil of the larger French islands. The many wars on the whole sustained the prosperity of the sugar industry and the planting interests were surprisingly unperturbed when the attack developed on the slave-trade; certainly the labour provided by the trade for the British islands was very 'adequate'; abolition when it came made no labour shortage that was seriously felt except in the newer acquisitions, Trinidad and British Guiana; natural increase was relied on to maintain the labour supply. Slavery itself was unquestioned, as if it were of the nature of things and must continue because this almost first of British industries was unthinkable without it. As for the slaves, by the very definition of slavery, they had no legal rights; dubious local laws might even make their evidence inadmissible in court. Schooling was frowned upon, so that their hopes of bettering themselves were slender at best, and capricious. Yet some might learn trades and attain comfortable prosperity, and manumissions, especially of favourite women slaves or their children, created a considerable free class of mixed or 'brown' people. The value of slaves as property made it on the whole unlikely that the treatment of slaves would be very different from that which the rough manners of the age tolerated elsewhere; but here there was neither effective appeal against the acts of white overseers and supervisors nor much hope of redress—for justice was dispensed by voluntary J.P.s, and order enforced by the local white militia. Sporadic slave risings occurred and were ruthlessly suppressed, but except in Haiti they were aimless and fruitless. The very idea of radical reform could only come from without. Battle was joined in the first place in Britain, with the British shipping interests, to stop the slave trade. In a second phase it was concluded that slavery itself, like the slave trade, could never be mended but must end. The first pronouncement against slavery was made by the Society of Friends in America as early as 1727. The first effective blow was struck only in 1772, by Granville Sharp: this essentially English character, a resident like others of what came to be called the 'sect' in comfortable suburban Clapham, and perhaps in fact a 'crank', took on himself to intervene on behalf of a runaway slave 'boy', Jack Somersett, who had been recaptured by his master and forcibly detained in London. Giving judgment, only after prolonged consideration, on a writ of habeas corpus, Lord Mansfield laid down principles which meant in effect that any slave setting foot in England became a free man:

> 'The state of slavery . . . is incapable of being introduced on any reasons, moral or political. . . . It is so odious that nothing can be suffered to support it, but positive law. Whatever inconveniences, therefore, may follow from this decision, I cannot say this case is allowed or approved by the law of England: and therefore the black must be discharged.'

Slaves being few in England, the judgment did no more at first than stimulate the Christian philanthropy of men like Sharp. A colony for freed slaves was planted at Freetown in Sierra Leone in 1787 and put a little more firmly on its feet by Zachary Macaulay, another of the Clapham 'Sect', in 1793. The 1780s, however, saw also a curious diversion of interest. The publication of Rousseau's *Contrat Social* in 1760 had asserted the rights of abstract *man*, 'born free and everywhere in chains'—its supporters were rationalist and radical. At the same moment, but independently, and with little radical help, Christian enthusiasts, conservative in politics, took up the cause of the real men suffering specific wrongs at the hands of slave-traders in far-away Africa and in the colonies. This real issue became at any rate so much of a 'talking point' that in 1785 the dons of Cambridge posed the morality of slavery as the topic for the Chancellor's annual essay prize. An organized crusade against slavery developed quickly when Thomas Clarkson, whose winning essay was published in 1786 and provided a textbook, decided to devote his life to the cause he had been thus led to take up. This dedicated secretary, working with Sharp and others, at once found an influential and no less ardent president in the 'converted' William Wilberforce, whose like-minded neighbours were a ready-made committee. Ministered to by the Rev. John Venn (Rector of Clapham, 1792–1813), and enjoying the hospitality of Henry Thornton, banker and M.P., the group included experienced Indian administrators like the elder Charles Grant, at least one able lawyer, Dr. Lushington, and two men with direct West Indian knowledge, the elder James Stephen and Zachary Macaulay (father of Lord Macaulay), several more M.P.s and well-to-do business men, notably Fowell Buxton; led by Wilberforce, a close friend of Pitt who had the sympathy and support also of Burke and Charles Fox, this powerful group was well placed to follow up its deliberations by parliamentary action. Commons resolutions against the slave trade in 1788 and 1789 were followed in 1792 by one backed in a memorable speech by Pitt himself. Yet bills to control or regulate the trade were tossed to and fro between Lords and Commons without result; Pitt's preoccupation with revolution and war caused the campaign almost to languish. There were other reasons too. Slavery had long disappeared from western Europe but the serfdom of men 'tied to the land' persisted in several parts, and slavery as such had never been abolished, never before so much as expressly condemned; it was widely if only tacitly accepted that even the slave must do his duty 'in the state unto which it shall please God to call him'. The new crusaders were original and even revolutionary in appealing to moral principle to buttress their condemnation at once of ancient custom and current practice, and revolutionary teaching was particularly unpopular in England at that time; its source, too, the scarcely even liberal-conservative 'Clapham Sect', was a handicap; while real radicals were suspicious or incredulous, the 'sect's' conservative friends and neighbours, who included many slave-owners, were inclined to say that these 'saints', like the earliest Christians before them, turned the world upside down. Well aware that their critics had as yet no solid political backing, the shipping interests were content to fight a delaying action and merely obstruct, demanding evidence in place of hearsay. The earlier debates were conducted on almost a matter-of-fact level. 'How useful!' said the *Edinburgh Review* of July 1805, in a caustic summary of the arguments:

> 'Not to mention other things, the subordination, which the vulgar call slavery, is the source of good government, peace, sugar and coffee, national prosperity, ships, and fine colonies.'

But the shippers were a power in the land; the threat of material damage to their long-established interests was serious enough to make Wilberforce himself at one moment in 1805 protest that total emancipation of the slaves was no more than an *ultimate* hope or—in a later version—the '*remote* and *ultimate* end'.

By this time the main stream of opinion had turned perhaps more than was realized in the reformers' favour. The stresses of the revolutionary years were bringing utilitarian teaching uppermost and, though Jeremy Bentham and his disciples were little interested in slavery, as such, the principle of utility, the greatest good of the greatest number, 'required' (the word is Professor Dicey's) the freedom of the slaves. Quite suddenly it appeared that the case, at all events for the trade, was undermined. In 1805 an Order in Council was enforced abolishing the trade in the newly acquired colonies. When the death of Pitt brought Fox into office he at once sponsored a Government resolution asking for abolition—it was within a few days of his own death. There was only slender opposition to the General Act for the Abolition of the Slave Trade which became law in 1807. A sustained struggle to make the Act effective tended chiefly to show that so long as slavery was legal and slaves in demand it was almost impossible to stop the traffic altogether, and administratively no less difficult to carry out the necessary registration of slaves who were legitimately owned. So far as trade restrictions made slaves scarce, they were more valuable; this was alleged to make conditions worse than ever, tempting shippers to overcrowd the slave cargoes. The growing pressure of public opinion made slave-trading a felony in 1811; it also moved Lord Castlereagh to make himself almost a nuisance as an advocate of international action at the Congress of Vienna; but this needed the co-operation at least and especially of France and America, and they held aloof. It was almost in desperation that Buxton, taking over from Wilberforce in 1823, pronounced at last for total emancipation as the only practicable way of ending the slave trade.

It contributed materially, if not to Buxton's decision then certainly to the vigour of the anti-slavery campaign which followed, that a lively new force was now at work. In the course of the 1790s evangelical enthusiasm found expression in the Protestant missionary movement and this was now functioning strongly. The well-known societies, the S.P.G. and S.P.C.K., had been long in being but they ministered chiefly to Anglicans in exile; mere slaves, and the 'native' peoples of the colonies, had so far languished in darkness except for the work of the great Catholic orders or of a few scattered Moravians. It was as if the force of militant Protestantism had spent itself in the age of the Puritans, first in the effort that established its brief ascendancy, then in a struggle to survive at all. Now the Puritan remnant and a section in the Establishment itself became seized of the duty of Christians to bring the message of the Gospel to God's children everywhere. As early as 1788 William Carey produced a pamphlet on this Christian obligation to 'the heathen' and in 1792 he founded the Baptist Missionary Society. The London Missionary Society (L.M.S.) followed in 1795, the Church Missionary Society (C.M.S.) in 1796—the Methodist and various smaller Scots societies as well as the closely allied British and Foreign Bible Society not long after. The Congregationalist L.M.S. is perhaps the typical representative of the new movement in its early phase. 'Independency', a direct legacy from the seventeenth-century Puritans, was its great strength; untrammelled by central organization its congregational units spread unusually far and fast, the light skirmishers of the advancing missionary army—as notably in southern Africa. These individualists were strong, again, in having a political tradition; John Philip, for example, in South Africa, had few inhibitions about 'meddling in politics' when meddling seemed to be called for. The tolerant Congregationalism of the L.M.S. incidentally attracted a succession of other notable Scots at a time when the Church of Scotland, as such, had no missions to use the services of such men as David Livingstone. Yet independency had its weak side when it came to digging in—and the undeveloped state of most of the colonial peoples made the consolidation of early gains peculiarly necessary.

The zeal and devotion that went to the almost precipitate launching of so many evangelical missionary societies is characteristic of these Bible Christians who preached salvation by faith not works but were themselves earnest in the performance of good works. The missions were their supreme effort, but their 'enthusiasm' became an epithet on the lips of those who preferred the studied moderation of the Age of Reason; to many of these, 'evangelicalism' and evangelicals became almost abhorrent. Yet the missionaries were far from being moved and guided only by blind enthusiasm. The pioneering Carey, for example, became a noted Orientalist, being speedily made aware, in the field, of the necessity of education. At a later date, when the 'Disruption' of 1843 ended the reign of the 'moderates' who had hitherto curbed the 'enthusiasm' of evangelicals in the Scots establishment, the Free Kirk played an outstanding part in the development of education in India, and made a mark too in southern Africa where any educated African was known as, and till very lately probably was, a 'Lovedale boy'. It was indubitably the missionaries who, almost unaided, first carried Western education round the world.

The mere presence of missionaries in the colonial field for the first time supplied witnesses who were in a position to give direct independent evidence on conditions in the slave colonies, and soon the missionary interest was playing a notable part in an essentially political war. The anti-slavery campaign has by common consent a place of its own in the history of organized political agitation; the technique of *ad hoc* committees, of public meetings, and resolutions and petitions was originally of its devising. Nonconformist chapels all over the country were ready-made anti-slavery centres, where missionary letters and visiting missionaries themselves might rouse both enthusiasm and indignation. The strongest congregations were the most mission-minded, and the Evangelical wing of the Establishment made a special contribution. At a time when the social gulf between Church and Chapel was deep and wide the Chapel parties, for all their self-reliance, set great store by 'respectable' associations and leadership, and welcomed Churchmen like Wilberforce and Buxton, peers of the realm, even the occasional Royal Duke, to speak or preside and give agitation a *cachet*, especially at the crowded May Meetings held normally in a building off the Strand known as Exeter Hall. The body of opinion sometimes derided as the 'nonconformist conscience' got 'Exeter Hall' for its name, and was to win its most spectacular triumph as the militant wing of the anti-slavery movement.

The evangelical fervour of the emancipationists (as they now became) was not the sole factor in giving their new campaign all the intensity of a crusade. The fight against slavery, like that formerly waged against the slave-trade, was decided in Britain; but this time West Indian interests were more directly and, above all, more personally involved. The shipping interests formerly concerned were well able to fend for themselves and find alternative outlets; but the attack on slavery struck at the slave-owners on the plantations and at the very fabric of the society they had painfully built up over two centuries. The West Indian community of white planters, with their commercial and other associates and helpers, was at once a larger and a far more coherent unit than the white 1 per cent of the total population in the multi-racial society of today. Barbados soon lost many of the 18,000 whites it had in 1640, but in 1791 Jamaica still had some 30,000. It is corrective of the impression left by the habit of speaking of planters' *estates* to realize that in the cultivable, empoldered area of British Guiana (lately some 271,000 acres in all) there were once as many as 400, each presumably with its own mill; the Jamaican land register lately showed 'estates' of no more than fifty acres (a significant proportion being listed as 'ruinate'). In the great days of the sugar industry the proud, self-conscious, not very large-scale gentlemen farmers were everywhere the unchallenged and unchallengeable ruling influence. But the essentially 'frontier' conditions they faced were peculiarly unstable; the fluctuations in their fortunes were such that the 'gold-rush' of the early Pinney days in Nevis (see p. 14) never really 'expired': one lasting impression of my first visit to the islands in the 1930s was of the Micawber-like spirit that still survived—like that of farmers I have known, living from hand to mouth on the edge of the African 'bush', yet always hoping for something to turn up (scilicet, a prospector to whom to sell off their land or at least a mining 'option' on it). In keeping with their expectations, the planters' standards were uniformly high; their best domestic architecture, the Creole cookery, were real contributions to the difficult art of living well in tropical conditions. They clung too to their Western heritage; much of the absenteeism alleged against them has a credit side; parents often had to follow to keep an eye on children sent ahead on the long Atlantic crossing for better education, in more stable conditions, than even Barbados afforded. The slave majority, having no status in this society, had a long upward climb ahead (Chapter 4); but the Jamaica of Lady Nugent (*c.* 1807) and of 'Monk' Lewis, a little later, has been described by Professor W. L. Burn as a 'happy and jolly place', and the writer of *Tom Cringle's Log*, 1815, was not alone in cherishing memories of 'that land of fun and fever'. The slaves manifestly shared in and contributed greatly to the 'fun'; the plantation 'great' houses are unthinkable without the cabins of *Uncle Remus* and his many kin.

This old West Indian society was, however, also more sure of itself than the circumstances of the 1820s really warranted. Estimable sojourners like Lady Nugent saw no reason to question either its stability or the fundamentals on which it was based, but no one would have thought of repeating in 1828, or even in 1823, Pitt's 1798 estimate (p. 48) of the West Indies' place in the Empire economy. When criticism arose the high standards of the planters actually counted against them. Gilded West Indian youths and Creole heiresses were fewer in London than of old, and the sugar interests less influential in the City; but many well-to-do West Indian merchants survived to keep the Islands' eighteenth-century reputation alive, and the English superstition that any sugar estate was a potential gold-mine. The sugar industry had manifest weaknesses: soil-exhaustion in the smaller islands, rising competition from East Indian and bounty-fed European beet sugar, and always the 'one crop' basis of the economy—the late Sir Frank Stockdale, himself an agriculturist, often spoke of the impossible difficulty of building 'development and welfare' (see p. 211) for the inordinately large population originally brought to the Islands only by the sugar industry, and for it he saw no practicable substitute. The Pinney history shows that good management rather than the luck of the seasons might continue to earn substantial rewards, but also that such cautious and far-sighted managers were even then for 'pulling out' and successfully doing so. Under the influence of the newer fashion in economic thinking, critics were already inclined to be censorious of mere failure, making it inadvisable for the planters to seem to shirk the freest competition. The emancipationists, when they began, had no thought but that West Indian sugar was a strongly competitive industry; all they asked was that, like any other, it should rely on free paid labour, no longer on slaves; they clearly assumed also that, like the 'lower orders' anywhere else, the freed slaves would have no alternative but to give their labour as before. The planters, for their part, were more wide awake to the difficulties and dangers of any such transition (and in many of the islands, the fear of starvation turned out in fact to have little compelling force). Increasingly, therefore, seeing their livelihood at stake, the planters manœuvred themselves into the position of men apparently ready to die in the last ditch in defence of an effete institution, and of their right to property in slaves. Lively, deeply felt Island tradition insists to this day that the former prosperity of the West Indies was shattered by three successive blows dealt them by the ruling power—first the inevitably unsettling campaign for abolition, then the prolonged and contentious period of uncertainty before emancipation, finally, just when they were laboriously adjusting themselves to the new conditions, the 'unilateral' repudiation (for British convenience) of the two-centuries-old preferential tariff on which the sugar industry was built. It was actually the tide of world economics that had turned against them.

When in 1823 Buxton moved his motion in Parliament, Canning, for the Government, agreed at once that emancipation should be the goal but, with more understanding of the difficulties, he also insisted first on giving 'amelioration' a full trial: a gradual reform of the conditions of the slaves, together with freedom for all children, from birth, might bring slavery at last to a quiet and decent burial. Canning may have underrated the strength of the forces behind Buxton, and though he well knew the right of the many Island legislatures to enact their own local laws, his next steps made little allowance for widely varying local circumstances; able and enlightened officials at the Colonial Office, uneasily aware of the unsatisfactory status of the many under-privileged people for whom they felt themselves responsible, and sensitive to the growing criticism of slavery, were steadily for reform; but their draft orders invited opposition by failing to differentiate between Jamaica and Trinidad, or even the Cape. Legislative assemblies, where they existed, had thus ample excuse for obstructing the reforms pressed on them wholesale from afar. In the newer colonies compliance could be enforced by direct Orders-in-Council and caused fierce resentment; in Demerara a London missionary, John Smith, was put under restraint and in 1824 died what was widely taken to be a martyr's death. The hesitant Government then faced a furious reaction from the aroused hosts of 'Exeter Hall'; tales of barbarity and of the grievous wrongs perpetrated circulated wildly. In the end the uniformly peaceful passing of slavery was proof that these were grossly exaggerated; but in the echoes that reached them over 4,000 miles of sea the planters heard themselves pilloried by the ardent advocates of justice for others as the defenders and perpetuators of the injustice of slavery.

At home the agitation slackened temporarily during the fight for the Reform Bill but revived at once when, in spite of Ministers' promises, implied or real, the King's speech at the opening of the reformed Parliament made no mention of emancipation. Then came proof of the residual power behind the anti-slavery crusade; 'affronted and vexed', as he himself records, Fowell Buxton bearded the Ministers and forced them to 'name a day'—April 23rd. Working overtime (and for once in his life on the Sabbath day!), James Stephen hurriedly prepared the Emancipation Bill. In their hour of triumph the leaders, including Buxton, risked serious unpopularity with their own followers by supporting the grant of compensation to the then formidable tune of £20,000,000, and with the blow thus softened the Bill became an Act on 18th August 1833. The restrained mood continued—and there was much to be said for a cautious policy of gradualness. Stephen and others at the Colonial Office, hoping to ease the revolutionary change they knew the transition from slavery must be, had originally worked hard for 'amelioration'; now, in 1833, they threw themselves (as the event proved, almost too whole-heartedly) into getting an apprenticeship system to work to their satisfaction. The compensation voted to slave-owners made it an agreed starting point that the Island economies be as little disturbed as possible; if only to maintain the public revenues the estates must be kept in production; the workers, therefore, must be persuaded to give or cajoled into not withholding their services. For a short term of years, and on terms to be fixed, the freed labourers were required to give their former owners forty hours' work a week, and to be paid wages for overtime, as in the season of 'crop'. Landlords, at the same time, must not use their monopoly of land to provide themselves with forced labour serving in worse conditions than the slavery the workers had newly escaped from; to settle disputes, and exercise supervision, 'special' magistrates were appointed. These men, some recruited locally, others from Britain, were paid by the Home Government and by all accounts did their work well; but the terms of apprenticeship were imperfectly defined; even the distinction between predial (seven years) and non-predial (five years) apprentices was never fully settled, artisans being suddenly pronounced by the courts to be non-predial only in 1838. There was much else to harass the magistrates; in fixing a fair wage they had to take into account whether or not the free workers were still entitled to free housing, and to the traditional ration of salt-fish (this last, as almost their only source of protein, was peculiarly necessary). The amount to be earned by overtime was at any rate no great inducement, and some missionaries advised against accepting the rate the masters offered. The 'target' worker also soon appeared—the man, that is, who works only to meet his immediately felt personal wants and, having provided these in three days, goes home for the rest of the week in total disregard of the urgency of any work waiting to be done. This meant that labour was always short when it was most needed, in time of crop, and continuously so where 'crop' was prolonged, as in British Guiana. It is a strange commentary that, in Island tradition, the planters came to look back on apprenticeship days as a 'good' time when they were reasonably assured at least of getting labour. The continuous vexations the planters suffered are again underrated. As always, they had to wait to be paid for their own produce; but formerly labour was kept, in kind, on goods advanced by their 'factors' against goods in transit; now they must equip themselves to pay, 'on the nail', in ready cash. But cash was clearly also in short supply; most of the compensation money undoubtedly went to creditors abroad. Bankruptcies were numerous and new-comers who bought up bankrupt estates cheaply were no steadying influence. The situation could not be handled with the care it needed by regulations imposed from afar. But responsible feelings of concern kept the Colonial Office more than merely watchful. When it appeared that recalcitrant apprentices could be punished only by imprisonment, and that the public prisons were inadequate, it was London that insisted on taking control by means of an overriding Prisons Bill. Thereupon, tiring not so much of the law's uncertainties as of having their own legislature superseded by such 'outside interference', the planters opted, in one island after another, to be done with the experiment. The 'special' magistrates remained as 'stipendiaries', and, as such, were protectors of the weak, and useful government agents in outer districts; but in 1838, two years earlier than the Act required, the slaves were free.

This summary ending of slavery marks a milestone in history. An institution of such immemorial antiquity, and so universal, could be overthrown at a blow, in any society, only by a benevolent dictator or, as here, by some impartial external authority—the same imperial authority that was later also the chief agent in stopping the supply of slaves at its African source. The reform was beneficent and, for that reason, dangerously flattering to the self-complacency of people cherishing the idea that theirs was an imperial *mission*; it was rather, in the full Scots sense of the phrase, 'an awful responsibility' for outsiders to undertake the ordering of the lives of so many dependants. The pattern of events woven in the bitter contention of the fight for emancipation was repeated till it became an almost unvarying part of the British colonial tradition. Whenever the imperial power was called on to play the honourable role of protector to peoples incapable of ordering their own affairs, the same triangular duel was to be expected; voices would be raised, as from 'Exeter Hall', pressing abuses on the attention of the Colonial Office; the Office, sympathetically disposed but bound to impartiality, then faced the protests of local interests acting defensively rather than constructively—for the reforming critics habitually ascribe the inevitable stresses of colonial societies to the wrong-doing of other people; over-simplifying difficult issues they make it somebody's 'fault' that straightforward 'solutions' of the 'problems' are impossible. The Emancipationists themselves helped to speed up a necessary social revolution; but, lacking full knowledge and understanding, they contributed little or nothing to the social reconstruction their own action had made imperative. They even mistook a beginning for an end. It is not that none looked further ahead; but a continuing obsession with the slave trade made Fowell Buxton, for instance, seek a remedy, not where the slaves were but at its source in Africa, and to cherish a project for trade and economic development in the basin of the River Niger; it is pathetic to read of his hopeful interest in anti-malarial precautions that were to give his men protection by having them breathe chlorinated air—'tween decks in the stifling heat of the Niger creeks! When the Niger expedition failed, calamitously, Buxton retired—beaten. It was said in Parliament in 1846 that 'Emancipation has succeeded morally, it has failed economically'; Mr. Leonard Barnes once put it that the 'positive' side of the Emancipators' work 'was never fully tried'. It was in fact too lightly assumed that as labourers the ex-slaves would 'offer their labour' to the nearest market, and that that market, the sugar producers, would remain to absorb it. Neither side adequately filled the role assigned to it, the negroes because they would not, the planters because in the last resort they could not. It was overlooked that once the slaves had been freed it remained to re-equip them for their life as free men.

Chapter 3

THE ROAD TO SELF-GOVERNMENT

*

Once the Emancipation Act was law the driving force behind the antislavery crusade died away. Thereupon the stronger, homogeneous colonies of overseas settlement took the place comparatively near the centre of the stage briefly occupied by those of the 'mixed' kind, the communities, that is to say, in which 'backward' peoples or groups are in a majority. In the next thirty-odd years the outstanding 'colonial' development was the attainment by most of the former group of responsible self-government; unlike America, they retained close links with the imperial power and continued to have the benefit of its support and protection; but by the effective co-operation especially of British and Canadian statesmen the people first of Canada, then of other relatively advanced communities, came to enjoy independent and unfettered control of their own affairs. The newly-freed slaves of the West Indies were manifestly unready to carry such a responsibility.

As usual throughout the colonial story, local facts and factors played the decisive part. Individual British statesmen contributed materially to the Canadian settlement but there was no consistently enlightened imperial policy. The leaders of British opinion were preoccupied, if anything more even than usual, with a variety of weighty affairs of their own. Throughout the earlier nineteenth century colonies of any kind were much out of favour with the British public, in spite of the antislavery crusade or perhaps, where the West Indies were concerned, a little because of it; a steadily growing trade with free America supported the teaching of Adam Smith on the futility of mercantilist empire, and the break-away of Spanish America seemed to confirm the lesson. Spanish-American independence was in fact one more blow to the fortunes of the West Indies, of Jamaica in particular which had an old and remunerative trade with the mainland; Britain was satisfied to take her supplies where she could get them most cheaply and the sugar industry as a whole suffered competition from new and intensive cultivation in Cuba and Puerto Rico. Some even at the Colonial Office (who certainly found the planters troublesome to govern), cherished a fond impression that the West Indies could get on well enough without the sugar industry. There being no evident recovery, the place of the West Indies as the major British overseas interest seemed gone past repair; the spirit of enterprise, almost at a peak in the 1830s, was finding many more profitable outlets than the declining fortunes of these Islands offered. In spite, again, of general support for the Emancipation Act public opinion, other than missionary, was preoccupied with almost anything rather than tiresome colonies; the 'Saints' in truth won that battle less by their own strength than because emancipation was in tune with the secular humanitarianism of the day. The philosophy of the age was self-help—comfortable doctrine, perhaps, for pioneers of the Canadian West or the Australian bush, but hard indeed for newly-freed slaves. Once they were freed they were quickly and easily forgotten.

Officials at the Colonial Office were almost alone in appreciating the need to follow up emancipation with measures of social reconstruction, but they could not well take action without stronger backing than was to be looked for from the friends of the Negroes. These enthusiasts were positively suspect in the eyes of home-staying radicals and reformers: Cobbett hurled his most venomous darts at Wilberforce, and the not-so-radical Carlyle wrote amiably of 'niggers living on self-sown pumpkins, and rum'. The Colonial Office, accordingly, was content to play a sternly protective role and confined itself to supervising in great detail the administration of its own Act. Emancipation as an expression of the British national will had warranted parliamentary action, but Sir James Stephen was well aware that this could not lightly be called upon again; the everyday domestic law-making of the Islands was the prerogative of local assemblies; and, as he knew, nothing short of a revolution, centrally imposed like emancipation, could by-pass them. He and his colleague, Henry Taylor, probably believed this to be desirable, and Taylor seized the opportunity for a minute recommending that the constitution of Jamaica, the leading island, be abrogated when the Assembly doggedly refused to pass a prisons bill giving the Imperial Government the right to administer prisons throughout the West Indies by Order in Council. In 1838 the British Government compromised with a proposal to suspend the Jamaican constitution for five years. This Bill was so nearly defeated that the Cabinet resigned and all that emerged, in 1839, was a measure giving the Governor limited power to 'ordain' expiring laws if the Assembly failed to renew them.

It was like an intervention of fate that at this critical juncture, before the novelty of the West Indian situation had really made its impression, the political and constitutional crisis in Canada brought a change of wind that decisively diverted official attention and energies from the complexities of West Indian administration. The Colonial Office, a junior in the official hierarchy, was ill placed to fight at once on two fronts.

Canadian malcontents, when they became vocal, were not without British sympathizers. The teaching of Malthus had shaken mercantilist theories and got some thinking of 'surplus' population. In spite, too, of the general unpopularity of colonies the idea of overseas settlement had some vogue, even with radicals, as a means of relieving post-war social distress; thus Sir Robert Wilmot Horton and others sponsored emigration to Canada and even to the newly-acquired Cape of Good Hope. About 1829 the marriage affairs of a bright young man named Edward Gibbon Wakefield earned him a spell in Newgate, and there his ruminations on prospects in 'Botany Bay' were set out in a *Letter from Sydney*; the conclusion of a long series of writings was that the development of the new lands should be prosecuted both as a means of relieving the needy at home and as in itself a worthy objective. Wakefield put a finger on a weak spot in colonial practice when he pressed for less wasteful distribution of the land in newly-occupied countries, and he and his friends, banding themselves together to further 'systematic colonization', were instrumental in helping New Zealand and parts of Australia to a more carefully planned start than had been usual elsewhere. It was of more lasting importance that the views of the Wakefield 'school', well publicized by active supporters like Charles Buller, and also the radical Earl of Durham, focused criticism for the first time on the almost immemorial and thoroughly outdated machinery of colonial government. In particular, the 'colonial reformers' saw these struggling units as growings ocieties and threw all their weight in favour of allowing them to function as such. More than any other influence, and even if it left the intricate constitutional adjustments to practising experts, their work was chiefly instrumental in moulding public opinion to accept the fruitful idea of responsible self-government. It is only after a hundred years of practice that this devolution of power seems so right and obvious.

It may be that the Reformers made contribution enough for any single group by helping to create an atmosphere favourable to one of the outstanding achievements of their century. It was made, however, at some cost to the weaker communities, those not ready all at once to shoulder full responsibility for their own affairs. Thus a famous essay suggested in mild terms that the colonists be left to manage their own business. Charles Buller, the author, writing in 1840, had clearly never considered the position in the West Indies where the vast majority of the colonists were newly-freed slaves and all the business remained in the hands of their employers. Here, no less than in Canada, the traditional forms of government cried out for amendment; the planters and others of the employing class not only monopolized the privilege of electing representatives to the Assembly, but they also dominated the actual administration. The slaves, being private property and resident on the estates, were 'managed' as an integral part of these; even as freemen they had little real choice but to remain where they were; there was neither place nor function for them in the existing political system. It was its recognition of this anomaly that prompted the effort of the Colonial Office to keep protective control of the apprenticeship system in its own hands. By 1838, the apprenticeship being dead, the slaves were free, but the Canadian crisis was very much alive. Unfortunately Wakefield's chosen tactic in the campaign for 'systematic colonization', now at its height, was a whole-hearted arraignment of the Colonial Office as 'Mr. Mother-Country' (an antediluvian dominated by 'Mr. Over-Secretary Stephen'). This libel has won the Reformers' warm commendation from some Dominion historians as 'saviours of the Empire'. Stephen and his 'bureaucracy', it was said, would have left New Zealand to the Maoris and the missionary—or even as Wakefield was not slow to suggest, to be harried by lawless traders. Such loss of face on New Zealand, and in South Africa (Chapter 6), gravely weakened the Colonial Office and from this point West Indian affairs were left merely to drift for most of a generation. Since the Islands were on the whole quiet and peaceful this was as if H.M.G., the responsible authority, felt itself absolved from acting except under strong pressure; but even the anti-slavery crusade was now a spent force. One abortive attempt was made to apply the idea of 'responsible government' in Jamaica in 1853, but a change of system was at last set in train (see Chapter 4) only under the pressure of the 'Jamaica Rebellion' of 1865; and it began very nearly where Sir Henry Taylor's minute had left off nearly thirty years earlier.

The new Jamaica constitution became in time the basis of a plan for better government of 'dependencies' in general and was the work of the Colonial Office playing at last a hand of its own. But till that later day the Canadian model continued to be looked on by British opinion as setting standards which admitted of no exception. It was accepted doctrine that self-government was to be pressed wherever possible, above all for the prospect it offered of easing the home country's burden of responsibility and expense. Canada and her sisters became indeed, and remained virtually till the days of World War I, '*The Colonies*'; the others seemed more than ever small and very far away but apt to be costly—at best dependencies, and of little account. A strong body of opinion would have cut them adrift; it was in 1865, for example, that a Committee of the House of Commons was pressed to withdraw altogether from the Gold Coast; it came to the significant conclusion that it should be 'the object of policy' to encourage in 'the natives' those qualities which would

> 'make it possible for us more and more to transfer to them the administration of all the government'.

This goal remained very distant till, in our own day, West Indians, and others of less experience, came to demand this transfer of power as their right. The tendency of many of these to overlook what history teaches are the conditions of success, and to under-rate the difficulties, makes it necessary to examine that history. The conventional phrase which speaks of the imperial power 'granting' self-government is misleading; Canada, first, and others later, were many years facing their difficulties for themselves and patiently working out a higher destiny.

Canada, as the great laboratory or forcing house of self-government, was already more than the French Canada that gave a more complex whole its name; Nova Scotia and its smaller maritime neighbours long counted for proportionately more than they do today. Tactful administration and the confirmation of French religious and legal rights by the Quebec Act of 1774 safely carried British rule in Quebec through the American War. Then the centre of gravity began to move slowly west. An appreciable number of 'United Empire Loyalists', colonists who repudiated the republican creed, sought to escape the new American order by moving north; a few settled in Eastern Quebec; many more began to break new ground in Upper or Western Canada, now Ontario, and important consequences followed. These 'loyal' Americans could not well be made to forfeit the political rights they were used to; accordingly, a Canada Act of 1791 granted 'representative' institutions on the old model to Upper Canada. Thereupon, rather than discriminate, the Home Government set up similar forms in Quebec, thus ending the direct paternalism that had served so far. There were all the makings here of serious political disequilibrium. Almost for the first time this new Ontario constituted a province (or was it to be a separate colony?) completely dependent for access to the sea and the outside world on a neighbour colony of radically different political character. The Home Government temporized by appointing one Governor-General for the two separate provinces, yet allowing him, in practice, to give most of his attention to Quebec. Inevitable provincial quarrels over the customs duties collected at Montreal even necessitated a Canada Trade Act, in 1822, to secure Upper Canada a fair deal. In the long run the geographical facts made Canada perhaps more favourable soil for developing the idea of a federal solution than, for example, sea-girt Australia was likely to be; but, immediately, local tensions continued to grow unhindered. French nationalist moves in Quebec, and internal dissensions beyond, at last created a most uneasy situation. The year 1837 saw small-scale but overt rebellions break out not only in Quebec but in British Upper Canada as well.

The breakdown, as this double collapse suggests, was due to weaknesses inherent in the traditional 'system' of colonial government. Much old-style bickering between governors and elected assemblies over 'supply' preceded or accompanied this climax in both provinces, but this time political reform was in fashion and the underlying causes of friction got more reasoned consideration. Basically, we see in retrospect, discontent was likely on account of the 'time-lag' we spoke of. All the colonial assemblies were still in the position of the Parliament of early Stuart times; those old Parliaments jealously asserted their financial powers, and they might register such a protest as the Petition of Right, but the King's remained the real, sole, and independent executive power. By a long slow process the King's prerogatives in Britain were devolved on responsible ministers, ultimately on a united Cabinet dependent on parliamentary support. The executive power in the colonies stood vested in the governor as it always had been; by the book and the letter of the law Americans are within their rights who still denounce the tyranny of 'King George III'; it was in his name that their governors habitually acted, taking as much or as little account of the views of popular representatives as they themselves saw fit or felt obliged to. Two centuries of British constitutional development had left the colonies merely at a standstill.

Awareness of this truth clearly underlies a statement of the nature of the local concerns and interests and of the reasoned claims of colonists, by a young Nova Scotian journalist, Joseph Howe; a statesman of some note, Howe was yet to play a part in working out a peaceable agreement. In open letters addressed to Lord John Russell in 1839 he modestly claimed for his countrymen

'the right to influence, through their representatives, the Government under which they live, in the matters touching their internal affairs (of which their fellow subjects elsewhere know nothing)'.

The Canadian colonists, it is to be remembered, were not and never had been 'directly' ruled from without: in practice, all but two or three of the senior officials were local men, the nominees favoured by such as the Government House coterie I mentioned before. Accordingly, deprecating the view that the interests of colony and mother country 'must be continually in conflict', and coming to the heart of the matter, Howe demanded

> 'control of their own revenues, and the means of influencing the appointment and acts of the men who are to dispense them, and who are, besides, to distribute hundreds of petty offices, and discharge functions manifold and various within the Colony itself (in which the people of England have no interest)'.

The perpetual feud with the Assembly was to be ended by having H.M. represented in every colony by an executive able by virtue of parliamentary support to carry whatever legislation it thought necessary. Howe asked, in other words, that the time-lag be taken in, and colonial practice brought back into harmony with that ruling in Britain itself. It is perhaps clearer in retrospect than it was at the time that the moment such colonial constitutional reform became a live issue the Home Government was faced once more with the challenge that cost it America. The climate of opinion this time favoured change but Sir F. Rogers (Lord Blachford), a later Head of the Colonial Office, like Sir James Stephen before him, inclined to believe that grown-up daughters must ultimately come to a clean break with the mother country—only hoping it might be by mutual consent. The very large number of small colonies concerned may have had some influence in modifying this attitude. Both Canada and Australia then comprised, each of them, as many as six separate and distinct units. As in America these little communities for the most part shared a common speech and outlook; they also had no lack of individuals capable of conducting their own modest day-to-day affairs; but their resources, human and financial, were very limited. The facts of geography still dominated. Transport by sea was so much easier than overland that the pioneers of the new continents tended to disperse themselves along the seaboard; James VI might have been speaking of Australia when he described his kingdom of Fife and its flourishing chain of seaports as 'a worsted petticoat with a fringe of gold'. No one was inclined to claim full sovereign independence for so many scattered units. The difficulty was to work out the practical limits of the virtual sovereignty now proposed for them.

The Home Government, for its part, was better advised than its predecessors of the 1770s. It may be the failing of a weak government finding itself in a quandary to defer taking a decision by referring its perplexities to a commission of inquiry. Rebellions in each of two neighbouring colonies put ministers in a quandary indeed, but it was to ministers' credit that they saw the need to inform themselves before taking action, and to inform also the public and Parliament which must approve any remedy proposed. The causes of such a breakdown, and also the views of such as Joseph Howe, manifestly called for explanation. The much-denounced colonial connection, it may be added, has one insufficiently appreciated advantage; the younger country can always draw for such inquiries on the richer or certainly the more abundant talent and experience of the parent country. The Home Government now chose a man of great talent, and of thoroughly 'modern' views, the Earl of Durham—one who had undoubtedly also a mind of his own. Along with him went expert advisers, Gibbon Wakefield no less, and Charles Buller. The Durham Report which resulted stands as the first of a long and distinguished line of official papers. Often since that time 'Reports' have given such a clear, well-informed lead as had been conspicuously lacking till Durham's day; it is this lack that makes the record of earlier colonial 'policy' on the whole a rather dreary story. Durham's analysis being full and detailed as never before, the fresh view of such an independent outsider gave even Canadians a new understanding of their own country. It is evidence only of human limitations that history quickly ruled against many of Durham's actual recommendations; Upper and Lower Canada were to be reunited (and for a time they were) in order that British example and influence might overcome 'the idle and narrow notion of a petty and visionary nationality' (that of the French). On the other hand, the country as a whole must, so he advised, have self-government on the British model. For the first time this was taken to necessitate not merely a council to aid the Governor but a body of responsible departmental heads who would in fact be ministers, if not yet so called. It was not so good that British sovereignty was to be safeguarded by reserving to it the control of external affairs, of foreign trade, and (clearly under the influence of Wakefield) also of land; Wakefield's ultimate land theory came in truth parlously near 'colonialism' in legendary form; vacant colonial land made, in his view, 'the ample appanage' of the crowded masses in the mother country. The solid body of the Durham Report, the strong lead for 'self-government', happily outweighed such trappings.

A strong lead was very necessary, for Lord John Russell's immediate reaction was to write from Downing Street (October 1839) asking how the Governor, the appointed representative of the sovereign power, was to take orders from a local assembly without himself becoming an independent sovereign. This poser came near to wrecking the hope of a peaceful settlement. Governor Lord Sydenham made a start with a rather stage-managed experiment in trusting a Canadian majority with the responsibility of office; but by 1843 Sir Robert Peel's ministry had taken fright and sent Lord Metcalfe to tighten up imperial control. The result was that by 1845 chaos was come again—a condition bordering on renewed revolt. The answer was supplied at last by the admirable team work of Earl Grey, who came to the Colonial Office in 1846, Sir John Harvey of Nova Scotia, and a great Governor-General, the Earl of Elgin. The native caution of the Colonial Office had fortunately made it demur to embodying Durham's reservations of power in a formal written constitution. The next steps were thus unfettered. In fact they were almost rule-of-thumb—a manner of carrying through a revolutionary change that may justly be claimed, this once at least, as a triumph of British constitutional lack-of-method. There was no such thing as a 'Responsible Government Act' for Canada; years later, in 1872, the essentials of the Canadian settlement found their clearest expression at the Cape of Good Hope; when that colony became fully self-governing it was by virtue only of the short 'Responsible Government Act' of its own Parliament which decreed that henceforth certain officers (viz. Colonial Secretary, Treasurer, Attorney-General, Commissioner of Lands and Works, and Secretary for Native Affairs), 'shall be eligible to be' (in effect it became *must* be) elected Members of Parliament; a rider added that these offices were no longer pensionable. There was little more to it in Canada; this short list of officers covered then and still covers the nucleus of any cabinet. As for the rider—in an instruction written by Earl Grey to the Governor of Nova Scotia in March 1847 the Secretary of State had originally, almost incidentally, drawn the important distinction between 'political' officers and the permanent staff of the civil service; when authorizing the appointment of Canadian party ministers he suggested, rather than stipulated, that any office-holders dismissed merely on the demand of incoming ministers must be compensated for loss and damage suffered. This reasonable requirement (or the prospective cost of meeting it) had its effect in moderating the claims of Canadian politicians. The acceptance of this principle also meant that Canada and its later imitators were assured the benefits of a stabilized civil service. The alternative was of course the

American 'spoils system'. A clean sweep of officials with every change of party administration may have some dubious advantages as a means of keeping officials lively by denying them the security our system offers; but the assured control of a handful of key offices gave Canadians all the control they really needed. The way was now clear for Lord Elgin, with Earl Grey's steady backing, to feel his way to abdicate from the position of Chief Executive and to assume the status of a constitutional monarch. So simply, in the end, the constitutional practice of the Canadian group of colonies was brought back into line with that ruling in Britain itself, and part of the answer found to the question on which Britain and America had split apart within the lifetime of men then still living.

The example was quickly followed. One after another the numerous British overseas settlements were equipped, or re-equipped, with 'responsible' government on the new model—and times have changed so much that it actually needed some gentle suasion from the British end to induce one or two of them to accept the heavier responsibilities that went with such self-government. None of the colonies was really in a position to be assertive of its sovereign independence, at any rate as an isolated unit. Yet it was almost easier for a colony to work amicably with the mother country than for neighbouring colonies to make common cause and stand together, as they had need, for common ends; (they were usually also near relations!) Here again it was Canada that gave a lead. It happened that in and after 1846, when Lord Elgin took office, events in Britain had unusually wide repercussions. The 'hungry forties' which caused a steady flow of emigration to Canada culminated in a major financial crisis, and in the sudden adoption of free trade; Canadian interests, resenting the loss of their preferential status in British markets, looked for a compensating new deal with the United States. The very existence of the U.S.A. was always a challenge to Elgin to demonstrate the merits of a non-republican form of democracy; it was urgent, he felt, to make self-government a success. He was at pains, therefore, to ease the economic position by negotiating a trade agreement with America and the bargain he made helped Canada to forget her free-trade grievances. Meanwhile hard times persisted at home and the resulting flood of new migrants to the West gave Canadians compelling reason to look to their own internal relationships. Durham's Union of the two Canadas never worked very smoothly; the give and take it made necessary might be beneficial, but now the security of very touchy French cultural interests in Quebec was increasingly threatened by the growing predominance of non-French elements in the West; at the same time this ever-expanding West must always be dependent on the St. Lawrence ports of entry, and its very different communities were likely soon to stretch all the way across North America to the Pacific.

The fifties saw no change, but in 1861, as if to point a warning of the dangers of mere drift in such matters, the Civil War broke out in the great American Union. When this struggle was at its height, and under its influence, Sir John Macdonald was able in October 1864 to convene a national convention at Quebec. A federal agreement, in the first place for Canada and the Maritime Provinces, was successfully arrived at and this wholly Canadian document was immediately endorsed (as by law anything affecting more than one colony required to be) by the Home Parliament. The Quebec draft thus became the British North America Act of 1867 which duly constituted the Dominion of Canada. The accession of British Columbia in 1871 brought all the far-stretched Provinces together into one effective whole. Local rights were well secured; but Canadians also took warning from America's recent experience and actually gave the 'Dominion of Canada' a more strongly entrenched central government than that of the U.S.A.

The Canadian move preserved the unity of the Empire and was one way round the old American difficulty. But it was something more—a decisive contribution, in fact, to that adaptation of British, or essentially English institutions which has transformed an Empire into a Commonwealth; internal divisions within a colony, or between colonial neighbours, have more than anything else given occasion for arbitral but usually unpopular imperial intervention; it was this that set eighteenth-century America aflame (Chapter 1). When Canadians shouldered the responsibility for smoothing out their own divisions they made this arbitral imperial role superfluous; perhaps the magnanimity of British statesmen and their practical good sense in abating claims to sovereignty had otherwise been of less avail. Only a few years earlier, in 1858, an experienced Governor, Sir George Grey, wrote a famous dispatch asking for a free hand to repair 'the dismemberment of South Africa' to which a recent British decision confirming her people in their divisions had contributed. Grey was very nearly summarily dismissed for his temerity but, as he foresaw, the divisions persisted; they were at last directly responsible (see Chapter 7) for dragging Britain herself into a major war; the old sores have indeed continued to fester in the body politic of the South African Union which only that war availed to bring into being. 'Responsible' government certainly spread fast and far, but so long as the colonies thus dignified included adjacent but divided fragments this was not enough; the federal idea, which the Home Government would not and perhaps could not herself impose, was essentially complementary. Yet it failed to commend itself. Thus, even, if the consequences of delay were less serious, the more self-contained Australian colonies were nearly as slow to learn as the South African fragments. At any time the mere enhancement of a single colony's status by responsible or self-government will be dangerously satisfying to local pride. The sovereign indeed, having made way for self-government, can hardly do other than leave the colony to take its own course. The colony, on the other hand, is likely to be jealous of its new dignity. More than once in our own day even the formal unity imposed by the imperial power has been quickly shattered—as in India—by self-government. The converse will always be unusual. Only political sense of a high order will avail, as it did so early in Canada, to bring self-governing neighbours together of their own free will.

The newly self-governing colonies of the later middle nineteenth century were in truth weaker and less mature than their modern stature would suggest. They usurped the very name of colonies, and monopolized the services of the one Colonial Office, but their emergence even as dominions was only a gradual progress. Now that so many former dependants are stronger and themselves graduating to self-government, it has become usual to make it one jump from colonial dependence to full, independent Commonwealth status. The not-so-independent colonies of that earlier day were more modest; they were even glad, it would appear, to be able, as young growing communities need, to conserve their strength for their own internal development. Even Canada, the strongest of them, endured till only the other day a long 'colonial' phase, without obvious strain. All colonies, great and small, enjoyed the protection of what was then the strongest world power. The Royal Navy was a reassurance to the lesser, outlying units and even the stronger called at one time or another on British military aid. All had their interests sufficiently represented all over the world by British diplomatic and consular agents; none, therefore, felt much urge to be building up, and paying for, its own Department of External Affairs and its own foreign service. Canada was perhaps the least vulnerable of them; she and her great neighbour kept unbroken peace for a whole century on the undefended 49th parallel; but even Canada was better placed for having British backing in her dealings with her sometimes emphatic American neighbours. If it was only by force of habit, important services were given on the one side and received on the other with almost equally little question. But British overlordship was more than formal; the legislation of the colonial governments, even certain of the appointments they made, required Her Majesty's, in effect Her ministers' approval, and this was by no means to be assumed. The Colonial Office, indeed, learnt to walk warily. Serving officers I have known considered that in the 1930s a strong Crown Colony governor was able to take a stand against London from his dependency and 'get away with it' as if he were a John Macdonald or a Cecil Rhodes! The C.O. learnt discretion in a tough school, but habitual caution is not to be mistaken for total abdication. A right to veto legislation persisted. This clumsy weapon went virtually unused; but it constituted also a right to be consulted, and the records have yet to reveal how much dubious colonial legislation was sensibly modified, or even withdrawn altogether, in face of criticisms made by London before ever the local (e.g. Rhodesian) legislatures came to handle it.

The British yoke was light indeed; it is nevertheless surprising what a long apprenticeship so many increasingly vigorous young states were content to serve. The limits of the self-government they practised were nowhere defined—again it proved fortunate that the powers Lord Durham proposed to reserve to the imperial authority were never written into any constitution. So when Canada took control of her own lands and of her foreign trade, and in 1859 even asserted her right to tax British manufactures, she was at any rate within the letter of the law; there was, therefore, little occasion for public debate and Canadian practice was quietly accepted, with serious demur almost only at the breach of free trade principle. An Australian, Mr. H. Duncan Hall, justly remarked in the days of the First World War, when closer definition was at last being sought, on the essential 'instability' of responsible government; there was nothing but her own convenience to hinder a strong state like Canada from assuming full control of her own external relations, or for that matter, 'cutting the painter'. Ties both of interest and of sentiment sufficed to bind even Canada in a nominal dependence which left her free to concentrate all her energy on her own internal development. The sister states of the Australian group were still too many, those in South Africa too sharply divided, to cherish wider national ambitions. As late as 1905 Mr. Richard Jebb was writing essays on 'Colonial Nationalism' as of a new and almost surprising phenomenon.

The overseas settlements might be self-governing but their consciously pioneering phase was not yet ended; till the speed of modern transport and communications annihilated distance even internal intercourse was slow and hampered. An enduring sense of physical isolation made it unlikely that any considerable body of opinion would be strongly nationalist; links with the parent country were links also with the distant, civilized outer world. These ties were at this time unusually close and personal. Recent arrivals, the many forced out of Britain by the recurrent economic crises of the mid-century, and their children, were almost everywhere a factor of strong account. The practice, which persisted, of speaking of Britain as 'Home' certainly gave mild offence to older settlers at the Cape and perhaps elsewhere, but even Cape Afrikaners neither envied nor deferred to their kinsfolk in the neighbouring republics. At the same time, Cape Coloured people and also many West Indians were almost assertively 'British' in sentiment. Those contemplating this scene from the British end showed excusable self-complacency at the orderly progress and evident 'loyalty' of so many promising daughter states. For the colonists themselves the practice of self-government was a satisfying exercise to be going on with. The next would-be forward movement came, accordingly, from the British end where gratification was further stimulated by hopeful reports from the large body of recent emigrants. More than ever before these were drawn from all ranks of society, and steamer mails were now regular, very cheap, and fast enough to keep widely separated families and friends in intimate touch. Enthusiastic reports of the 'great possibilities' open in the new lands were often backed by more substantial evidence: Highland crofter homes, for example, often benefited. 'The colonies' thus came to inspire hope and expectancy as well as national pride, and also a lively and genuine concern for their welfare. The Colonial Institute, for example, later the Royal Empire Society, was founded in 1868 and, besides building up an important library, provided a central forum.

The rise of colonial nationalism noted by Mr. Jebb in 1905 was in part a rebound from the cult of Empire in which this British enthusiasm issued; British imperialism, which had an obvious focus in the august figure of Queen Victoria, earned its name and made its mark, if ever it did, in the last years of her long reign, suitable occasions offering when Her Majesty, who was proclaimed Empress of India in 1878, celebrated a Jubilee in 1887, and a still more resplendent Diamond Jubilee in 1897. It was characteristic of the times that in 1895 Joseph Chamberlain, a front-rank national statesman, deliberately elected to serve in the hitherto soberly regarded Secretaryship of State for the Colonies, and that a modest Conference of Colonial Prime Ministers brought together for the first time in 1887 had by 1897 become, under his leadership, the Imperial Conference. British Ministers, faced now by questions of foreign policy or defence which were of common concern to more than one self-governing state, tended to think of these as calling for some super-government; it was as if the parts needed to be reunited to the parent body, and this allowed enthusiasts to campaign for outright imperial federation. Chamberlain, in particular, hoped to bind the whole of this Empire on which the sun never sets into an effective world state centred in London. The daughters, for their part, were warmly attached to the Mother Country; they rallied enthusiastically to send 'Colonial' contingents to help her after the 'Black Week' of the Boer War in December 1899; but the idea of joining to build a super-state made no appeal—the international barometer was no longer steadily set fair and the prospect of being drawn into war in British quarrels was disquieting; increasingly conscious, too, of matters which were their own peculiar concern they were impatient even of their weaker sisters, the dependencies; in 1907 their influence had the Colonial Office split into separate 'Colonies' and 'Dominions' divisions. They were ready enough to join in consultations, but steadily obstructed efforts to give the Imperial Conference some continuity, refusing even to agree to its setting up a permanent secretariat.

Even so, it was at last only the First World War that gave imperial evolution its decisively modern direction. The declaration made by Great Britain in 1914 automatically involved the whole Empire in war; but it was for the last time; Canada, strongly backed by South Africa, set the course firmly for 'Dominion status', so defined as to mean virtual independence. The Peace Conference at Versailles prepared the way for the Dominions (now strictly so named) to become individual members of the League of Nations. The late Mr. Lionel Curtis and his fellow knights of the modern *Round Table* still fought a stout rearguard action; effective imperial unity was, they insisted, essential to buttress world peace; they prevailed so far that they gave currency to the idea and established the name of the *Commonwealth*; but it was the Dominions politicians who gave the idea expression. The Balfour Declaration of 1926 pronounced the Commonwealth to be a body of sovereign independent states, equal in status, in no way subordinate one to another, freely associated of their own free will for their common good. The consequential Statute of Westminster of 1931 was required only to underwrite *independence* by removing all remaining semblances of legal dependence. The emphasis, disregarding actual achievement of power, is on equality; the idea of unity almost drops out—even if on the showing of the late Mr. L. S. Amery, in the All Souls smoking-room one Sunday morning during the sittings of the 1926 Conference, the archetype of the phrasing was the Athanasian Creed! Any pronouncement on status was likely to be acceptable only if it was an assertion also of the member states' new freedom from imperial guidance and control. The United Kingdom, still much the strongest and far the most widely experienced member of the Commonwealth, had most to contribute but found its own freedom of action and even of expression limited by the need to defer always to sensitive and sometimes over self-conscious fellows. Once at least a U.K. representative (again it was Mr. Amery) was constrained to beg Prime Ministers to 'remember that the U.K. too enjoys full Dominion status!' Such unsleeping egalitarianism has continued to embarrass the efforts any of the freely associated equals may have wished to make to give substantive meaning to their undertaking to work together for their common good.

The long series of Commonwealth Conferences in great variety may, however, be more promising evidence of active life than is always appreciated; their work is carefully prepared in advance 'at the official level' where the work of any government is done, and treasurers, defence ministers, even over-burdened prime ministers have been assiduous in their attendance. So much is possible only because officials are constantly pooling information and comparing notes at Commonwealth capitals throughout the world; matters of any kind of mutual interest, from foreign affairs and relationships to subjects of purely departmental concern, become the occasion for close and, above all, *continuous* consultation. As a settled routine, this is something new in the everyday diplomacy of sovereign independent states. As between the members of the Commonwealth it only conserves the old links; the one innovation is that any meeting of the members is now a meeting of equals, the senior no longer having the decisive last word; and it is an advantage that the parts are now in touch with each other as well as with the old sovereign power. Commonwealth collaboration is rooted thus in the old associations, the common working language, and the common institutions inherited from the colonial or, in important instances, the imperial past. The practice may well be a model for wider imitation; but it must be more difficult when even such gradually evolved co-ordinating machinery as the Commonwealth Relations Office has to be improvised, and where there is no guiding tradition of joint activity.

The Commonwealth is not and as constituted could not be a body fitted to make decisions and take action on them; action is for its sovereign individuals alone. Its newer members, those graduating directly from colonial to Commonwealth status, have close and recent traditions associating them with the former imperial power, but they are likely to be even more jealous of their new independence than some of the original members; having less power of their own to sustain independence they may be even less inclined to work actively for 'their common good'. As things are, the Commonwealth has rarely if ever got so far as to make any helpful common pronouncement of its own on world affairs. The newer members have the best reason to remember, and may perhaps take warning from the earliest phase of Commonwealth history from which we started; the effort that went originally to the setting up of the superstructure of responsible self-government distracted attention altogether from the necessity of looking also to its social foundations. It is nothing new for the pursuit of self-government to become an exciting and all too absorbing end in itself. The outstanding example is the neglect earlier dependencies suffered in the years that should have been above all the years of reconstruction in the West Indies.

Chapter 4

THE WEST INDIES

*

The newly-free people of the West Indies started their life as citizens leaderless and divided. Few of their scattered islands are within sight of a neighbour. The largest, Jamaica, is distant two days even by modern steamship from any other British island, and historical differences are intensified by this physical separation. Though local affairs have always been in charge of at least five or six separate administrations, even the foster mother, the Colonial Office, was apt to generalize as if the islands were a natural unit. The social developments in the critical thirty years following emancipation would properly need to be pursued not only island by island but almost district by district.

The immediate effects of emancipation can be exaggerated; the slaves had never lived like miserable exiles and habits change slowly. Established customary privileges were some substitute for rights; 'ownership' made every plantation a community, almost a family—distinct from other plantations as from foreign lands; and life there was no barracked existence, like that of many bare African mining compounds of not so long ago; 'Monk' Lewis thought the thatched cottages and gardens compared well with those of British labourers. Housing may indeed have been insanitary, and would have been almost for choice near mosquito-infested water-courses; malaria and yellow fever were the curse of most of the islands and took heavy toll also of the Europeans. The pattern of labour on the estates remains even today very much as it always was. Workers are organized in gangs under a leader, often of their own choice; all work is piece-work and one 'task' is never a full day's work. In 'crop', which in most of the colonies lasted for only three or four months, temper-fraying exertions put severe strain on all, including the managerial and factory staff; the overtime then required was responsible for a good many of the labour troubles that followed emancipation. In British Guiana there was more than one crop and more continuous labour was required than the emancipated slaves were willing to supply. In Jamaica, on the other hand, where there is a long season between the sugar crops, the slaves had long been allotted 'provision grounds' and encouraged to grow their own food, being given regular time off to attend to these. The long week-end thus became a tradition and the Sunday markets at which produce was sold were great social occasions; by sale of their produce and by the exercise of crafts and skills on their own account slaves were able to earn and save money and might even buy themselves free. The irregular wage-earning which still makes West Indian output low and labour costs relatively high have a historical background; even if it means going without food West Indians still reckon a three-day working week enough to give to the service of any employer.

The predominance of males in the slave society is certainly exaggerated; customary 'marriages' were usual and indeed encouraged, if only to prevent the men from roaming. From earliest times, as Sir Hans Sloane bears witness, planters made it their policy to keep the balance even between the sexes; there was nothing like the seven-to-one proportion of males which still makes for instability in many African urban areas. Infantile mortality was very high, as everywhere in the tropics until very recent times, and this checked the expected natural increase of population, in spite, in later years at least, of considerable attention given to the health of mothers. In the principal islands there were also many who had never been slaves, in effect a slowly growing middle class. Unions between lonely European males and slave women or women of mixed blood were socially accepted, numerous, and by no means only casual; the children were as a rule well cared for and educated, and they even became well-to-do—a few inherited land and slaves in their own right. Most if not all the islands, except perhaps Barbados, thus had many coloured or 'brown' people, the children of European fathers or the descendants of such. By the time of Catholic Emancipation at home a 'coloured party' was an active force in Jamaica where the 'brown men' had been joined in the battle for civic rights by the wealthy and influential Jewish community. But as leaders and champions of the people these men had limitations; expenditure on education and development got little support from politicians who in the old parliamentary tradition were wont to resist taxation and to denounce all government spending. The 'brown' men's standing in society was not yet secure and they were self-centred, holding aloof from the darker-skinned masses very much as in very early days when almost the only 'colonists' had been white.

The original colonists had contended successfully that by right of British birth they were entitled to remain subject only to laws enacted by the British Parliament or by themselves; it has been said to be logical enough that they should enjoy the rights of European colonists anywhere else. But as the slave population grew the normal functions even of local government continued to be exercised by the white minority. Except in such an emergency as a slave rising each plantation relied on its own staff to keep law and order, and each owner was responsible for the behaviour of his slaves—it was even difficult to get rid of a criminal since (as became evident after emancipation) public prisons were few and inadequate. When the 600,000 slaves became free citizens this private jurisdiction was inadmissible. Yet it was without attempting to revise the existing constitutions that the Colonial Office made its attempt to use 'apprenticeship' as the means of securing an orderly transition. In 1833 the young Howick (later, as Earl Grey, a notable Secretary of State) served as Under-Secretary to the Colonial Office and worked closely with James Stephen and Henry Taylor on the details of this system; but, administered as it was direct from home, imposed on yet not abrogating the planters' political rights, the plan almost inevitably misfired. It was thus that in 1838 the Office was driven as a desperate last throw to propose the abrogation of the Jamaican constitution; that too having failed there was need to think again—but the Canadian crisis intervened.

One remaining consideration was now coming uppermost, that the estates, no longer sure of labour, might collapse altogether, and the island revenues along with them. It turned out that this fear was not insubstantial. As the makers of the centrally conceived plan of apprenticeship were apt to forget, much depended on local conditions which varied greatly even from one district to the next. Thus in Barbados, a small, flat and easily traversed island about the size of the Isle of Wight, the soil grows cane uniformly well, but little else, and its almost temperate climate attracted and kept more resident estate owners than usual, so that estates, of modest size, were under close supervision. There being little or no waste land for slaves to use for provision grounds, the large population of freed slaves had really no choice but to carry on as before, working the canefields for a living. So too in the two small islands, Antigua and St. Kitts, less reliable rainfall made against peasant cultivation. The Barbados planters came to terms with their labour and on the whole kept their side of the bargain. Being sure of labour, they kept up their output, their own solvency and that of their government. Their position as the natural leaders of the island community went almost unchallenged. Even the 300-year-old constitution stood substantially unchanged till only the other day.

The experience of Jamaica is more typical. Most of that much larger island is as Columbus described it when he likened its contours to those of the paper he crumpled in his hand before Queen Isabella. Much rugged mountain land that was useless for cane was capable of producing a variety of other crops; the soil is light and has limited fertility, but a heavy rainfall makes quick growth. The freed slaves, accustomed to cultivating for themselves, took up new ground in the hill country. After apprenticeship, when the planters began to demand rent for houses and gardens on the plantations, this movement was accentuated, missionaries helping enthusiastically to organize 'free villages'. The 'free peasantry' which established itself was often to be cited as a model when practice elsewhere, especially in Nevis and Montserrat, had degenerated into a most unsatisfactory system of share-cropping or *métayage*. But, notably in Jamaica, the first effect was that labourers withdrew from the estates in large numbers and, in fact, the economy of most of the islands was severely shaken. In British Guiana on the mainland estates that had brought in a regular £4,000 a year were by 1848 making a loss. In 1850 the Jamaican parish of Portland had only four plantations producing where there had been twenty-eight; coffee production, too, had virtually ceased. The estate owners were not the only losers; the total number of doctors in Jamaica fell shortly after 1834 from some 200 to fifty, recovering to the 200 level only a century later. The decline of the plantocracy thus left gaps that yawned open in the troubled post-emancipation years. The gulf between ruler and ruled has not even yet been satisfactorily bridged.

The revenues of the Islands' governments also suffered in the general breakdown. From the very start the taxation payable by owners for the slaves on their muster-rolls lapsed, and now the decline in estate imports made the receipts from customs dwindle away. The Home Government was prevailed on after prolonged argument to sanction a novel experiment and to introduce Indian immigrant labourers; these were the means of saving a complete collapse in Trinidad (a newly conquered, therefore directly ruled colony), and in British Guiana, where unusually continuous employment on the irrigation furrows made labour consistently scarce. It has been described as tragic that the most lasting memorial of Earl Grey's zealous administration in 1846–51 was the introduction of indentured Indian labour; but Grey knew the realities of the situation better than most and the desperate political and economic situation in Demerara virtually forced him to act; the possibility of untoward social and political consequences never occurred to the originators of this scheme. Seeing clearly the need, for example, of social services, Grey concluded that, solvency being imperative, his first duty must be to restore the output of the estates. Knowing, too, that Treasury help was out of the question (he was himself a faithful follower of *laissez-faire* economics), he was moved by the hope that general prosperity would enable the workers themselves to contribute more adequately to the cost of the schools and hospitals they obviously needed. For Jamaica no escape-door was opened, in some part just because the resources and the interests of this island were more varied. In the Assembly the strong 'coloured party' threw its weight definitely against immigration, being inclined, like some liberals in or about the Colonial Office, to think that peasant proprietorship was equal to carrying the economy, and that sugar might be allowed to die a natural death. In the event the economic situation clearly went from bad to worse; after 1846, when the British sugar preference was withdrawn, Jamaica was virtually bankrupt. The political crisis which then ensued —something like open war between harassed governors and indignant, impoverished assemblies over questions of supply—was resolved only in the 1860s.

In all these years of financial embarrassment and strain the services needed for the re-equipment of the common people were inevitably a casualty. So long as the rule stood that every colony must 'live of its own' little help was to be looked for from H.M.G. Even the British political conscience then took little count of social duties; it was only in 1867 that Robert Lowe proclaimed the need at least to educate our masters. The West Indies of those days were no health or holiday resort; the '40s and '50s saw terrible epidemics of cholera and smallpox; but even had theory permitted, the state, represented by many ill-supplied island governments, was little able to attempt a remedy. When opportunity offered the Home Government was not unsympathetic; sometimes it did good almost by stealth, as when, to strengthen the established Anglican Church, the West Indian diocese was subdivided (1842), or again when the substantial accumulated funds of the unused Mico Charity, intended for Barbary slaves, were diverted to promote Negro education in Jamaica. But the civilizing mission of Empire devolved for the greater part on voluntary helpers.

The economics of the day, 'the dismal science', was after all an attempt to analyse and clarify, tackling one thing at a time; thus 'business is business', and more humane feelings must find expression, separately, in good works and so-called 'philanthropy'. George Canning made glorious fun of 'The Needy Knife-grinder and the Friend of Humanity', but the philanthropic movement had its active side and did much constructive work in places like the West Indies. The philanthropic sentiments of prosperous English business people were the mainstay of the missionary movement; and even if many missionaries were perforce of those passing rich on forty pounds a year, the planting of a world-wide system of missions, a stupendous and costly enterprise, was successfully carried through. In the West Indies, after some Moravians who had made little headway in the dry uplands of St. Elizabeth in Jamaica, an American Negro Baptist began work in that island in 1782 and was instrumental in bringing the Baptist Missionary Society of Britain to establish itself there. Methodist and Presbyterian missions followed from 1814 onwards. The L.M.S. was less prominent here than in Africa, except in Demerara and Berbice. The C.M.S. left the Anglican field to the older S.P.G.; the latter society did well by the Negroes on the Codrington College estates in Barbados and won approval at a time when Anglicans in general, being of the established Church, were thought to be identified with the plantocracy; the stand made by Free Church pioneers for the slaves' rights made their early years contentious. But the evangelical home front was assiduous to keep in touch: sponsored deputies of the Foreign Missions Committees and societies frequently toured the mission-stations, even those in the dangerous climate of West Africa. Private individuals, too, like Joseph Sturge of the Society of Friends, made comprehensive tours; Sturge's published and widely read report on 'The West Indies in 1837', whatever its qualities or defects, was instrumental in bringing the prisons and apprenticeship debates to a head. Mission views of whatever was afoot in any of the fields thus never lacked spokesmen in the highest quarters; the predominantly Liberal political influence of the mission-minded Free Churches was comparable till as late as the election of 1906 with that of the trade unions.

The Missions certainly made their major social contribution in education, but their earliest efforts were sharply challenged in the West Indies. The indictment laid in 1824 against Smith of Demerara (see p. 58) alleged that his teaching:

> 'did promote discontent and dissatisfaction in the minds of the Negro slaves towards their lawful masters . . . thereby intending to excite the said Negroes to open revolt and rebellion'.

Brougham's rhetoric in the House of Commons debate on this Demerara episode put the case simply:

> 'The question is not "shall the Negroes be taught by missionaries?" but, "Shall they or shall they not be taught at all?" '

Both of Brougham's questions were soon answered in the affirmative and the Missions long continued to equip and run almost all the schools there were. Both the strength and the weakness of the missionary movement lay in the self-confident optimism which was the mark of that age, when religion and politics were always closely interlocked. The most 'advanced' social reformers, for example in the trade unions, were usually active Christians, to whom the sentiment of Bishop Heber's 'From Greenland's icy mountains' came easily and naturally. Cecil Rhodes's sturdy L.M.S. antagonist, John Mackenzie, a keen man of affairs, was so sure of the merits of our common civilized ways that he assumed British settlers to be the best and quickest means of spreading enlightenment even in complex southern Africa; I distinctly remember the approval given in a missionary household about the year 1900 to A. R. Wallace's book on the nineteenth century—*The Wonderful Century*. The fruits of civilized achievement were thus for any to share who would. But the teachers chose to lead West Indians by the hard way, with little to adapt or water down even secular teaching to local needs; it was almost 'take it or leave it'. No one seriously studied non-Christian 'custom', or even realized the influence of physical and environmental factors. Faced in the West Indies and in still newer countries, or even in India, with situations of the greatest social complexity, the missionaries did not set themselves to study customs but to uproot them, and to substitute Christian civilization as they knew it—the individualist, fiercely competitive civilization of their homeland.

The view that the pietism of the earliest Evangelicals was a paralysing influence cannot be reconciled with evidence of the regard still cherished for the Baptist, William Knibb, and others for the work they did for peasant cultivation in Jamaica. The missionaries clearly did most of what little was done, positively, to raise the social level in the West Indies. Their unaided resources could not hope to build a nation-wide school system; illiteracy remained at 50 per cent and is 25 per cent even today; a later governor put it that the people were freed, but a society was not born. It is true that the people of African descent who were the Missions' concern came all but unanimously to profess and call themselves Christians; the islanders even became, in the Scots phrase, 'kirk-greedy'. Yet Church organization was strangely ineffective; perhaps missionaries were too few. Church discipline failed conspicuously to make Christian marriage more than a remote and ultimate ideal for the majority of the people; to this day 70 per cent of the population are born either of casual encounters or of so-called 'common-law marriages' which are by no means always life-long unions; few of these children even know their fathers. One foremost authority on West

Indian life and custom is of opinion that the men's deplorably weak sense of paternal responsibility, and hence the lack of family ambition, is one of the greatest obstacles to West Indian advancement. Nevertheless, West Indians have retained their own ideas of kinship responsibility among a wider family group, and so far as it functions this can be a stabilizing influence, making land ownership a family rather than an individual interest. The independent and responsible role played by the women may similarly reflect African matrilineal tradition. The pity is that the missions were at small pains to understand the people and their ingrained customs in those chaotic thirty years when they had the field to themselves. Be that as it may, the devoted life of many of the missionaries and the example they set still made them worthy ambassadors of civilization. The vaunted prosperity of the eighteenth century, even for those who shared it, was war-torn and precarious; but now there was complete security against threats from without and, in spite of strains, peace ruled within. The conditions being stable, the mission schools, inadequate as they might be, were able to train and equip workers to carry on what was begun; over the years they powerfully helped the magic of the Queen's name and the devotion of many governors to bind the West Indian people in such close and spontaneous attachment to their British associations that 'alien' rule entirely ceased to be felt as alien. West Indian values became not only wholly Western but essentially British values. Freedom from want, unhappily, the people have never fully known; but it was not for nothing that they went to school with the Britain of the great Victorian age; freedom of speech and of thought and, in the end, political freedom, were the distinctive contributions of secular Britain.

The troubles of the West Indies were basically economic, and the Victorians habitually sought a political remedy even for social and economic ills. But the very success of the prescription used in Canada, though the same would not answer here, hindered experiment on other lines even when the war of the elected representatives with the governor in Jamaica was at its worst. The doings of the Assembly in the late '40s and early '50s were often irresponsible and factious; it was a local cynic who commented that the best and ablest citizens could not afford to play politics, and those actually in the game could not afford *not* to! But for a time cholera and smallpox raged and stark ruin faced the planters. These had sometimes been obstructive in the past but now the Kingston traders were also concerned, and the strong, rather more complacent 'coloured party' always took a hand. The state of representation was such that by 1863, when the total population of the island was some 450,000, there were only 1,794 registered voters; yet the elected members were, after all, a reasonably good cross-section of the country's major interests. Even the fortunes of the great voiceless black majority were involved in the national bankruptcy which was the real occasion of the Assembly's stopping of supply. It is often said that only the ability and tact of a succession of distinguished governors kept the machine on the rails at all (it was a legacy of the palmier days that the office of 'Captain-General and Governor' was a 'plum' of the Service and attracted able men, Sir Charles (Lord) Metcalfe and the Earl of Elgin among their number); but this means, too, that the turbulent Assembly could be reasonable or could be 'managed'. Earl Grey, before vacating office, even thought to bait the Assembly into voting supply by offering 'responsible' government on the Canadian model, and sent an able governor, Sir Henry Barkly, to try his hand, even arming him with the promise of a Treasury loan—'not to exceed £60,000'—to tide over the financial crisis. In 1853 Barkly set up a more broadly based Executive Committee; by including elected members he hoped to give the executive its own spokesmen in the Assembly, and so to reduce the paralysing effect the obstructing legislature often had on the executive arm. In practice the salaried nominees were repudiated as costly government 'stooges', but in 1856 the *elected* Assembly actually passed a modestly liberal education measure of Governor Barkly's, only to have it rejected by the *nominated* Upper Chamber for its 'iniquitous' adjunct, a house-tax! The paralysis of the executive remained; only an easing of economic stress (due to better prices) brought some respite.

At last, just as the federal moves in Canada were approaching finality, the Colonial Office found itself compelled to come to grips with the situation (and Sir Henry Taylor, who had long ago minuted for the abrogation of the Jamaican constitution, was now half-retired but still almost first in counsel). An untrammelled and effective executive was now the goal and, dearly loving a precedent, the Office had found one, in the Gambia; that little outpost had a governor who was legally supreme in administration and everything else, and it gave no trouble. But *Campbell* v. *Hall* (see p. 30), the Court's vindication of the rights of the 'plantocracy' of Grenada, still stood in the way of direct action. It was hard, too, whatever the Office might advise, for Secretaries of State to press responsible self-government on Parliament as a panacea for Canada and other leading colonies, and yet to recommend a directly opposite course in another—and Jamaica was still almost better known.

While the authorities hesitated events took charge. In October 1865 a popular demonstration near Morant Bay culminated in a serious riot,

The 'prompt' official counter-action amounted to reprisals; a total of over 600 died—some were shot but 354 were executed after trial by courts martial. Hot dispute has raged on this episode—a respected governor of Jamaica, the late Lord Olivier, has indignantly denounced both Eyre and the use of the epithet 'rebellion'. A more recent colonial administrator, Sir Alan Burns (who has also seen more politically inspired violence), passes judgment that though the riots were purely local in origin the guardians of law and order were bound to check such violence severely for fear of the example spreading among the highly excitable people of the ill-defended Island. Fear clearly intensified the bias and indiscipline of the West Indian militia, to which a recent West Indian historian ascribes the excessive rigour of the repressive measures actually taken. It stands out as a considered governmental action that George William Gordon, a leading coloured member of the Assembly, was summarily hanged as (in Eyre's own words a year later) 'the proximate occasion of the insurrection'. Such short shrift as Gordon got is not infrequently demanded by die-hards, but our age is more familiar with the shock tactics of 'political agitators' than the Victorians were, and more tolerant of their ways. The hot-heads who rushed the Governor were in no position and in no mood to assess fairly the discontent of the masses—their sense of grievance, intensified momentarily by the effects of the American civil war, went deeper than Eyre or any of his ruling-class advisers realized or allowed for. The hopeful energy stimulated in many of the people by emancipation was now much weakened; but the thirty years of freedom had kept hope and expectancy alive. Leaders like Gordon stirred their hopes of acquiring 'more land', and other good things, by their own political effort.

The Governor at least turned the situation to account. The politicians had for some time known very well that a change in their own status was inevitable. The Assembly, agreeing that 'strong' government was essential—if only, as they themselves said, for fear of Jamaica becoming a second Haiti—at once passed an act which proposed a single Council, half its members nominated and half elected. Before this could take effect instructions from home prompted Eyre to ask for more. At thinly attended meetings, in the off-month of December, he succeeded in getting a second Act passed authorizing H.M. to create and constitute a new government 'in such form as may seem fitting', and to take power also 'from time to time to alter and amend it'. It was thus that the Assembly itself freed the Crown from the cramping restraints of *Campbell* v. *Hall*, clearing the way for direct action by Order in Council. This time the Colonial Office was not caught unprepared. In June 1866 a new constitution was in being which, with one significant modification in 1884, carried Jamaica through many vicissitudes till our own day, 1944. The new Crown Colony system was distinctive—and I draw here on unpublished researches of Dr. F. R. Augier which clearly reveal both the general plan and how decisively it was modified by the experience gained in Jamaica between 1866 and 1884. Unlike earlier rule by the Crown, and however much it professed only to follow precedent, this was a conscious effort to meet special needs and to provide a working alternative to 'responsible' self-government as practised in the more mature parts of the Empire. The considered attempt to fill this obvious gap is the essence of the matter—a meticulous attention to local variations of the one pattern has too much obscured its significance. Governor Eyre's approaches to the Assembly when the island fell into the disorders of 1865 were directly in line with the policy suggested by the Gambia. A still more poorly equipped representative Assembly in the smaller island of Dominica had newly been replaced, in 1863, by a wholly nominated council; similarly in Jamaica the election of members was discontinued; a body of senior officials, directly answerable to the Governor, now sat *ex officio*, together with men nominated by the Governor from among the general public. As a rule, though not invariably, these 'unofficials' were one fewer in number—so that the official side had the decisive word. The composition of the Council might vary later from one Colony to another but the principle followed was always that practised in Jamaica from 1866 onwards. In the often quoted words of a Secretary of State, Lord Carnarvon, the very ambitious aim was to provide 'that direct protection by the Crown of the unrepresented classes which takes the place of representation'. The Governor, that is to say, now became directly and solely responsible for the administration of his Colony; legislation normally still required the consent of the Council. The Governor could if he saw fit direct the voting of his official majority; but, the Governor's overriding power being reserved necessarily for real and rare emergencies, the new plan preserved at all events one of the most distinctive merits of the British colonial system; so long as its legislation required local ratification every colony was assured of preserving its own individuality.

At last freed of his old dependence on an elected assembly which he did not control, the Governor became at the same time more directly and continuously answerable for his actions to the Secretary of State in London. The Secretary of State being himself responsible to the British Parliament, the doings of colonial governments were liable now, as never before, to be ventilated in Parliament. This opened a chapter of which the last pages are yet to be written. No one then went far in asserting the direct responsibility of the metropolitan power for the economic reconstruction of the dependent territories. It was of the 1870s that Dr. de Kiewiet noted how, in face of Colonial Office requests for help, it had become 'almost a Treasury rule to pay only for disasters' —by corollary, rarely to pay to forestall disaster. This was in tune with the *laissez-faire* rule that the best hope of progress in any colony is to leave the best-equipped individuals to work out their own salvation, and carry the others with them, as they best can. If, however, anything went at all seriously wrong there was now the certainty that critics were watching to fix the blame and, on the model set in the days of emancipation, to demand action. This concentration of criticism on the sorely-tried Colonial Office fostered a steady growth of the delusion that the distant metropolitan power is directly responsible for and can itself remedy all that is amiss in the colonies. Such habitual criticism of other people has done too much, as Mr. Guy Wint has said of the Asians, to weaken or destroy the powers of self-criticism of those who indulge it. The metropolitan power can at most help to equip the people on the spot to carry the burden themselves.

The constitutional experiment of 1866 in Jamaica ran for a time in comparatively smooth water. Britain had freed the slaves and her prestige stood high; the Negroes who were the neediest class, and not only the Negroes, had high hopes of the benefits to be looked for by the change from Assembly to direct *British* rule. Education and public works at once began to get more attention, and a larger share of the revenue. The first Governor, Sir John Peter Grant, was able to make good use of his powers, and of a run of good seasons, to provide better services and make new ventures; the Rio Cobre irrigation scheme was his and, with such help, the life of the community was set on less utterly insecure foundations. The peasantry in subsequent years were doing well enough to become the white hope, at the turn of the century, of notable governors like Sir Henry Norman and Lord Olivier. The increased local production of food and the marketing presently of bananas were, of course, in themselves an appreciable and unusual source of strength. The near-virgin soil yielded at first a fair subsistence, but it progressively wasted and deteriorated under the rough usage it suffered. When in the mid-1930s I suggested that holdings were now too small and tillage too indifferent to maintain the higher standards of a modern state, Lord Olivier was still so firm a believer in peasants that he chided me severely. It was not even then well understood how the quality of peasant agriculture must depend (fully more than that of plantations) on capital equipment, on aids and services or even helpful supervision such as only the state can furnish. The struggle for stability has had to be renewed in our own day.

Direct rule was a very heavy burden on the small body of officials, but it was the rigidity of the current economic theory, not a failure of persons, that actually put a term to it; the British Treasury was all too well able to enforce its rules. Sugar and subsidiary crops kept the revenue 'buoyant', but only till about 1873; then prices fell and the difficulties grew. Direct rulers must maintain strict impartiality and care for the interests of the island as a whole; always holding the balance even, they must not penalize the planters in the interest even of the poorest classes. It was when the struggles of the Government to make ends meet had already brought murmurs against arbitrary rule, especially against government extravagance, that an extraordinary, almost fantastic exercise of financial control from home played straight into the critics' hands. In 1881 the ship *Florence*, carrying arms to Cuba (where revolt was brewing against Spain), was seized by Governor Musgrave, but the courts ruled that the seizure was illegal and awarded the owners some £8,000 in damages. The seizure had been made in imperial interests and it was not unreasonably claimed that it was for Britain to pay. The Treasury's idea of compromise was to 'go halves'. When the Governor was required to use his official majority to recover £4,000 from the island revenues the rival parties sank their differences. Even the coloured politicians took up the cry and the fat was in the fire; if this was the British rule they had hoped so much from, the sooner the islanders recovered a say in the management of their own affairs the better. Direct rule had been found wanting. The experiment of 1866 sought not only to end the age-old conflict of governors with the Assembly but also, and more positively, to make the executive the special guardian of the unrepresented masses. Now the conscientious effort of officials to maintain strict impartiality had left them isolated, estranged from the public they must serve. The Home Government, having raised the storm, had qualms and appointed a Royal Commission to review the whole West Indian situation and make recommendations. The Commission's advice was that the time had come to make a modest advance in constitutional practice and try

> 'a system . . . tending towards more representative institutions and judiciously meeting the legitimate desires of the inhabitants'.

Recognizing that the most benevolent rule needs popular backing H.M.G. at once reconstituted the Jamaican Council by bringing in nine directly elected members to balance the four officials and five government nominees; the Governor was chairman but had a vote. After 1895 the official group was increased to fifteen to allow for fourteen elected representatives, one from each of the island parishes. High franchise qualifications restricted the electorate and left the interests relatively strong, but now only as a restraining influence—there was no return to 'plantocracy'. The masses were in truth so backward as to be insufficiently self-assertive; but, for many years, at least the politically conscious minority found fair opportunity for self-expression. The elected members' influence on affairs was by no means ineffective; it was agreed from the beginning that the official majority must not vote as one body unless on a measure certified by the Governor to be of urgent public importance. Since a governor could never make it everyday practice to use his official majority the elected members had a virtual veto on legislation. It was in Northern Rhodesia, about 1931, that I learnt in an aside from an M.P. friend how the elected members there would wring concessions from the Governor by daring him to use 'the steam-roller'—they knew very well he must almost inevitably give way rather than face embarrassing questions from London!

The date of this readaptation of the Jamaican constitution, 1884, was more important than anyone could then foresee. In no time delegates were gathering for the Berlin Conference which precipitated the partition of Africa. The Colonial Office had assiduously applied its brains and experience to the affairs of Jamaica and was soon using the Jamaican model, if it was only by inertia, as the standard pattern of Crown Colony rule for a growing number of its new wards in Africa and elsewhere. Evidence of the persisting influence of Jamaican usage comes again from Northern Rhodesia; about 1947 a Labour Secretary of State, Mr. Creech Jones, surprised many by deferring to its elected members so far as to agree that legislation to which they were unitedly opposed should be disallowed. This was only the Colonial Office being true, as always, to established precedent—the half-century-old practice in Jamaica. The powers and privileges enjoyed by the elected representatives of Jamaica were, however, reserved for relatively advanced peoples, not an invariable part of the standard Crown Colony pattern. Barbados and Bermuda actually carried on with only slightly modified versions of the very oldest constitutional model. These and other quite considerable local variations notwithstanding, Crown Colony government was the fruit of experience expressly and consciously applied to produce forms suited to the peculiar conditions.

It limited the use of the complete Jamaica model that the electoral principle was hard to apply anywhere outside the West Indian group of colonies. In Africa, particularly, the natural spokesmen of the people were the tribal chiefs; where they functioned they and their tribal officers could not well be by-passed. Normally, too, the potential electorate was almost wholly illiterate—the plan of making people vote for painted symbols is a very modern (and dubious) invention. Even so, the citizens of Freetown, Lagos, Accra, and others who sat loose to any tribal authority, chose their own members, and they manifestly learnt more than the rudiments of Western political ideas. They did so not only from books and papers but from actual practice; the people's use of political machinery was always assumed to be a rehearsal for bigger things. The voters were at any rate of any and every class, race and colour—and for many years what little demand there was for popular control was satisfied. The great drive for more and more self-government is wholly new; Jamaica itself began the post-1884 phase with one special privilege, and it was withdrawn without serious challenge: till 1899 the Government refrained from filling all the official vacancies and functioned without its official majority. It was actually Joseph Chamberlain who then insisted on filling the vacant places by way of security for Treasury help given to tide the Colony over a series of lean years—that most enthusiastic of Secretaries of State was also a hard man of business. Everywhere it was assumed, till the days of the Second World War, that the executive must be entrenched; the divisions and discords of the normal colonial society were such that the Government, which alone held the parts together, must be strong enough to put the sanctity of law and order beyond challenge.

The Governor, 'H.E.', was thus always and everywhere the linchpin of the system—the Queen's representative, and yet so much more than a titular head. The power of a capable governor to make a clear-cut decision—and even the pomp and ceremony that went with his office—must be held to have served a good purpose. There is recent evidence in abundance of the ill-effects of indecision in the Government especially of politically immature, not to say primitive peoples—and most of us enjoy a little pomp and ceremony. On the other hand, too much depended on the personal initiative of the Governor—the exclusive responsibility he bore inclined him almost to look for reasons for *not* doing things rather than to embark on *action* for which he could be called to account. The term of office being normally only five years, there was also a deplorable lack of continuity: successive governorships have even been said to amount to 'a series of new beginnings'. The Legislative Assembly was a safety-valve and provided an outlet for popular feelings—though just because the ultimate responsibility was always the Governor's, the elected members, for their part, suffered no penalty for giving bad advice or for the mere obstruction of which they were often guilty. At any rate no British governor could play the autocrat: *Fabrigas* v. *Mostyn* (p. 30) had settled that in principle long ago and there was, besides, always the right to appeal to London and to get grievances ventilated in the British Parliament. In the end it was perhaps not so much the system, but once more the *laissez-faire* economics of the age that was at fault. Joseph Chamberlain saw the dependencies as 'neglected estates' and sought a remedy (see Chapter 9), but the preoccupations of the South African War of 1899, and its cost, intervened. After him *laissez-faire* ruled again and purposeful colonial development virtually ceased for thirty years.

The economic stagnation of the colonies thus became ever more marked. Yet the Crown Colony system stood for fifty years and in the perspective of history appears as a reasonably successful attempt to come to grips with a peculiar situation. It was in the West Indies that the system took its essential shape and had its longest clear run. The governors were less well served there than their African colleagues—these came to rely largely on the unified Colonial Service—and years of over-centralization left only weak local institutions to carry the weight of a modern government. But, starting as they did from the social chaos of the 1830s, the people of the West Indies were tided over a formative period and have emerged—whether from Jamaica or Barbados or Nevis—as evidently one people, a nation in their own right. The Victorians, I have said, left them to learn the hard way. Many took that way, and they were more than enough to provide the sound administrative service on which the work of government must depend. No erstwhile 'colonial' society—and I speak from direct observation—is so well equipped to manage its own affairs. Others may have reason yet to envy West Indians the long apprenticeship they served as Crown Colonists.

Chapter 5

THE RULE OF LAW AT THE CAPE OF GOOD HOPE

*

The answers to the questions posed by conditions of the colonial kind considered in the first chapter of this study have so far been been substantially those supplied by statesmen of the far-away British imperial power. The negative lesson of the American Revolution never perhaps fully impressed itself; there are still those who fail to see that control becomes impossible when any strong section of the local community has become politically self-conscious. Nevertheless, the caution induced at home by experience in America had its influence in smoothing the way for the highly original and sufficiently British experiment of self-government within the Empire. The Crown Colony system (Chapter 4) was clearly also of British devising. These two not inconsiderable successes engendered a degree of complacency that was almost a disability in dealing with circumstances apparently of the same kind yet substantially different. The further development of the colonial theme was to be worked out in fact largely in Africa south of the Sahara, and the best maps of the 1860s show how little this Negro or negroid Africa was known even so lately. More than three centuries of the Colonial Age left it still the Dark Continent, for good reasons: till the interior plateau was penetrated the main stream of world traffic passed it by; little or nothing came out of Africa except exported man-power—slaves—and very few indeed of any race ventured beyond its coasts. The inland plateau, most of it at 4,000 feet or more, is healthy, and is a more connected whole than might appear. In South America the forest regions are divided one from another and remain still almost untouched from outside, but the African interior, though lacking America's river highways, is almost without natural barriers. It is possible that Zulu raiders from the far south may at some point have clashed with the equally warlike Masai of the north; it is certain that the activities of such marauding Africans, of Arabs, and later of Europeans, had repercussions far beyond their points of origin. Far from giving access to this healthier plateau region, the coastal country known to sailors even barred the way; two thousand miles of desert separated Morocco from Cape Verde, and nearly as many more stretched from south of the Congo to the Orange River. The Congo, navigable for only a short distance, remained unexplored, and a well-known shanty warned sailors against the notorious Guinea Coast:

The Bight of Benin! The Bight of Benin!
Few come out, but many go in!

Till Mungo Park and his successors dared to venture inland, Europeans sailed the Bight for centuries without ever connecting the creeks they got so many slaves from with the river already known from the Sahara side as the Niger. The stoutly-built European castles of the Guinea Coast were mere trading-forts, at most of long-term significance; the influence of Portuguese both east and west was purely local. Certainly the more distant east coast was regularly visited by Arab sailors, but it too was very unhealthy; even its dangerous seas long remained uncharted and Europeans gave it a wide berth. Thus the Dutch made no mistake when, as early as 1652, seeking no more than a refreshment station for their ships' companies on the long voyage to India, they lit upon Africa's one readily accessible oasis, one blessed, too, with a good Mediterranean climate—the peninsula near the shores of Table Bay.

The modest original venture at the Cape of Good Hope was at least carefully considered—as was to be expected of its sponsors, the Dutch East India Company. The directors' decision to plant a station was taken promptly in the end, but only after a marooned ship's company had reported almost with enthusiasm on their experience of an enforced stay at Table Bay two or three years earlier. A colony, properly so called, was in their innocence the last thing the Company wanted to be burdened with; from the beginning the Council of Seventeen tried to keep close control; the first 'settlers' were their own paid servants. The leader, Jan van Riebeeck, was hard put to it to do his part, so he complained, as 'his own engineer, delver, gardener, farmer, carpenter, smith'; he at least quickly learnt what it meant to wrestle with 'new' country; no one has bettered his protest that he was expected 'to bring forth everything out of nothing'. After five years of toil he persuaded his directors to take the inevitable but momentous step of strengthening his hand by inspanning a small body of 'free burghers', or, in effect, colonists. By 1662 the little community mustered a total of '1,394 souls'. Soon these were furnishing passing ships with fresh meat and other provisions, according to plan; at first there was also a little tobacco, but mercantilist principles ruled against luxury production in a purely utilitarian venture. Yet utility was not all: the varied fruits and the famous oak trees of the Cape Peninsula were a very early Dutch contribution. Soon the Cape was becoming known, too, as a health resort for men worn out or invalided by service in the more strenuous East Indies. Van Riebeeck appreciated that ultimate success must depend on his burghers learning to think of their new sphere as their own permanent home. This need not have caused him concern had he survived to see the 600 effective burghers of that day reinforced, after the Edict of Nantes, by some 200 French Huguenot refugees. The superior education of this accession, and their moral fibre, immeasurably strengthened the community. Designedly dispersed among the earlier comers, Dutch and German, they did much to make the Afrikaner people what they became, a distinct, a God-fearing and, increasingly, above all in their own consciousness, a peculiar people.

The Cape, so far, might almost have been a settlement on an Atlantic island for any contact it made with the realities of the African continent. It was destined to remain so more than long enough to confirm the new inhabitants in set ways and views that were all their own. The aboriginal inhabitants were too weak, if not also too few, to make much impression. The pigmy race of bushmen have left many remarkable rock paintings as a legacy, but they were widely scattered, primitive people living entirely on wild products and by hunting. The defence of 'their' fountains and water-holes, their best hunting-ground, soon brought them into collision with the farmers who appropriated these for cattle. The Hottentots were one step in advance of the bushmen; they too were nomads, ignorant of tillage, but they had herds of cattle which they readily bartered (so long as their stock lasted) and thus greatly helped the Dutch new-comers to get themselves established. Hottentot tribal organization, such as it was, very soon collapsed and the known ravages of smallpox, besides much sickness that went unrecorded and unchecked, soon wrought great damage among them. It is understandable that having no agriculture of their own they made poor farm labourers; but cattle-rearing soon became a major Dutch activity and Hottentots were useful cattlemen. All in all, the farmers came to rely on this despised source of labour more than has always been admitted. The Cape was typically African at least in one way: from the very start all European employers felt reason to complain of the poor quality, if not also of a shortage of general labourers; even Hottentots were therefore under pressure to do their share. The Company itself quickly tired of the experiment of using its own paid European servants. The very year of the first free burghers saw also the beginnings of a regular import of slaves. Most of these seem to have been East African but there was also a steady intake of Malays, convicts and others from the East. Males naturally predominating among all these immigrants, they tended to take to themselves Hottentot women and before long the 'pure' Hottentots had disappeared. The resulting class of mixed-breeds, largely perhaps Hottentot, African and Malay, had also a strong admixture of European blood and was a new people long before it came to be known as Cape Coloured. The Company, meantime, always ready to do business, had seen fit to ease the labour situation by selling slaves to burghers willing to pay their price. Only the stronger farmers of the west could afford slave labour, the rest making do with Hottentots; but all were thus confirmed in their own 'superiority complex'. The Hottentots were judged so inferior as to be not even worth enslaving; they remained, I have written elsewhere, 'in the Colony but never of it'. It is evidence, none the less (to use a phrase much bandied in modern debate) of the 'integration' of the despised Hottentots into the life of the country that Cape Dutch, *Afrikaans*, was acquired from their farmer-employers and displaced spoken Hottentot as their only language.

For a century and more the new Dutch colonists were left at peace to settle in. Slaves helped with the heavier work and Hottentots, so far as they were not made use of, could be safely ignored. Only the bushmen were troublesome, often contesting the appropriation of springs and water-holes; and one isolated episode was a warning of danger ahead. By the turn of the century Hottentot cattle were becoming fewer and in 1702 a party of colonists, venturing 300 or 400 miles to the east in search of barter, brushed for the first time with a band of 'Kafirs', members of the great Bantu-speaking family of African tribes. These too may have been scouts, or even raiders: undoubtedly they were the head of a counter-invasion by Africans coming from the north. They may well, however, have been longer settled, at least in the neighbourhood of Algon Bay, than is always agreed: the dialects of this corner of south-east Africa are unique in making use of the distinctive tones known as 'clicks', and these are taken to have been acquired from the Hottentot speech—this evidence telling against the view that they too were complete new-comers. They gave at any rate no immediate cause for concern.

The new colony was notoriously slow-moving, for obvious geographical reasons that also took effect in ways that are less obvious. Long before the ox-wagon had become a political symbol the traffic of the colonists (who were certainly not immobilized) tended to be one-way only, outwards from Cape Town, and even then the direction it followed was almost pre-determined. Travellers on the shortest journey to or from Cape Town itself used to have to reckon with a good many miles of barren, pastureless sand on its very outskirts; even the beautiful valleys about Stellenbosch, barely thirty miles away, began to be occupied only after nearly thirty years, in 1679. This western oasis where the Dutch began, the country sure of regular winter rains, extends inland only on a radius of at most 100 miles. The one break in the great semicircle of mountains round Cape Town, and perhaps the lure of potential wheat country, first drew explorers along the coast towards the north. Copper was identified far away in Namaqualand as early as 1685; but the Orange River, just beyond, was first crossed only in 1760—the arid conditions quickly discouraged activity in that direction; the more distant of the mountains rising towards the north-east, clearly visible at least from Table Mountain, guard what is in fact the great African plateau. The Karroo which lies just beyond is, however, far from being its most fruitful part; this great expanse has good soil and nutritious drought-resistant scrub, but the annual rainfall may average perhaps only ten inches, and even modern farmers have to count on from ten to twenty acres to graze a single sheep. The cattle-rearing of the Hottentots had evident limits. The Dutch colonists, for their part, or the many who found the Company's regulations and restrictions irksome, could only turn eastwards, pushing out along the south coast, between the Indian Ocean and the Karroo escarpment running roughly parallel to it most of the way. This was to bring them, by the shortest possible route, into head-on collision, on the narrowest possible front, with the oncoming 'Kafirs'. These likewise hugged the coast.

The south coastal belt where the farmers entered it, and as far as Algon Bay or beyond, was itself a second best—broken country, uniformly pleasant, but with poor, 'sour' soil. The lovely but very small belt of forest in the extreme south, about Knysna, normally gets a double share of rain, in winter from the north-west and in summer from the south-east, but most of this country is liable to miss both onsets and go short. Its early farmers, steadily moving farther away from the only market, inevitably came to depend on cattle; their agriculture produced only corn (maize), and a little fruit, both for their own use. Grazing was their one need, but fencing to conserve this was unknown; here, therefore, the unit of 3,000 or 4,000 *morgen* (some ten square miles) came to be accepted as the minimum required for a single farm in all the outer districts. Many justly famous eighteenth-century houses stand memorial to the solid achievement of stable wine-farmers in the old West; there are few or none of these after Swellendam, on the fringe of this region. Farther east, 'farming' brought in little more than subsistence, and houses were makeshift; the colonists made do, perforce, with a manner of living that was easy and pleasant, especially when birds and game helped the larder. Hides, and cattle sent to market on the hoof, provided for modest extras, to be bought of the wandering pedlar, or *smous*: who also brought his version of the news. This life made a self-reliant people, jealous of their own independence, but so highly individualist as to become almost anti-social. Families were large and, doubtless, normally included so many near kindred as to make most farms a small community. Even so, distances were formidable: the conditions ruled against regular schools: teaching therefore devolved on rare wandering scholars, of sorts, and on the Church. Quarterly pilgrimages to the nearest village, to *Nagmaal* (Communion), were prolonged to allow for classes in Bible and Catechism, as well as for business and social activities. It is a tribute to the quality of these colonists that they remained a literate people, firmly grounded in the catechism and well versed in their one Book, the Bible. Their religious beliefs were unavoidably sheltered from changes of stress at home in Europe and retained the seventeenth-century outlook. The Evangelical Movement, which touched their fellow-Protestants in Germany and Holland as well as in England, little affected them, and certainly the fashionable secular teaching of the times that all men are equal, was unacceptable when the term men included 'savages'. When the colonists' growth in numbers, and their insatiable search for grazing, brought them at last into competition for the land with African tribesmen whose chief want was the same, they had long got used to slaves and submissive Hottentots; they therefore readily persuaded themselves that these rivals too were mere Canaanites, for ever under the curse of Ham, and to be dealt with summarily. Bushmen raids on their cattle had by this time accustomed them to using improvised local levies of mounted infantry to harry the 'enemy'. These so-called 'commandos' had official sanction (the company rulers were frugal!) so that means were not wanting of self-defence, and of self-assertion. True frontiersmen that they were they were not going to give way now to the tribesmen who were certainly unreliable and sometimes dangerous neighbours.

The stage was thus set for a contest that was in obvious ways like that on the North-American Indian frontier; yet a real parallel would require revolutionary America to have consisted of one colony, with a total white population equal perhaps to that of Rhode Island spread out over the whole of New England, and first meeting Indian resistance in the region of the great lakes only in the later years of King George II. Cape and North American colonists were individually of similar stock and had much the same outlook, but those at the Cape were in fact both absolutely and relatively few, and collectively far less strongly based, having but one distant and poorly developed seaport behind them. The opposing tribes, on the other hand, were closely massed, at the beginning, on a narrow 100-mile front. Having cattle as well as hunting-grounds, they were generally better fed than the Indians: even later, when the front came to be much extended, their country was outflanked rather than penetrated, and they were never dispersed; normally well provided in their own countries with beer from millet of their own, they seldom sought the white man's drink, and disease has never reduced materially even their relative numbers. There was accordingly never much possibility of a North American 'solution' of the difficulty presented by the meeting of such unequally equipped peoples.

The Company Government was always weak, and in the early days of the actual contest nearly impotent. The dispersal of colonists over so wide an area was itself flatly against the rules; these aimed always to keep the Cape no more than a victualling station, and the nearest Company post was far back, a bare 100 miles from Cape Town; close administration of the frontier, let alone the police supervision it needed, was impossible from this distance; there was certainly not the staff to attempt it. Land-holdings, however, were subject to quit-rent, so from time to time new and wider boundaries were recognized, if only to legalize the collection of such dues. In the year 1778 Governor van Plettenberg felt it necessary to 'show the flag' on the frontier and attempt a personal settlement. It is significant that his journey took him far north, to the later Colesberg, and near this place he raised a boundary beacon. The frontiersmen were in fact circling the arid Karroo and striking towards the better watered north-east where, thanks to summer rains, grass begins to replace the stunted Karroo-bush. Shortly afterwards—in 1786—a government post for the frontier was at last established, not as might have been expected in the neighbourhood of Algoa Bay but at Graaff-Reinet, in a valley blessed with permanent water from the nearby Sneeuwbergen (snow mountains) but actually in the barren Karroo. The coast belt becomes increasingly favourable farther east, but the Xosa tribes, if not quite barring the way, at least made any further advance in that direction acutely uncomfortable.

This 'Kafir' frontier was the Governor's major pre-occupation. As the fruit of his 1778 journey, and hoping to avoid the threatening conflict, he announced an agreement making 'the Fish River' a boundary separating the spheres of white and black. Van Plettenberg's diplomacy fell short on two counts. Like many another he failed to make sure that the chief or chiefs he dealt with had power to bind the very loose tribal confederacy as a whole. The moment his back was turned disputes about cattle, which were really disputes for possession of the land, reached a crisis; the next year, 1779, stands in the conventional histories as the date of 'the first Kafir War'. His failure also to define the actual boundary line further bedevilled a situation which of its own nature could hardly have been more difficult. For fifty years and more the term 'Fish River' was accepted on the colonial side as sufficiently marking the limit of 'Kafirland'. Certainly at the point where Van Plettenberg saw it (and impressively as it still appears when seen from the air), the deep valley which is the seaward end of the river properly known as the Great Fish makes a clear-cut mark. Even if the river flows as a rule for barely half the year its great gorge cuts decisively for perhaps sixty miles straight across the country whose possession the colonists were contesting with their rivals. It was as convenient as it was perhaps natural to think of this line as running straight all the way between the nearby mountain barrier and the sea. The colony, too, was always specially concerned about the inhospitable thorn-scrub of this lower part of the river; it was seen as a favourable hide-out for 'Kafirs' waiting to pounce on the cattle of innocent farmers. But the thieves also were in the first place cattle-farmers and their judgment was not at fault in coveting, really, the higher-lying land about the foothills to the north; these provide good grazing and, unluckily for the Governor's 'settlement', they were on the *Kafir* side of any boundary fixed on the Fish River; an almost right-angled bend carries the upper reaches of the river not *across* but straight *along* the east and west line of advance of either contestant. For a long time the use of this veritable land of Goshen for cattle grazing was the real bone of contention, and understandably, the first 'Kafir' war was quickly followed by a second in 1789 and a third in 1799. The tribes in truth made a prolonged fight of it, and always under the name now discarded but used here because all that time it commanded rather fearful respect—the 'Kafirs'. The 'Fish River' country was finally brought within the Colony only in 1846, and a ninth and last Kafir war in 1878, a minor rebellion, was followed by the very serious Zulu War of 1879, a full 100 years after the original clash.

A famous pamphlet of Boer War days set and established in certain quarters the fashion of treating this century of conflict, together with the many troubles attending on or following from it, as constituting a

'Century of Wrong'. This habit of attributing all to the sins of a long succession of British governments calls for a historical re-appraisal. These frontier rivals were at first not unevenly matched, but basically they were very unequal. No possible government could have hoped to find a ready basis of agreement between them, still less to settle by decree their respective rights as members of one duly constituted state. The seventeenth-century outlook engrained in the Boer frontiersmen drove a fatal wedge between them and any more modern government, even one speaking their own Dutch language. The Company in its last years (it was finally dissolved in 1798) was weakened by political dissensions at home in Holland, but the attitude of certain of its officials showed unmistakably how the wind was setting in a new direction. For the protection he gave to Hottentot servants, and for the humanitarian methods he tried with the Kafirs, one H. C. Maynier in particular came under fire in language indistinguishable from that reserved later for the missionary and philanthropic 'misleaders' of British governments. Not content with words, certain of the frontiersmen felt driven by official 'philanthropy' to try to take charge themselves and, before the end, to set up an independent republic of their own at Graaff-Reinet. The first British Government soon found itself involved in the third Kafir war, 1799, and quickly concluded a temporizing peace. Its better established successor, on the other hand, came nearer to taking—on the frontier at least—the sort of action frontiersmen were likely to approve: in 1812 it set out systematically to 'clear the Zuurveld', hilly country well on the colonial side of any Fish River boundary. In this pleasant but infertile ('sour') country it planted a fort named Grahamstown, and when in 1819 a Kafir attack swept up to the gates of the new fort more decisive action followed. The country between the Fish River and its eastward neighbour, the Keiskamma, was by another dubious 'agreement' pronounced a *neutral* belt. The debatable land in the region of the mountains was still most imperfectly defined but, to make more sure, troops were posted in forts and frontier block-houses to keep the peace. The attack on Grahamstown in 1819 was evidence that the people in the frontier districts faced actual physical danger which the authorities must guard against. This attack was itself unusual in being inspired by a Kafir 'prophet', the first of several who, sensing the significance of the colonial advance, tried to rouse the tribes to stiffer resistance. Makanna, as his name was, judged rightly. Next year, in 1820, some 5,000 British-born settlers were introduced, to people Grahamstown and to strengthen the hold of the Colony on its frontier districts.

For some time before this early attempt at segregation, and before it

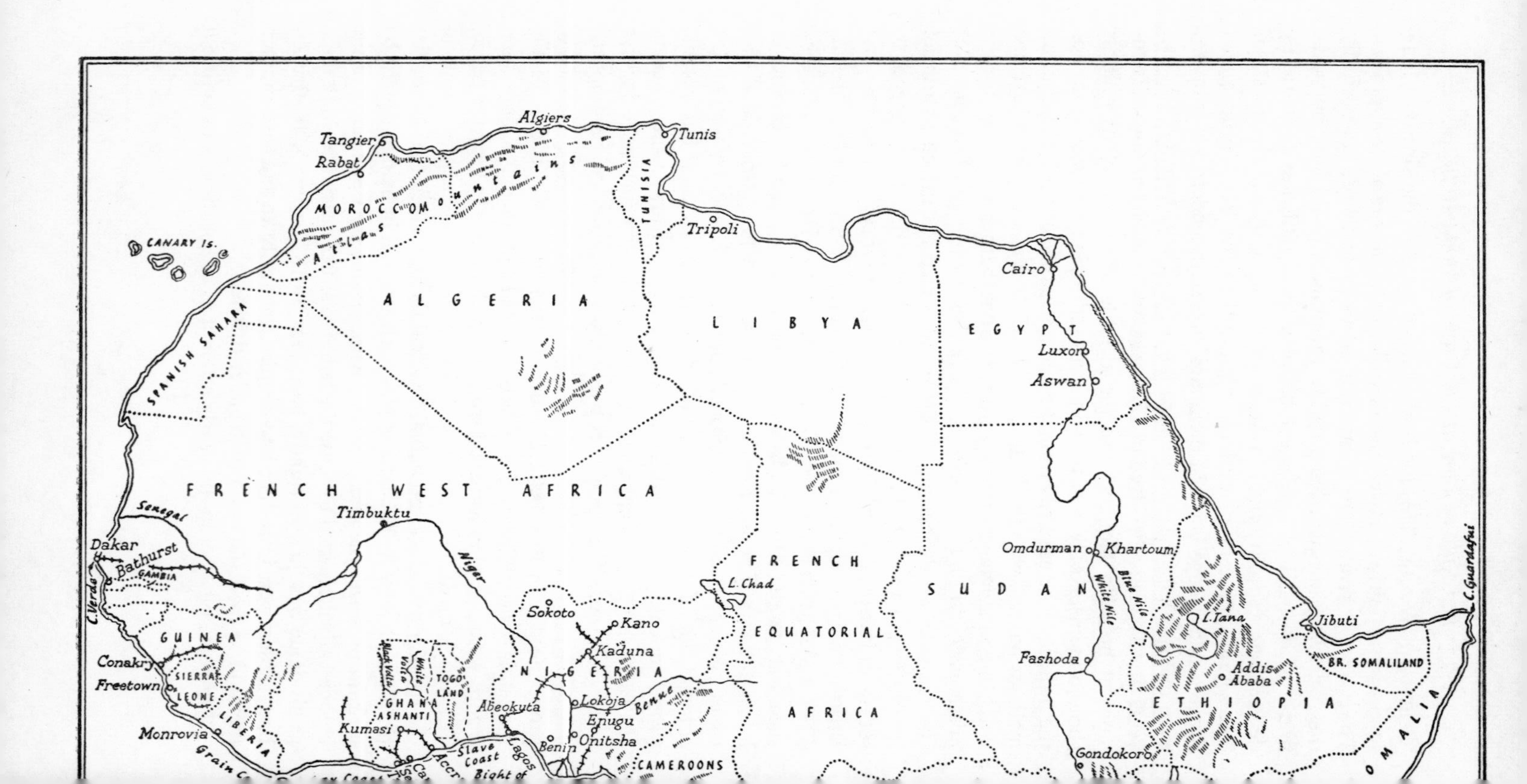
Algiers
Tangier
Tunis
Rabat
MOROCCO
Atlas Mountains
TUNISIA
Tripoli
CANARY Is.
Cairo
ALGERIA
LIBYA
EGYPT
Luxor
Aswan
SPANISH SAHARA
FRENCH WEST AFRICA
Senegal
Timbuktu
Dakar
Bathurst
GAMBIA
C. Verde
Niger
FRENCH
L. Chad
SUDAN
Omdurman
Khartoum
Blue Nile
White Nile
C. Guardafui
Sokoto
Kano
EQUATORIAL
L. Tana
Jibuti
GUINEA
Kaduna
Conakry
Fashoda
NIGERIA
Addis Ababa
BR. SOMALILAND
SIERRA LEONE
Freetown
Black Volta
White Volta
TOGO LAND
GHANA
ASHANTI
Abeokuta
Lokoja
Benue
AFRICA
ETHIOPIA
Enugu
LIBERIA
Monrovia
Kumasi
Onitsha
Slave Coast
Lagos
Benin
Bight of
Grain Coast
CAMEROONS
Gondokoro
OMALIA

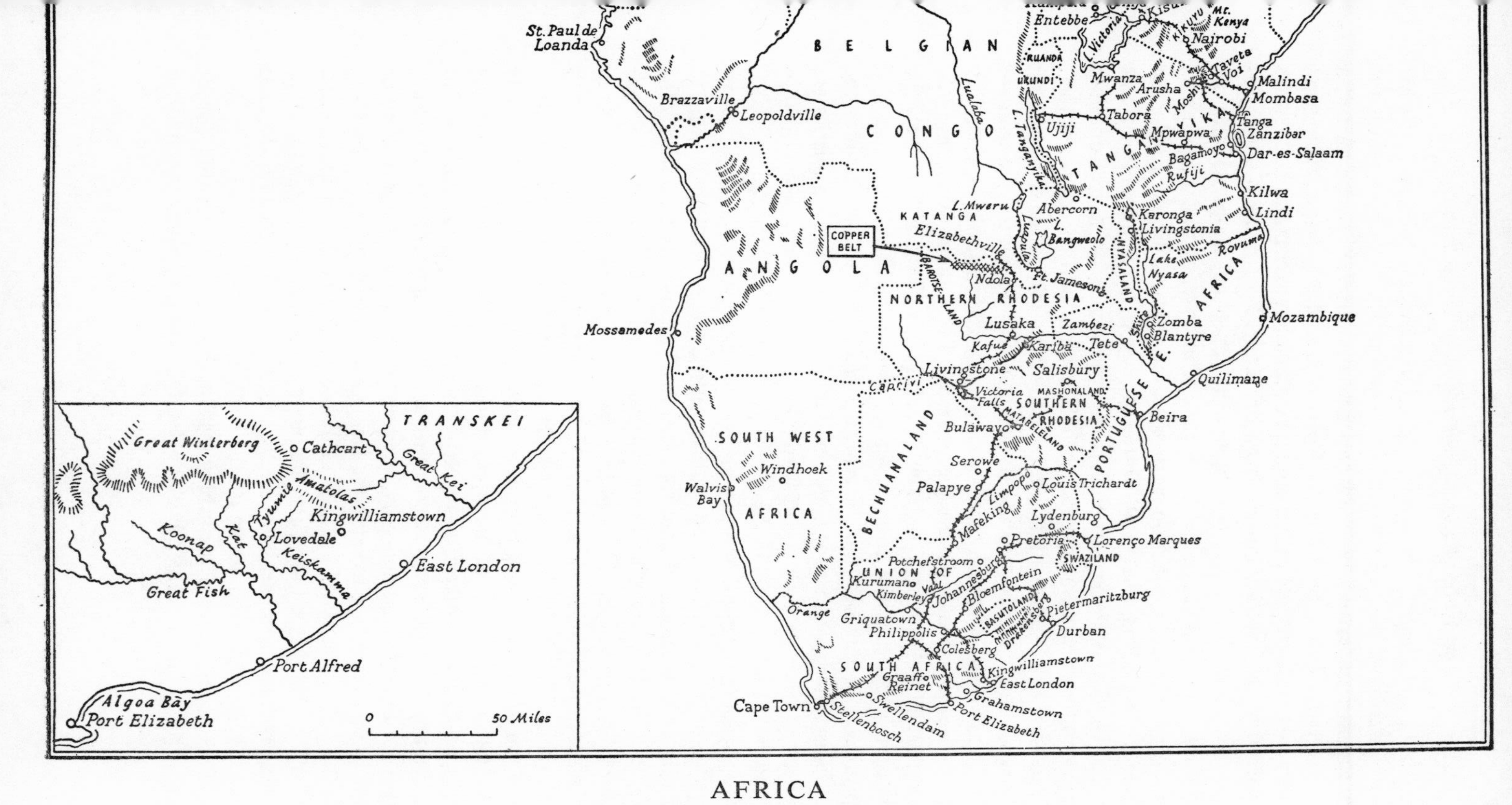

AFRICA

The inset illustrates the Cape 'Fish River' frontier

could be fully tested, attention switched to the domestic aspect of what was essentially the same 'colonial' question. The strong measures the authorities undertook on the frontier in and after 1812 were part of a concerted attempt to bring the Colony as a whole under such strict administrative control as the original Company government had always shied off. The external danger from the Kafirs became itself a compelling reason for looking to the state of the dependent peoples within the borders; the troubles of the 1790s gave clear warning that malcontents within might make common cause with the enemy without. Unlike the North Americans, the small scattered European community of this Cape of Good Hope accepted their dependence on a metropolitan power almost without question. Field-cornets of their own number, who were like English J.P.s, satisfactorily handled routine local affairs; burgher councillors were their spokesmen with the central government at Cape Town; salaried officers known as *landdrosts* took responsibility for government interests in the districts. The system was admirably simple and well understood; it could hardly have been better if only the burghers had had the country all to themselves. But 150 years had produced in this new land a typically *colonial* situation; besides the colonists there were slaves and, especially, the Hottentots. Statistics are uncertain; the slave class can hardly have grown from some 17,000 in the year 1800 to 29,000 in the census year, 1805; but the total of 39,000 for whom compensation was claimed after 1834 would perhaps not be understated. The Hottentots, still so called, but presently beginning to figure as 'free people of colour', are rather surprisingly estimated to be fewer still. There is at any rate no reason to judge that the total 'coloured' population much more than balanced that of the Europeans in the older western districts where the two are still roughly equal; they were not, like the American Negroes, concentrated in a few localities, but the four-to-one 'non-European' majority is modern, following only on the incorporation of the tribes of the east; the farmers of that day had no nightmare-like fear of being 'swamped' by mere numbers. But when the slave trade came under fire, and the supply of slaves dried up, the Hottentots were the only alternative source of labour and came under some pressure to serve the farmers for very low wages; the Cape was a poor country till the days of diamonds and gold. European wars, as after 1793, helped to prime the pump by causing mild inflation that made business comparatively lively; but this also increased the demand for labour, and the pressure on the Hottentots.

The slaves had no disturbing legal rights, and were cared for as property of some value; but the Hottentots who, similarly, had no legal rights, got no such proprietary consideration. Their position as a class was, in the literal sense, anomalous. Slaves merged with Hottentots so quickly after emancipation, and so completely, that the nominal freedom enjoyed by the Hottentots was manifestly of little significance. Originally, as cattle-keeping nomads, they roamed at large; now most if not all the land had been allocated to farmers; if any Hottentot still owned cattle it was on sufferance. Only the very few skilled tradesmen could hope to fend for themselves. Any with oxen and a cart could engage in 'transport riding'—always a profitable trade in undeveloped country—provided they had a secure base; but it was for the landowners to make room or not as they pleased. The aged, the infirm and the very young were more numerous than farmers could conveniently keep, and some farmers were ready to impose stringent terms and conditions. Most Hottentots were in fact such 'servants' as had engaged the solicitude of the reforming *landdrost*, Maynier, and got him into trouble.

The authorities felt it desirable or even necessary to placate the farmers, especially to check the Hottentots' habit of resorting to a roaming life of so-called 'vagabondage', which was still quite possible. But the Government, aware also of the danger of driving not only 'vagabonds' but servants who had real grievances to join the Kafirs, recognized that the Hottentots in general must have more than the rough justice meted out by farmer-employers and the field-cornets. The changing climate of opinion in the Western world also had its influence, especially after 1798, when some early Moravians were followed by the first London (L.M.S.) missionary, Dr. J. T. van der Kemp, a well-connected, perhaps mildly eccentric, Hollander. It was coming to be recognized that the old way, which kept the Hottentots in the Colony but never of it, must give place to the Rule of Law.

The first British Government, 1795–1802, made the preparatory move. By this time even Kafirs were beginning to scent economic opportunities and to infiltrate, and, as in North America, administrative officials, many of them Dutch, were the first to scent danger; at British behest one of these, the Fiscal (Treasurer) van Ryneveld, made the first comprehensive report on Hottentot conditions in 1802. This, together with missionary van der Kemp's representations, at once engaged the attention of two eminent officials of the succeeding Government of the Batavian Republic, 1802–6, the visiting Commissioner de Mist and the new Governor, General Janssens, a college acquaintance of van der Kemp. The drive for a more comprehensive order of government now became marked and British successors later only carried on what the

Batavian Republic began. Governor Janssens insisted, for example, on officially approved contracts of service for Hottentot employees; his tenure of office was too short for him to do more than announce the outlines of his policy, yet he also took the momentous step of initiating what were in effect Hottentot 'reserves'. At the instance of Dr. van der Kemp, the Governor granted the L.M.S. a farm near Algoa Bay, of indifferent quality, but of standard size; under the name of Bethelsdorp this became the first of several 'Institutions', specifically recognized as mission-supervised homes for Hottentots other than 'servants'. Soon there were nine or ten, mostly in the coast belt, two or three of them on the sites of traditional Hottentot *kraals*; van der Kemp's original commission empowered him, moreover, to innovate so far as to open a school or schools for Hottentot children.

Janssens' successor, again British, clearly only 'took over' where he left off. The successive changes of régime left many key officials where they were, and so much of the preparatory work was already done that Governor the Earl of Caledon was able to promulgate a full Hottentot Code within three years. It was now laid down that every Hottentot must have 'a fixed place of abode', and carry a 'pass' if or when he moved from home; since the pass was obtainable only from an employer this check on vagabondage was restrictive and, for a time, riveted on the Cape a system that became notorious in the later Boer republics. The Code of 1809, moreover, still made no provision for Hottentots to acquire land of their own and even a place in one of the new missionary institutions required official sanction. But the principle stood that employers must make approved contracts of service. If only by implication the State undertook to enforce the terms of contract and conditions of work, and to protect servants in their rights and persons. Hottentots were now subject, if not to the law of the land, at least to law—to some pains and penalties perhaps, but also to legally enforceable protection. But the battle was not yet won; an amendment made in 1812 recognized, for example, a dubious practice by which young dependants growing up on a master's premises might be bound for a term of years as 'apprentices'—this and other provisions even of the new law were liable to abuse, at any rate till the whole administrative system could be geared to meet the considerable new calls made upon it.

The re-gearing process proved troublesome. It at once became evident that the new Government was seriously bent on bringing the frontier districts at last within its orbit and under systematic control; hitherto a High Court had functioned only in Cape Town; in 1811 two of its judges were deputed to go on tour through the outer districts.

The Government acted unprompted: it was an obvious step to take, and even necessary, to make the services of the High Court available to all citizens. The judges, it is true, were not only to hold regular sessions: they were also to report on conditions in the country and on the work of the district officials: and it may or may not have occurred to the authorities that the law of 1809 invited a crop of Hottentot pleas. The friends and advisers of these people, Dr. van der Kemp in particular, were standing by to test the law on their behalf. On the eve of the new court's sittings Dr. van der Kemp died and the marshalling of Hottentot complaints devolved on his less experienced colleague, an artisan missionary, the Rev. James Read. At the second or 'Black' Circuit of 1812, a great number of farmer-employers from all over the outer districts found themselves arraigned on charges of committing offences ranging from the illegal withholding of servants' wages all the way to murder. The worthy James Read, showing more zeal than discretion, allowed more charges to go forward than the weight of the evidence could substantiate—especially as Hottentot witnesses were likely to be at a loss in the unfamiliar atmosphere of a court of law. Commotion of course followed; it was new and strange for these lords and masters to be called on to answer charges levied by or on behalf of Hottentots; some who had to face the ordeal of a trial in court on undeserved or even frivolous complaints may excusably have been indignant. The frontier people as a whole had reason this same year to welcome the strong measures taken to clear the Zuurveld of Kafirs and give them greater security; but 'interference' with the individual farmer's control of his own servants was another matter; a sturdy remnant was no readier to be bridled in this respect than in the days of Maynier. In the end only a small number of convictions was recorded; none, by all accounts, was unduly severely dealt with; but enough came of it to give any responsible government serious cause for concern about Hottentot conditions of service.

A second incident brought no reassurance on this score. In 1815 a frontier Boer who had for two years ignored a summons of court to meet a Hottentot complaint was shot when resisting arrest, and shot—it is often complained—by a Hottentot soldier. A small party of his friends then took up arms in what is ominously known (by the name of a hill-pass where it ended) as the Slagter's (butcher's) Nek Rebellion. This sorry affair is best described in terms used of a much later episode; the Boer War hero, General de Wet, excused a grave rebellion in 1914 as being originally no more than an 'armed protest'; it was traditional for Boers riding out to make any demonstration to carry their arms with them. Five of the 'rebels', taken in fact by burgher commandos, were presently tried, by Dutch judges, and hanged. It was the year of Waterloo, when this was the end to be expected to follow open rebellion; but the public hanging was miserably bungled; it is not clear whether it was that at the first attempt the rope was rotten or that a beam broke. Many burghers were present at this grim scene by official command and their distress was natural; but this also inspired a tradition which makes too light of the original offence. It was a trivial rebellion, but in their flat defiance of the law its perpetrators even had obscure but risky dealings with the Kafirs, besides setting them a dangerous example.

It is pitiful that Afrikaner children are still nurtured on versions that make these two incidents outstanding examples of the wrongs suffered by frontier Boers at the hand of their alien British rulers and, accordingly, landmarks in the rise of Afrikaner nationalism. An Afrikaner historian has said the last word; in *The Cape Coloured People*, Dr. J. S. Marais writes of 'the educative influence', adding in a footnote, '*and educative necessity*', of the trials of 1812. Slagter's Nek, he continues, was 'nothing else than resistance to the new conception of justice which was gradually becoming effective'. It has indeed cost the country dear, one may add, that for so many long years its Company rulers left its key citizens without any civic restraint whatsoever. With a sure touch Dr. Marais goes straight on to put these incidents into their proper context, showing how the upset they caused decisively speeded up an essential reform. Only a few years later, in 1828, a professionally qualified Supreme Court replaced the older, amateurish High Court. The transition thus successfully accomplished was from the rather wholesale demonstration of the authority of the law by the Black Circuit, or at Slagter's Nek, to its sober ordering by an efficient Supreme Court. This Supreme Court was finally freed from the control of the Governor; it soon attained, and has maintained, the highest standards of sound learning and strict impartiality. Thus the need supplied the answer—the justice the court dispenses is the outstanding feature of South African administration to this day.

The legal reforms of 1828 came about, however, only after ten or twelve years of activity of a kind quite new to the politically very immature Cape. All these years the troops in forts and block-houses kept the frontier in relative quiet such as should have left the Government free to continue taking in the slack left by years of Company rule and tightening the general administration; but instead, the reinforcement of the original Dutch population by the arrival of the 1820 British settlers suddenly brought the Government itself under more direct criticism than it had ever known. The new settlers found the agricultural conditions defeating and gave a fillip rather to the life of the towns, Grahamstown, Port Elizabeth and even distant Cape Town. The Cape, as a colony newly acquired by conquest, was still subject to direct rule, by Order in Council, besides being under an autocratic governor. The newcomers, who had a political tradition, at once began to ask inconvenient questions and to demand a voice in the counsels of their government. This unusual political liveliness gave the British Government good reason to divert two Eastern Commissioners from tours of New South Wales and Ceylon to the Cape to examine and report. They arrived in Cape Town towards the end of 1823, in good time for a private view of one particularly vigorous episode in the fight for constitutional rights. In 1824 a Scots settler, Thomas Pringle, a poet and a former neighbour of Sir Walter Scott, moved to Cape Town and set up the first Cape newspaper. The Governor, Lord Charles Somerset (the last of a line of eighteenth-century aristocrats to hold this office), whose High Toryism made him as good a target for attack as he was intolerant of criticism, very soon took offence and had the newspaper summarily suppressed and the press confiscated. This happened to bring the printer and the mission owners of the press into the quarrel, as well as the promoters. First the printer and, after the paper had had a second run, its co-editor, John Fairbairn, went seeking redress and security to London. There the Governor's brand of Toryism was now losing its hold. The Commissioners meantime had taken cognizance and in 1828, on their advice, the new model Supreme Court was set up which answered at least some of the critics' questions. The freedom of the Press, like that of the Hottentots, was taken out of the Governor's hands and made subject to positive law as interpreted by this independent Supreme Court.

The pity was that the Commissioners' reform of local government was less happy: the old *landdrosts* and their burgher councillors or *heemraaden* were replaced by a more streamlined magistracy. This change, dictated entirely by considerations of economy and convenience, was accompanied by a decree making English the official language of the country and may well have looked like needless anglicization; it certainly took time to strike roots in the soil and was yet to be counted against its originators as a piece of colonialism. It came, as it happened, at a moment when the administration could least afford any weakening of its links with the farmers in the outlying districts. The status of the dependent people had so far been the only public question that really stirred them. Earlier moves caused trouble enough when they were the unprompted action of the administration itself. Now the rise of the towns, and the presence in them of active politicians of a radical turn of mind like the founders of the press, made it likely that the debate on the Hottentot and kindred questions would follow new patterns. One significant fact finds little place in the story as usually told. The normal way out of the constitutional agitation of the middle 1820s would have been the institution of an elected assembly. After some delay the Cape got its legislative council in 1834, but its unofficial members were all nominated. In 1824 the newspaper men, the politically-minded settlers and even the missionaries had all been in the fight together and were certainly canvassing the idea of representative institutions. The Dutch-speaking country people were, it is true, rather passive onlookers and their aloofness discouraged a venture into elective parliamentarianism. But the English-speaking political allies themselves split asunder. The reason was that Fairbairn, now sole editor of the *Commercial Advertiser*, stood firmly for the enfranchisement of qualified coloured persons. At last he withdrew altogether from the campaign for a parliament till this principle should be accepted. The pressure for the rights of dependants, that is to say, was coming now from spokesmen within the colony itself. These liberals were perhaps more formidable but no less a party of colonists for being in alliance with a strong body of opinion in Great Britain. When just before this, in 1823, the concentrated attack of the British anti-slavery movement was turned on slavery, as such, the Cape was automatically involved as a slave-owning country; the leaders of the crusade, moreover, were readily moved to take up the cause also of the nominally free Hottentots. The settled, slave-owning western farmers actually took fairly calmly the slave regulations that came pouring in, but memories of the Black Circuit still rankled with the frontiersmen, who employed only Hottentots. After that first serious clash with frontier opinion the ill-planned zeal of the missionary Read made him the obvious target for outraged feelings and set the fashion of making the missions the scapegoat; that the Government took the initiative in 1812 out of its concern for order counted for nothing, still less did 'the educative necessity' of making the power of the law felt throughout the country. Read's notoriety at any rate upset some of his own colleagues and came near to bringing about the ruin of the L.M.S. and all its work. The dissensions of the brethren caused resignations, and so much scandal that the Governor intervened; at his instance the directors in London were moved to send two senior representatives to look into matters; one of these, ranking as a resident director, was deputed to stay in Cape Town and thence to supervise the work of L.M.S. stations throughout the country. In 1819 this brought on the scene a strong leader of the mission interest and a formidable champion of the Hottentots in the person of Dr. John Philip, who also became the father-in-law of John Fairbairn. By 1823 when British anti-slavery enthusiasts were taking unction to their souls by denouncing the sins of West Indian planters, South African tradition had begun to repay the debt with interest by saddling interfering missionaries with sole responsibility for all the troubles of southern Africa.

From the time of John Philip's arrival in 1819 till ill health overtook him two or three years before his death in 1851 he was a close and competent observer of all that went forward; often a protagonist, he seldom if ever, in spite of his critics, had the decisive last word in policy-making. In this small-town world the numbers of those engaged in political controversy were small and personal rancours disproportionately acute, but none, even there, has suffered more persistent detraction.[1] Philip never joined battle uninformed, and no governor, official or farmer had comparable first-hand knowledge of the southern Africa of that day. His persuasive powers may not always have matched his mastery of the facts: there is little evidence that the assurance which marked his plunge into controversy was mellowed by any strong sense of humour. He was, however, never left to fight alone. His mission responsibilities, as a director, left him leisure to minister to a regular congregation when in Cape Town, and he ministered there, in the phrase used by the pious of those days, 'with acceptance'. In his very first years he made friends, as a leading Evangelical, with influential visitors, including senior East Indian and Service officers, and some of these were soon directly instrumental in bringing him into an important alliance, if not with Wilberforce, then certainly with the Buxton family. His congregation, which included John Fairbairn (the son-in-law and stalwart supporter, who was also a personality in his own right), was then and long afterwards the nursery of a succession of Solomons,

[1] About 1920 it fell to me to supervise the study of Philip's personal letters and records, a mass of documents hitherto seen only by members of his family. The first results were embodied in two large books which I think made clear at least his ideas of the policy the conditions called for, and his success, or ill success, in getting his views accepted. Rightly or wrongly the political significance of this evidence was given priority; the state of historical studies in the 1920s seemed to demand it. An estimate even of such an important personality could apparently afford to wait; but it is now impossible. Many of Philip's documents are duplicated in the Public Archives or in the well-kept records of the L.M.S.; but every shred of the voluminous private correspondence was consumed in the University Library fire at Johannesburg in 1931. There was much work still to be done, for example, on a pile of papers embodying journals written between the *schofts* of prolonged ox-wagon treks that took him at frequent intervals all over the Colony, and beyond it into Kafirland, Bechuanaland and Basutoland.

Buchanans and others; these makers of the Cape Colony all accepted as the very first principle of politics the liberal teachings Philip above all men was instrumental in buttressing.

Philip began to take his bearings in his new environment with all the circumspection due from a man of experience who was also of good standing in his Church; he was now 44 years of age. It is one real advantage of life in such small colonial communities that the chief executive officers, from the Governor downwards, are normally far easier of access than at home. Philip (formerly an Independent pastor in Kirkcaldy, Hoxton and Newbury, later the minister of a more important charge in Aberdeen) was distinctly sensitive to 'the smiles of the great' and much appreciated his new standing. He certainly always worked, for choice, with the authorities rather than against them; but he soon began to ask questions. The control exercised by officials over frontier and trans-frontier mission stations seemed largely inspired by fear of their tempting labourers away from the farms. Two years after his arrival he was on good enough terms with the acting Governor, Sir Rufane Donkin, to thrust upon him a request that at Bethelsdorp he would look into allegations of forced labour that had reached him, again from Read. This casual request caused Donkin some embarrassment; the Eastern officials were ready with their own defence and the Governor rebuked his questioner for making unsubstantiated charges. Philip thereupon set out on tour rather disconsolate, till one day, at Bethelsdorp, he found, 'thrown aside in a corner of the mission office', a bundle of papers showing irrefutably that even the *landdrost* was in fact in the habit of using his power over Hottentot movements in a way that left individuals with little option but to work as and where they were bid. For one reason or another there seems to have been at this time a strong demand for labour, if not a shortage.

When Philip returned to Cape Town at the end of 1821 his first instinct was to collect more evidence on the workings of the laws: instructions were sent to missionaries to comply with official orders concerning Hottentots, but to insist on having them in writing; they were also to make regular reports to mission headquarters. Very soon, in consultation with his naval friend Captain Owen, Philip concluded that the law itself must be at fault when its administration permitted such abuses. Improving on Read's practice, he now made a very shrewd move. Recognizing the futility of continuing to confront employers in the dock with another succession of Hottentots who would always be ill at ease in the witness-box, he pronounced: 'Our cause had better, if possible, rest on generals rather than on particulars'—he would attack the principles underlying the existing law, that is to say, rather than be distracted by incidents arising in the course of its administration. If the law was in question, the Cape was a directly ruled colony and the Home Government must be moved to action. From about this time, accordingly, many of Philip's letters in the L.M.S. Archives begin to be endorsed 'for Wilberforce and Buxton'; others went direct to Sir Jahleel Brenton, a friend at the Admiralty. It remains uncertain which of these channels was more effective, but as early as July 1822 Wilberforce was moving on Hottentot grievances in the House of Commons. There is no doubt that this suasion had its share of influence in getting the Eastern Commissioners directed to the Cape. By 1824 Philip was marshalling evidence to press on these visitors. In 1825 he set out on a major, year-long tour that took him, always in search of evidence, as far afield as Bechuanaland. In 1826, thus fortified with information, he set out to spend nearly three years prosecuting his 'cause' in England. A book of *Researches*, written at high speed and published in 1828, was 'almost' reviewed by Macaulay; but it is an example, rather, of the merit of his own rule to base such a cause 'on generals rather than on particulars'; at least one 'particular' got him mulct in damages for libelling an officer who still had the letter of the obsolescent law on his side. On the other hand he knew his Adam Smith, and his grasp of the situation was strikingly modern. None before him was so clear in his appreciation of the need to think of these backward peoples not merely as a convenience, 'animated tools', but rather as potential *consumers* who would be better for consuming more. In conference in 1828 with one notably able but unhappily short-lived Secretary of State, William Huskisson, he emerged with credit:

> 'Tell me in one sentence what you want for the Hottentots,' said Huskisson; to which he replied, 'I want nothing for the Hottentots but the power of bringing their labour to a fair market.' 'That', was the answer, 'is all you require. It includes everything else.'

But the Cape administration itself now took up the running. Huskisson almost at once gave place to Sir George Murray and, while Philip and Buxton were preparing certain resolutions for the Commons, the new Secretary suddenly sent Philip a copy of the Cape's own proposals, the draft of a law that was to make history as the 50th Ordinance. This measure, actually promulgated at the Cape in this same July, was no bolt from the blue. In late 1821 or early 1822, after Philip's Bethelsdorp 'discovery', the Secretary of the day, Colonel Bird, admitted 'strong things against us now', and Philip himself continued quietly to keep the matter alive. In the following years the Crown Commissioners were under constant pressure to look into Hottentot matters. It may be even more important that frontier officials charged with the actual administration of such peoples' affairs are rarely unsympathetic, and Philip himself conferred at length in 1825 with one such, Andries Stockenström; at Graaff-Reinet these two found themselves in cordial 'general agreement'—and the new proposals were largely the work of this same Stockenström. All previous legislation was now to be abrogated, 'passes' and other 'discriminatory' restrictions abolished, the right to hold land assured (though no fresh land was provided); verbal contracts of service (which were normal) were to run only from month to month, and written contracts no longer than one year. Other provisions confirmed existing restraints on 'truck', and transferred all but petty (20s.) cases to the Courts of the new regular magistrates. In face of all this, Philip, when consulted, protested only that he 'disliked a separate legislation'; like most modern reformers he would have one equal law for people of all sorts. Taking counsel with the leading anti-slavery lawyer, Dr. Lushington, he finally agreed to accept the Ordinance as a settlement, on one condition, that it had 'the seal of the King in Council'. After some demur the Government gave way and in January 1829 the desired Order in Council put it beyond the power of the local Government to amend its own Ordinance except with the consent and approval of H.M.G. This proved to be another shrewd move.

At the Cape itself the new Ordinance, even without the additional clause, was strongly resented. The reaction might have taken even more serious form had not Philip returned just in time to get all the blame and make a focus for public resentment. His critics are still wont to make him directly responsible for the new law, as well as for the slave regulations pouring in about the same time, and yet also to be at pains to emphasize (correctly) that the drafting of the 50th Ordinance was the work of others. Immediately, a libel action arising out of Philip's *Researches*, and a pandemonium of denunciation, eased the pressure. The chief grievance was an outbreak of 'vagrancy' on the part of some Hottentots exulting in their new-found freedom from the burden of carrying 'passes'. The implementing of one more of the Crown Commissioners' recommendations was in time to give local opinion some outlet; the Legislative Council of 1834, though non-elective, included for the first time a number of unofficial members and at once, with the backing of an acting Governor, it approved a draft Vagrancy Law. As an amendment of the 50th Ordinance this required endorsement by Order in Council and a new Governor disallowed it;

Philip's prescience in securing the original Order in Council was justified. The sequel was surprising. In the last days of the same eventful year, 1834, hard on the heels of emancipation which passed off on December 1st with perfect decorum, the eastern Kafir frontier exploded. A serious invasion of the frontier districts (see Chapter 6) broke suddenly and led to such a distracting exodus of frontiersmen that the menace of Hottentot vagrancy was completely and finally forgotten. Seven years later the 50th Ordinance, which Philip had disliked in so far as it was 'separate legislation', was quietly repealed. A Masters and Servants Law which superseded Ordinance 50 in 1842 was 'colour-blind'; this measure put European 'servants' (if there were such) on the same legal footing as the vast majority of coloured people who were its prime concern. And not a mouse stirred! The Cape had won through to a system of equal laws. Philip had his way at last; but he was far away in Basutoland and, so far as his papers show, had himself made no move about it. Cape public opinion had indeed mellowed, at all events in the steady and dominant western districts where Fairbairn's educative influence had done its work. The way was clear for the no less 'colour-blind' constitution of 1853, and for the Cape Parliament, of which Fairbairn himself became a leading member.

The real colonial question, wherever it arises, is just such a challenge to order the relations and to establish the peaceful co-existence of diverse peoples like the Cape farmers, the mixed Hottentots and the steadily increasing number of Bantu-speaking tribesmen—people with widely different traditions, standards and personal habits, incidentally of almost every shade of colour, and most of them completely illiterate in any one of the two or three or many more languages spoken and current. As Cape governments early realized, like British officials before them in North America, the 'problem' is not *one*, but first and last a complex of problems in administration. Law and the making of laws have their place. More especially because of the difficulty of verbal communication the law must be equable, clear and easily understood; unless the law wins general acceptance the best administration must fail. Cape practice passed most of these tests; but the frontier remained to be settled and here even it failed calamitously.

It is in large measure the feuds surviving from long-drawn-out frontier disputes that continue to bedevil the South African situation, diverting attention from the real issue. The original difficulty was that African tribal society, though 'settled' according to rules of its own, was predominantly pastoral; custom gave it ill-defined claims to a great deal of imperfectly used land, inevitably provoking challenge from neighbours. The strongest challengers happened at last to be white men. Even within the colony this land issue was one-sidedly dealt with, but the pressure on land space was not yet really intense and a working arrangement was come to that was at any rate legally ordered and went unchallenged. This made it possible to establish a firm civil administration; the law was brought home to and reasonably well understood even by illiterate people speaking a variety of languages. It was the more readily accepted for the reason that, before long, the civilized members of any of the dependent peoples had a political outlet and the means of giving expression to their views and feelings. The need on the frontier, the point at which the rival societies met, was essentially the same, but from the beginning the authorities bungled the issue or evaded it altogether. From the beginning both Dutch and British rulers inclined to the counsel of despair since given the name of segregation: the attempt to keep the rivals separated brought no settlement even on the old, narrow 100-mile front. On the new and much wider 'frontier' the real call was still to gear the machinery of government to deal with the routine affairs of everyday life in the inevitably more complex conditions. Persistent evasion has issued at last in the impracticable twentieth-century dream of total separation of the races, or *apartheid.* The modern world has reason to ponder again the experience of the old Colony of the Cape of Good Hope.

Chapter 6

THE GREAT SOUTH AFRICAN SCHISM

*

The frontier explosion of 1835 was the not surprising sequel to the attempt made in and after 1819 to 'segregate' the rivals competing for the grazing in the foothills of the Winterberg stretch of the Karroo escarpment. In theory there was to be a neutral belt maintained by troops posted in forts built on the Keiskamma, a new line that was perhaps also less equivocal than the Fish River (Chapter 5, p. 102). At the very beginning, however, Governor Somerset himself set the disingenuous official fashion of writing of the no-man's-land as the *Ceded* Territory, and by 1829 a great part of it had been quietly incorporated in the Colony. The region is extensive and very broken and the authorities could not if they would have kept close control. Hottentots were at any rate judged safer than Kafirs and, partly as a defensive measure, the L.M.S. were allowed in 1829 to establish an 'Institution' for these people, under James Read, in a highly favourable part of the upper Kat River. Even Kafirs were tolerated in the forbidden area if their chiefs were considered reliable, but there was a cat-and-mouse game with one, the genial but wily Maqomo, who 'crept back' or was several times allowed back to Kat River country, and as often forcibly ejected. Peaceful intercourse was encouraged: a trade fair set up at Fort Willshire on the Keiskamma was discontinued after 1830 because by this time it was thought safe for independent traders to enter Kafirland provided they avoided the risk of disturbance on the frontier by following a route north of the Winterberg (which happened also to be less rugged). Missionaries too pursued their calling: one or two had entered Kafirland before 1819 and the Wesleyan, Glasgow and London Societies had a number of representatives soon after that date. James Brownlee of the L.M.S. was even sponsored by the Government on the site of King William Town from 1819 to 1825.

The general effect was thus more rather than less 'contact'. The Kafirs were never a bloodthirsty people and farmers were seldom in danger of their lives, but their cattle were obvious game—and cattle lifting tended even to increase. For answer the authorities invoked the sanction of tribal custom: free burghers were allowed to form 'commandos', to follow the spoor of stolen cattle and recover for themselves if they could. Commandos might also be sponsored by the army and these were the more likely to exact punishment and burn villages. Frontier life was thus becoming increasingly insecure, on both sides of the border, when Dr. Philip took occasion to inform himself, if only about the new L.M.S. Institution, and came on tour in 1832. This time he examined the Kafir frontier really closely but, clinging to his principle of 'generals rather than particulars', said little or nothing about it in public. Relations were strained with the Governor of the moment but Buxton's request, '*Pray keep me well informed*', was not overlooked; a letter from Miss Buxton, dated 21st September 1833, reported shortly that her father had been 'several times' lately with the Colonial Secretary, Mr. Stanley, 'about your horrid commandos'! Shortly after these talks, in January 1834, a new Governor arrived bearing detailed instructions to look to the frontier. Sir Benjamin D'Urban was now to consider how best

> 'to protect colonists from unprovoked aggression and to consider also the propriety of using Government agents, salaries to chiefs, or other means of regulating and improving trade and intercourse.'

This new Governor was often slow off the mark and had much to occupy him, including slavery and vagrancy. On March 20th he personally and promptly acknowledged receipt from Philip of a memorandum on the frontier situation; but it was not till May 31st that he could write, 'The time is now come to take into my most serious consideration the whole of the frontier system . . .', and call Philip in to confer. A series of increasingly cordial personal notes flowed to the Mission House, bearing witness to the intimate contacts of the next three months. At the end of them Philip set out, with approval, to 'prepare the ground' with chiefs and others for the Governor's own consultations on the frontier in or before September. A veil of secrecy then falls—further communications passed, seemingly, only between Lady D'Urban and Mrs. Philip—and the Governor dallied. Philip, for his part, had good grounds for trying to reassure the chiefs with confident promises that the Governor was bent on establishing a new and better order. He may also have been consequential in his talk about 'having the ear' of the Governor on the whole subject; by the long accepted colonial account this phrase was rendered by the chief, Tyali, as a promise to 'speak in the Governor's ear' for their benefit! When D'Urban arrived at last, only after war had come, he himself was inclined to take Tyali's view and blame Philip for provocative indiscretion. Philip, on the other hand, never put the blame for the breakdown on D'Urban's delays, as he well might—hope deferred certainly played its part; he even excused delay on the ground that the Hottentot Vagrancy Law was still in the balance; had it passed, he wrote, 'thousands' of Hottentots might have fled to the side of the Kafirs. Philip had at last turned homeward in mid-November, to be back for Christmas if not for Emancipation Day (December 1st). A year-long drought was apparently just over, and this had brought a sharp intensification of the old rule by commando. On December 9th James Read (frontiersman if ever there was one) wrote from the Kat River his version of certain unusually lively patrol actions:

> '(Colonel) Somerset is now clearing the country from Willshire to the sea . . . now again just in the time of harvest when the corn is in the field. . . . I am sorry for the case at the moment, as the chiefs will think we have deceived them.'

Two weeks more and, banding themselves together, the Kafirs fell on the colony itself in full force.

When D'Urban reached Grahamstown early in 1835 he was not unnaturally shocked at the material havoc, and the administrator in him inevitably made way for the soldier. The enemy was elusive and the 'campaign' amounted to no more than 'clearing' the country to allow abandoned farms, and even some of the forts, to be reoccupied: but there was one unfortunate incident—the great chief, Hintza, was shot in what was accepted to be a 'chance-medley' when trying to escape. In May D'Urban proclaimed his policy. The whole of the country up to the Kei River, named the Province of Queen Adelaide, was to be annexed and settled by European colonists. The pronouncement was bald and its startling effect in missionary circles, and presently in London, was not mitigated by two accompanying phrases reflecting D'Urban's continuing horror at the havoc he had seen: to pronounce the Kafirs 'irreclaimable savages' was verbiage, and it was little better to add that, by way of punishment, they were to be 'expelled for ever' from the country they had so misused; the troops at the Governor's disposal could not possibly have made expulsion effective. By September he had second thoughts about it. With little said to London he now came to terms with the errant chiefs; they would still make room for settlers, but they were now to have their own fixed 'locations' (and Philip for one agreed that each tribe should 'know its own limits'). The chiefs were also to accept Government 'agents' and take responsibility for the good behaviour of their people. This was in tune with his instructions, but in the stress of business the Governor found little time for writing dispatches. It is extraordinary how ill at any time he gauged the reaction of his superiors in London, being always inclined to rely on enclosures that overwhelmed them with local detail. It was November before he reported at all on his September dealings and then, as if reluctant to admit a decided change (including the recognition of the 'expelled' Kafirs as 'British subjects'), he harped on his older themes; the Kafirs had been 'chastised—not extremely but perhaps sufficiently'. As if dimly aware of the notorious reluctance of London to accept new territorial responsibilities he was enthusiastic (as well he might be) about the quality of the newly acquired land; but it was unhelpful to add that much of it would still be available for the 'occupation and speculations of Europeans'. Having thus disburdened himself D'Urban set to work, devolving a good deal on his second-in-command, Colonel Harry Smith, to prepare tribal locations with para-military white farm-holdings dispersed among them, in accordance with the plan both men spoke of as their System. The November dispatch reached London some time in January 1836, but by this time London, which had only the May report to work on, had arrived at very nearly final conclusions of its own.

The result of deliberations at the Colonial Office, which thus all this year 1835 had no official guidance except the plan of expulsion *cum* settlement, was the forcible dispatch released by Lord Glenelg on December 26th; it reached D'Urban in March 1836 and, whatever its genesis, devastated him. Strong language used in this document about the wrongs suffered by the Kafirs took much space; but its essence was a challenge to D'Urban either to 'prepare the public mind' for the abandonment of the new Province before the end of 1836, or at least to show good reason for retaining it. Whatever a stronger and clearer-thinking governor might have done, D'Urban seems never to have considered that he had any choice left him. The appointment of another old frontier hand, Andries Stockenström, to a new post under the style of Lieutenant-Governor on the frontier, may have further dashed his pride and assurance. That officer complained, for his part, that he was no better than 'fifth wheel to the waggon', but between them they agreed that the new Province must be evacuated. Stockenström then proceeded to organize peace by means of treaties binding the chiefs to maintain order, while D'Urban withdrew to labour in his own defence on a vast, heavily documented dispatch, which Glenelg received by way of reply to his December 1835 bombshell only in April or May 1837.

The abandonment of the new Province, virtually complete by this late date, was an almost unrelieved blunder. The Colonial Secretary was ultimately responsible, but D'Urban's dalliance was at least a contributing factor. Anyone with experience of frontier administration knew very well by now that the best hope of law and order was for civil magistrates and police to take over from the soldiers; the more conservative Wesleyans often disagreed with Philip, but were at one with him on this point. The Kafirs, in spite of the Glenelg dispatch, had gravely offended and must have expected a change; when the opportunity presented itself of establishing a civil order it should have been acted upon without further delay; the breakdown only showed how necessary it was to try a new system such as D'Urban himself had official instructions to consider. The entirely innocent advent of Europeans of itself created a situation wholly disruptive of the tribal institutions it was proposed to rely on—one only a stable government could hope to control. This was the re-emergence—in a different climate of opinion—of the colonial question in its old American form, and the Colonial Office instinctively ran away from it. For D'Urban to carry on his own alternative system in face of official disapproval was a heavier responsibility than any governor could be expected to bear—the discretion the dispatch left him may at any rate have been little more than a concession to the hurt pride of King William IV. The disinclination of the Colonial Office to assume new responsibilities was certainly its own; in dismay at finding themselves suddenly faced with direct responsibility for a, manifestly, highly disturbed new Province, Lord Glenelg's advisers built up a case for withdrawal largely by the citation of incidents tending to prove the contrary; these reasons annexed in the dispatch itself are conventionally attributed to missionary influence, and in particular to the machinations (yet again!) of Dr. John Philip.

The influence of the missionaries is not in question, but the way of it has been greatly misapprehended. In January 1835 Philip, beyond doubt the chief figure, was silenced by the outbreak of war, and remained silent for some months; the 'poor Kafirs', according to Mrs. Philip, had put themselves out of court, and he himself was scrupulous not to weaken the arm of authority; the Governor, he wrote, was on trial and he hoped he might yet find a satisfactory solution. The 'expulsion order' in the May Proclamations staggered Philip, as well a proposal might that would mean clearing nearly 200 miles of rugged, thickly wooded country of Kafirs and resettling it with Europeans. In June, and not till then, he wrote pressing his directors to call in Buxton and take issue with the Colonial Office on D'Urban's proposals. His long report, with circumstantial matter, arrived towards the end of September, only three or four weeks after D'Urban's own curt announcement of his original plan of action. The Colonial Office was very ready to welcome additional information, but it was the Rev. William Ellis, the Mission Secretary, not Philip, who handled it. This made a difference; Mr. Ellis clearly 'had the time of his life'! The moment Philip's dossier arrived Ellis rushed it direct to Buxton, who demanded and got an immediate interview with Lord Glenelg. A few days later Ellis wrote proudly that he had just had 'four hours at the Colonial Office' and, significantly, that he had been taking up 'the seizure of the Caffre territory, the expulsion of the chiefs, the death of Hintza, *etc.*'. The *etc.*, his letter shows, concerned a paper of Philip's on 'the origins of the war' which went over old ground: the abuse of the commando system was Philip's strong reason for urging a total *change* of system; but in Ellis's hands his document became, rather, a recital of *The Wrongs of the Caffre Nation* (the title of a contemporary booklet). The heady emotionalism of the purest 'Exeter Hall' had the field to itself, Philip's more constructive contribution going for nothing. Philip himself was getting ready to answer Buxton's urgent summons to London while the Glenelg dispatch was preparing, and he was in London when it reached D'Urban; his direct reactions never appear. In London in 1836–7 he worked hard preparing a South African chapter for Buxton's Aborigines Select Committee, but D'Urban's long-delayed 'reply' arrived when the King was on his death-bed. The demise of the King entailed the dissolution of Parliament, so if, therefore, the Committee was to report at all, the chapter on South Africa must be, and was, dropped altogether

Lord Glenelg's policy was at any rate none of Philip's. This stalwart was rarely terse; his letters to the L.M.S. and to Buxton were accompanied by memoranda, newspapers and other enclosures and Ellis may be excused if he found them hard to digest. To Buxton, however, and still more clearly, with italics of his own, in a letter of advice to a younger James Read, he wrote in October 1835:

> 'On the subject of it being desirable that the Caffres should be retained as British subjects I have long made up my mind. . . . *The Caffres cannot otherwise be saved from annihilation.*'

Philip was shocked at 'expulsion', but he was no advocate of 'retrocession'. The point of his catalogue of 'wrongs', on which both Ellis and Glenelg fastened, was to show the abuses inevitable under military rule: his own consistent plea was for civil administration buttressed by law. His best claim to prescience is his resolute insistence that the essential prerequisite to any such new order was '*a clear land settlement*'. Unlike some modern critics of colonial policy, he was a realist and never opposed 'white settlement' as such; but like other of his own later critics he firmly believed in tribes preserving their identity and internal unity: he therefore strongly resisted the 'chess-board' like penetration of tribal areas, while at the same time laying it down, as I have already quoted, that 'every tribe must know its own limits'. All this went for nothing with the Colonial Office. Within ten years the authorities had to think again—in the much more complex southern Africa of 1846.

The withdrawal from the Province of Queen Adelaide was the signal for the mass emigration of frontier farmers known as the Great Boer Trek, a tale of derring-do, and an epic of courage and endurance in its own right. The moment the Glenelg dispatch was seen to dash all hope of relieving land hunger, on the Katberg or in the beautiful Amatola Basin, emigration, which had so long been sporadic, swelled into a mass movement. The undoing of the D'Urban settlement accordingly stands out as a chief 'cause' of the Trek, but an organized movement was clearly preparing well before 1836. There is a difficulty about these antecedents. The farmers of the West were the slave-owners and they, like the Church, if they did not disapprove of the exodus, held back from it. The trekkers themselves owned hardly a slave between them. Emancipation, therefore, provoked no mass protest and was not a 'cause' of the Trek. The trekkers themselves, however, made no bones about it that the 'interference of missionaries and other interested persons' was good reason for wanting a state of their own which would ensure, in a famous phrase, 'proper relations between master and servant'. The 50th Ordinance, the unforgotten Black Circuit, and certainly the disallowing of the Vagrancy Law in 1834, were lively grievances; the news of emancipation cannot but have disturbed these farmer-employers who, though little affected by slave-regulations, strongly resented so much fussy 'sentimentalism'. The due place of the Hottentots was in their view to be serfs, if not 'tied to the land', at least strictly bound to the service of the land-owners. The emigrants, Afrikaans-speaking Boers to the last man, were individually kind and considerate masters; but they were themselves tied to a seventeenth-century body of belief and carried it with them, never seriously modified, into the great new beyond.

'Causes' apart, the fundamental motive of the Trek, one at the same time unimpeachable, was beyond doubt no more than the Boers' natural impulse to explore and make use of the illimitable veld, later their beloved *platteland* (open or flat lands). It is a mistake to think of the 'frontier' as sealed; there was no Iron Curtain to stop coming and going—there was a good deal of it! Stray hunters, and a very few runagates, roamed far and wide. The Kafir resistance checked the advance but never stopped it. Ordinary farmers herded their cattle, even in

'Kafirland', in such times of drought as 1834. The coming and going was not all one way. So many Kafirs were coming in search of work and opportunity that Ordinance No. 49 of 1828 actually instituted a system of 'passes' for such visitors—and these undoubtedly brought scraps of news. At least as early as 1834 Boer inquiries and movements became more systematic; the dispatch of three 'commissions' to investigate and report must have cost still earlier preparation. One report said a firm 'No' to the *dorst* (thirst)-land of the lower Orange River. Another, with good reason, spoke enthusiastically of the country to the north-east; the virtues of this grass-covered High Veld must have been widely known. It was with eager expectancy, not in blind desperation, that the emigrants abandoned their homes and started out, banding themselves together in unprecedentedly large and well-organized parties to join in the rush to possess a distant but better country.

There was justification too for the report of the 1834 commission that this delectable land now lay 'empty'; a monster upheaval had lately occurred far beyond the frontier and scattered the inhabitants. The shock of the Glenelg dispatch came by chance at the moment when this scattering of the tribes of the interior gave the frontiersmen every encouragement to strike in themselves. The inevitable opening up of the interior had come sooner rather than later. The pity of it is that these pioneering heroes, already gravely out of touch with any except their own kind, were now to be still more completely cut off for another fifty years from the development of political thought in the Western world they represented. Even a little later, the penetration of the interior might have been the joint effort of farmers and at least gold or diamond seekers. A more cosmopolitan outlook would have been helpful.

The Great Trek at any rate followed hard on a mysterious and certainly barbaric upheaval among the tribes in lands far off. The (dubious) South African theory is that the Amaxosa were themselves the vanguard of a mass migration; if so it was to be expected that the check to their advance on the Fish River must cause repercussions farther back, and undoubtedly a certain internal restlessness contributed to the Kafirs' outbreak in 1834. Refugees pressing in upon them were an unwelcome additional strain on their pasture land; the first of these new-comers were denounced by the Xosa as Fingos (dogs). Whatever the contributory causes—and slave-raiding from the African East Coast may well be one—the disorders flowed from the rise of the Zulu power under the despot, Chaka. This savage warrior inherited from his patron and overlord, Dingiswayo, a sternly disciplined army—a force that owed much of its effectiveness to the use of the short stabbing spear when others had only throwing assagais. One firm date is 1828, when Chaka was murdered and superseded by his brother Dingaan. For some ten years before this his *impis* (regiments) operated widely from his headquarters in the east-centre of what is now Natal. The consequences of his reign of terror are imperfectly calculable but were widespread. A chronic state of war kept food short and set neighbours plundering neighbours in a crescendo. The valleys and bush of Natal itself afforded appreciable cover, but not enough; so that refugees fled across the Drakensbergen to the open plains where there was much less (although some) cover, and both refugees and organized groups moved far and fast. One fragment of eye-witness evidence lifts the veil on how in 1823 Robert Moffat, lately established at Kuruman, a station that was to become famous, was obliged to stand to arms in its defence against raiders; he even called in the help of certain Bastards, so-called, coloured men armed with guns, who were not above adding to the unrest by doing a little plundering on their own account. The Bechuana tribes in his neighbourhood undoubtedly fell back or were driven towards the Kalahari, which is arid, but fair cattle country much of it, and no mere desert. The Makololo, who later were to provide Livingstone with faithful followers, pushed right through Bechuanaland to the Okavango swamps and settled there, near the Zambesi. Zulu raiders, the Angoni, penetrated even so far as southern Tanganyika where, though intermarriage with local women changed their ways, huts and other appurtenances of obviously Zulu type are their witnesses to this day.

The open High Veld in particular (the later Free State, Southern Transvaal and Northern Natal) was thus crossed and re-crossed and its people dispersed; and here was the trekkers' promised land. Because of the cold, dry winters its inhabitants were, in spite of the grass, perhaps never very numerous; but the emergency produced one dark statesman, the famous chief, Moshesh, who established an impregnable fortress in the Maluti Mountains and gathered round him, or indeed made, the upstanding people known as the Basuto. Another less estimable was the leader of a rebel Zulu army; this was that Moselekatze whom Robert Moffat first visited in 1829; the long, strange friendship of this pair began with a visit to the chief when he was settled near the site of what is now Pretoria. The trekkers, therefore, quickly found that, in spite of burnt villages and unburied corpses, this new home was *not* empty. Their very first township, seat of their first republic, was named Winburg in honour of the first victory (1836) in a series of hard-fought fights with Moselekatze's warriors. That tyrant had soon had enough; Winburg is in the south of the later Free State; by 1838 he had removed to Mosega in the far west of the Transvaal; shortly afterwards he and his followers trekked, *en masse,* all the way to Bulawayo; only there he found safety and set up his own kingdom of Matabeleland. This removal left the central High Veld comparatively clear; but well-watered Natal was even more seductive and the main body of trekkers, under Piet Retief, had already made a spectacular crossing of the Drakensbergen. When Retief went ahead to strike a bargain with Chaka's supplanter, Dingaan, still graver trouble befell; one February morning Retief and some seventy followers were barbarously murdered. Ten months later, in December 1838, Retief's body, with a signed treaty safe in a leather wallet, was recovered by his victorious avengers after the battle that gave a name to the *Blood* River. The Republic of Natal was now apparently secure. The trekkers, however, were widely dispersed and they often disagreed among themselves. Several more republics arose but there was still no end to their 'native troubles' on either side of the mountains; by 1840 the Natal republicans had found the African inhabitants inconveniently numerous. The remedy they proposed was the first of what was to become a long series of *Plakkers* (squatters) laws that limited the number of African families on any one farm to a maximum of five. To relieve the pressure on their own farms they further proposed to move the 'surplus' away to the west, into Pondoland. The one plan, to limit squatters, was impracticable; the other, the proposal to remove them, was reckless. Such high-handed self-assertion against tribes living so near the troubled frontier of the Cape was a portent.

The trekkers, never consciously or overtly taking the offensive, were in fact themselves involved, even if it was defensively, in a continuous tribal war. Though not yet unchallenged masters, they were now the dominant factor from the Orange River to beyond the Vaal, and southwards again into Natal. Thus inside four years the whole South African situation was revolutionized; the main body of the Kafirs and their neighbours was in a military sense completely outflanked. The disorders on the narrow 100-mile front had been a sore embarrassment to many Cape governments; now the frontier had come at one blow to stretch indeterminately for 500 miles and more in almost every possible direction. Yet at law the invaders were citizens of the Cape Colony; the Cape Government was still legally and morally responsible for any untoward consequences arising from the activities of its own voluntary exiles; news of the irresponsible proposal to quarter surplus population on the Pondo brought it home to their government that these might be dangerous.

For some time the sheer difficulty of communications made it impossible to get a clear picture of the ever-changing situation on this extended frontier, and no government can be blamed for failing to assess it quickly and as a whole. The limited resources of the Cape authorities left them almost powerless; perhaps the only remedy would have been to shepherd the scattering sheep back into the fold—and that was impossible. Events followed one another headlong, out of all control, and the policy of the Government the events so much concerned came tumbling after—this is often the only real answer to questions that vex the schools about the causes of historical catastrophes; the 'policy' of the luckless Government responsible can never keep pace. The distant Colonial Office was never avid for adventure; its pathetic gesture was the so-called Cape of Good Hope Punishment Act of 1836 which made colonial citizens responsible under Cape Law for any wrongs they might commit beyond the borders up to 25° S. This law was actually prompted not by the Great Trek itself but by ill deeds attributed to certain runagates of pre-Trek days; it was still-born for want of the means of compassing the offenders; the far interior was well out of reach. The move into Natal, to within easy reach of the sea and the Navy, was therefore fateful. Port Natal had for some time been a trading post and in 1835 was given the Governor's name (Durban), but still no official recognition or support. At least it was a channel for news like that of the murder of Retief, and for rumours of the Republic's disturbing 'native policy'. Well-founded reports of coal deposits up country also followed, and these ensured the interest of the Admiralty, the more readily when about the same time foreign ships, Dutch and American, began doing business with the Boers of the Republic. Comparatively promptly, in 1842, a company of British soldiers was sent to garrison Durban. Following a Boer 'siege' of this tiny force, and its relief by a naval frigate, the situation was deemed to need a Special Commissioner. In 1843 this Colonel Cloete annexed Natal to the Cape Colony and, after further prolonged negotiations, set it up as a separate colony in 1845. But, rather than submit, a large part of the emigrants packed up once more and made for freedom on the landward side of the mountains. This open country, too, the essential High Veld, was in a very disturbed state. The mild climate of Natal got venturesome people at least talking about tobacco and cotton or other profitable sub-tropical crops as 'possibilities', but the colder inland plateau was good for little but grazing and maize; wheat grows well in favoured spots but that came later. In the early days the trekkers who elected to remain there included a considerable proportion of farmers of the semi-nomadic type, the essential *trek-Boere* who habitually roamed the country driving their herds with them. The need to make room for those returned from Natal did nothing to promote unity. In the '40s there was really ample space even for a few nomads, but there were still tribal remnants and other challengers, and some of the Boers' high-handed ways with these gave the Government continuing cause for anxiety. To get out of reach of British 'interference' a party of these restless and ill-equipped pioneers made one venture into the seductively attractive *low* veld of the tropical northern Transvaal. They quickly fell back, beaten by malaria, to the safer 6,000-feet altitude of the place they named Lydenburg (Town of Suffering). In face of so much coming and going the Cape Government was bound by obdurate orders from home to avoid entanglements. The Glenelg 'policy' held that its responsibilities must on no account be added to by the annexation of more territory; Natal touched real British interests and was an unwillingly admitted exception. Elsewhere, as on the post-1836 Cape frontier, chiefs might at most be admitted by treaty into defensive alliance on condition that they took responsibility for keeping peace and order within their own borders.

This forlorn hope led Dr. Philip to make one last bid. At least the south-east of the Orange River country was quiet enough to allow him in the course of 1841–2 to make an extensive and peaceful tour of his missions in that area; he even pushed on to visit the Basuto, and Moshesh. His journal was unusually placid and made frequent friendly references to Boer farmers for whom he even conducted Sunday services. The L.M.S. stations at Griquatown and Philippolis were of some consequence, the first because the Griquas, or Bastards, having much white blood and being themselves *trek-Boere*, were the most independent of the coloured people; Philippolis was a major crossing of the Orange River. The visit to Moshesh was justly due: when he was on trek in 1832 that chief had sent him a present of cattle to 'buy' a missionary and Philip was able to divert the French Evangelical mission to Basutoland—a most helpful move. Philip now singled out the Griquas and Basuto as comparatively stable units, but he judged that even they could not stand by themselves in dealing with their Boer neighbours. On his way back to the Colony he took real alarm at the news that met him from Natal about the 'siege' of Durban and once more pressed on the authorities the need to keep a firm hand on the situation; he often recommended the Indian States as a model, and distinctly heralded 'indirect rule'. The most he could get was a pair of stock-pattern treaties. The Griqualand and Basutoland of the next years are still inappropriately known as 'Dr. Philip's Treaty States'. Later events abundantly justified him in urging the imperative necessity of taking firm control of the frontier as a whole.

The weakness of the treaty system was soon now to reveal itself at the very point where it first took shape. The duty laid on the frontier chiefs was really to act as police, to control their own followers and protect the farmers' cattle. The burden was too heavy for them. 'They have to court the people rather than be courted,' wrote Livingstone of their central African fellows. The Xosa had no effective leader, and the evidence is that the police obligations laid on these chiefs cost them much even of such authority as they had. At last, in 1846, a lawless act of aggression by some of the Kafirs' own bands plunged the frontier once more into a general war. This time there was a stronger Secretary of State at the helm, Earl Grey, and events moved with unusual precision. The Governor of the Cape was at last made High Commissioner for southern Africa, a belated recognition of the wider responsibilities he had to carry. In 1847 all the land up to the Kei was annexed as British Kaffraria, and that old hand Colonel, now Governor, Sir Harry Smith, set about ordering the new Province. This Governor always had initiative and drive; he was the hero of a ride to the frontier in 1835—500 miles in just over five days. In 1848, at his behest, the territory from the Orange to the Vaal, where disorders persisted, was proclaimed the Orange River Sovereignty. This was unusually drastic action and met some opposition, but a sufficiency of the Orange River people were, may one say, sufficiently good *South Africans* to welcome the renewal of association with the Cape. In the old colony, at this moment, a strong and united blast of public opinion forced the Home Government to abandon a project for making it a penal settlement. The victorious anti-convict agitators then went on to press a claim for constitutional rights. It was a propitious moment, when the many parts were at least momentarily linked together. The remoteness of the capital, Cape Town, was a difficulty, but for a while there was good hope of a happy issue: a draft plan proposed that a connected group of colonies, Eastern and Western Cape Provinces, Kaffraria, Natal, and the Orange River Sovereignty should enjoy mutual free trade, and all were to acknowledge the unimpeachable authority of the Supreme Court of Appeal at Cape Town.

Yet again events on the old frontier intervened. At Christmas in 1850, before Smith's civilizing efforts for the resettlement of the Kaffrarian tribes could have a fair trial, a major revolt broke out. This continued for most of three years and it was the British politicians who now lost patience. The cost to British taxpayers caused still more outcry when the administration of the Orange Sovereignty muddled into a land and boundary quarrel with Moshesh; in 1852 a British force rather cavalierly sent to warn him to be on better behaviour even suffered a sharp check. Reformers at home were consistent believers in self-government; the manifest reluctance of the white burghers to take their share in the hard work of suppressing the Kafir rebellion made them join the Manchester school and insist the more on the need to throw the burden on the people concerned. Pressure from Lord John Russell made even Earl Grey conclude that Britain was 'not wanted', and he wilted so far as to wonder if his widening of the sphere of British responsibility had been 'Quixotic Philanthropy'; by 1851 he agreed that even the Orange Territory was not a British interest. The Philip-Buxton alliance had never allowed such doctrine to go unchallenged, but there was no Philip now. The last of his considered reports to the L.M.S. accepted the incorporation of Kaffraria with the remark that '*everyone here is now of my opinion*' that the annexation of ten years earlier ought to have stood. The burnt Philip MSS. included letters from key points all over the country showing where Sir Harry Smith's well-intentioned moves were going awry. But there was no one to marshal and use this solid material; Philip himself retired to a station far in the country and died at Hankey in 1851; his own directors were frightened off politics by the unjust odium he incurred and he had no effective successor. Early in 1852 Sir Harry Smith was recalled and the die was cast. Smith's own failing was to be overmuch the soldier, but he stood firm for the unity of the country. Now that there was no one to contradict it, the view prevailed that made the African tribes not a standing challenge to good administration but only a military menace. A new Governor, Sir George Cathcart, wrote presently in a new vein; an independent state in the interior, he considered, would not readily fall foul of the British might; it would certainly be less expensive and '*a more secure barrier against barbarians*' than any British political interference could be without costly military backing. In 1852 commissioners concluded a convention which recognized the Republic and conceded the Transvaal Boers' claim to 'manage their own affairs'.

This Sand River Convention was hasty and ill considered. There was no thought or mention of 'sovereign independence'; 'suzerainty' (a troublesome term that emerged at a later date) was clearly taken for granted; this was the hey-day of Lord Palmerston who, though himself in and out, was never far from the changing ministries of that day. The clause by which the Boers renounced slavery was little more to the point than the British undertaking to bar the sale of guns to native peoples. The underlying assumption was, as Governor Cathcart had indicated, in the spirit of Palmerston, that British power could and would assert itself if and when necessary. The Colonial Office, forgetting its own earlier project for free trade and a common Court of Appeal, was at that moment preparing a constitution, but when promulgated in 1853 it was for the Cape alone. This constitution stopped short of self-government—though in 1872, it will be remembered, a simple Act of the Parliament now set up sufficed to complete the final step in that direction. It assumed, however, the legal equality established in 1842, and conceded the parliamentary vote to any qualified person, whatever the colour of his skin. The free Boers of the Transvaal set leisurely to work drafting their own constitution or Grondwet, and in 1858, in flat contradiction of the Cape principles, they launched a famous pronouncement:

> '*Het volk wil geen gelijkstelling*' . . . 'The people will (i.e. will tolerate) no equality between coloured people and the white inhabitants whether in Church or in State.'

This was indeed a parting of the ways, a schism that was the more complete since within two years of Sand River, in 1854, the British Government had precipitately abandoned the Orange River Sovereignty; washing its hands of the consequences of its 'policy', and as if for good measure, it left a body of well-disposed burghers to manage their affairs in an independent Orange Free State which was no longer even loosely associated with the parent Cape. All was not yet lost. A new Governor, Sir George Grey, quickly inspired confidence, winning support even in the Free State where the Boer leader, Pretorius, was making strenuous efforts of his own to unite the divided trekker republics. It was in the end of 1858 that Grey wrote his great Federation dispatch warning the Home Government against the dangers of the 'dismemberment' that had overtaken South Africa:

> 'They have', he wrote, 'the same sympathies, the same prejudices, the same habits, and frequently the same feelings regarding the native races, although marked and rapid changes in public opinion are taking place. . . . The only bond of union which at present holds together these states, European and native, is the High Commissioner. . . . A slight failure of temper or judgement on his part might at any time bring on a native war, a general rising of the natives, or a European rebellion. . . . The affairs which (the republics') legislatures handle are so small that they can raise no class of statesmen to take enlarged and liberal views. . . . They can possess no able bar, no learned judges. . . . Trade and commerce must therefore necessarily

languish. . . . Life and property thus become insecure and a general lawlessness follows.'

Grey had his supporters. Nearly forty years later a visit to the old man was still the 'high-light' of a European tour made by the author of *Commando* as a boy with his father F. W. Reitz, then newly retired from being President of the Orange Free State. All Grey got in 1859 was a severe reprimand, and with it a curt reminder that H.M.G. had already made its decision.

The venture into the African interior which had thus split the tiny European society left it with a political lack of system that must, if this was the last word, deepen the cleavage and perpetuate it. The saga of the Great Boer Trek has been recited loud and long as the saga of a heroic adventure deserved to be; but the move must be recognized also for a political disaster of the first magnitude. The effects matured only slowly. Too much can be made of the significance even of the original Transvaal Grondwet pronouncement on the status of coloured persons. This flat contradiction not only of Cape practice but of the principles of Roman Dutch law which ruled in the Republic's own courts (when it came to have courts) was no more than an assertion of their own prejudice by a recalcitrant minority. In their hour of triumph the frontiersmen felt able to repudiate the Rule of Law as it was administered by their own country's courts; but for many years they were struggling far too hard for their own individual existence to do anything serious about organizing a settled administration. It was an unwelcome surprise not to get their 'empty' El Dorado to themselves, and at once, on the principle that attack is the surest defence, they had set about 'clearing' the Matabele off the central High Veld. The tribesmen's reaction to the presence of intruders being much the same, life was very hard and dangerous; the Boers' long guns outmatched the tribesmen's assagais and were the only means of keeping law and order. These Transvaal Boers were, however, so far away that the sovereign authority, burdened with cares nearer home, felt it safe to leave them to it. It was already forgotten how once before, in 1840, when the Boers' outward movement was only four years old, the proposed dumping of 'surplus' tribesmen on the Pondo threatened the peace of the eastern frontier and forced an earlier and equally unwilling government to take notice. The sequel to this more comprehensive washing of hands is a classic example of how a minority left to 'manage their own affairs' can disregard the interests of their more numerous neighbours.

The double British surrender of sovereignty in the 1850s was not and, in the absence of properly constituted and viable succession states, could not be complete; the Cape Governor was still High Commissioner for southern Africa and, as such, his authority was sometimes an irritant, as Grey had foretold, but never a unifying force. H.M.G. studiously refrained from interfering in internal affairs but could not ignore matters of common interest. The annexation of Basutoland in 1868 (when 'protectorates' were not yet in fashion) was resented by the Free Staters as upsetting a settlement of their own making; but H.M.G. had recognized the Basuto in 1843, and any break-up threatened repercussions that must affect adjoining states, both the Cape and Natal. The next moment H.M.G. had even fuller reason, all too late, to take Sir George Grey's warning to heart. The economic possibilities of the interior went curiously unsuspected till the discovery of diamonds (which was of more than local import: Chapter 8) brought a 'rush' to the Kimberley fields in 1870. The strike being made at a point perfectly placed to warrant rival claims to possession at once by the Cape, the Transvaal and the Free State, H.M.G. was inevitably involved: its own action had left no authority competent to deal even with a dispute involving three separate and distinct units, therefore the country as a whole. The diamond rush at once, moreover, threatened social and political complications to which the Cape and H.M.G. itself could not remain indifferent, and this time the High Commissioner did not hesitate to take direct control. Following on this action Lord Carnarovn, the Secretary of State, even began to preach and plan for the Federation H.M.G. had so lately rejected. It was an unpropitious moment. The Free State was compensated, not excessively, for the loss of its diamond interests; but though it was thus relieved of two administrative problems (Basutoland and the diamond fields) which must have changed its own essential character, the Republic was left with a sense of grievance that rankled. The Cape was, at best, very lukewarm towards Carnarvon's plan.

It was, however, the affairs of the Transvaal that presently came uppermost. Bent now on Federation, Lord Carnarvon sent a strong Governor, Sir Bartle Frere, to press this policy. This Republic was hard put to it by wars with its tribesmen and virtually bankrupt—so apparently helpless that in 1877 Frere's Commissioner, Sir Theophilus Shepstone, marching in with a force of twenty-five police, saw no remedy but to proclaim an (unopposed) annexation of the Transvaal. Yet again 'native affairs' intervened. An unimportant rising in the Cape in 1878, a major Zulu war in 1879, and 'trouble' in Basutoland, created a state of commotion which embarrassed Frere's moves. The overthrow (1879) of the Zulu power, their near neighbour, so improved the prospects of the Transvaal that towards the end of 1880 recalcitrant Boers declared their independence, took to arms, shot up garrison troops caught on the march and (February 1881) very gallantly stormed the main British relieving force on Majuba Hill. The Gladstone Ministry, newly elected to power on an anti-Imperialist cry, spared all its sympathy for the freedom-loving Boers and conceded independence, retaining only an ill-defined British 'suzerainty'; this term was disliked and in 1884 a revised Convention dropped it. Two years later the opening of the great Rand gold-fields found the Boers still flushed with victory after Majuba, and stout for the independence two Conventions had newly confirmed. It was a novel feature of the Rand system that the process of extracting the gold (which is present in minute percentages in great masses of banket rock) was too complex to be undertaken by the old-fashioned digger working independently and called from the start for highly capitalized organization. The activity this caused, and the wealth accruing, tipped the economic balance of the country in favour of the Transvaal, against the more sober Cape, and gave the republicans good reason to feel even more sure of themselves; their poor little republic suddenly became the centre of the only considerable industry in the whole country. Unyielding about the status of British or other *uitlanders*, who were in the mining industry, and unaccommodating even about railway rates and customs, they were not innocent of using their new-found wealth to arm themselves against eventualities. The successors of the British rulers who had taken the easy way in 1852, in the day of small things, were soon now to pay the bill for having left so much to the disregardful isolationism of the valiant but inexperienced Boer trekkers. There was no United States Congress here to deal with the acute local differences that resulted from the absence of any competent over-ruling authority, and H.M.G. was obliged to step in to fill the political vacuum it had left, thus concentrating on itself most of the blame for an inevitably strained situation. The Americans, who for a time successfully evaded their own Indian question, came to blows at last about its slavery variant; but the federal principle survived, and preserved that minimum of unity which is essential to internal peace and orderly progress in such wide open spaces. But both the warning of the Civil War and the example of Canadian Federation had come just too late. In the end H.M.G. was involved as principal (1899–1902) in a South African counterpart of the American Civil War.

The basic cause of the continuous friction that ended so disastrously was and continued to be a conflict about the rights of African and coloured peoples. The Transvaal republicans were, however, almost equally intolerant of the *uitlanders* whose presence threatened to disturb their very rigid way of life. The trouble was, rather, that the sheer physical isolation they won for themselves left them too much leisure to brood on real and alleged past wrongs; the repetition among them of highly varnished accounts of the Black Circuit and of Slagter's Nek, of the folly of Lord Glenelg and the wickedness of Dr. Philip, bred in them an isolationist philosophy of unparalleled and unyielding intensity. In earlier days, before this doctrine had ossified, Sir Harry Smith came near to restoring the situation when he reasserted the authority of the state the trekkers had repudiated; only the Transvaalers were a small hard core of resistance, bent on 'independence' at all costs: many other equally good Afrikaner frontiersmen were not ill settled in new homes; a monolithic state was not the only alternative and an accommodation was actually in sight till the Kafirs, the original victims of European pressure, rose again in desperate rebellion at the end of 1850. The Kafirs, who cannot have been unaffected by the rumours that reached them of lawlessness and war in the lands beyond them, had grievances of their own against the white man; it gives some idea of what they were that the Scripture lesson still read at an annual Xosa commemorative service is from *Lamentations*:

'*We have drunken our water for money; our wood is sold unto us.*'

Soon afterwards, in 1855, they acted again; led astray by one of their prophets, they slaughtered all their cattle by way of preparation for the coming of a mighty Avenger. This crazy act finally destroyed their military power. But by this time the costly burden of South African responsibility had made impatient British politicians put pressure on their Government, and H.M.G. had abdicated. The tragedy of it is that the parent state, the Cape of Good Hope, was then well on the way to showing that there is an equitable way through the difficulties presented by racial inequality. Even before the cattle-killing Sir George Grey, the first civilian Governor and one of the best of the line, had at once embarked with zest on the essential work of the civilized power, at last setting up a civil administration and pressing on to build schools and hospitals. The demarcation of native 'reserves' of land was made with the best of intentions but, cut off as these islands were, they got little of the benefit even of roads and railways and could not share in the expanding economic life of the country as a whole; even the casual 'squatter' system used in the republics was at least less destructive of the soil-surfaces. It was all the more important that the steadily growing number of qualified Africans were consciously free to exercise the political rights the liberal Cape policy allowed them. The coloured and African voters, for their part, were fully 'integrated', never a mere racial *bloc*; I have more than once seen their rival electoral processions, one shouting for a 'Progressive', the other for his 'Afrikaner Bond' opponent! It is only modern self-deception that would make Cape liberalism a burden imposed from without. It was nothing of the kind. For thirty years and more of its Parliament's very honourable life, the Cape unquestionably led; the official Dutch Church frowned on the Trek and lost some ground to the straiter Calvinists of Potchefstroom, known as 'Doppers', but these were little assertive of their views; even in the 1920s Cape educational and intellectual pre-eminence was unchallenged. In spite of the ruinous political schism the high prestige of the Cape gave every hope that its example would prevail generally. Pupils of Dr. John Philip helped to shape Cape policy, but men of all races accepted it and cherished it as their own. Its doughtiest defenders at the crisis, only in 1936, were two leading Afrikaners, F. S. Malan and Jan H. Hofmeyr.

It greatly contributed to the dénouement that in all the recurrent crises of the later years the basic question, the status of the dependent African peoples, though never far from the surface, was steadily sidetracked. As in America the debate came to turn more and more on the purely political issues. Had this really turned attention to mending the political divisions of the country as a whole there had been something gained. But the protagonists were, as a rule, the Imperial Government on one side and always one if not both of the exclusively Boer Republics on the other; and this accidental circumstance confused the issue—the 'problem' was increasingly taken to be the conflict between Briton and Boer, and the reconciliation of the white races. The example of habitual disregard for African interests in the Transvaal in 1852 was followed again in the negotiations after 1881, when the only recognition that African rights were involved was H.M.G.'s stipulation that the Republic should provide adequate 'native reserves'. In fact, war with their northern tribes kept the Republicans busy till the end of the chapter; they did little or nothing about the reserves, but no more was said. By 1899 the Lloyd George Liberals were making all turn on the greed of capitalist mining magnates; the Briton or Boer theme was dominant. The peace of 1902 expressly left the question of a Native franchise for consideration only when self-government should be restored to the ex-republics—as it was in 1906. At the next stage the young men of the Milner 'Kindergarten' turned the limelight on the relations of the states, the visible occasion of much friction: their formative document, the

Selborne Memorandum of 1907, and their journal named *The State*, consciously avoided the thorny subject, in the conviction that agreement on railway rates and a customs union was a safer road to British and Boer reconciliation. The British Parliament hesitated when in 1909 it was called on to approve the South Africa Act; but, solacing its doubts by retaining direct control, through its own High Commissioner, of Basutoland, a *colony* actually within the Union's borders, and of the two protectorates, Swaziland and Bechuanaland which are just beyond it, it let the Cape-inspired 'entrenched' (coloured franchise) clauses of the locally drafted constitution suffice, once more and finally declining to demand the enfranchisement at least, in Cecil Rhodes's phrase, of all the new state's *civilized* citizens. The Union thus began its life on foundations that were basically unsound.

The country has always been physically one, if only because internal communications are so difficult: the same two or three indifferent seaports were all that linked its people with the Western world they specially claim to represent—and for too many of them the tenuous link snapped altogether. The white colonists are now less completely one than when Sir George Grey wrote his sharp warning, and the people of colour have been steadily extruded (Chapter 10) from their share in the conduct of affairs. This came of the old Cape having lost its frontiersmen; for, having lost them, it lost touch with and control also of its own frontier; and the Cape that suffered such 'dismemberment' was *South Africa.* The long chapter which ended thus in schism was, inauspiciously, also the opening chapter in the modern history of the African continent.

Chapter 7

NEW THINGS INTO AFRICA

*

The essential Africa, the area peopled by negroids, extends for the greater part of the more than 4,000 miles that lie between Durban and Cairo, and includes also much of the other 5,000 miles stretching from Cape Verde in the west to Guardafui in the east. The longest distance between any two points in the fraction of all this which is the Union proper, from the Cape to its northernmost border, may be about 1,000 miles.[1] The penetration of this greater Africa by civilizing influences was stopped dead in early classical times by the barrier of the Sahara. The peoples of the tropical parts beyond were bound to be drawn some day into association with the outside world, but unprofitable experience, not least in the far south, discouraged enterprise elsewhere and the process was begun again seriously only by Livingstone's travels (starting from the Cape soon after the Great Trek) and gathered head, still later, about the time of the opening of the Rand gold-fields. Many who now made their ventures naturally looked for guidance to experience in the one part of Africa that was already well known; but South Africans in general paid the penalty for absorption in 'managing their own affairs' and played no proper part in helping the development of neighbouring country. These new lands were so little known that for most of those who did participate the 2,000-year-old saying of Pliny never lost its force—*ex Africa semper aliquid novi*. We know better now the natural disabilities of the peoples of the tropical regions, and how unequally they battled with them: having no formal education, and not a glimmering of scientific knowledge, they were a prey to much grievous, ill-understood suffering and to insidious fears and gross superstition. It is one enduring effect that these lands are only thinly populated, but till lately it was little appreciated even that the disabilities came of Africa itself. Many still suppose

[1] I found myself driven at last to inviting students to visualize these relative dimensions by covering the southern end of the map of Africa in any school atlas with the flat of a thumb!

that abundant cheap labour is one solid asset; but untrained, irregular labour is highly inefficient, and, therefore, as most would now agree, *dear*; and as for its being plentiful—at an official conference not many years ago I heard the Secretary of State's Labour Adviser, the late Sir St. John Orde-Browne, argue with cogent authority, though he then got little support, that inefficiency and ill health leave Africa actually short of man-power for the immense labour required to make its tropical parts reasonably fit for civilized habitation.

The involvement of the African peoples in world affairs was at first only very slow and gradual. The difficulty of travel and movement at least made for peace, and the quiet early years built up against later tensions a great fund of goodwill between black and white. For fully a century before the modern invasion very lonely individuals were able, by sheer force of personality, to win the confidence of their African hosts and, with their help, to lay bare more of the facts; the so-called profit motive counted for little even with those who first revealed the economic potentialities by their blood, sweat and tears; a handful of devotees made a self-appointed task a labour of love. A natural curiosity to reveal the unknown was sometimes inspired by zeal for advancing scientific knowledge, but just as often the prime motive was the instinct for sheer adventure; all African travel was arduous—Shanks's mare was as a rule the only possible way of it—but there was always the indescribable lure of the African bush: as the Arabs said so well: whoever has once drunk of its fountains will always thirst for more. Africa, moreover, was unmatched as a game park and big-game hunters played their part, as did pick-and-shovel prospectors and many lonely traders; missionaries followed, always solitary, and before the end many devoted government servants.

There had, of course, been British stations on the West Coast since at least the time of Charles II. In a legal sense these were 'colonies', but even for them the new chapter began in some sort only with Mungo Park's travels in West Africa in and after 1785 when strategical considerations and the attack on the slave trade brought this coast into notice. The British Government was now disposed to countenance Sharp's or other philanthropists' plans for a settlement in Sierra Leone; the rugged twenty-mile-long headland, still known as the Colony peninsula, was acquired and planted in 1787 with a small community of freed slaves, or Creoles. There were other moves and influences. Sir Joseph Banks, former associate of Captain Cook, became in 1788 the chairman of a London dining club known as the African Association, a group interested in African exploration; Mungo Park, a young Scots doctor, was his protégé—this was a time too when the storm rising against the slave trade inclined the shipping interests to look for alternative economic possibilities in the slave-trading countries. The West of Africa was the most accessible part and so, for half a century or more, in spite of the climatic terrors, the only serious European attempts to penetrate into the interior were made from what is still spoken of as The Coast.

The common objective of a long series of expeditions was to determine the course of the River Niger. The climate took heavy toll of the explorers. Four attempts failed and three of the leaders died in Africa before Mungo Park was called in from service in the East. His deliberate and considered choice of the Gambia as a starting point for his journeys in 1795 and again in 1805 deserved to succeed; the secure anchorage of the Gambia is at the mouth of a long navigable river which makes it a natural point of entry and gave Park a good start; he reached the Niger and discovered its eastward trend. At a second attempt, in 1806, after sailing eastwards half its length, he was drowned trying to escape through rapids from hostile Africans. It is some measure of the difficulties and dangers Park faced that definite news of his end was obtained only six years later by one of his former native guides, whose special mission took most of two years to accomplish; but at least Park's *Journals* were saved and published and kept interest very much alive. The Gambia went out of fashion as a base; Tripoli was used more than once, and even the lower Congo was tried—in case this other unknown river should turn out to be the Niger. By 1822 the sources of the Niger had, however, been definitely located in the highlands not far behind Sierra Leone: in the following years its course was gradually made clearer; Lake Chad was now known, and Timbuktu; but it was not till 1830 that one of two brothers named Lander, striking inland at last from Badagri, near Lagos, completed the journey down stream to one of its several mouths.

The results were negligible; knowledge had to be its own reward. The immense distances made freight costs prohibitive; at the same time the risks to health ruled out any large or direct European participation even in trading; white settlement was unthinkable. One last British Government expedition started from Tripoli in 1850 and was notable for the work of the German scientist, Heinrich Barth; for over five years this sole survivor of the team that began the quest roamed alone by way of Timbuktu to the country farther south—the Benue, the Niger's great eastern tributary, was his discovery; his well-illustrated book, published in 1857, is a classic for this immense stretch of country.

An incidental outcome was even more significant: Dr. W. B. Baikie, leading a party in search of Barth, not only steamed a long way up the Niger; his success also in keeping his men in good health was the first demonstration of the value of regular prophylactic doses of quinine as a curb on the worst ravages of malaria; and by this time attention was turning back once more from the savannah to the Coast proper, where preventive medicine was of the highest consequence. The interior engaged British attention again only years later—when international rivalry threatened traders with the loss of such markets as they had been able to build up from their coastal bases. Meantime, from the '30s till the '60s the Royal Navy's hunt against the slave trade, the major Coast activity, was making it urgent for traders with Coast interests to find some alternative exportable commodity. Their best hope was the Coast's one great natural forest product, red palm-oil, which besides being valuable as at once a food and a medicine, is an important industrial lubricant. The years 1832–4 brought Macgregor Laird, a young Liverpool merchant, exploring the possibilities. The Niger Expedition of 1841, which Fowell Buxton fondly hoped was to remedy the slave trade, failed; but in the '50s Macgregor Laird was back organizing posts on the Niger, in the region which came to be known as the Oil Rivers. About the same time the Navy's effective suppression of slave-running was deemed to require the occupation and, in 1861, the annexation of Lagos. The string of British forts and trading posts was now complete—the Gambia, Cape Coast and its neighbours, comprising the Gold Coast, and Lagos, an island set in lagoons, and at one point only a stone's-throw from the mainland. There was also Sierra Leone which, *sui generis*, was a real colony; the plantation of non-tribal British-protected Africans settled into a community rather like that of a West Indian island. Its early years were a struggle for existence, but in time, when European example had begun to rouse more interest in West Africa, Freetown became a considerable educational and cultural influence; the services of its educated people were in some demand further afield, and its mission-sponsored (C.M.S.) College at Fourah Bay for many years sent out a steady trickle of professional men and administrators to neighbouring colonies.

But for years, also, British sovereignty was effective only within range of the guns mounted on the walls of its several castles. A very few strong personalities made a mark, but in the conditions that ruled on the Coast some such limited assumption of sovereignty was little more than a means of giving traders the protection there was no local authority strong enough to ensure. Settled administration was all but impossible except within easy walking distance of headquarters. The mortality rate among officials, and still more in the garrisons, was fantastically high; well on into the nineteenth century the lists of governors show an average tenure of office of less than one year. A very few white men (it would almost seem to be a *genus*) were or became immune to fever; some of these helped perhaps to inculcate some idea of and respect for western law and justice; but the most remarkable of them, Captain George Maclean, though he acted as Governor in the Gold Coast for thirteen years (1830–43) and won real authority in the course of a still longer stay, was never confirmed in his office. Official British influence being thus almost negligible, the function of introducing the local peoples to the ways of the civilized world inevitably devolved on cosmopolitan unofficial visitors, even if the slave-traders might include worthies like John Newton, the hymn-writer, their presentation could only be unimpressive. But the enduring legacy of centuries is not to be discounted. The peoples of the Coast after all this time were no longer unaffectedly simple 'bush' men. The well-populated forest country must always be one of the hardest in the world to see; not even a Heinrich Barth could ever cover it at one comprehensive glance. The European participants in the chief trade of the earlier years rarely if ever dared to set foot inland to collect the human chattels for themselves; their share was little more than the shipping of the cargoes brought to them on the beaches. The major and profitable operation of collecting or chaffering for slaves was a monopoly—it would seem the jealously guarded monopoly—of Africans, many of them professional traders. Slavery was indigenous and very lightly borne; Mungo Park and his successors soon found, if that much was not already known, that the stronger African states, some of them 'empires', were the preserve of a privileged class, thriving (if they did thrive) on the labour of numerous slaves—as most of the rest of the world had always done. Those in power parted with surplus slaves when the chance of greater gain presented itself. Their chance arose from the labour needs of the more productive countries of western Europeans who in their own home-lands were working gradually towards an alternative system of free labour. In Africa the European slave-traders acted chiefly as the receivers of stolen goods, accessories, therefore, to the cruelty and the crimes to which this rape gave rise. When the insatiable demand for the labour of slaves increased the overseas traffic and perpetuated the cruelties, Britain became the leading offender. British writers, as well as British statesmen, have done some penance, and finally they did more than any others to put an end to slavery itself. It now falls to responsible and forward-looking Africans, most appropriately to those of their new university colleges, to clear all our minds by examining the African part in this sorry story.

Some of the social effects are clear. The traffic can have afforded the few white men at the receiving stations only a miserable and uncomfortable existence, but it was clearly a considerable source of employment for many Africans, and of substantial profit for the privileged few. It is not merely that the Coast people, almost in general, show a genius for trading and bargaining; a strong and well-established 'middle' class is the unique feature of what were once the active centres of the slave-trade in Nigeria or the Gold Coast. Life in the forest strongly favoured independence rather than autocracy—nowhere else have chiefs, where there are any, been so completely 'kept in their place'; the effective power was with men who were not always themselves of chiefly rank, but yet certainly more than mere subsistence peasants. The little towns that stud the foreshore have clearly seen better days; the handsome remains in the centre of Cape Coast were not built yesterday. Several specialist tribes still produce superlative seamen, and in this tsetse-infested, meatless country cured fish is a staple of diet and the fish-trade profitable; but the towns are more than fishing villages. The gold of the Gold Coast was no great export, but much circulated internally, helping to stimulate the towns which are evidently the product of what must long have been a very active economic life. There can be no doubt that the slave-trade was the main support of this activity, and the influence which originally moulded the life of the Coast and the ways of its people. The vested interests undoubtedly struggled long and hard against abolition, and not all of these were European.

It was at last in the depths of a long 'depression' consequent on the ending of the slave-trade that the more benign western influences began to affect the Coast. Dr. Baikie's success in introducing the prophylactic use of quinine must rank high among these influences; officials and traders, and besides these an increasing number of missionaries, were presently able to face longer or more frequent tours of residence. In the earlier nineteenth century several ventures were made, with appalling loss of life; once at least the Gambia had to be settled afresh: four of the first five Methodists sent to the Gold Coast (1835–6) were dead inside a year (even if, as by a miracle, the fifth was one of those rare exceptions and survived on the Coast for sixty years!). The well-known Scots mission at Calabar in Nigeria was originally planted by volunteers from Jamaica about 1841; and these and others gradually struck root. As in the West Indies, missions brought schools—as well as the beginnings of medical care and sorely needed hospitals. An active internal trade continued—dealings not only in palm-oil and in gunpowder and gin, but a clandestine traffic even in slaves—but since the Coast no longer drew very close attention its peoples were left very much to themselves and could spend the years quietly learning. The old, vigorous trading middle class, especially, did more than merely survive. British administration remained weak and ineffective, largely because governments habitually relied on the chiefs, ignoring these assertive middle-class people or by-passing them as up-starts. Their day was to come later—if indeed it ever really passed.

While mounting numbers of the West Coast people were adapting themselves to new ways and new conditions, European interest switched decidedly, in the middle years of the century, to the hitherto unknown parts of Africa, south-central and east. The first moves were actually made from the south. About 1800 Sir John Barrow, an Admiralty and for a while a Cape official, who also became the founder of the Royal Geographical Society, was one of several who recorded impressions of native peoples and described the rich wild life of the country. The naturalist, William Burchell, followed, a great collector who penetrated, in 1811–12, to the Bechuana country. He was not quite the first in that field; when his hosts, who coveted the guns on which he depended for food, gave him some miserable weeks fending off their importunities, he escaped worse usage, so he suggests, only because ill treatment of one lone traveller would have frightened off the traders and pedlars on whom the Bechuana had already come to rely, for desirable imports. The slow seepage of outside influences must have been at least speeded up by the repercussions of Boer doings in the later 1830s.

In 1841 a fateful chance brought a ceaselessly inquiring missionary named David Livingstone to this same neighbourhood, to a station just inside the Transvaal but on the verge of the Kalahari. North-east of this point the country is more attractive, but it is much broken by hills, besides being malarial, notorious for what is comprehensively known as 'horse-sickness', and also infested by tsetse-flies whose bite is quickly fatal to cattle; there was no road that way, even by ox-wagon; to the west the bush steadily gives way to desert. Livingstone's station was at the one point whence a northward road, though hard and heavy, leads on through level, almost flat country; the scarcity of surface water makes travel by wagon difficult, but keeps it nearly free of tsetse-fly and of mosquitoes and malaria. The newly-arrived missionary had reason almost at once to want to try out its possibilities. The unsettlement inevitably caused by the advance of the Transvaal Boers, and by their competition with Livingstone's parishioners for possession of the land, sufficiently explains Livingstone's own apparent restlessness; he wrote warmly of the Cape farmers he met on his coastal journeys, but was soon at loggerheads with his Transvaal neighbours, both on his own account, as a member of the hated L.M.S., and on behalf of his Bechuana followers. When in 1852 he returned from a trek to find his home at Kolobeng ransacked by a Boer mob, a 'commando', he began to think in good earnest on the lines that were to take him so much further afield. One obvious aim was no more than to find his flock a secure home on some outlying extension of the healthy High Veld; but an alternative to the long southward trek to the sea might also make a shorter link with the outside world—'commerce and Christianity' would then flow more freely into Central Africa. The Zambezi naturally suggested itself when experience of the deadliness of the tsetse made it likely that only a waterway would serve. Another chance gave Livingstone the help he needed to make a beginning. The Kalahari was by this time coming to be the Mecca of big-game hunters; one of these, Gordon Cumming, displeased Livingstone by his slaughter of elephants—he was written off as 'a mad sort of Scotchman'—but another, William Oswell, became a life-long friend, helper and supporter. Already in 1849 they had joined forces on the preliminary trek through the Bamangwato country to Lake Ngami and the swamp-lands between it and the Zambezi. Then, alone, he set out on the great journey that brought him first to the Zambezi at the Victoria Falls. So far the ox-wagon carried his supplies and provided a 'home'; he could still occasionally use a riding-ox, sometimes a canoe, but most of his journeys ever after could only be made on foot. The *Missionary Travels*, published at the end of 1857, describe the tremendous progress by way of the upper Zambezi into Angola and on to Loanda, then back with his porters to their Zambezi home, and down to the sea again at Quilimane. This first record of a crossing of the Dark Continent, packed with close and accurate observation, gave any fillip needed to stimulate more active African exploration. It was of more immediate import that on this journey Livingstone for the first time met the slave-trade in action in the Zambezi country. Arrived in England in 1857 he was received by the Queen and generally acclaimed as a national hero; besides writing a book, therefore, he had unique opportunities of proclaiming this sinister discovery and his own cherished remedial project—a road for a healthier commerce, to be conducted, as he hoped, by Christians on Christian principles. The famous address delivered in the Senate House at Cambridge in 1857 was, by all accounts, no masterpiece of eloquence, and yet one of the most impressive and effective speeches any orator has ever made:

> 'I direct your attention to Africa . . . which is now open. Do not let it be shut again. . . . Do you carry out the work I have begun. I leave it with you.'

The human and emotional content of this appeal, driven home less by the speaker's choice of words than by his personality, was something new. Here was one having authority who spoke of the life and well-being of the people for whom the unknown continent was home, not merely of its physical expanse or its economic potentialities. The Royal Geographical Society had lately taken up straight exploration with enthusiasm fired anew; the C.M.S. had been for some time at work near the East Coast; but the country behind the old Portuguese fort of Mombasa where they began is desert, and the better parts farther inland, being then dominated by warrior Masai, were avoided till two missionaries, the Germans Krapf and Rebmann, reported the discovery of a snow-clad mountain almost on the Equator. This was exciting, even if it was met with incredulity. It was, of course, Kilimanjaro. Arabs and others also rumoured the existence of great lakes; and there was always the puzzle of the Nile source to be solved. In 1857, before Livingstone's book appeared, the Arabian and Eastern traveller, Richard Burton, who had lately explored Somaliland, joined John Speke (under R.G.S. auspices) on an expedition that took them tramping together for over seven months through the hot dry central plains of Tanganyika. Following Arab trails they reached the Rift (like a bigger Loch Ness) which is Lake Tanganyika. The great Burton, ill with fever, was displeased and sceptical when Speke by himself sighted Lake Victoria and (rightly) divined it to be the source of the Nile; unlike Tanganyika this vast sheet of water lies in flat country and is difficult to glimpse from afar; but in 1861 Speke returned with Captain Grant, successfully skirted the western side of the Lake, reached its Nile effluent, and continued as far as Gondokoro where they met Samuel Baker lately arrived up stream; in the service of the Khedive, all the way from Cairo. Though the newly discovered northern, leeward shore of Lake Victoria was Buganda, even the unusual economic potential of this fertile, well-watered and potentially healthy country gave it little immediate interest except to a few Arab traders—it was then not only full of fever, but distant most of six-months' tramp from any seaport. Buganda, however, was revealed as commanding the approach to one main source of the Nile, and the Nile and its waters were traditionally of interest to rival great powers in Europe. For the first time there was reason for events in far-away Central Africa to engage at least the watchful attention of these rivals.

Any serious clash of interests was not yet, but the British Government had for some time been directing a little of its own attention to the East African Coast which Livingstone's slave-raiding revelations now brought into special notice—and indeed, when slavery was in question H.M.G. needed little urging: by the '60s the long fight with the Atlantic traffic was all but won and it was fixed policy to prevent it showing its head again in the Indian Ocean or anywhere else. The India Office, moreover, had interests at a highly strategical point, Zanzibar. The African continent was still so forbidding that islands were commonly preferred by traders as a safer base of operations; the Portuguese lost Mombasa, but survived (at one time almost only) in Mozambique, and Zanzibar was far superior to either; lying some forty miles off shore it is at once relatively healthy and far roomier: cloves, above all, and a forest of coconuts, make it valuable in itself, and the water-supply is superlative—sundowner talk is still that its springs must, surely, be fed from the snows of Kilimanjaro! Early in the century the Sultan Sayid, seeking for and sought as an ally against the French, transferred his headquarters from Muscat to Zanzibar, and from 1841 the British ally had a consul posted to his court. It was this officer's duty to enforce anti-slavery treaties and keep a check on the export of slaves to India (where slavery was made illegal in 1843); at the same time, paradoxically, he must protect the interests of British Indian merchants whose business of providing stores and trade-cloth to Arab traders made them in fact the bankers and financiers of Arab slaving caravans. Arab trade, based on Zanzibar, was carried on actively both north and south, and its outposts on the mainland coast acknowledged the Sultan as their overlord. The British Government accordingly was ready to take an occasion to extend its representation on this coast; when Livingstone himself set out again, early in 1858, it was as an accredited British Consul, in charge of a Government-sponsored expedition deputed to explore the Zambezi waterway.

The explorer was too great an individualist to be also a good leader of men; this expedition was neither happy nor successful; but it was momentous. Rapids stopped progress on the Zambezi itself and sent the party up the Shire to discover Lake Nyasa and, south-east of it, the marvellously attractive Shire Highlands; the Portuguese who had been in the near neighbourhood for upwards of three centuries would seem to have missed one of the most habitable and well-populated regions anywhere in Africa. Arab traders knew better; Livingstone and his companions quickly learnt that Arabs, and bands led by people described as Portuguese half-castes, were making this lovely country the very centre of their slave trade. The representatives of the strongly supported Universities Mission to Central Africa (U.M.C.A.), the direct first-fruits of the Cambridge speech, arrived in 1861 and made for this country; but the unrest prevailing was too great. Physical hardships largely due to the disturbed condition of the country greatly aggravated the fever that attacked them. The leader, Bishop Mackenzie, was one of several victims and the U.M.C.A. fell back to base its work on the only stable town in the region, Zanzibar. In 1864 the official Zambesi expedition was itself recalled without having attained its objectives; but the drive against the slave trade continued. The ablest of Livingstone's Zambezi company, Dr. (later Sir) John Kirk, was one of the many who, having once drunk of African fountains, wanted more: in 1866 he became agency surgeon, in 1867 Vice-Consul, and in 1873 Consul-General at Zanzibar. There, in 1872, his diplomacy, and steady pressure from the British ally, prevailed at last on the Sultan to decree the end of the slave trade in his dominions; since these included the line of East African ports, and the activities of the Arab traders extended to the Red Sea and the Persian Gulf, this was a resounding success; for it was still the sea-borne slave trade that chiefly drew the attention of the outside world.

It remained for the missionary and humanitarian forces to demonstrate the need to attack the evils of the traffic at the source inside Africa. Recalled from the Zambezi, Livingstone returned after only a short break and, entering from farther north, by the Rovuma, was lost in the bush from 1866 (except for one moment when H. M. Stanley 'found' him in 1871) till his death in 1873; the evidence of the ravages of the slave trade collected on the most prolonged of his journeys became available only some time after this. On the eve of Kirk's success at Zanzibar, however, his memorable message to Stanley's patron, Gordon Bennett, made its mark—the appeal for help to cure 'the open sore of the world'—and the drama of his death and Westminster Abbey burial roused missionary zeal to a new pitch of enthusiasm. By 1875 the U.M.C.A. and two strong Scottish missions were back in Nyasaland and there they held their ground as witnesses of the slave trade in action—without any protecting government to help them till after 1890. A move into Uganda followed quickly on the beginnings in Nyasaland—at the instance, this time, of H. M. Stanley who, after 'finding' Livingstone, had been drawn whole-heartedly to African discovery; a letter sent post-haste from Uganda and published towards the end of 1875 in the *Daily Telegraph* strongly commended to the missions the opportunity afforded them by the apparently stable conditions prevailing under the rule of King Mtesa. The C.M.S. sent out a strong team which included Alexander Mackay, one whose practical bent made him an outstanding figure. Simultaneously, in 1878, the Catholic Order of 'White Fathers' came into Uganda from the north, a second strong mission of international make-up at this nerve centre by the head-waters of the Nile; Cardinal Lavigerie, the forward-looking founder of the White Fathers, had seen Africa as a continent with a future and made it his special concern. In 1878 tropical Africa was still too inaccessible, even fertile Buganda too unproductive, to count in world commerce: the Rhodesian High Veld and the Kenya Highlands could be reached only by covering vast distances on foot and were unknown: none yet dreamt of finding a field for colonies of European settlement. A few scouts were out—Stanley was at that moment completing a first transit of the Congo region—but it was still largely from missionary sources that evidence accumulated on the malaise of Africa, on how, though African society may have been self-contained, it was anything but 'free'.

Commerce was thought to be the remedy; but over a wide area slave-raiding was creating chronic disorders and a general state of insecurity, in effect a reign of terror which made peaceful commerce impossible. Few of those, it may be, who were inclined to moralize on the duty laid on the strong to protect the weak, fully appreciated why Livingstone so insistently prescribed commerce as well as Christianity. Slaves, as he saw, were a commodity, the only commodity available for use in acquiring for the more privileged Africans a share of the goods they well knew only the outer world could supply. Two considerable and still active trading companies, the African Lakes Corporation and the Uganda Company, were originally attempts by Christian missions to act on Livingstone's advice and substitute a more orderly commerce. But in those days backward peoples were considered to be just 'backward' and, as such, Africans got very little study. Evidently very few saw the economic reasons for the extraordinary hold the slave trade retained in all parts of the continent. (There is a wide field for research by students of the newer colleges in Central and East as in West Africa.) The emphasis at the time was, naturally enough, on the lurid (and indubitable) facts; thus it called for vigorous, but only negatively preventive action that a gang of fifty slaves seen marching to the Coast might be the outcome of raids involving the destruction of ten or twelve villages. Throughout south-central Africa, the scene of Livingstone's last travels, such violence was specially frequent; the predominantly agricultural tribes round Lake Nyasa and the Rovuma basin, being tied to the soil, were easily preyed upon by organized bands; this area has never fully recovered from the depredations of Arab-led Yao or marauding Angoni; Kilwa and Malindi, Milton's 'Quiloa and Melind', have long been nearly derelict, like most of the not infertile Southern Province of Tanganyika.

A map by Sir Harry Johnston, printed in the 1899 edition of his *Colonization of Africa* but later discarded, gives an informed eye-witness's impression of the much wider scenes of the slave-trade's operations, and of its main traffic lanes. The number of Africans transplanted beyond the sea may be counted in millions, but external demand is at any rate no sufficient explanation of the later phases of this horrific traffic, or of the huge area affected in Africa itself. *Ex Africa semper aliquid novi*, perhaps; but Africans themselves certainly love new things; Burchell's experience in the Bechuanaland of 1811 (p. 146) was wholly typical. It was when, as Burchell found, Africans were no longer satisfied with beads and trumpery but demanded cloth—or guns—that the demand for slaves grew. There were local differences. When Europeans first appeared on the West Coast they brought their wares with them but, being physically unable themselves to hawk them round that country, they opened wide a door through which African 'trade boys' entered to take over and become both traders and middlemen. The Arabs on the east coast were from the beginning their own middlemen, ultimately even in the far interior; their indispensable economic services thus gave them power unchecked by that of any East African middle class. This was a grave disadvantage to the East in the new phase that opened when, in the course of the nineteenth century, the demand for ivory was stepped up by the development of European luxury trades. Elephants were plentiful and widely distributed, but in roadless country the transport of one good tusk down the long trail to the coast needed at least two porters; when cheaper and better guns made hunting more efficient the demand for porters, i.e. slaves, grew immeasurably. The increased use of guns was itself of revolutionary effect; spears and poisoned arrows became antiquated and any rough balance of power there may once have been was gravely upset; bands of Africans armed and trained by Arab leaders denuded the country of game and preyed even on the garden produce of peaceful tribes, this in turn stepping up the demand for guns, for defence. Lawless disorder was at a height when Livingstone met it and bewailed the slave trade as an 'open sore'.

Yet the enterprise of Arab traders was after all doing Africans a service. Its beginnings are lost in obscurity and may be very old; the glories of Kilwa and other old ports can hardly have owed nothing to links with the interior. Caravan routes were well defined; one from Kilwa to Lake Nyasa has been almost obliterated, but the stages on the famous, much-trodden track from Bagamoyo, directly opposite Zanzibar, to Lake Victoria, are still well marked by forests of gigantic mango trees. These were an Arab contribution, and distinguish Tabora, (the great inland base, unattractive in itself, but later recognized by the Germans as the ideal jumping-off ground for the populous country of the three great lakes), the marvellous spring or 'eye' at Kondoa Irangi, Mpwapwa, and other stations where water, fresh supplies of food, trade goods—and porters—awaited the caravans. If only on account of their monopoly of the supply of arms, Arab traders came before the end to wield power almost in a political sense. It was not as if insecurity, though greater than ever in some parts, was new; slaves in the service of Arabs (such as survived their first uprooting and the hideous tramp to the coast) lived in security and comparative freedom; they were paid no wages, but life was much as it had always been—there was no question here of their being driven by time-keepers and overseers and kept to long hours of unremitting toil; the victims of the system were completely passive. For many Africans, and not only the Haves among them, the slave caravans were the only purveyors of goods from the outside world; the slave trade was, basically, their own bid to satisfy this spontaneous and natural want. These traders' wasteful practice could not compete with or even survive alongside of free enterprise, but it was still a rival economic system. The systematic pursuit of African economic possibilities by Europeans was actually gathering head in the last days of slavery and got almost exclusive possession of the stage once it started. But their place was originally secondary: the shocked surprise of those who first saw the devastation caused by the slave trade turned to fierce indignation and was the decisive factor in bringing about the forcible intervention of the powers of Europe. As in the West Indies, only an independent arbiter had the moral authority, and the physical capacity, to compel such a revolutionary change. The ordering of the chaos left by the slave-trade was quite beyond the competence of any native African authority—there are obvious limits to the efficacy of the smooth modern formula, 'self-determination'. The alternative of bringing western Europeans into Africa was then the only possible way to help Africans to find their place in the wider world.

This process went along of its own momentum once it had got such a start as the discovery of diamonds in Griqualand West gave it. The rush of a cosmopolitan crowd of diggers to Kimberley in 1870 threatened such complications as quickly brought about one abrupt change—the British Government which had so lately washed its hands of responsibility for the neighbouring Boer republics accepted without demur the Cape Governor's outright annexation of the diamond fields. This find was made in an arid part of the interior; old tradition tells how the stone that gave the first clue was spotted by a quick-eyed pedlar among a child's playthings on a Hopetown farm. In 1867, however, a German geologist, Carl Mauch, had already caused some stir by reporting a workable find of gold at Tati in the far north of Bechuanaland. Two years earlier still, old gold-workings were discovered much farther away by one Henry Hartley. Frontiersmen and others must have been beginning to dream, as they have done ever since, of mineral wealth hidden in the bush—none the less that (according to a chart once shown me by a colleague at the University of the Witwatersrand) poor Hartley, who lost his life prospecting for gold in Mashonaland, was or had been the owner of what the map showed as 'Hartley's Farm', a portion of the Central Witwatersrand! The South African sequel followed a pattern of its own (Chapter 6); but at any rate the hunt was on.

Natural resources in the no-man's-land of the remoter tropical regions remained longer completely unproven, but hard on the discoveries of the early '60s the Khedive of Egypt deemed it expedient to assert his country's interest in the valley of the Nile as a whole. Baker's travels revealed something of the depredations of slave-raiders in the country he traversed and the Khedive conformed strictly to the moral principles of the age; his soldiers were put under the command of European officers of high standing—Baker himself, General Gordon, and the hardly less well-known Emin Pasha—and their officers were hopefully commissioned to suppress slave-trading and establish sound administration. Sir Samuel Baker, after toiling for three years (1870–3), was succeeded by General Gordon in 1874 as Governor of Equatoria, a province based on Gondokoro. At once Gordon's imaginative genius fastened on Mtesa's Uganda as the natural centre of this region and he went on to contemplate driving a shorter way, even a railway, through Uganda to the sea at Mombasa. Gordon was no British stooge. H.M.G., as he knew, had no wish to see Egypt established on the Indian Ocean; Kirk was sitting all this time at Zanzibar, and a great shipowner, Sir William Mackinnon, was thinking of the commercial possibilities. Gordon's dream meant something like an Egyptian East Africa, and was certainly precipitate; Lake Victoria itself was accurately mapped only by Stanley, in 1875, on the first stage of his second and greatest journey; the missionaries he asked for had reached Uganda before he himself had completed the great trek in which, having crossed to the Lualaba, he earned his African nickname (Bula Matari, the breaker of roads) by carrying on along the Congo to the sea at its mouth; he reached England again only in 1878. The map of Africa was now taking full shape; Stanley, like Gordon, judged the Lake Victoria country to be its heart, and the Congo the key to the approaches. Stanley's expedition, moreover, was a large-scale undertaking; unlike the lonely Livingstone he occasionally had to blast a way through native opposition. The inference was that the pacification of Africa and the development of its resources called for more than individual enterprise; but the year was 1878 and the British Foreign Office was too deeply involved in the 'Eastern Question' to be ready for any new adventure. Stanley, for his part, was no diplomat; there is reason to believe that he was aware of having no old-school-tie and was unduly sensitive. Very soon, at all events, he took himself off to Brussels and got a reception more in accordance with what he felt to be his deserts from H.M. Leopold II, King of the Belgians.

The Kimberley diamonds were largely a British affair, but any move in the north was bound now to be of international concern. King Leopold at once called a Geographical Conference, which proceeded, in the best Livingstone tradition, to form an 'International Association for the Exploration and Civilization of Central Africa'. In 1879 Stanley set out as its representative to promote his own suggestion of a confederation of chiefs under European leadership; the outcome was a Congo Free State, presided over by King Leopold, and without the British co-operation Stanley had hoped for. The British attitude was emphatically that Britain had quite enough 'formal' African Empire and wanted no more; but what has since been called her 'informal' concern to safeguard her interests in Egypt disposed her to leave Germany a free hand in tropical Africa in a bid for German support against rival French claims in Egypt and elsewhere. A French officer, de Brazza, was responsible in 1881 for the first real move in the open 'scramble' for Africa; by a brilliant jungle dash he forestalled Congo Free State emissaries by planting the French flag on the north side of Stanley Pool, on the Congo where Brazzaville, the capital of French Equatorial Africa, now stands as a memorial of this feat, only a mile or two from Leopoldville, the capital of the Belgian Congo. But even in those early '80s German commercial and shipping interests too were asserting claims to share in openly avowed *colonial* enterprise. Chancellor Bismarck held back at first but suddenly, in 1883, struck—without warning; without the warrant even of German cultural or commercial interests, he seized points of vantage in south-west Africa, Togoland and the Cameroons. In 1884, when Britain and Portugal came to an agreement that would have recognized Portugal's historical claims to extend to the mouth of the Congo, Bismarck objected to this bilateral arrangement, but then, having by his own actions done more than anyone else to 'put the cat among the pigeons', he saw danger ahead and called an international conference to deliberate on these African questions in Berlin. Inside ten years Africa and the interests of its peoples had thus become an item in a purely European political contest. The main business of the conference was to lay down rules to order rivalries that were becoming a danger to European peace. The old principle of 'effective occupation' was invoked, but with a new rider; boundary commissions being impracticable, 'effective occupation' of key points on the coast was to entitle the occupant to a 'sphere of influence' in the *hinterland*—a new phrase which betrays the Germanic origin of this doctrine.

The British influence is recognizable in a clause which required equal trading rights in a completely ungeographical 'Congo Basin', wider than but including the Congo Free State. The Niger Delta was acknowledged a British 'sphere' and, *inter alia*, Togoland and the Cameroons became German: Germany already had British recognition for South-West Africa, long a 'sphere of influence' of the Cape whose Government had done no more than annex Walfisch Bay and its anchorage in 1878. The agreed rules of 1885 at once gave occasion for an unseemly rush by rival national interests for 'treaties', exclusive trading rights and concessions, but almost before the conference ended Germany also seized a share of East Africa. By the end of the century, if not in substance by 1890, the 'Partition of Africa' was virtually completed on the Berlin 'principles'.

From a European viewpoint it was at any rate an achievement that so many thorny deals only once provoked a major 'crisis', the Fashoda incident of 1898; when a west-to-east desert crossing by Major Marchand challenged Lord Kitchener's newly accomplished reconquest of the Sudan, a Franco-British war came very near. In Africa, on the other hand, 'spheres of influence', arbitrarily fixed, added appreciably to the anomalies inevitably arising in the chaos of unrelated tribes and peoples which make the colonial world. There are always large, underpopulated masses of territory, and tiny overcrowded fragments, equally incapable either of self-government or of fitting neatly into a federation, especially when they include strong minorities, like several groups of East Indians, who cling to their own ways and resist assimilation with new neighbours. But only the partitioners of Africa could unashamedly, all in a year or two, put members of a single tribe under two or even three different rulers, leave the Gambia cut off from its hinterland, and create a monstrosity like the *Caprivi Zipfel*: in 1890 a strip of land over 500 miles long and perhaps fifty miles wide was marked on a map to meet a German demand for access from South-West Africa to the Zambesi; its shape and its inaccessibility make it impossible to administer efficiently even as the game reserve it is by nature.

The selfish ambitions of European rivals are on the surface, but they sprang nevertheless from the disordered state of Africa itself. European powers undertaking African responsibilities at this stage faced long unprofitable toil; they acted now in large part in answer to appeals that came as strongly from Cardinal Lavigerie of the White Fathers as from any British Protestant anti-slavery crusader; and the conference powers' undertakings to suppress slave-trading were positive; to talk of Europe's as a 'civilizing mission' in Africa was not cant. There was justification too for the apologetic term 'protectorate'—it became current, according to the New Oxford Dictionary, in or after the year 1884; few or none of the new acquisitions were annexed outright as 'colonies'. It has disadvantages that 'protected persons' are not 'subjects' and citizens of the protecting power, but there were new dangers threatening Africans not only from within but from without: few or none could face these by themselves, but 'protection' to be effective must be authorized; Mr. Sidney Webb once told me how, in his Colonial Office youth, the Great Seal of the Realm, the almost legendary symbol of the royal prerogative, had to be brought into use as the only lawful warrant for the compassing of a British wrong-doer roaming at large on the West African coast. This cumbersome procedure was not for everyday use; but in much of Africa, apart even from slave-raiding, which persisted, the tensions of the changing times continued to mount, normally in strict proportion to the force available from without to assert the authority of law and to keep disorders in check; the inaccessible Sudan fell into chaos when Egyptian troops lost control after 1883.

The temptations mere adventurers faced, and the risk of their resorting to lawless practices in such essentially 'frontier' conditions, may be inferred from the recorded experience of many of the representatives of European governments; the most responsible of these had to take weighty decisions under the severe physical and mental strain caused by the sleepless anxiety of months spent in guiding their train of followers

—o'er moor and fen, more often through parched deserts alternating with dank, malarial swamps—to the rendezvous with suspicious, unpredictable, usually capricious local rulers. The British governments of the day were, all of them, most unwilling starters in the race for more 'possessions'; trade was to be encouraged and defended, but trade was the function of private enterprise. Recognizing, however, that those making their ventures in the uncivilized, lawless parts of Africa faced abnormal risks, a predominantly Conservative Government met the difficulty by reverting to the use of the 'chartered' company and endowed three of these with administrative powers and exclusive rights in their chosen fields. The Royal Niger Company, 1886, the Imperial British East Africa Company, or *I.B.E.A.*, 1888, and the British South Africa Company, 1889, were sponsored respectively by Sir George Taubman Goldie, Sir William Mackinnon and Cecil John Rhodes, three outstanding personalities. All these spheres of influence showed red on the map even before they came, eventually, under the direct control of the Crown; but the charters, none the less, were originally an attempt to avoid this necessity, not a plot to prepare the way for imperial expansion. Before any company was fully functioning, civil war, the direct outcome of slaving activities, threatened the survival of the British missions in Nyasaland. The Portuguese of Mozambique disliked intruders in their sphere of influence and were so unhelpful that in 1890, rather than abandon the missionaries, H.M.G. stepped in and proclaimed a protectorate. Tradition is misleading on the significance of all this; there was more to it than a 'scramble' by greedy European powers to be in on the 'partition' of a defenceless Africa.

The story of Uganda is the classical example of how partition came about, and shows also why something of the kind was inevitable. The contrast between the Uganda people and countryside and any on the road thither could not fail to make its impression; but Stanley, who was so much struck by the relative stability of Mtesa's kingdom as it was in 1875, had clearly not taken stock of Speke's experience of murder rampant not many years earlier, when the King had felt himself less secure. The missionaries who hurried in to act on Stanley's recommendation made an auspicious start in 1878, but peace and order were not indigenous. In October 1884 Mtesa died. The passing of this firmly established despot synchronized, as it happened, with the so-called German 'irruption' into Tanganyika, an event, incidentally, which threatened the old Arab traffic lane to Tabora. The Arabs may well have been in touch, through Tabora, also with Nyasaland, and they at once scented danger to their interests, not only from the Germans but from the growing influence of the anti-slavery Christian missions. Mtesa's successor, Mwanga, setting out after the manner of tyrants to safeguard his own position, was led, partly by Arabs, to ally himself with the Muslim interests, in the first place against the Christians, Catholic and Protestant alike. For Christianity had struck root; some dozens of Christians braved martyrdom for their new faith, and confusion and civil war reigned.

Before this, and since the mid-1870s, Sir William Mackinnon, then of the British India line of steamers, had been making Zanzibar a base from which to try out the possibilities of East African trade—with no great success. After 1885 the pressure of strong German competition forced him back entirely on the trackless country north of the old main highway which took off from Bagamoyo. This challenge necessitated the strengthening of his organization and in 1888 produced I.B.E.A. The new company's sphere of influence was unproductive and, except for distant Uganda, almost unknown; the Kenya Highlands, now so famous, were first visited only in 1883 by Joseph Thomson; their discovery revealed also that the short cut to Uganda dreamt of by General Gordon would not only have the Masai to reckon with, but must cross the Great Rift, a long but not wide valley two or three thousand feet deep, with almost precipitous 'walls'. In Uganda the new ruler, Mwanga, was warned by a soothsayer to look for danger from the north-east; when in 1885 the newly consecrated C.M.S. Bishop Hannington made his approach by the new short route he was murdered at Mumias on the eastern approaches and something like a reign of terror ensued. The leading C.M.S. missionary, Mackay, became virtually an exile, dying at the south end of the Lake in 1890. But Mwanga was more than once an exile himself. I.B.E.A. was nearly helpless and sought to keep clear of trouble, but later in 1890 its agent (Sir) F. J. Jackson, came near enough for Mwanga to appeal to him for help. Jackson still kept his distance, but he took the opportunity to reply by sending Mwanga a British flag; it was understood that acceptance of this symbol was to pledge I.B.E.A. to give the help asked for, but also to bind Mwanga himself to a 'treaty'. While Jackson moved away to scour the Mount Elgon country for trade-ivory, a highly expert treaty-maker, the German Karl Peters, found and read Jackson's correspondence left at Mumias, and hurried on to Mengo (Kampala). There he forestalled Jackson by getting a written treaty and he went on his way rejoicing, only to find that diplomats at home had 'done a deal' on Berlin principles. The Germans, setting much store by the cession of Heligoland, had withdrawn claims on Zanzibar and accepted a final demarcation of the British and German spheres. One of the lines ruled on the map by office clerks ran straight across Lake Victoria and left the whole of Uganda in the British zone.

By this time straight colonial rivalry was at its peak all over the world. I.B.E.A. and the other companies looked upon themselves as British instruments, and their young men unquestionably enjoyed playing a part as the champions of national interests. Among the rest, Captain F. D. (Lord) Lugard, fresh from fighting Arab slavers in Nyasaland, arrived in Kampala in December 1890 to assert I.B.E.A.'s newly recognized claims, only to find the Christian parties fallen out and civil war raging now between Protestants and Catholics, known respectively as 'British' and 'French'. The originally triumphant Muslims had lost, but the Catholic-Protestant feud now turned, characteristically, on the distribution of places of profit under the restored king. Mwanga had accepted the British flag; but Lugard had only his 100 men and his orders were to remain strictly impartial; so he seized a period of relative calm to 'show the flag' in still more remote parts of his company's zone. Returning to Kampala in the last days of December 1891 he found the situation grown even more tense. By this time I.B.E.A.'s years of profitless struggle on long lines of communication had left its funds exhausted and it was inclined to withdraw. The company's order of recall actually awaited Lugard, but he felt obliged to turn a blind eye. Within a week a letter cancelling the recall brought a reprieve—for the remarkable reason that the missionary leaders at home, taking alarm at the danger to their missionaries, had themselves raised the funds that enabled I.B.E.A. to carry on. Lugard still could not hope to enforce peace and order with 100 men, and on January 24th it came to a pitched battle. Having privately strengthened the friendlier Protestant party with a gift of old muskets he kept aloof, till a manœuvre of the combatants threatened to leave him and his men isolated. Then his not very efficient Maxim-gun served to turn the tide of battle and secured the victory to the Protestants.

This, of itself, settled little even in Buganda, and in terms of the latest agreement an orderly and secure peace must now take account of East Africa as a whole. The task was too big for I.B.E.A. Lugard himself returned home almost at once, there to use his unusually wide experience, and his pen, in support of the missionary demand that H.M.G. itself assume the burden. The Government temporized by sending Sir George Portal in 1893 on a mission to investigate. The significant part of his report was his evidence that the resources of I.B.E.A. were in fact utterly unequal to its responsibilities. There was little trade to warrant great expenditure and prospects of its increasing were poor; the 'stations' on the long line of communications were so weakly manned that there were no beginnings of an administrative system. But missionaries' lives were in danger; and the 1890 agreement which left Uganda in the British sphere had produced also a fresh pronouncement, from Brussels this time, against the slave trade. Largely by Cardinal Lavigerie's insistence the powers reaffirmed their determination to suppress this traffic, and the British Government gave a provisional undertaking to clear the way for orderly commerce by building an East African railway. The economic prospects were too slender themselves to commend such a project to the Treasury or the House of Commons; but the commitment of 1890 was steadily pressed by humanitarian opinion and in spite of the economic hazards the railway project gradually won support, for a mixture of reasons, humanitarian and strategical. More than £5 millions was a very large sum in the 1890s, but the railway was at any rate an administrative necessity. Successive Liberal governments still hesitated, or actively resisted the pressure for a forward move of any kind; when at last, in 1894, Lord Rosebery agreed that I.B.E.A. must be bought out, a famous cartoon by Sir John Tenniel aptly portrayed John Bull emerging from his doorway to find 'another unwanted baby'—'Uganda'.

These wholly African-peopled dependencies might be unimportant additions to an already far-flung Empire but they presented in fact an entirely new exercise in the art of government. They were also totally different one from the other: Nyasaland was a small mission enclave with uneconomic, treaty-fabricated boundaries; Buganda on the other hand was one relatively coherent unit in a distant part of a vast agglomeration of tribes and diverse territories now lumped together as the 'British East African Protectorate'—a domain with no vestige of the unity suggested by the contiguity of its parts on the map. East Africa was recognized, perhaps, to be a little of a puzzle—it remained till 1904 in charge of the Foreign Office. It was at least an advantage to have this stronger department dealing with the Treasury; the Uganda railway would, it argued, provide a solid asset in return for outlay to which the country was in any case committed for anti-slavery police work; it was strategically desirable also to open a back-door into the Sudan where Lord Kitchener was then preparing a campaign to restore order. The Uganda line was off the route of Mr. Rhodes's latest pet scheme, a Cape-to-Cairo railway, but his ardent advocacy of railways helped to put them in popular favour, and the challenge presented by the Great Rift Valley ensured the active interest of ambitious engineers. After

1895 the project definitely went forward. In 1901 the railway reached the Lake at Kisumu, bringing Uganda within some twelve hours' steamer range of railhead. The engineers successfully traversed the Great Rift, but the authorities boggled at the expense of bridging even the stripling Nile at Jinja; lake transport served very well and the Uganda railway reached Uganda proper only some fifty years later.

The coming of a new order could not be quite yet; even in an exceptionally strong African unit like Buganda the new forces that were at work everywhere had the effect at first only of demonstrating the bankruptcy of the old system: between them all, the activities of Arab traders, the clash of British and not very distant German interests, the operations of divided if not rival Christian missions, reduced the country to a state of faction-riddled confusion from which there could be no smooth and speedy transition. Not far away, both in the Sudan and in the south, slave-raiding persisted; the reliable tradition is that the last slave caravan was broken up in the Northern Rhodesian bush only about 1897. Till then, at least, the humanitarians of the day were emphatic that the first duty of the civilized world was the suppression of slavery. In the end, slavery died so comparatively speedily that the trade motive came uppermost and the humanitarians of later times, unlike their predecessors, usually see in the sequel no more than the unredeemed wickedness they call the 'scramble for Africa'. Both views make too little of how both the slave trade and its confused sequel grew out of the unsatisfied wants and aspirations of the indigenous African peoples. The Arabs themselves were traders, first and last, keen dealers in cloth, wares, ivory or anything else that offered; slaves were a means, not the end, of their business, and they were world traders. From early in the nineteenth century their dhows were no longer quite alone; not only British but also French and American ships occasionally visited the east coast, and it was neither for slaves nor for health reasons.

Such world trade was bound to grow once it started. By the early '80s the trend was beyond all possible doubt. Trade, moreover, soon became the prime objective of the European rivals. Colonies, or even protectorates, were sometimes an anti-slavery move, but still more often, and increasingly, no more than a means of ensuring the possibility of being able to carry on trade in reasonable security. The alternative to such external control was likely to be chaotic disorder. H.M.G., for example, insisted throughout the '90s on leaving Swaziland 'free', a no-man's-land it would neither itself take over nor allow the neighbouring Transvaal Republic to try to administer. Slave raids never seriously disturbed the Swazi, but they too had wants and were not alone in discovering that the goods they wanted more than ever might now be bought by pledging their land. The mining and agricultural 'concessions' for which King Mbandine took payment, often in brandy—and the figures were impressed upon me by a frequent golfing companion, the judge who was sent after 1900 to straighten out the tangle—added up to a total three times the area of the whole of Swaziland. Or again, much was heard after 1900 of 'atrocities' perpetrated in the Congo on Africans set to collect wild rubber. So far from being an example of brutally strong government, excesses were in fact due to the weakness of the overburdened and much too slender administrative staff of the Congo Free State. After 1908 the Belgian Government took charge and put things straight, with so much success as to prove that the untoward consequences of modern 'contact' are to be avoided only by bringing all the new forces at work in the old Africa under strict law. The trading profits hoped for from this undeveloped, devastated continent seldom materialized, as the British Government learnt to its cost quite early; the Niger Company was the only one of the three African chartered companies to show some profit. But in 1898 H.M.G. revoked its charter, judging that its political responsibilities had already grown to be such as only the state itself could rightly discharge. There was really no other answer possible. The European States immediately involved largely by the doings of their own nationals were bound to assume, as they alone could, direct responsibility for the administration of the law.

In the British colonial sphere the refurbished West Indian Crown Colony system (Chapter 4) was generally applied, but from the beginning, also, the presence in Africa of effectively functioning tribal authorities was recognized and put to use. Everywhere local institutions were fully respected, changes being rarely forced from above and without. The standing of chiefs like the well-known Bamangwato, Khama, was enhanced rather than weakened by British protection—he and many others were actually freed from or set above the restraints normally imposed by tribal custom. In Uganda the local authority won express recognition by treaty. Soon after H.M.G. assumed direct responsibility a fresh outbreak of dissensions and disturbances arose from the presence of Sudanese troops who (with their families) had been left behind by Emin Pasha, brought out of Equatoria by Lugard, and planted to fend for themselves, virtually as colonists. In 1900 Sir Harry Johnston, an old hand who had newly pacified much-raided Nyasaland, was sent to try his magic in Uganda. Building on local institutions as he found them, and supplying perhaps a little of his own, he gave the lesser chiefs a semi-feudal status, making them landlords; centrally, a Buganda Native Authority, thus reconstituted, was left to manage local affairs under its King or Kabaka, with the advice and under the benevolent supervision of a British Resident. The Uganda Agreement of 1900 which embodied this settlement functioned smoothly and stood unchanged for upwards of fifty years, as did treaties establishing similar relations between the Protectorate Government and the neighbouring African states, Ankole, Toro and Bunyoro.

West Africa was basically not very different, even if European rivalries were there more on the surface. The Royal Niger Company, unlike I.B.E.A. and the B.S.A. companies, developed important trade interests, and under Sir George Taubman Goldie its agents had made good their claim to an effective sphere of influence in the Niger Delta as early as the Berlin Conference of 1885. Thereafter competition continued with the French who were moving far and fast in West Africa. Because the French held no truck with free trade principles any extension of their empire meant the exclusion of all rivals; it was therefore all or nothing for the Royal Niger Company under its defence officer—at that time Sir Frederick (later Lord) Lugard. So, when its territorial expansion was deemed too great and its responsibilities were taken over by H.M.G., the old colonies of Lagos and the Oil Rivers then came to have added to them most of what is now Nigeria, a populous territory of 372,000 square miles (rather larger than Tanganyika).

On the Gold Coast there was no company to take the initiative; but trading interests were threatened by the continuance of an old feud between Ashanti and the coastal Fantis, and in 1900 a British force settled the matter by a march to Kumasi and the conquest of Ashanti. Still in the interests of stability, and to counter French moves, the now enlarged Gold Coast incorporated a Muslim fringe, the semi-arid Northern Territories. The old Colony at Freetown, Sierra Leone, similarly became the base of a mainland Protectorate about the size of Scotland. Once again 'scramble' may be the right word; but the alternative to insisting that Lagos, and the rest, must have elbow-room, was to see them cut off from their hinterland like the Gambia. No local state or combination of states was any better fitted here than was Buganda in East Africa to ensure the orderly entry of the peoples into inevitably closer association with the wider outside world.

British rule once begun was carried on with very little parade of military force. Everywhere its representatives lived with the people and among them, alike in remote bush stations and in crowded urban centres; even their revolvers (if they possessed any) rusted in cupboards. The officers of the ruling power were only a handful, a skeleton staff of district commissioners, a few doctors (fully occupied often enough in serving their own colleagues), law officers, a governor; but these, with a European-officered body of African police, were able to establish and maintain very effective law and order. The Uganda Company successfully promoted cotton-growing and Europeans introduced tea-planting in Nyasaland. Gold-Coasters themselves learned to produce cocoa; tradition has it that the first cocoa-bean was smuggled into the country in 1879 by a worker returning from Fernando Po. Resident Basel missionaries who were keen and skilled gardeners may have helped, and by 1885 systematic experiment had official encouragement; but a Government Botanic Garden was begun only in 1889, and then at Aburi, on the escarpment outside the forest. This chosen site was a pleasant hill-station much favoured by governors, but quite untypical of cocoa country. The further progress of the cocoa industry was the work rather of peasants, who relied on the direction and the financial backing of traders and other middle-class townsmen; by 1910, when results were beginning to show (see Chapter 9), the venture had acquired an unusually broad national basis. Officially backed economic development, however, was not yet; and this Africa remained the very much untamed Africa; some 200,000 persons died about 1908 in an epidemic of sleeping sickness near Lake Victoria—where bubonic plague was still endemic in 1930. Colonial rule was tentative and hesitant; but it gave both East and West Africans a full half-century of peace and security and in this interval numbers of them were accustoming themselves to new things, learning new ways and absorbing new ideas.

Chapter 8

'TAKE UP THE WHITE MAN'S BURDEN'

*

In the late Victorian days only the West could supply the African peoples' old but undefined wants. Africans were free at last of slave-raiding, but still they produced no readily exchangeable commodity to offer in return for goods except their labour; even their soil could produce nothing suitable without better directed work than they knew. Their own immaturity threw it inevitably on the new-comers to supply the direction needed, and on European governments to take the responsibility of ordering the desirable and necessary intercourse which slowly grew; the end for which the greedy powers were supposedly contending turned out to be not the spoils but the *burden* of Africa. British people, with little regard, it may be, for the Africans' share, were ready to do their part: the new imperialism, then at its height, was nurtured on memories of just such work done by the sons of Britain in other parts of the world. In the middle '90s Rudyard Kipling gave the challenge an evangelical turn when he bid our young men 'Take up the White Man's burden'. The appropriate leader was already there, Cecil John Rhodes, founder and maker of the British South Africa Company. Interest accordingly focused on Rhodes: in a phrase of Sir Robert Ensor's, the guiding star of the new imperialism was not in the east but in the south: and there, for years, it stayed.

Cecil Rhodes, the invalid son of an English rector, was dreaming dreams of Africa as a field for development and planning ahead long before any 'scramble' began. His dreams were all his own; they came of his imagination being fired by his first big African journey, a leisurely, 300-mile trek in 1871 from a brother's Natal farm, over the Drakensbergen and across the fine pasture lands of the sparsely peopled High Veld, to the dusty turmoil of the newly opened diamond fields—I have heard many good judges who happened to get their first impression at the right season go into rhapsody over the lush grass of this country. But Rhodes was original; surely no one since Francis Bacon has seen so clearly the conditions of successful development, and its capital cost.

Finding himself in the diamond industry, 'on the ground floor', he put dreams aside and worked to build a fortune, not for the wealth's sake but always as the means to an ever more clearly defined end. By 1881, at the age of 28, he had built the de Beers Company (partly by buying up claims fallen to ruin, one over another, in the great open hole that is the Kimberley mine), and was commanding an income of about £1 million a year: then, having completed a course of summer terms at Oxford and taken his degree, he was elected to the Cape Parliament. From the very start his interests were African, not merely South African; a revealing entry in *Who's Who*, obviously his own or prepared under his eye, records that he became 'very great friends with General Gordon, beginning in 1881'. The founding of the de Beers Company was only a rehearsal for the dramatic moves that outmanœuvred the financial genius of Barney Barnato and virtually unified the diamond industry in *de Beers Consolidated.* The motive force of this great combine was Rhodes's magnetic personality; when Sir Alfred (Lord) Milner, another man of the first rank, took over the governorship of the Cape in 1897, his first recorded impression of Rhodes was of 'a really *big* man . . . among dwarfs'; his own circle occasionally spoke of him as the *Colossus,* but more normally used the full formal title, *Mr.* Rhodes! His extraordinary powers of cajolery and persuasion ruled even the directors of de Beers; they actually empowered him to use the company's resources for any purpose he thought fit. This bigger de Beers was born in March 1889; by October of the same year H.M.G. had granted the charter of the British South Africa Company. The resources even of de Beers would not quite suffice; but when Rhodes commended African development to the City of London as an opportunity for 'philanthropy at 5 per cent', he was speaking a language the men of the '90s well understood. Thereafter shares in 'Chartereds' alternately boomed and slumped on world stock exchanges; though investors drew no dividend till after 1924 faith in Rhodes's venture never really died.

Twenty years of active life, 1881–1902, went whole-heartedly to the 'big idea' that came to Rhodes in the early '70s—to his mission, the development of Africa. His own liberal Cape must take the lead and this required that South Africa, the base, stand strong and united. At once he found South African divisions obstructing the only road to the north, the 'Missionaries' Road' blazed by Livingstone and Moffat through Bechuanaland—'the Suez Canal to the North', as he called it; in 1882 Boers from the newly-freed Transvaal streamed over their loosely defined western border and planted themselves in two new republics, Stellaland (Vryburg) and Goshen (Mafeking), leaving Kuruman, the old headquarters of the L.M.S. and the starting point of his road, virtually isolated. In 1883 the German occupation of South-West Africa threatened to cut off the Cape altogether from his 'North'; a link-up between Boers and Germans was to be expected, in spite of the difficulty of crossing the Kalahari. Rhodes at once stepped in as champion of Cape interests. A campaign conducted by telegram with Cape Town was followed by his famous pronouncement in the Cape Parliament in August 1883:

> 'We want to get rid of the Imperial Factor in this question and to deal with it ourselves, jointly with the Transvaal.'

It was a hard saying. The appeal successfully rallied the Cape Dutch to his side, and the alliance with the first J. H. Hofmeyr, Leader of the Dutch party known as the Afrikaner Bond, carried Rhodes to the Prime Ministership in 1890. Rhodes, so often thought of as the arch-imperialist, was before his time in speaking the language of the later Commonwealth; he was an Englishman, first and last, and far too sure of himself ever to take orders from Downing Street. Joseph Chamberlain, the rising apostle of pure Empire, was profoundly shocked and never really trusted Rhodes, less than ever when—Commonwealth man as he was and Federal Home Ruler—he made a princely contribution to Irish Party funds! But Rhodes, the Englishman, never dreamt of giving up the flag; there were German claims to be countered and the Imperial Factor could be helpful, or even necessary. The Boer Republicans, on the other hand, have rarely appreciated the advantages of a broad-based unity. To them Rhodes's ideal meant accepting the British flag, and it was the flag, of all things, they most affected to abhor. They therefore refused even the 'Commonwealth' bait and stood moodily aloof—or were actively obstructive, as in Bechuanaland.

Rhodes himself made one serious miscalculation by never allowing for what might be called the African (or 'Native') Factor. His all-African policy was strong in its economic grasp, strong too in assuming the well-tried Cape policy of equal law as its basis; but it took little account of social consequences. Africans as he knew them at Kimberley might be useful but, being inefficient, were often a hindrance to a man in such a hurry; and since African politics were not yet born, any necessary safeguarding of African interests must inevitably fall to 'the Imperial Factor'. At the very outset, when he found Boer farmers in occupation (with Transvaal titles) of tribal lands they had cut up into farms, his instinct was to leave them to it; there was room for all, and the Boers were the better farmers; the North road alone mattered. John

MacKenzie, the missionary at Kuruman, thought otherwise, and from 1883 to 1886 struggled on behalf of the dispossessed tribes for an alliance with the Governor in his capacity of High Commissioner and local representative of the Imperial Government. The issue was apparently more purely local than those that engaged Philip before him; MacKenzie has had his detractors as yet another interfering missionary;[1] but the outcome of two or three years of confusing comings and goings is not in question. British control of the Road was finally asserted by imperialists of the older school; in 1886 a strong expedition under Sir Charles Warren went in and annexed most of the two republics as British Bechuanaland, and this, instead of being incorporated in Rhodes's Cape, was made a directly ruled Crown Colony. At the same time a Crown Protectorate was proclaimed over as much more of the Bechuana country as marched with the Transvaal, up to 22° S. Ten years later Rhodes so far prevailed as to get the Crown Colony annexed to the Cape; but Chamberlain, and the Crown, yielded to the appeal of the Bamangwato Chief Khama and retained direct control of an enlarged Bechuanaland Protectorate, expressly excluding it from his company's field of operations. The success of a visit by Khama to London did much to consolidate the tradition, which has lived on, that 'native' interests are the special responsibility of the 'Imperial Factor'.

The dealings in Bechuanaland were unlooked for and preparatory only. Bechuanaland was a vast, barren expanse of country which no one coveted; only the road to the North must not be blocked by tolls or customs houses, or by the active obstruction of Boers or Germans; for evidence of mineral wealth had come, it will be remembered, from faraway Mashonaland. The way there lay past Matabeleland where Moselekatze's successor, Lobengula, was now the great power. At the very moment the road was finally cleared, in 1885, the Berlin Conference announced the rules of the game and the 'scramble' was on; rights must be based on occupancy. Rhodes was well ahead of rivals with his ideas, but found himself once again forestalled by the quietly expansionist Boers of the Transvaal; in 1887 one Grobler persuaded Lobengula to accept a Transvaal consul and to concede privileges. President Kruger and his advisers were becoming conscious that a seaport was desirable and they badly wanted Swaziland as a step seawards; but they had mines enough to be going on with and Grobler was probably concerned only about grazing rights and shooting. Rhodes quickly set out to make

[1] Shortly after I had acquired his private papers, and before they had been exhaustively studied, the collection went up in the same University fire of 1931 that consumed the Philip MSS. (see p. 113n).

sure. His emissary, J. S. Moffat, son of Robert, was well equipped to speak to the son of Moselekatze, and in February of the next year Lobengula agreed to make no treaties except such as should be approved by Queen Victoria's Government; this in itself was at least some protection against the wiles of concession-hunters. Then, in October 1888, Moffat himself helped Rhodes's business representative (C. T. Rudd) to conclude the agreement that availed to convince H.M.G. that a charter was warranted; later it became the basis of the Company's operations. The terms of the Rudd Concession suggest how essential it was that even the most responsible of these African dealings with foreigners be under the eye of such foreigners' own law and government. The exclusive mining rights now granted were the main and not unreasonable objective; a single mining authority is a necessity in any conditions and certainly was in Lobengula's country; but a time limit was desirable—this and other safeguards were imposed by a Rhodesian Government some seventy years later and are now a normal accompaniment of the exclusive rights which any government that wants mining started will recognize as an inducement it must be prepared to offer.

It remained for Rudd and company, two or three Europeans negotiating in wild country a thousand miles from anywhere, to put a value on mineral rights whose worth was not yet proven. They had in the first place to satisfy the African seller: the 1,000 Martini rifles and 100,000 rounds to shoot with, were the form of wealth most Africans in those days coveted. The £1,200 to be paid annually was at any rate something solid, and not inconsiderable. A third item was surely an attempt to meet the expectations aroused by the talk that went on—a steamer on the Zambesi! These treaty-makers, however, had their minds so set on distant objectives that they made no mention of rights in land—even in the land to be worked for minerals—and another sharp concession-hunter saw his opportunity, approached Lobengula two years later, in 1891, when he was still well away from company control, and secured the land rights for himself. Rhodes solved this problem (in the way the speculator must have hoped for) by buying the so-called 'Lippert Concession'. Meantime de Beers Consolidated was good for initial capital needs, and the Rudd Concession was something definite for Rhodes's company to go to work on. In effect (as the Courts explicitly ruled many years later) the B.S.A. Company became from October 1889 H.M.G.'s agent, responsible as such for *good* government and for the advancement of civilization. The Company's powers were as wide as its jurisdictional functions made necessary—a few pre-existing rights were safeguarded and there were provisions that trade be reasonably free, except in liquor which was to be kept under control—but all its actions were subject to the distant, yet never-to-be-disregarded, overruling authority of one of H.M.'s Principal Secretaries of State.

The sphere of the Company's operations was, and could be, only vaguely specified and had yet to be determined. By 1890 the scramble for Africa was at its height and if this had to be done it were best done quickly. Only the white men 'scrambled'—African interests suffered little damage; but Rhodes wasted no time. A carefully-picked pioneer column of some 200 men which set out in June 1890 had by September planted the flag at Fort Salisbury in the uplands of Mashonaland. It is characteristic of this adventure that the offer of fifteen mining claims was more of a magnet than the promise of a 5,000-acre farm. The claims proved to be of little worth and farming got going only slowly; but there was enough to keep all hands busy establishing a base—and the Company had rivals. The great hunter, F. C. Selous, had been called in to guide the pioneer column by a new route avoiding Matabeleland, ostensibly in order not to disturb Lobengula; but the Salisbury stance, as the promoters also knew, left them better placed to make a bid for delectable country to the east, against Portuguese claimants who had suddenly become aware of their 'hinterland'. Rhodes's ambition was to acquire Beira, in spite of its pestilential climate, to serve as his seaport, but Portuguese claims were strong. Empty land was never the quest—Colonel Grogan, a pioneer still active in Kenya in 1956, wrote in the late '90s deploring the loss not only of Beira but of Tongaland, Shangaan country and a great reservoir of African labour. The Company was able at least to secure Umtali and the fine highland country in its neighbourhood, where there were also some useful goldmines.

Farther north the Company had successes, and one major disappointment. In 1890 the Home Government was unwillingly making itself responsible (p. 158) for the mission zone of Nyasaland—so unwillingly that Sir Harry Johnston, its representative, was kept going at all only by Rhodes surreptitiously subsidizing him with a grant of £10,000 a year. East and south the Nyasaland boundaries were fixed by H.M.G. with the Portuguese; on the other side, with the Shire country as a 'jumping-off' ground, the Company made good a claim to what became 'North-Eastern' Rhodesia (Fort Jameson). In the far north-west the Barotse king in the well-favoured upper valley of the Zambesi was prevailed on, with help from a well-known French Protestant missionary, François Coillard, to choose British suzerainty. The Company's agents also improved their boundary with German Tanganyika by making sure of what is now Abercorn. But they lost the highly mineralized region of Katanga; the story goes that Rhodes's men were beaten to it, by days, by an English officer in the service of the Congo Free State—they were held up by the Luapula, a mighty river even before it becomes first the Lualaba, then the Congo. Shorn thus of the coveted Katanga, known as the Congo 'pedicle', which breaks into the rough right angle made by the Rhodesian border near the modern Copper Belt, the limits of the Company's sphere were now set; but its representative in North-West Rhodesia (Barotseland) was delayed by more pressing business and took up his duties only in 1897. There remained Lobengula, a thorn in the Company's flesh nearer headquarters. The Company's officers clearly went on the assumption that the Matabele private military despotism could only and must be broken. Lacking the patience and perhaps the means to build the administrative system needed for civilized government, they allowed an accumulation of 'incidents' to become the occasion for a Matabele War. A sharp campaign in 1893 ended tragically; the Matabele were broken and Lobengula died miserably of smallpox, a fugitive in the bush.

Rhodes meanwhile, as Prime Minister of the Cape, was caught up in the chain of events finally responsible—by way of a South African railway 'war' and the Jameson Raid of 1896—for the disastrous political fixation which made the troubles of southern Africa turn entirely on the feud (Chapter 6) of Boers and Britons. The new poor relations of the prosperous Transvaal were desperate to get what share they could at least of the carrying trade to the Rand hive of industry—the South African railway system grew up, not as a network carefully planned to help local development, but rather as a straggle of lines all making as directly as possible from the five principal seaports to the gold-fields. President Kruger and his advisers, foiled in their effort to get a seaport of their own, favoured a Delagoa Bay line which, besides being the shortest route to the sea, ran most of its length through the Transvaal. Their obstinacy in vetoing a direct line from the Cape and refusing to permit even the fifty miles of line needed to link the Free State terminus with Johannesburg reached a peak in August 1895 when the President went so far as to close the 'drifts' or Vaal River crossings used by wagons carrying goods from railhead to the Rand. It then came so near open war that Kruger alienated sympathy throughout the country, making it likely that, even if he ran at all, a younger and less conservative candidate would win the election due in 1897 and make a comprehensive settlement on a broadly South African basis. It was not to be. The 'drifts' crisis dragged on till November. In December Rhodes lost patience and decided to strike (or to stand aside and let his second-in-command in Rhodesia strike) into the Transvaal with a sketchy force of 500 men. Rhodes, who knew little of the Rand, deceived himself, or was deceived, into supposing that the grievances of its British and other *uitlanders* had them on the verge of revolt. In fact, busily prosperous in spite of political handicaps, they were disinclined to risk what they held by launching a revolution. The Jameson Raid was a bid to stimulate incipient revolt and bring the Transvaal into a United South Africa —the forlorn hope of a man, conscious that his time was short, who died only six years later lamenting, 'so much to do, so little done'. So far from bringing unity to the country, the abortive revolution roused righteous indignation, particularly in the Cape. The alliance with Hofmeyr which, had it lasted, must have made the Boer War impossible, broke down overnight. The less responsible Boers' sense of having triumphed once again made them less willing than ever to compromise: British negotiators toiled hard in the years that followed to undo the harm done by the Raid, but even if it was (as a friend who was in Boer counsels at the time always maintained) when nerves were set on edge by the heat of Pretoria on the eve of the rains that would not break, it was a Boer ultimatum that precipitated war in October 1899.

The ill consequences are with us yet (Chapter 10); but it was one better outcome of the Raid that Rhodes, thus calamitously freed from the burden of the Cape premiership, now gave all his attention to 'my North', and first of all to 'native' grievances. The Matabele were broken in 1893 but not crushed. In the fateful year 1896, when also a disastrous epidemic of rinderpest swept like a fire through the cattle of half the continent, they rebelled, and the Mashona with them. The Mashona had been freed from Matabele domination and raids, but are said to have complained that Matabele raiders came *and went*—whereas their European deliverers stayed indefinitely! Rhodes earned and well deserved praise for his patient 'indabas'—especially when he met the Matabele alone and unarmed in the Matopos, a tumbled cluster of low hills hidden away in a depression that makes them a fastness near but invisible from Bulawayo. Rhodes's diplomacy was so successful that about 1930 a lawyer friend in Salisbury assured me there had been no 'native trouble' since the Mashona rebellion.

The status of the African population all these years was perhaps equivocal. The new order, besides putting an end to tribal warfare, provided new opportunities for individuals; but the majority lived very much as before, staying on where they had always been; land that became native 'reserve' was not even visited much more than once a year, when the Commissioner came to collect the conventional poll-tax. Land in the Highlands, if it was also on the railway, was most of it alienated to settlers, but there too the original inhabitants stayed on as 'squatters'; much of this had been in native occupation but chiefly as pasture. The High Veld favoured by the Europeans is not necessarily the best land; the climate and the rainfall may be better, but not the permanent water-supply. A red soil was chosen as better for maize than the lighter grey, but the grey turned out to be better for tobacco which became the country's staple cash crop. The native population had always been scattered and displacement was local, causing little hardship at first; any real crowding on the land came of natural increase and was not marked before the 1930s. By that time, however, African progress had also begun to make access to the railways more necessary. The complaint arose that native-grown maize had an extra long journey to market, and got an unfairly low price whatever its quality. African progress owed something to white example, and more to certain mission schools which gave instruction in agriculture. The work of the missions got Government blessing and support, but in the first place the country was run by the European population as *their* country.

Rhodesia rightly bears its founder's name; Rhodes's personal influence was everywhere and in everything. He dreamt and planned for the country, just as he, personally, pacified its African people. The spacious layout of Salisbury was his, as were the amply wide streets of Bulawayo—the ox-wagon drawn by sixteen oxen was then the normal means of transport and must, he said, have room to turn! Even though the hoped-for mining turned out to be an affair, for the most part, of three-stamp or even one-stamp batteries, and though the vision of a Cape-to-Cairo railway remained a dream, Rhodes worked energetically and got the Cairo telegraph, and railway lines to serve his own farmers or miners; one connecting the Cape, through Salisbury, with Beira, was complete by 1899, another to the north reached Broken Hill in 1906 by the bridge (1904) which he insisted must catch the spray of the Victoria Falls. Mr. Rhodes's avowed aim was to found a colony like New Zealand, and the man who capitalized and revolutionized farming in the old Western Cape by setting up the 'Rhodes Fruit Farms', was not the one to neglect the agricultural foundations of Rhodesia. By the early 1900s his settlers, besides rearing cattle, were producing tobacco and citrus; they were not perhaps very prosperous, but many of the best farmers had pensions or business connections to help them, and soon they very decidedly evolved a distinctive Rhodesian way of life: well into the '20s and '30s the slogan was that new-comers were welcome but they must be 'of the right type'. Like Rhodes himself, the settlers really hoped and worked to build a society of gentlemen-farmers to exercise the lordship, most enlightened and benevolent, over something like twenty times their own number of African peasant-labourers.

The new colony was taking form even before Rhodes's death at the age of 49 in 1902; the Boer War was no serious interruption—Rhodesia saw little or no fighting and military expenditure circulated some cash. But the moment his guiding hand was removed the political atmosphere changed; the benevolent autocracy of Mr. Rhodes was one thing, rule by a company of merchants, or even of mining magnates, quite another. Administration was necessarily burdensome and costly; the Company's huge domain was, half of it, tsetse-infested, almost trackless, and cut in two by the unbridged Zambezi; mere distance made a centralized government impossible in the early days; when three originally separate units became two (southern and northern), in 1911, the north still brought in little revenue and its staff was a mere skeleton. When the south, which was little more profitable, began also to be politically restive, the Company was very ready to have its Charter revised as it was due to be, after its twenty-five years, in 1914. But this year war intervened, delaying also the conclusion of a major lawsuit in which the Privy Council was called to adjudicate on the Company's land-rights. Judgment was delivered only in 1919, to the effect that the Company had all this time been no more than the agent of the Crown; un-alienated land, therefore, was Crown land, not the Company's. On the other hand, the agent was entitled to compensation for the administrative work so long done on the Crown's behalf; and for two or three years longer the so-called Cave Commission wrestled to calculate the amount of these dues, and to determine how they were to be met.

The great days of the Chartered Company as a governing authority were ended. Even if it meant dividing the Rhodes heritage, none questioned that the poverty-stricken, undeveloped north must pass to H.M.G. and the Colonial Office; the Covenant of the League of Nations had newly recognized its like as constituting a sacred trust of civilization. By this time the B.S.A. Company's directors were themselves losing faith. As I had it from one of them, just three years after a change-over became effective, the Company had been willing or even anxious to be rid also of its encumbrance of mineral rights, those of Northern Rhodesia for a modest sum, 2 or 3 millions. The politicians of Southern Rhodesia quickly seized this chance when it came their way; but

H.M.G., which had none of their cautious foresight, and still less of Rhodes's imaginative faith, forgot even the traditional rule—to be prepared for the unexpected to come out of Africa. The Colonial Office, which also much mistrusted mining magnates, sturdily refused to look at the offer. By 1927 the figure of the price to be put on those Northern Rhodesian 'rights' had grown from 2 millions, as my friend put it, to 'something astronomical'! The Company had in the interval initiated skilled and intensive prospecting which about 1925 located great deposits of copper *sulphide*: till now, as in the nearby Katanga, only the oxide had been profitable, but mineralogists had lately evolved a process by which the sulphide yielded its copper when treated with oil. Seizing its opportunity, the Company came into its own as a most effective development corporation; rid now of its political burden, it set some of the greatest of the mining companies to open up that 'Copper Belt' which I singled out in the beginning (p. 22) as perhaps the most spectacular single example of modern 'development' in any part of the colonial world. On the strength of its copper Northern Rhodesia was able to rejoin its southern neighbour, in 1953, as a not unequal partner in the new Federation of the Rhodesias and Nyasaland (Chapter 11).

By the time of the passing of the Chartered Company's administration the other half of its domain, Southern Rhodesia, had become established as a colony of settlement, but of a new type; its white immigrants, true colonists, generally distinguished as 'settlers', produced nearly all its revenue, but numbered only some 50,000 all told, and shared the land with nearer a million Africans. Being concentrated in the narrow belt of high veld bordering the railway lines, the settlers were, however, a united and effective community; even in Company days they had been strong enough, like so many previous settlements, to be endowed with their own elected legislative council. African interests might seem to have called for the Crown Colony solution applied in the north; but by old British tradition a legally constituted parliament could not be set aside, and this way of it was never seriously canvassed; the franchise was on the Cape model—few but whites qualified to vote, but there was no Colour Bar—and Cape practice was as yet unchallenged. There can be no doubt of the answer Rhodes himself would have given; his beloved north was an extension of the Cape and linked in his mind with the United South Africa he lived and worked for. The South African Union of 1922 was not, however, all Rhodes had hoped for, and particularly unsatisfying to settlers strongly attached to the British connexion. British political leaders, who shared a certain mistrust, used their influence to secure the Rhodesian electors the alternative of deciding by referendum whether to join the Union or to stand by themselves as a self-governing unit. In the course of 1922 General Smuts, then still Prime Minister, personally canvassed the country in support of union with South Africa. But he himself, together with Mr. Lionel Curtis and others of the Milner 'Kindergarten', had made Union only too effective; fearful of internal dissensions breaking out again they had rejected anything like a federal solution and built a monolithic state which left the provinces little or no power; alarmed at the prospect of losing their separate identity, a substantial three to two majority of some 13,000 electors voted against union. In October 1923, accordingly, Southern Rhodesia graduated to full responsible government, to the extent even of being attached to the Dominions Office and no longer to the Colonial Office. But this was the end of a chapter. The doctrine that Africa is 'the White Man's burden' had by this time brought into being in Kenya a similar though smaller East African colony of 'white settlers'. That very year the Colonial Secretary of the day came to a remarkably different conclusion about its future.

The unproductive country served by the Uganda railway (the same that originally piled up expenses and broke the back of I.B.E.A. (Chapter 7), was now the separate colony of Kenya. The Highlands, where settlement concentrated, is an irregularly shaped wedge of country, no one part of it much more than 100 miles distant from any other; the rainfall is reliable, and though it is nearly on the Equator its altitude (from 6,000 to 10,000 feet above sea-level), gives it a healthy and stimulating, even a brilliant climate, also 'wide horizons' that are unmatched; at points on the main road in or near Nairobi there is a chance of seeing at once *two* snow-capped mountains, Kilimanjaro 100 miles to the south, Mt. Kenya almost as far to the north. Smaller peaks rising from the southern plain impress the Masai as Ol Donyo Sabuk, or the great hill, and even Ol Donyo Lengai, the hill of God. The future Lord Lugard first wrote of the Highlands as suitable for European settlement as early as 1893. Not much of the soil is rich and deep; but in 1897 Lord Delamere, who approached from the north in search of big game, marked at once the contrast with Somaliland whence he had set out, and returned two years later, with a bride, to examine it more closely. In 1900, to satisfy the promoters of the railway who were wondering what their line was to carry, a young and enthusiastic Governor, Sir Charles Eliot, began to plan for European immigration to stimulate agricultural production. The disbandment of the forces at the end of the Boer War in 1902 brought ready volunteers, including even a party of Boers; with them, or just before them, his mind made up, came Lord Delamere, a born leader, now just over 30 years old. These young men had almost everything to learn about farming in the Kenya Highlands which, by what was no more than a gentlemen's agreement with Lord Elgin, Colonial Secretary in and after 1906, became in effect the white 'tribal reserve'. In conditions where anything from English primroses to bananas will grow somewhere, it was often a problem, as one said, to know what *not* to grow. It fell above all to Delamere to find this out, even to play in Kenya the part of Rhodesia's Cecil Rhodes, as best he could from the resources of a private fortune; there were no diamonds or gold, he had no de Beers behind him and—like Rhodes in one respect—he was an invalid, several times incapacitated for months or even years on end by spinal trouble. Delamere actually used up his own fortune—by some accounts he did so more than once—but his persuasive powers were such (or his bank was so deeply committed) that overdrafts carried him through to the end. By tireless effort, and at great expense, he was able to introduce and prove wheat and to rear grade cattle and sheep; a French Catholic mission pioneered coffee, a staple of great importance, especially in the lean early years. By 1911 the white population of this newest colony had grown from roughly 400 in 1902 to about 10,000, and 2,000 of these, besides their dependants, lived on and off the land.

There were at once the makings of political friction in this situation. The settlers were 'frontiersmen', if ever there were such, facing a hard struggle to make a living for themselves in strange, new conditions. Temperamentally they were difficult material for authoritarian colonial rule, slow to take direction from above but impatient of the pace of the official machine; the bureaucracy, as they called it, was too slow to take the most necessary decisions. They were a small community, but most of them were concentrated within reach of the seat of government and well able to make the pressure of their presence sharply felt. The administration, for its part, was perhaps always in two minds about the 'settler' experiment, and sometimes capricious; individuals, including Lord Delamere, acquired large or very large holdings, but new-comers were sometimes kept waiting for land titles, living on their capital. Economic development, it was agreed, was necessary and desirable, and governors were on the whole sympathetic; but district officers, naturally and rightly feeling themselves peculiarly responsible for 'native' interests, were a good deal more hesitant.

By chance the settlement had begun just when the cattle losses caused by rinderpest in the '90s had certainly relieved the pressure on land, and perhaps reduced even the population itself; the Masai in particular were irretrievably weakened. Tribes like the Kikuyu consequently had less need to seek pasture on the high altitudes, which Africans normally shun as 'cold', and were readier than they might have been to leave these to settlers. The Masai were the first to feel some effect; the turn of the Kikuyu came later (Chapter 11). This warrior tribe of nomads had never, in Dr. Philip's phrase, 'known its own limits', and habitually imposed its will on weaker neighbours; it was they who forced the Kikuyu and their neighbours, the Wakamba, farther into the hills than these might have chosen, and they were restless and inconvenient near neighbours to the settlers on whom the revenues of the country increasingly depended. Acknowledged Masai grazing land in the Rift Valley ran across the precious railway, and at certain times of year vast herds were driven across it, forcing the Government to face the necessity of imposing a limit on Masai freedom of movement. In spite of an earlier treaty, and even if their holdings were greatly extended in compensation, they were required in 1911 to relinquish their northern lands and confine themselves to the south side of the railway. The close co-existence of nomadism and settled agriculture was hardly possible.

This first considerable clash between old and new was followed before long by the First World War. The prolonged and costly East African campaign gravely weakened the economic fabric of this new society, but also made it necessary for the administration to solicit all the help it possibly could. This chance meant that Lord Delamere and the settler representatives attained an influential if not a dominant position in the Legislative Council (an advisory and legislative body of the normal, only partly elected Crown Colony type). The end of the war, like the Boer War before it, brought Kenya an appreciable number of new settlers. By 1923, if not earlier, the white population was about 18,000. This body, politically much stronger than before, found its position challenged, not by Africans but by the rising claims of rival Indians. Originally introduced to build the railway, Indian immigrants were now doing a large part of the internal commerce of East Africa and supplied almost all the skilled artisans. The settlers, however, claiming to be the sole makers of the new Kenya, claimed also the decisive share in its government, refusing to agree, for example, to the opening of the White Highlands to Indian purchasers, or to the institution of a common electoral roll for Europeans and the more numerous Indians; at one point they went so far as to plot to kidnap the Governor and take direct control. But the Indians, besides being more numerous, were a power to reckon with; the rise of the Congress 'liberation' movement enabled them to embarrass the India Office in London, and through it the Colonial Office, with complaints from Kenya. It was under this pressure that the no less harassed Colonial Office was driven to set aside the Rhodesian precedent. The famous Devonshire Declaration of 1923 was provoked in the first place by Asian claims, but the pronouncement began with a blunt general reminder: 'Primarily, Kenya is *African* territory.' Having laid it down that in any such predominantly African colony African interests must rank *paramount*, the statement concluded:

> 'H.M.G. cannot but regard the grant of responsible self-government as out of the question within any period of time which need now be taken into consideration.'

The seven years following the Devonshire blast—in Mrs. Huxley's phrase, a period of 'spot-light on Kenya'—saw more reports produced than ever before in this colonial story, and so many books besides, that the heat of the debate hindered more than it helped clear thinking. By no fault of its own the Report of the East African (Ormsby-Gore) commission revealed the confusion. This body was appointed only in 1924 but its origins lie further back and were essentially East African. In 1920 when, after four years of war, the former German East Africa became British Mandated Territory, its administration was in a bad plight and its economic system broken down—at my first glimpse of the central railway from Dar-es-Salaam in that year it was running *one* train a *week*. Shortly afterwards the port of Tanga, whence a line runs to the Kilimanjaro country, was alleged to be losing traffic because a short link-line, built from Voi to Taveta to connect the Tanga railway with the Kenya-Uganda main line for war purposes, was attracting traffic to use the bigger and better Kenya port, Mombasa. It is extraordinary that in this ill-served country the Government was prevailed on to agree, by way of remedy, to having the Voi link dismantled and torn up. Lord Delamere's farther-sighted protest led to a Commons motion suggesting, rather, the federation of the three neighbours, Kenya, Uganda, and Tanganyika, and asking for a Commission to examine the possibilities. By this time, however, more specific questions were obtruding themselves, and Mr. J. H. Thomas, the Labour Colonial Secretary, widened the terms of reference to include the economic potential of East Africa, the labour situation and 'native policy'. The result was that the Report, when it came, provided the first comprehensive survey of this great region: it was illuminating, even inspiring; but it left the original question of federation in the air. Mr. L. S. Amery, who was now Colonial Secretary, decided in 1927 to follow up with a new inquiry; he himself wanted to know how, precisely, closer union should be set to work. The cabinet, however, asked also to be assured that union was in itself desirable.

This cabinet hesitancy was because the 'spot-light' was now playing very strongly. First Dr. Norman Leys, a wholly selfless doctor who had resigned after fifteen years' service in Kenya, started a vigorous agitation against what he considered to be settler encroachments, and the countenance and support given them by the administration's adherence to the policy of developing the country by means of 'white settlement'; his full-scale attack alleged repeated deviations from the newly proclaimed principle, the 'paramountcy' of African interests. Leys's views in the book *Kenya*, published in 1924, at once got sympathetic support from an active wing of the Labour Party. Informed missionary opinion —and it was something more than the old 'Exeter Hall'—was very ready to take notice; a few years earlier, in 1920, the American Phelps-Stokes Foundation had begun sending representatives to tour much of West, South and East Africa, and reports by Dr. T. Jesse Jones, and a notable Gold Coaster, Dr. J. K. Aggrey, were just then appearing; their special theme, education, was still an almost exclusively mission activity. Critical comments on over-academic teaching, on the parrot-like learning of Africans, and the need of more 'practical' methods, were to be expected; and in their ardent advocacy of '*community*-building' the Negroes scattered over the plantations of the Deep South were perhaps more in their minds than African villagers. But these reports asked also for a greater readiness to work *with* Africans and not only *for* them, and were evidence that the African point of view was now commanding more precise attention. In recognition of this new concern for African interests, Dr. J. H. Oldham, of the International Missionary Council, was appointed to the *Closer Union* Commission.

This next report, however, only made the debate range more widely; three of the members out-voted the Chairman, Sir Hilton Young, and again deliberately left the particulars of *closer union* in the air; their submissions insisted rather on the need, first, to define the 'native policy' of all the territories in such terms as would safeguard African interests in any future 'closer union'. Believing, as he did, that even native policy could be better handled by a competent central authority, Mr. Amery refused to accept defeat on the strictly administrative preliminary reform he thought the situation demanded. When the Hilton Young Report was published in January 1929 he at once despatched his Permanent Secretary, Sir Samuel Wilson, to pick up the threads left loose.

Working with great speed and skill, Sir Samuel returned in April with a workable plan which the governors and most of the interests were prepared to accept. It was too late. The Government was defeated at a general election and by June Lord Passfield (Sidney Webb) ruled in Mr. Amery's stead. The new Government's *Statement of Conclusions* was delayed until June 1930—it then appeared together with a *Memorandum on Native Policy* reasserting the doctrine of 'trusteeship'; the 'paramountcy' of native interests was declared to be:

> 'a trust which cannot be devolved and from which H.M.G. cannot be relieved; the ultimate responsibility for the exercise of this trusteeship must accordingly rest with them alone.'

The 'Labour' origin of these 'black papers', as they were called, won them a poor reception in the settler world, where they were taken to be a condemnation of settlement, as such; protests came even from far-away Northern Rhodesia. Without settler direction the countries where they had built a new and thriving society must, it was now declared, return to their former state of barbarism; in a dignified sermon I happened to hear broadcast in Nairobi, on the Sunday following the Passfield pronouncement, the story of the Creation was ingeniously applied to the settlers' civilizing mission:

> '. . . for the Lord God had not caused it to rain upon the earth, and there was not a man to till the ground; but there went up a mist from the earth, and watered the whole face of the ground.'

Settler grievances were being trumpeted at this same time with mounting indignation in a central assembly that went by the almost Cromwellian title of the *Convention of Associations*; the activities of one local group even had the Governor of Tanganyika, Sir Donald Cameron, speaking of the Kilimanjaro country as 'my *un*settled area'! Yet still Lord Passfield's was not the last word. The tradition ruled that colonial policy is not a party issue and the Labour ministry was only rather self-consciously assertive of doctrine broadly accepted by men of all parties. Having now said its own say, the Government took the unusual step of submitting the whole issue to a Joint Select Committee of Lords and Commons. This representative body sat and took evidence through most of 1931; when it reported at last, it was to yet another new Government, the National administration which took over in the economic crisis of that year. Its findings were very much as before, but economic depression at any rate turned all minds to the politics of bread and butter. Closer union, which the Ormsby-Gore team was deflected from considering, and the so-called Closer Union Commission played down, was no longer a live issue. These sprawling territories were neighbours with many common interests; it was most desirable that they should work together, and there was reason to hope that if co-operation was learnt in their infancy it would become settled habit before they reached maturity. A decisive lead from the sovereign power never came and the opportunity passed. The Kenya Government made time only for one major effort; to put its land policy beyond further question it set yet another (Morris Carter) Commission to work, and this produced a mammoth report in 1934. Closer union was so much out of fashion that Kenya actually won approval for sub-dividing itself, in terms of this Land Report, into a score or more of almost water-tight tribal compartments.

The economic blizzard of the early '30s, followed hard by the Second World War, effectively cooled the political atmosphere in Kenya as elsewhere, but the withdrawal of settler support had already killed the movement for closer union; when the Passfield white papers threatened tighter imperial control the settler interests were inclined to struggle to swim separately rather than sink all together. Control from without was always their bugbear; the idea of closer union was originally their reaction to the nervous official fumbling (and insensate economics) of the proposal to eliminate inter-territorial competition by tearing up the serviceable Voi-Taveta railway line; the 'anti-colonialism' of a later day is no monopoly of the dependent colonial peoples; the vigour of this sentiment in settler circles is rooted in their history. When the story of the modern dependencies comes to be told, like that of the Dominions before them, by their own people, their historians—whatever their colour—will give the settlers more credit for their positive contribution than they have had from their critics at any time since the 1920s. From the beginning settlement in Kenya was made in conditions which debarred its pioneers from enjoying the political privileges of their predecessors in America or Australia: the politically dumb African majority could not be directly subjected to the immigrant minority; even settler domination of the Legislative Assembly only further slowed up but never changed the administrative system. In the settler view of it they alone kept the state solvent, but were expected to work in a strait waistcoast, under the sole direction of inaccessible office-sitting civil servants, who not only administered but made the country's laws. On the other hand, the experiment began, with the general (if often hesitant) blessing of successive governments, at a time when no one seriously doubted that African advancement depended above all on the work and the example of Europeans. Suddenly, the comfortable but always dubious doctrine that made African development the White Man's burden went out of favour—with such violence, that opinion tended to make White settlement, rather, the root of all evil.

The old American assumption, that only the immigrants' interests need be considered, has modern support and needed to be repudiated; but the more humane opposite view, which makes the same exclusive claims for the rights of the weaker peoples, is equally fallacious. The earnest musings of the Hilton Young majority set the new fashion (which has persisted); their conscientious concentration on the points where minority interests conflict with those of the African majority made too little of the real community of interests that also exists. Africans, in those days, inevitably concentrated, as they still do, on the affairs of their own local units. The settlers' view ranged more widely; battling as they had to if they and the country were to keep solvent, the immigrants were disposed to demand labour services from Africans, particularly the Kikuyu, whose rights in land of their own were still imperfectly defined. But also, alone in seeing the country as a whole, they stood out for unified control of railways and ports and customs, common essential services whose functioning mattered greatly, yet meant little, to the mass of Africans. They were essentially right that the prosperity and well-being of all races alike must always depend on harmonious development. The pity of it is that the long debate had the effect of throwing this small, possibly quarrelsome, but also forward-looking white community almost fiercely on the defensive: from this point the inevitably lively social and economic perplexities of these dependencies came more and more to be looked on as arising from a conflict of the races.

It is to be said for the settlers, even on the racial score, that white leadership was everywhere cheerfully accepted. My fate, or good fortune, I may repeat, was to divide my time in the twenty inter-war years almost equally between Britain and the world overseas, and to have the stimulating experience of conferring with a great variety of the people either at work in the field or concerned with it at the British end. I received an outstanding impression that 'race relations' (not yet so called) were excellent, and few can have ranged more widely than I did. Certainly the Africans of that day were placid, even submissive: the great test of meeting the claims of Africa *emergent* was yet to come. For almost the first time the witnesses called by the Joint Select Committee of 1931 included a number of Africans well able to speak for themselves; it might not after all be the only answer to their questionings for the white man to carry the burden of African development. It began to be said that we must *build* rather, and build on African foundations,

The farmers and settlers on the spot were naturally uneasy at the trend of the debate, being inevitably more acutely aware of African deficiencies, and of the inherent weaknesses of such African foundations. Feeling their work threatened, and themselves superseded, they were increasingly defensive: for the clearest if not the only clear outcome of the specific debate on Kenya was the confirmation by four successive governments of the 1923 administration's blunt refusal to consider setting up responsible self-government in Kenya on the lately approved Southern Rhodesian model.

Chapter 9

BETWEEN TWO WORLDS

*

The inconclusiveness of the series of East African blue books and white papers shows a lost sense of direction, as of men groping where light has suddenly failed. For twenty years and more the future of Africa had been confidently assumed to depend on old-fashioned European colonization; colonies which lacked such help and direction were doing all that could be expected of them if they gave no trouble. In those confident years the white communities of Rhodesia and Kenya, and smaller groups in Nyasaland and Tanganyika, became established, and indeed put Africa on the map. But by 1920 a Great War had swept away the world that saw Rhodes's pioneers ride into Salisbury in 1890, discrediting even the liberalism which had redeemed ventures that now came to be regarded as crudely imperialist. The affairs of Kenya came to be judged by new standards and, increasingly, in the light of newer experience.

Some of this experience was drawn from West Africa where a great expansion of British influence had followed hard on the proclamation of the East African Protectorate; new tracts there had been 'won for the Empire', and then almost forgotten. The special needs of these tropical colonies had some passing attention from the protecting power during the Colonial Secretaryship of Joseph Chamberlain. Guaranteed loans at only 2¾ per cent helped railway building, relieving West Africa of its dependence on human porterage, hitherto the only possible means of transport. Even so, Sierra Leone could afford only a badly engineered line of two feet gauge; doggerel lines described it in 'pidgin':

Di train for Bo
No 'gree for go!

But as in Uganda and Kenya, railways at any rate made agricultural exports possible, and a special Department of Agriculture set up in Trinidad by the West Indian Royal Commission of 1897 produced the Imperial College of Tropical Agriculture to provide a training ground for agricultural officers in all parts of the Empire. Niggardly support from the Treasury made Chamberlain's Schools of Tropical Medicine in London and Liverpool a long-term venture serving at first the needs only of the colonial service itself. Little more was done, for though Chamberlain himself spoke of the Empire as an undeveloped estate, the South African War had the effect of putting an end for many years to any further such planned development. One notable exception proves the rule, the successful Gezira cotton-growing experiment conducted by the Sudan Plantations Syndicate in co-operation with the Government and with working peasants. Mr. Arthur Gaitskell's studies of Gezira history suggest that the participation of the Foreign Office (the governing authority for the Sudan) in the scheme was assured only after a chance meeting of some of the promoters with Mr. Asquith in Malta, which persuaded the Prime Minister that voters in Liberal Lancashire might be interested! Very few dependencies were ever in a position to press their needs on the attention of ministers hard at work after 1906 planning the welfare state and Home Rule for Ireland. Elected originally as anti-imperialist defenders of free trade, the pre-1914 Liberals felt keenly only one 'colonial' obligation, to right the wrong they believed imperialism had done the Boers in South Africa: it was they who made the great refusal when they disclaimed imperial responsibility for 'native' interests (see p. 139). This act of complaisance was poorly rewarded. Within a month of the outbreak of war in August 1914 malcontent Boers rose against their old generals, Botha and Smuts, in a major rebellion.

From the beginning the total war of the western European overlords involved the African dependencies. First General Botha carried the campaign against his own rebels into South-West Africa, from whose Germans they had drawn aid and comfort; not without provocation given, this country was conquered by South African troops. Other German colonies, Togoland and the Cameroons, fell quickly, but the Allies met more formidable resistance in German East Africa. It is just to recognize the loyalty and willing service, military as well as civic, given by the people of all the British dependencies; but the Germans too were well served by their *askaris*; having survived a number of major actions planned to end the war in the healthy Kilimanjaro country, a handful of Germans under a skilful leader, von Lettow-Vorbeck, held out successfully, with loyal African help, 'for the duration'. A prolonged campaign of hide-and-seek carried the war from the Kenya borders to all parts of Tanganyika, including the province of Ruanda-Urundi, a rugged but populous region which fell in the end to Belgian forces from the Congo and became later incorporated in the Belgian colony. Von Lettow's little army of about 1,500 surrendered at last, well inside Rhodesia, and only after the armistice in November 1918. When the plan of a short sharp campaign failed, the transport system—in the old raw Africa—completely broke down; tsetse-fly made transport animals useless, immobilizing the more numerous Allied troops, British and South African, who were left entirely dependent on African porters. These, like the troops, were decimated by sickness and of about 200,000 enlisted in a Carrier Corps some 46,000 died—a hard experience, shared by many doctors, which taught some lessons of hygiene and nutrition. In spite of this many Europeans learnt also the extraordinary fascination of East Africa. Lessons, however, were not soon or easily applied—for the war also brought a breakdown in colonial administration. In the British colonies understaffed officers were overwhelmed with special war work, and in Tanganyika there could be little but military improvisation—this Territory's solvency had not been fully re-established when I saw the country in the '30s.

Africans were wearied and bored by the war, and not unaware of the weakening effect on their masters of its years of slaughter; but some of them also did well out of new opportunities; wherever there were troops on the move the general shortage of supplies ensured ready markets and good prices for produce of any kind. A few of the more fortunate were able to meet the demands of world markets. During the short post-war boom a number of the dependencies surprised the world by appearing for the first time as prosperous primary producers. The value of cotton exported from Uganda, which in 1907 was 80 or 90 per cent of a total export of only £147,000, and in 1913–14 £757,000, advanced by 1923 to over £2 million. The benefit to individuals mattered less than the improved revenues which allowed the Government to supplement the lake steamer and the railway by building a system of exceptionally good roads.

The Gold Coast again had begun very modestly; agriculture had never been its people's forte; the natural forest provided the palm-oil which almost alone kept trade in being in the post-slave-trade era (and it is the forest also which nurtures the cocoa). An older and perhaps more congenial tradition was revived when the '90s brought a boom in gold-mining shares, known on the Stock Exchange as 'the Jungle'; much money was made and lost both on the markets and by some unscrupulous dealings in concessions, but the rich Ashanti mine and some smaller units settled down to a steady output worth about £1 million a year. In 1909 a new export, cocoa, was worth £755,000; by 1913 it was worth £2·5 million, in 1916 £3·8 million, by 1920 it had risen to £8·278 million—about half the world supply. The total exports of the Gold Coast, which by then included diamonds and manganese, reached a value of £12·3 million, and between the wars stayed near the £10 million mark, cocoa remaining about 80 per cent of the total. The Gold Coast still successfully resisted direct taxation and continued to do so till it got ministers of its own; but cocoa paid an export duty and the governorship of Sir Gordon Guggisberg (1919–27) was marked by a spending spree which the great prosperity seemed to warrant. Roads and telegraphs were extended, public buildings were put up and a great new central hospital; a £6 million harbour opened at Takoradi in 1928 spared most of the precious cocoa the rough and sometimes wet handling in open surf boats. Achimota College opened in 1925, with a government guaranteed income in place of endowments, and the avowed object of giving children a full course of preparatory and public school education as good as they could get in England. The public debt was considerably increased, and speakers in the contemporary debate on Kenya noted wonderingly that this great outlay could be financed from internal revenues produced by the unaided activities of the people of an African dependency.

Clearly not only Africa but the African peoples had greater possibilities than had been allowed for even by the framers of the Covenant of the League of Nations which, only in 1920, had proclaimed as new doctrine, in words that consciously or unconsciously echoed Fowell Buxton, that

> 'The well-being and development of peoples not yet able to stand by themselves form a sacred trust of civilization.'

The old empire-building self-confidence was gone—and not only in Britain; it must have been in the later '20s that I once heard General Smuts, as he ruminated on the age, break into Matthew Arnold's lines:

> *Wandering between two worlds, one dead*
> *The other powerless to be born.*

The distinctly anti-imperialist Labour Party which was displacing the old Liberals in British political life was very ready to conclude that if the Africans of the Gold Coast could do better economically than those of South Africa or Rhodesia imperial rule must be at fault, and the remedy should be to leave all Africans to themselves. It was just then (in 1922) that Lord Lugard's *Dual Mandate in Tropical Africa* was published and caught the tide. Starting from the novel but not new basic theme that colonial development must be at once 'for the benefit of the inhabitants and the general welfare of mankind', and drawing on his own experience, Lord Lugard now enunciated the principles of administration he and his staff had worked out over many years in Northern Nigeria. This West African practice suggested the alternative policy to colonization that so many were looking for, the plan already named 'indirect rule' by C. L. Temple, one of Lugard's officers, in a book published as early as 1918. Big book as it was, Lugard's *Dual Mandate* went at once (1923) into a second edition. This included a new passage commenting directly on 'the Kenya question', which may well have had its influence on the Devonshire declaration of that year (p. 180); the Hilton Young Commission two or three years later certainly took full account of Lord Lugard's gentle animadversions on the weakness of Kenya 'native policy'.

The public audience was still confused and uncertain; during the next decade there were men in all the parties very willing to 'appease' the blatantly 'colonialist' claims of Hitler and Mussolini at African expense; some of these were at the same time uncritical in acclaiming the unaided progress made by Africans. Agricultural officers, on the other hand, who knew how rough usage had killed the forest trees which in the '90s had produced an appreciable income from rubber, worked patiently to maintain the quality required if African cocoa or cotton was to keep its place in world markets; they also dreamt bad dreams of untutored peasants being called on to fight the spread of unexpected plant diseases—a test that came later when swollen-shoot attacked the cocoa. The best economies of the momentarily prosperous colonies were narrowly based monocultures, and therefore vulnerable when prices slumped, as they did in 1922 and again in the general collapse about 1931. The social consequences of economic progress meant little to inexperienced observers; but those on the spot knew the strain on native land tenure, the over-taxing of the soil itself, the rush to produce 'cash crops' at the expense of essential food. Lord Lugard himself unmistakably looked on the necessary development of Africa as still mandatory on men of the white race.

It therefore needed a spur of another kind to effect a complete change of direction and bring official policy to accept the 'indirect' part now assigned to the ruler. This spur was supplied, there is no doubt (and I speak from close knowledge of many of the principal actors), by the notorious deterioration of social conditions in South Africa where the effects of schism were now to be felt. In the winter of 1923–4 those interested in such matters in London were, for the first time in my experience, asking eagerly for first-hand evidence on the domestic situation in South Africa. Barely two years later the same circles were determinedly set to check any tendency for other African colonies to follow the courses that seemed to have brought the Union to disaster.

The critics of South Africa would have been more helpful had they consistently shown awareness of the real perplexities of its rival societies. There are indeed those who see here a microcosm of the world situation which in the '50s has race divided against race in many lands; but even those who, varying the metaphor, see South Africa as a 'laboratory of race relations', may forget that experiments have to be worked not in the abstract, from a comfortable distance, but in intimate daily contact. By 1947, for example, the interests of nearly 3 million whites had still to be harmonized with those of over 9 million Africans and fully 1 million Coloureds (Eurafricans), besides something under half a million Asians. So far as mere numbers go, the great American republic has not always done generously by its Negro minorities even though the white races outnumber these, except in local pockets, by ten to one; in the only partly developed tropical African colonies the tiny white minorities, having started the building of new states, know they can continue only with the consent of the original inhabitants who are from ten to a hundred times as numerous. In South Africa, where the disproportion of numbers is less than in either of these examples, the state is already well developed; foundations were laid, moreover, when the major groups, the Africans and the Europeans, were *two* rival but distinct *rural* communities, and the effective numbers of white and non-white much more nearly equal. Till well into the present century Cape Town, which now has some 100,000 African workers, rarely saw an African face. This certainly is the extreme example, but it points the moral that the adjustment now required is, as nowhere else and never before, one of different races thrown together in *one* society. Having intimate reason to know the immaturity of the African majority, the whites have reason to fear for the stability of the state, which they also have excuse for thinking is of their making. In the towns, moreover, as never in the simpler pastoral age, the less skilled or unskilled whites have to face the direct and disconcerting fifty-fifty competition of totally unskilled blacks.

It was, significantly, not native grievances or discontents, but the very genuine distress of white rural workers that first compelled attention. As early as 1908, in the reconstruction period after the Boer War, one of the brightest of Lord Milner's young men, Mr. Philip Kerr (later the Marquess of Lothian), was the principal architect of a report on (white) *Indigency in the Transvaal.* It was the prevailing view that degeneracy was to be expected among people disinclined to demean themselves by doing 'Kafir' work, but blame was now fastened on the inefficiency of Boer farming methods. In 1915, when the Bishop of Grahamstown turned my attention to conditions in his largely English cathedral city, I was able to show that indigency was at least not due to any peculiar Boer weakness. In 1916 the rising Afrikaner leader, Dr. D. F. Malan, made one of his first public appearances (other than in his pulpit) expressly to urge a general conference at Cradock to strive for the *oplossing* (solution) of the 'Poor White Problem'. Meantime investigations carried into a great many country districts produced clear evidence that perhaps a twentieth of the white population were (in the phrase used in Mr. Rowntree's study of York) more or less permanently 'submerged' below the poverty line; figures I transferred to a map showed a very general migration in process from the farms to the towns. By 1919, when the early immigrant Cornish and Australian miners had dribbled off to the war and away from the mines, they had been replaced to the extent of 80 per cent or 90 per cent by these white Afrikaners from the rural districts; the charge that they were 'won't works' was unjust. But the mines could supply only a partial solution; for many there was nothing but unskilled employment. Such lack of choice was felt to be hard on the rural population of nineteenth-century Britain which was a homogeneous society; but in South Africa the unskilled white worker had to compete with a flood of displaced rural Africans ready and able to do the same work and keep themselves on a fraction of the wage the white man needed to maintain a level even far below his expected standard of living.

It was too much to hope that excessively anxious South African politicians and governments, who readily accepted proof that rural conditions and a faulty land system, rather than mental and moral degeneracy, were responsible for the flood of 'poor whites', would also accept that (in words I quoted to them from Thomas Hardy) 'the tendency of the rural populations to the great towns' was, for blacks as well as whites, 'the tendency of water to flow uphill when forced by machinery'. Till the 1920s the African people of the Union were conveniently out of sight of their white neighbours. The easily manageable number of natives who took out passes to go 'in search of work' were normally 'target workers', who came to the towns only to earn enough to pay tax or to buy cattle for a wife's dowry (*lobola*); their numbers were in fact considered to be chronically inadequate for the needs of white industry. The great mass of Africans were effectively 'segregated' in the rail-less and almost roadless 'reserves' of the Cape and Natal, or in the undeveloped black blocks of the Transvaal where many 'squatted' unmolested.

Even in the campaigning of the Boer War, which unsettled and dispersed the 'poor whites', both Boers and British studiously avoided making incursions into native areas; few had any knowledge of conditions there. The reserves provided a basic subsistence, though steadily less adequately; they were not yet desperately overcrowded, though fast becoming so. Besides providing a refuge in sickness and old age, and thus saving the State the necessity of providing social services, their very existence in effect subsidized wages. Yet wages were already low enough, since many or most of these unskilled workers worked for perhaps six months at a spell and had to start almost from the bottom each time they returned. Ignorance of native conditions, therefore, and an instinct for conserving this convenient separate existence, inspired the misbegotten Natives Land Act of 1913, which debarred natives from the hire or purchase of land except in certain for the most part *yet to be* scheduled areas; it was designed to require regular squatters to become registered farm labourers. In a former book I analysed the land situation and showed how the ill-drafted, ill-devised Natives Land Act put fresh pressure on the limited reserve land, so that the stream of immigrant labour became a flood. Immediately after 1913, when World War I sent all prices soaring upwards, rising costs both raised the workers' 'target', and drove so many more out to work for longer periods, that wage-rates inevitably stagnated instead of rising in sympathy with prices. It was at the same time, and for similar reasons, that white migration reached a peak. The concern caused by the results of the unholy competition between distressed people worked against serious study of the consequences suffered by the natives, till the missionary wing of the Dutch Reformed Church eventually did its part; the growing congestion of the reserves was first fully ventilated at a Conference of Europeans and Natives sponsored by that Church in 1923—a completely representative assembly in which African speakers took full part.

Two years later, in 1925, I was directly challenged by Prime Minister Hertzog and his advisers to verify the picture I had drawn in 1923 of the state of the native areas. The district of Herschel (situated at the point where the Cape, the O.F.S. and Basutoland meet) which they commended and honestly believed to be a model, was new ground to me, and I set out hopefully to make a survey. A few weeks of intensive work, carried out with official help, put the matter beyond doubt; Herschel's *only* export was *labour*; the local commissioner finally agreed in putting it that 75 per cent of the able-bodied men were absent at least half the year. The chief import was equally certainly the wages sent in, or brought back, to pay for maize, the staple food, of which they could not possibly grow enough for their needs; the soil erosion was fantastic soil destruction; as for cattle, the original grass-cover had been replaced by a tangled mass of poisonous weeds. Seven years later an official Economic Commission fully confirmed this finding and gave, besides, emphatic warning of the approach of 'desert conditions' throughout the reserves. These tragic odds and ends of land were originally defined in an honest attempt to secure the tribal homes; but in a half a century and more nothing had been done to adapt the people's methods to the needs of a steadily growing population. They were all still pure pastoralists, and though grazing can be conserved by making fenced paddocks, native land was and often is at once distinguishable from any other by the total absence of fences; which communal rights forbid. The state of these reserves is the conclusive condemnation of the policy that made them not homes but closed compounds or *kraals*.

In the end, concern was only aroused by the risk of head-on collision between 'poor whites' and still poorer blacks. The strains and stresses of the early '20s culminated in 1922 in a violent and revolutionary strike of white workers on the gold-mines. Originally the strike was the miners' bid to prevent the mine-owners replacing them by employing masses of cheaper native labour; but the 'syndicalist' leaders who spoke of a workers' republic gave the political approach a new twist by setting the Afrikaner workers dreaming more ardently of a restoration of their own Boer Republic; so the strike became a rebellion. The uprising was crushed; but this was the heaven-sent chance for the new National (and republican) Party, a body of Boer dissidents who had languished in opposition since their break with the old leaders soon after union in 1910. A general election in 1924 brought to power a Nationalist-cum-White-Labour Government pledged to protect the white workers from the wage-cutting competition of the unskilled African majority. The powerful mining industry attempted to adjust matters by a quota system in which it undertook to maintain a ratio of not more than ten blacks to one white worker; the African workers being then about 300,000, there would be employment for some 30,000 whites. This, however, was not enough for the new Government which applied to the railways, public works and lesser trades a sweeping, exclusive plan which it called a 'civilized labour policy'; this arbitrarily scheduled a variety of jobs as 'white' and ensured, as it was designed to do, that natives were extruded wherever the appropriate wage was fixed at the rate needed to maintain 'civilized' standards. The Government decided next that the quota was not enough to safeguard white interests even in the mines. Underground mining (dangerous work that calls for stringent safety precautions) had not unnaturally established practices which had hardened into regulations that gave Europeans of the Mine-workers' Union a monopoly of the highly paid and dangerous operations. But, ruling almost in the very words of Lord Mansfield, the Courts in the case of Hildick Smith, 1923, disallowed these regulations on the ground that only positive law can exclude a particular class. The Nationalist Government coming in the following year, 1924, set about altering this as soon as it could override a hostile Senate, and in 1926 passed the Mines and Works Amendment Act which scheduled the dangerous trades as for whites only, thus creating the first statutory 'colour bar'.

Onlookers, especially those in Britain who were conscious of their own African responsibilities, had long known that regressive ideas flourished in some South African circles; but the liberal Cape Policy (Chapter 5) had never before been seriously shaken and was still, as in 1910, believed to be strong enough to prevail in the end. Now five years of consideration of matters affecting the African population, and two years of a not exclusively Nationalist Government, had brought only restrictions, and the exclusions culminating in this unblushing colour bar. Yet revulsion against these methods blinded critics in Britain to the fact that it was the competition of poor whites with poor blacks from which the trouble had started. The difference of colour of the rivals made, and still makes, their interests harder to reconcile, but the conflict had its roots in the low and unequal attainments of Africans. Opinion in Britain was already predisposed to ignore such inequalities, and from this point onwards theorists neglected or played down the contribution which the white peoples could effectively make to the necessary raising of African standards. Refusing to see or acknowledge how much whites had already done to give Africans new opportunities, critics turned not only against any extension of white settlement, as in Kenya, but against the Europeans already there.

The settlers themselves certainly took note of South Africa's troubles, but in a negative way; they were not going to be caught making the same mistakes. So in 1930 I found Rhodesian leaders pressing for a Land Apportionment Act with the avowed and prime intention of making their native reserves really 'adequate'; four years later, in the same hope, and with the guidance of the same Commissioner, Sir Morris Carter, Kenya sub-divided itself (see p. 183) into separate tribal units. Tribal lands were doubtless still necessary, but even South

African experience had failed to demonstrate the impolicy of working on the assumption that the great mass of the people must be insulated from any active economic life; the really stubborn task is to regulate the inevitable contact of the races.

The South Africans then in the ascendant were bent on reliving their country's past; but officially their programme was proclaimed as *segregation*, the ending of the native difficulty by separating black from white, territorially and socially, in the sphere of economics as quickly as might be convenient, and—politically. An unrecorded, all too short chapter in the history of that phase in South Africa relates to the attempt of a few local critics to keep their politicians' attention on *present* realities, and shows how desirable it is always to keep such doctrinaires well baited with the hard facts they shun. This task was successfully carried out for a while by the bodies known as Joint Councils of Europeans and Natives, which had been set up in Johannesburg and other centres on the advice of the American Phelps Stokes Mission which toured the Union on the eve of the Rand troubles of 1922. These Councils gave African spokesmen, to whom Parliament was closed, a platform from which to air their grievances. They owed much of their effectiveness to the first chairman of the Johannesburg Council, the late Howard Pim; himself a Quaker, he instinctively avoided taking decisions by vote, feeling his way rather towards 'the sense of the meeting'; any knotty point unresolved was left over to another meeting when grievances hotly felt but really insubstantial had usually faded. Thus the mere 'airing' might be sufficient; the criticism of sympathetic Europeans often served to put things in a new light. But when an African grievance was substantial, sub-committees, which included some of the ablest lawyers in South Africa, set to work and embodied the essence of their complaint in such weighty memoranda as Africans by themselves could never have achieved (and which the Government found embarrassing!). The very success of the Councils, unfortunately, seemed to ask that the movement be put on a national basis; but in any meeting at a national centre African participation was harder to secure and the vitalizing African contribution was inevitably watered down or altogether lost. The Institute of Race Relations which succeeded the Joint Councils operated in a vaguer context and, in the spirit of the age, shifted the emphasis from the particulars of administrative detail to the generalities of race relations. This was to accept battle on the emotional plane the nationalist politicians had already chosen and were fast making their own.

The Nationalists in general had no flair for facts or fact-finding, but the pace-makers of their movement had a genius for side-stepping stubborn realities by an appeal to the national emotions. Their own Prime Minister, General Hertzog, who had in all sincerity pronounced for *segregation* as the remedy for the country's ills, felt himself bound in honour to make this proposal specific. In the 1927 session of Parliament he therefore tabled four related draft bills: additional land for native occupation (as promised when the 1913 Act was passed) was at last to be provided, and a Native Representative Council set up, but only on condition that disfranchisement was accepted and the Cape Native voters removed from the common electoral roll. A further bill proposed to accept as voters coloured men who passed a civilization test, but still on condition that the proposed separate African representation was accepted. For two sessions a Select Committee to which the bills were remitted wrestled with detailed criticisms like those embodied in a Joint Council memorandum. With the Chairman, and an African member, it was my privilege to give evidence in support of our memorandum. During three full morning sittings of the Committee the Nationalist members took virtually no part, till in the last half-hour, turning with relief from administrative complexities, they woke up to question us in a body on the electoral bills. The reason was transparent; the political thinking of these Nationalists (like the revolutionary strike of 1922 which made the party's fortune), had two main springs; one was the reasonable anxiety to protect poor whites against indiscriminate African competition, the other a passion to avenge the overthrow of the Boer republics. In the heat of discussion these two were easily fused into one. The Nationalist politicians could already claim to have done much to save the poor whites, at least for the present; but only let the Afrikaner *volk* stand united and their power would both avenge the two republics that fell in 1900 and safeguard the future by putting up one bigger, better Afrikaner republic, pledged, in the spirit of 1840 as embodied in the *Grondwet* of 1858 (see Chapter 6), to permit no equality between coloured and white in Church or State. Only an Afrikaner republic would serve: it was no matter that many thousands of their white countrymen, being of mixed Afrikaner and British blood, are mere *South Africans*—the Cape tradition was un-Afrikaner and intolerable; the non-white voters it permitted might tilt the balance against the republic and must be removed. Their mild and generous General Hertzog had gone further than the mass of the party liked by conceding political rights to coloured persons. But the republican motif had to be played softly—a republic would come by popular consent when the time was ripe. There is one Nationalist nightmare—the

President of the Kruger model republic was chief executive and not a mere titular head—the loading by the 1910 constitution of their *platteland* constituencies might give them a parliamentary majority, but a straight popular election might still give them a president of *the wrong political complexion!* Coloured voters they knew to be overwhelmingly anti-Nationalist; to get rid of their votes would help—and at any rate make up to a dozen marginal Cape seats safe for their party. When therefore the pivotal Franchise Bill failed to get the two-thirds majority required by the Union constitution for any invasion of Cape voting rights, the Party was easily reconciled to sacrificing all the Prime Minister's Bills; almost at once, in 1929, it appealed to the country for a comprehensive mandate, not to establish a republic, but to 'save white civilization'. The 'Black Peril' election returned the Nationalists to power with an independent majority that left them free of labour support.

By a series of historical chances the attempt to implement the Nationalist programme was delayed for most of twenty years, till its inner springs had become forgotten. In 1931 the country was hard hit by the economic depression and by 1932 the Government itself so badly shaken that, early in 1933, General Hertzog was driven to agree to form a national ('Fusion') Government with General Smuts as deputy premier. The straiter Nationalists, under Dr. D. F. Malan, were left in a small minority and retired to sulk in opposition. But just before 'Fusion' the country was forced off the gold standard (to which the Nationalists had obstinately adhered chiefly to vindicate their complete independence of Great Britain); then, to the discomfiture of the Nationalists in opposition, the new Government drew all the benefit of the higher price paid for Rand gold in the free market, and the country entered on a prolonged period of prosperity and 'full employment' in which the burden of poor whites ceased to count. In 1939 Hertzog broke with Smuts on the war issue and went into opposition (where Dr. Malan's Nationalists disavowed him), leaving Smuts to carry on as Prime Minister. Even had he not been preoccupied by the war Smuts believed emphatically in leaving well alone. His opponents often quoted against him the phrase 'Let things develop' (used by him of the 1922 strike before he marched against the strikers); they may never have heard how in 1926 he clinched our conversation about the colour bar when he deprecated the Nationalists' passion for 'native' legislation: 'They forget that in South Africa we are on the edge of an abyss.' When at last the Nationalists recovered power in the shrunken world of 1948 their policy was almost universally condemned, by a world taken by surprise, as anti-black racial discrimination; their critics still failed to realize that unchecked wage competition of black with white would be discrimination against white. Such far-off economic causes were forgotten in a very changed economic situation. Nationalist policy partly escaped thus the censure it deserved for the wanton appeal made to anti-black racial prejudice for reactionary party political ends. Their major aim was and still is a Republic on a *voortrekker* model.

Before ever South African reaction had gone, in 1933, almost underground, British African policy had begun to take a decided move forward. Changes and chances in Africa itself may have been decisive, but a necessary first step was directly facilitated by the decline at last of the old *laissez-faire* economics. The pre-1914 Liberals neglected the colonies, but their work for the welfare state at home now made it accepted doctrine that there is much a state should do that it alone can. The older Colonial Office conspicuously lacked anything fitting it to serve as an agent of social betterment; till well after 1918 its subdivisions were purely geographical, each concerned only with its own particular group of territories—they were like so many post offices receiving and despatching letters. Both Mr. L. S. Amery, the Secretary of State from November 1924 to 1929, and his Under-Secretary, Mr. Ormsby-Gore (Lord Harlech), had a concern for and some knowledge of the dependencies and of their basic human needs; these, it was obvious, could be supplied only from without, but first the Colonial Office itself had to be equipped to deal with matters like health and education with the consideration demanded by a steadily growing volume of thought and research. Permanent expert advisers were accordingly brought in, for education in 1925, for medicine in 1926, for agriculture in 1929. These and later appointees formed advisory committees of leading outside authorities to provide the Secretary of State with expert guidance on his specific problems; the Advisory Committee on Education, for example, issued in 1925 the first comprehensive study of African education. This important document owed some of its realism to the personality of its Secretary; Major (Sir) Hanns Visscher was one of many called in at this time to apply Lord Lugard's Northern Nigerian experience for the general good. Outside experience was not in fact always called in when it should have been; as late as 1933 the Office was toying with the idea of throwing open an important minefield to exploitation by small independent 'diggers'; as in Rhodesia earlier, it was still afraid of the strong and efficient mining 'groups': it was then a senior official let fall to me the cautious comment that such 'magnates' were 'the devils who made the Boer War'! The 'diggers' were not this time let loose, but the Office has never faced the expense of employing a full-time mining expert. A Labour Adviser was, however, appointed in 1938, and before war broke out in 1939 the work of the Office for Social Services had been supplemented by the establishment of an Economic Department to deal with 'Development'.

Once the Office was better placed to know what needed doing, the next step was to provide 'bodies'. The Colonial Service got its name in regulations issued as long ago as 1837; but old tradition died hard and, in practice, the older colonies, including the West Indies, made do largely with local talent. Living strictly 'of their own', they appointed their servants for life and paid them what they could afford (which was often very little). Transfer to other colonies was the exception; Mr. Amery told me at the time how disturbed he was by the weak staffing of the South African Protectorates he visited in 1926. The reason for Lord Lugard's resort to 'indirect' rule was precisely that the tropical colonies had no trained local talent to draw on. Not even Nigerian emirates, however, could provide efficient advisory and supervisory officers, and (after inquiry in 1929–30 by a Commission under Sir Warren Fisher of the Treasury) a Personnel Division set about organizing recruitment for what in 1932 became the unified Colonial Administrative Service; a well-selected team of men then became available for appointment by the Secretary of State to whatever colony or dependency might need their services. In the following years most of the professional, scientific and technical services were also unified—law, education, health, agriculture, some specialisms like survey and audit, or whatever else was necessary for state-building.

This re-equipment of the Colonial Office and of the Colonial Service reflected an awakening of public opinion above all in the academic circles from which officialdom is normally drawn. After a war in which many dons were civil servants colonial subjects now got some airing; in Oxford senior common rooms, in undergraduate societies, at special conferences, colonial governors and many lesser lights were in demand as speakers. It was at this time, too, after 1927, that the late Bronislav Malinowski (p. 23) gave a mighty stimulus to the study of African custom from his Chair of Social Anthropology at the London School of Economics. University curricula were not much affected but, as B. Litt. and Ph.D. degrees came more into fashion, colonial history and economics supplied obvious themes. Specialist studies sometimes turned men to look for outlets in the Colonial Service, but more often it was the rapidly growing popularity of this service that stimulated colonial studies. Between the wars the Colonial Service was drawing from all the universities men like those who formerly entered the

Indian Civil Service (I.C.S.); there were only not nearly enough of them for all the work waiting to be done.

For the guidance of the new service in the inter-war years there were, besides *The Dual Mandate*, Lord Lugard's *Political Memoranda* embodying the detailed rules worked out during his governorships, first in the north, and later in the unified Nigeria which he left only in 1918. Lugard had realized at once, back in 1902, that he could never hope to get a large enough white staff to govern this large country 'directly'. His men tramped hundreds of miles to reach their stations; to keep their health in a deadly and a then still undefeated climate, they must have adequate 'loads' (bed, bath, filter, kitchen-ware, food and stores of many kinds), which meant also an army of porters; the cost of any adequate white staff would be prohibitive. It happened, however, that the north was predominantly Muslim country, the one and only part of negroid Africa where there were solid foundations to build on. Here alone the indigenous rulers had *viziers* and treasurers, besides *mallams* learned in Koranic law and in the habit of administering it, and also an established system of direct taxation; at Kano and elsewhere there was even intensive cultivation of individually owned land. The answer was to keep the old order functioning. It should not be hard to win the confidence of the local rulers and, that done, the influence and prestige of the white officers might hope to check and reform abuses and to lead rulers and people in new and better ways. Lugard's guiding principle, accordingly, was that indirect rulers must not take charge: they must on no account give orders; even on tour officers must take the representative of emir or chief with them, and deal with village heads only through this agent. There were to be no Commissioners acting in the King's name, only Residents and *political* officers, attached to a recognized Native Administration (N.A.). The treasury, where it existed, was carefully nursed, and new treasuries were set up where there had been none before. The N.A. character even of the treasury was strongly asserted—audit was a function of the local political officer, not of the central Audit Department. The status of the N.A. was sometimes unduly magnified. When indirect rule had been developed and become an exhibit a waggish Frenchman is said to have defined the system as *Gouvernement de parapluie!* The white man was still the real ruler but thus discreetly put himself out of sight! The strict indirect rulers became so assertive of N.A. rights that Sir Donald Cameron, Governor after 1931, was once provoked to remind one of them: 'There is only *one* Nigeria!'

The new school of indirect rulers believed, with some justification, that theirs was a surer means of getting things done than 'direct' rule had ever been. A communist police-state will undoubtedly make its 'direct' authority sharply felt in every part of its sphere, but no British colonial administration was ever effectively dictatorial. I learnt my lesson once and for all in a sufficiently 'directly' ruled Rhodesian tribal district. One very wet day a keen Native Commissioner took me a bare ten-mile drive, on an unbelievable 'road', to call on his leading chief. By this time I was well used to the bustling activity of the more active sort of N.A.; here I quickly realized that such officers' annual tax tours were the occasion for a general palaver on tribal affairs, including much more than tax-collecting. Equally obviously, a 'directly' ruled chief might go eleven months of the year and neither see nor hear another 'ruler', except the odd police messenger. Lord Lugard's experiment was the first serious attempt to bridge the gap inevitably separating the African people from their white rulers. Some of the best authorities disapproved of the term indirect rule, always insisting that their great objective was, rather, to develop *local* government. It was in fact in the sphere of local government that the Nigerian experiment won its most notable successes; the Northern Nigerian Residents made amazingly little parade of force but clearly had central authority behind them when they cleared and re-formed the local prisons; so too when, if they did not quite end domestic slavery, they at least drove it underground. Undesirable practices doubtless continued of which the political officers knew little; but the records of the native courts were regularly checked; more and more courts were required to keep records; and in the last resort there was now an appeal to the Nigerian Courts. Northern Nigeria is to be credited, too, with a pioneering attempt to reform African taxation. By long tradition (originating at the Cape) a poll-tax at a flat rate was universal—except in Sierra Leone which had an even less desirable hut-tax; this regressive source of revenue had nothing but its simplicity to recommend it. The individual assessment of illiterate people being all but impossible, Nigerian officers attempted an assessment by districts; they even left it to villages to sort out their individual payments among themselves. The qualifications of political officers as valuators were unfortunately too unequal for the plan to be approved by the fiscal authorities; but a little was done to temper the wind to the lamb about to be shorn by grading the rate of tax to allow the people of the poorer districts to escape more lightly. This practice soon became almost normal in other colonies.

Experiment on Lugard's principles ran into difficulties among the very different and highly diverse peoples of Southern Nigeria. From the beginning the loosely tribal, or tribally mixed and, at the higher levels, quite advanced communities of Lagos and other towns could only be left to be ruled 'directly' as before. The more 'primitive' people of the oil-palm forest belt had to be provided with chiefs to get their N.A.s working efficiently, and ex-Army sergeant-majors were appointed by 'warrant' to supply this want. Chiefs of any kind were a novelty among this undisciplined people; when these strangers were set to assess their districts for direct taxation, this was too much! The simultaneous coming of chiefs and of equally unheard-of direct taxation produced at the end of 1929 the serious outbreak known as the Aba Riots, which also made the authorities uncomfortably aware of the necessity of allowing in any Southern N.A. for the unusual economic status of women. In spite of this set-back, a steady stream of Northern officers, versed in indirect rule, was directed in these years to governorships and secretaryships all over the Empire, even to distant Malaya; members of that established Service who knew little more of Africa than Pliny had done sometimes referred to such recruits as *aliquids*!

The most important transplantation came in 1925 when the very able West Indian, Sir Donald Cameron (not a Northerner at all but an old hand at the Lagos Secretariat), was appointed Governor of Tanganyika to bring order to that war-torn and still predominantly 'bush' mandated territory, in which the Germans had deposed many errant chiefs and set up others by 'warrant' in their stead. Realizing that the deposed chiefs still enjoyed the loyalty of their own people, Sir Donald made it a principle that the N.A. must be attached to the person of the *de jure* ruler whoever and wherever he might be; a new rule gained currency—'First find the Chief!' But Cameron (a 'secretariat wallah' and, as such, not entirely approved of by the purer indirect rulers), refused to be bound by the rules of the *Political Memoranda*; more than once I heard him protest that no one can hope to administer a district 'in a strait waistcoat'. His fixed purpose was to set up not native administrations but Native *Authorities*. Once 'found', the chief must be vested with real authority and held directly responsible for his official actions and those of his N.A. A burst of activity followed in Tanganyika comparable only with that of the stronger Nigerian emirates, where many public services such as water-supplies and lighting became N.A. functions. I was fortunate to travel through much of Tanganyika in 1930 when Sir Donald's energy was at a peak. His grasp of local detail clearly kept his officers 'on their toes'; as in Nigeria they were *political* officers, *D.O.s* and not D.C.s, and his test of efficiency was what a D.O. left behind him when he left, not what he himself did. By this time the recruiting of special service officers was improving and the best Tanganyikan districts were actively promoting N.A. schools and dispensaries, model farms or seed farms, roads and bridges; some tribally-organized, anti-tsetse bush-clearing was particularly striking. But the condition of the most active district of them all some twenty years later made it clear that the zeal so evident in 1930 had a good deal of it been due, after all, to the personality of the European D.O.

The vogue of indirect rule certainly won more attention for African reconstruction, perhaps even gave a greater stimulus in five or ten years than more direct methods had done in twenty or thirty. But there was a weakness. The rule was to build only on indigenous African custom; for according to the new functional anthropology a break with custom at any one point might upset the delicate balance of tribal institutions. New functions, therefore, must not be unduly pressed for fear of causing general disintegration. It was not African custom to pay regard to health, education, and agriculture; the reconstruction services were therefore at a disadvantage; a trained doctor called out to cope with an epidemic of plague or smallpox must not give the chief orders but only advise him. Native Authority 'bush dispensaries' were only better than nothing. The growing enthusiasm of the more academic indirect rulers for building on African institutions became a doctrine and made British policy for once almost doctrinaire and evasive of awkward realities. The Negro-inspired American stress on race, now a growing force, told in the same direction; the fashionable academic study came to be racial contact—evidently the root cause of African 'detribalization'. The ultimate question of how to link so many Native Authorities with the central government was never faced at all.

On this, the political aspect of reconstruction, Lord Lugard himself pronounced more than once that the ballot-box politics of parliamentary democracy would be inappropriate and undesirable. N.A., in some unspecified way, was to provide the alternative, but here was the essential weakness of the tribal approach. Many of the most influential Africans were civilized men with western ideas and western ways of life and thinking, and these middle-class citizens of great West African towns like Lagos or Accra, being ineligible for membership of any N.A., were left high and dry; for them indirect rule was clearly impossible, but even the strengthening of existing legislative assemblies ceased to interest the orthodox. On all these matters the rule was, with growing emphasis: 'Go slow!' Active development either of the reconstruction services or of the political machinery was frowned on, as if time were no object. One Jomo Kenyatta of the Kikuyu tribe (see Chapter 11) was among those who sat through seminars in London, drinking in all he heard about the perfect balance of African institutions. There were others who, when they came to plump at last for full self-government, did so without the training those locust-eaten years had failed or positively refused to provide for them.

Change, together with a speeding up of the racial 'contact' which the fashionable school feared and abhorred, was precipitated on a seismic scale by the war; but at least the change was not unheralded. More material factors than custom and institutions were coming under scrutiny for some years before that upheaval. The world depression of 1931 hit the dependencies hard. The Empire Marketing Board, while it lasted (1926–33), and the Ottawa Agreements of 1932 were primarily concerned with the Dominions, but both the disabilities of primary producers in world markets and the generally poor productivity of the dependencies could not quite escape notice. In the winter of 1932, after Ottawa, Mr. Lionel Curtis, leader of the influential *Round Table* group which gave the Commonwealth its name, took to heart a suggestion that their Journal of Commonwealth affairs, *The Round Table*, was unduly neglecting the dependencies of the Empire. His ponderings bore fruit in the following summer when plans were matured that sent Lord Hailey on the African mission first hinted at in General Smuts's Oxford lectures of 1930. Mr. Curtis's first idea was that an administrator with non-African experience should do a quick comparative 'once over' of the African dependencies and produce a report of the kind that would 'go on sale on the railway book-stalls at a price of five shillings'. The complexities of Africa, and the uncommon thoroughness and industry of Lord Hailey himself, ruled otherwise; experts and specialists of many sorts were inspanned to make their contributions and Lord Hailey returned from his own comprehensive travels to deal with volumes of reports and special memoranda. His encyclopaedic *African Survey* appeared ultimately in 1938; it stands as a challenge to others to make sure first of the basic facts of the African situation.

Any person of normal sensibility travelling in the tropical dependencies in the early '30s could not fail, I imagine, to recognize physical suffering due to disease and ill health as one of these basic facts. The good doctor was almost bound to be the hardest worked man on any station; he was commonly also the best of guides to the student of living conditions. It is fitting that the most notable advance made in the inter-war years was in the study of African health, in particular of the effects on the people's health of their indifferent nutrition. The bitter experience of the troops who served in the East African campaign was one lasting lesson. But the great mining houses, those both of the Rand and of the Belgian Katanga, were still earlier pioneers in this field. Their motives were utilitarian as well as humane: native workers were brought great distances at high cost and had to be well cared for. At once appreciating the significance of the discovery of the vitamins about 1912, they began experimenting; rations of mealie-meal were supplemented by cooked dinners; instead of the old monotony of carbohydrates, regular meat was served cooked with green vegetables; and cocoa was provided between the shifts. There was a visible improvement in physique and efficiency, showing that better nutrition was both desirable and necessary. Such organized experiments were possible only in the rather highly regimented compounds of the great southern mines, but the study of nutrition made progress elsewhere. In 1930 Dr. W. E. McCulloch made a report from Northern Nigeria on the *Dietaries of the Hausas and Town Fulani*, and in 1931 the Medical Research Council published a comparative study by J. B. Orr (Lord Boyd-Orr) and Dr. J. L. Gilks of the vegetarian Kikuyu and their blood-drinking neighbours, the Masai.

The hunt was taken up at a high official level and, also in 1931, the Colonial Office itself published the illuminating replies of various governments to a circular dispatch from Lord Passfield, *Papers relating to Health and Progress* among certain native populations, not exclusively African. Local committees now continued the work—bits and pieces appeared from time to time till in 1936 the *Economic* Advisory Council appointed a very strong sub-committee to correlate their reports. Health and nutrition thus became more than a hobby of medical specialists; those who made the final report included not only the leading nutritionists, but economists, at least one agriculturist of standing, Sir Frank Stockdale, various educationists including Sir Hanns Visscher, and Professor Malinowski's chief assistant, Dr. Raymond Firth.

A two-volume report on *Nutrition in the Colonial Empire* was ready only in July 1939, just in time to be almost forgotten when war followed in September: five years later I found that the devoted American doctors wrestling, at a well-appointed hospital in Liberia, with defective nutrition, and positive malnutrition, had never heard of it. The published evidence was conclusive that not only in our own dependencies, but throughout the tropical world, 'native' diet is defective and unbalanced, short of animal protein (meat and milk) and insufficiently protective against the onset of active disease. Afflictions with strange names like *kwashiorkor* are the result of chronic malnutrition, especially in childhood. The causes of this widespread malnutrition are ignorance, inexperience, poor husbandry and poor food-storage; its effects are indifferent physical health, loss of mental alertness, a generally low standard of material well-being; the remedy, clearly, must be education and welfare services rather than political and constitutional reforms. It was a fortunate chance that these broadly-based conclusions were clearly impressed at any rate on the official mind before the war brought its distractions. It was also fitting that the opportunity of trying (in official phrase) to 'implement' them—and also Lord Hailey's teaching—was provided in the end by events in the older colonies of the West Indies.

The truth is that all the dependencies were really very small beer throughout those inter-war years. The West Indies had long been out of the picture; in the early '30s the standard book was still J. A. Froude's complacent account of *The English in the West Indies*, published in 1888. But for that matter, though indirect rule and 'the Kenya Question' make a long story, even these African themes were the active concern chiefly of a small body of enthusiasts. The Colonial Development Act of 1929, fruit of Mr. Amery's efforts, provided only a beggarly £1 million a year, and that was to be spent with an eye always to its helping to ease the lot of unemployed at home. The general public heard a good deal about the Dominions and the development of the Commonwealth, but many were excusably uncertain where the new Commonwealth began or the older Empire ended. Even the Commonwealth Group *par excellence*, the *Round Table*, hardly helped; their awakening discovered Lord Hailey, but that was only in 1933. I have before me a letter from Mr. Geoffrey Dawson, Editor of *The Times*, a close associate of the group, telling me in May 1932 that (Sir) Reginald Coupland agreed with him that it would be inappropriate 'to revive the Native Problem in Africa' in *The Times* at that moment! The topic suggested was Rhodesian, and the Ottawa Conference may have made it a bad moment; but the use in a Rhodesian context of the South African phrase, 'Native Problem', throws light on the ruling 'climate of opinion'. Many humbler people were further confused by the colonial propaganda of the 'unsatisfied' powers, or of Hitler and Mussolini; the stirrings of the guilt-complex of the English Puritan tradition have often worked like a paralysis. Perhaps only Malaya was regarded with some complacency; tin and the rubber plantations brought in a good return, apparently for all classes, and Singapore flourished; but few had any idea how much even Malaya's passing prosperity owed to preventive health measures. Enlightened Malayan employers had been prompt to use the talent of Sir Malcolm Watson to apply anti-malarial measures against the anopheles mosquito. Their example had no serious imitators or followers, public or private, till development began in the '30s in the Rhodesian Copper Belt.

It is thus not surprising that the West Indies were still all but forgotten when Kenya and Rhodesia were beginning to cause concern. Lord Olivier, who should have known, was actually one of several who strongly urged me to check my African studies by going to see how much better things were managed in the West Indies. The condition of the islands as I found them in the early months of 1935 moved me to record my impressions in an unpremeditated book called *Warning from the West Indies*, published in 1936; the Colonial Office, I have reason to believe, was one of the few places where the book was read (at least till it was reissued in the *Penguin* series in 1938 when explosions of discontent had brought the islands well 'into the news'). Mr. Ormsby-Gore put it tersely in answering a parliamentary question in February 1938: 'Disturbances involving casualties occurred in Jamaica, St. Kitts and St. Vincent in 1935, and in the Bahamas, Barbados, Jamaica and Trinidad in 1937.' It was a clear example of revolution threatening, not in the smaller islands where distress was most acute, but rather where there was a visible prospect of better things: the oil-fields gave Trinidad substantial revenues, and hope for the future; Jamaica was always in fairly close touch with the outside world and now enjoyed the spirited leadership of the returned emigrant who was to become Sir Alexander Bustamante. Trinidad was the subject of an *ad hoc* inquiry in 1937, but in the end there was nothing for it but a full-scale Royal Commission. This body was appointed in July 1938. By the time its Report was ready in 1940 France was collapsing and Britain bracing herself to 'stand alone'. The Cabinet decided, in its wisdom, that publication at such a moment would be a gift to Nazi propaganda and kept dark this tale of colonial misery; no more appeared than a 'Statement of Conclusions'; but colonial grievances could not be ignored at such a crisis and the conclusions had point and force.

It was now that the indoctrination of the Colonial Office with the lessons of the Nutrition Reports and of the African Survey bore fruit. War had the effect at least of breaking down financial obstacles and Britain's very darkest hour saw the passing of the Colonial Development and Welfare Act of 1940. The age-old principle that each colony must 'live of its own' was tacitly dropped, and £5 million a year for five years set aside to finance

'the research and survey work, the schemes of major capital enter-

> prise and expansion of administrative or technical staffs which are necessary for the colonies' full and vigorous development',

including the more adequate health and education services such development was now seen to require; in addition, and this by Lord Hailey's teaching, £500,000 a year was set aside for research. In the war years effort was concentrated on the West Indies, where many began to learn with surprise that the spending of a round £1 million takes a good deal of planning and preparation; even there the Fund was often underspent. But the idea struck root. A second Act of 1945 raised the annual total to £10 million a year for ten years. British governments, with sufficient public support, had at last got some measure of the dimensions of the fundamental 'colonial problem'.

The lessons of colonial history were thus slow to sink in. It has the elements of tragedy that the full awakening to the effects of ignorance and poverty came only when British power was past its peak. With new understanding, and the best will in the world, we were short now both of man-power and of the resources needed for full-scale 'development', and had lost also the unchallenged prestige our representatives enjoyed in the pioneer days. And yet, as late as 1950 a Colonial Report carried a preface repeating a pronouncement of 1947–48:

> 'The central purpose of British Colonial policy is simple. It is to guide the colonial territories to responsible self-government within the Commonwealth in conditions that ensure to the people both a fair standard of living and freedom from aggression from any quarter.'

The old doctrine of the White Man's burden died hard; even in the new post-war world it was believed that H.M.G. would still lead. But this was to reckon without those unconsidered elements, the 'detribalized', largely 'westernized', middle-class politicians whom the anthropologists deplored, and British administrations studiously ignored or contrived to by-pass. These were now to assert their claim to recognition and set out, even clamorously, to take up the burden and carry it as they themselves saw fit. We stood thus, as suggested in the introduction to this book, on an '*emergents*' frontier'.

Chapter 10

THE POST-WAR DECADE

*

Almost before the Second World War was fully over the initiative was passing from those who would mend colonial rule to those who would end it altogether. This latest phase in colonial evolution may have something in common with that of the American Revolution, but the differences are significant. When the American colonists became a self-conscious community and saw the natural resources of their country obviously ample for their needs they themselves took charge; none could gainsay them. The natural resources of the colonies that remain colonies are slender, or else hard and costly to develop; none is a united community and only a most inadequate number of the people are qualified to man the services of a modern government. The American Revolution too was a spontaneous internal upheaval; the modern campaign for colonial freedom has taken much of its inspiration from without, from political theorists like the Indian leaders whose thesis would make the weakness and the disabilities of the colonial peoples not an original cause but an effect, the direct outcome of their subjection to colonial rule. Barely a generation ago there was general approval for the Covenant of the League of Nations' pronouncement that made colonial rule 'a sacred trust of civilization'. This judgment was dictated no doubt by the experience of Western statesmen and reflects the complete self-assurance which, in a phrase of the veteran Dr. Gilbert Murray, 'still dared to say that unequal things were unequal'; it could stand so long as western ascendancy was undisputed. Half the world is now in revolt against this Western assumption of superiority; yet the very idea of self-government, the professed aim of the new movement, is the purest western liberalism. The western powers, moreover, whatever their shortcomings, were the first consistent champions in history of the principle that world affairs should be governed by law. Our hope of a stable world order depends above all on how far the newer and less mature states attain to and develop standards approached, at their best, by the world's former leaders. The reaction which inevitably followed the self-immolation of western Europe in two world wars has overshot the mark.

It is only since the war that the planning of constitutional development has become a clear response to local demand. The principles were nothing new and fitted with comparative ease into the traditional scheme of things; self-government had long been the accepted goal (see Chapter 4), but the limited functions of the early *laissez-faire* governments were easily served without an elaboration of the machinery becoming a matter of any urgency; in spite of Joseph Chamberlain's lament that the colonies were like 'undeveloped estates' it was not till 1929 that his disciple, Leo Amery, secured his slender Development Act. The progressive Lord Olivier, Governor of Jamaica from 1907 to 1913, complained vigorously of the Treasury's addiction to annual budgets even for long-term items of expenditure, and he may have got his West Indian pupils imbued with the idea of state-aided *development*; forgetful of Chamberlain, he commended Mr. Lloyd George as the first to popularize 'the blessed word'. The constructive Fabianism Olivier himself professed found satisfaction in the Crown Colony system, which entrenched the executive yet did not offend his sense of what was due to the governed. To the end of his life his heroes were the 'strong' governors who preceded him, from John Peter Grant to Norman and Sir Henry Blake; as late as 1934, it will be remembered (p. 208), he felt no need for political change. The political peace and calm that reigned in the West Indies, in spite of their economic stagnation, stands to the credit of the Crown Colony system; even the discontents that blazed up in the later '30s had little political bite; but they served to force the appointment of the Royal Commission of 1938. Even so it took the solvent of war to clear the way for the Development and Welfare Act of 1940.

The systematic reconstruction to which colonial governments were committed by that Act was bound sooner rather than later to raise political questions and to necessitate constitutional adjustments. These implications were imperfectly diagnosed in advance; as a wholly British-born effort to meet the colonies' obvious needs the programme was to be planned to suit local peculiarities; but it was always with British funds and, therefore, always under home direction. In the West Indies, whose needs brooked no delay even in war-time, the first Comptroller, Sir Frank Stockdale, quickly found himself in a quandary; economic development was the obvious cure for the unemployment of a landless people, yet the physical disabilities of the workers made them unfit to carry new burdens till welfare services had in some measure relieved their immediate needs. The funds the Comptroller could hope for during the five years for which Parliament had provided were necessarily earmarked for getting things started; but such initial capital outlay at once created a need for more money to meet 'recurrent expenses'. Ultimate self-government, the avowed aim of policy, carries a corollary; any self-governing state must carry its own 'recurrents' and pay its own way. The Comptroller, therefore, must strike a just balance; welfare services being only indirectly if at all reproductive, their scale could not be determined solely by the people's needs but must be limited to what 'development' would give the islands some hope of carrying on by themselves. This and other lessons of early Colonial Development and Welfare experience have been much overlaid, in their haste, by later enthusiasts for immediate, untrammelled self-government. One evening Sir Frank threw out in conversation an illustration he could not be persuaded to use in a broadcast he was about to make; there was warrant, he admitted, for counting education, even compulsory education, to be development as much as welfare; but his staff had worked out that, in Jamaica alone, the staffing of schools for compulsory education would necessitate increasing the annual intake at training colleges from the actual 150 to 1,000. The island would need to build and equip schools and colleges on the enlarged scale, and to pay, recurrently, for the additional teachers; besides this, four or six times as many of its young people must be diverted into choosing school-teaching as their career. Ten years later this particular problem remained as intractable as ever. There is a distinction between enacting a new constitution, or even such a constructive piece of social legislation, and getting it effectively administered. Being new in their experience, the demands self-government must make on the colonial peoples can be expected to register only gradually.

The colonial governments were themselves caught rather unawares, and the West Indies Comptroller, for instance, served at least seven distinct administrations. Once London had checked and approved local projects, their officers found C.D. & W. funds at their disposal, in unusual amounts, often for cherished but hitherto unattainable objects. Many colonies, however, have continued to find it unexpectedly hard to spend large sums in strict accord with the standard set by H.M. Treasury; a straightforward educational programme will concern not only teachers and pupils, actual or potential, but also contracts with builders and contractors, the engagement of technicians and other 'bodies', as well as finding supplies and stores. Inevitable delays were not all of them due to war-time pressure on men's services, or to the shortage of supplies. In African territories there were sticklers for indirect rule who wanted development carried through only by the 'Native Authority'; when the N.A. failed, the central government was sometimes driven to make a gesture, such as the providing of 'public halls' that, it was hoped, would serve as 'community centres'; some of these were classifiable, for a time, only as of the genus white elephant! By 1945 the fashion was to think in terms of five-year plans—when in that year the annual grant was raised and its life extended to ten years there were some ten-year plans; even so, the C.D.W. fund long continued to be almost habitually underspent. The results of the experiment were inevitably less spectacular than some may have hoped; H.M.G. in fact earned less kudos than its gesture surely deserved.

The launching of the development programme had the unlooked-for effect of setting in train the first major overhaul of the institutional machinery of government. This came about not under political pressure —an important influence only after the war—but rather by the logic of necessity. When money flowed in, as never before, for the expansion of civil services or the betterment of agriculture, for roads and other public works, the technical departments had to be strengthened and new staff engaged. The lone D.C. could no longer cope single-handed with so much detail. Offices were in any case short of staff and overburdened with 'war work', and the Colonial Secretary man-of-all-work's back was finally broken, that old 'bottle-neck', the Secretariat, choked past hope of remedy. Here, the Financial Secretary was hurriedly up-graded to share the burden with the former Chief; there, departmental heads were given direct access to the Governor. One way or another, constitutional changes had to be made; and they were of a kind that at last made 'self-government' something more than the remote and ultimate ideal it had long been. When, later, colonial demands really became insistent, commanding sympathy also in the United Nations, the evolutionary process was already in full career. In this respect at least the ground was well prepared in advance.

The first considerable innovation was made largely to meet administrative necessity, but partly to satisfy the claims of the always restive white settler politicians of Kenya and Northern Rhodesia. The economic depression of the early '30s much abated these politicians' persistent sniping at their irresponsible executive governments; but the strains of war-time made it expedient to engage the sympathies of active colonists on whose goodwill the conserving of man-power and an increasing flow of supplies might depend. Much earlier, in 1931, political pressure and administrative convenience had both played a part in moving the

Donoughmore Commission to equip the premier Colony, Ceylon (which was virtually a nation state), with governmental committees planned to work on the L.C.C. system. This model was now passed over in favour of the so-called 'Member' system, a plan which had Indian precedent. With minor local variations the Member is, in effect, a minister charged with direct responsibility for one department, or more than one; but, unlike a 'responsible' minister, he need not be one of a parliamentary majority even if a member of the Assembly; he could also be a permanent official (e.g. the director of a functional department) or an 'unofficial' nominated private citizen. Yet some were popularly elected members of the Assembly: the director of man-power or supplies, for example, might usefully have political backing. The new system was improvised, and even anomalous; the Member might consider himself answerable to his constituents; but the Governor whom he served nevertheless remained the responsible head of the executive arm. One Governor, Sir Philip Mitchell, once described it as 'government by Quaker meeting'; the plan, in fact, worked tolerably smoothly so long as the lines of policy followed were in accord with the 'general sense' arrived at when Governor, officials and elected representatives sat to take counsel together. For the first time, at any rate, some of the public of a Crown Colony were directly associated with the government in framing their country's policy and in conducting its day-to-day administration.

The next move was in the comparatively experienced West Indies. The political consequences of the economic tensions of 1938 worked themselves out slowly and it was only in 1944 that a new constitution for Jamaica, the largest and most mature of the islands, was agreed upon. In principle it was the Member system that served here too, but the Members now became Ministers; five of these, together with the head of the largest party in the elected House of Representatives, a Chief Minister, joined three senior civil servants, sitting *ex-officio*, in the Executive Council. The Governor still presided over this enlarged body, but the demand for increased popular control was met by the introduction of universal adult suffrage. This unprecedented step was meant to ensure that the poorest and most depressed class, which is predominantly black, should pull its full weight; but it was taken at a time of stress which precluded the debate its importance merited. Jamaican conditions perhaps justified the venture; its peoples are divided indeed, but all are emphatically Jamaican first of all; if they are 'two nations', black and brown, these are also the basis of a ready-made two-party system. By the time the first elections under adult suffrage were due, popular political feeling was at last violently aroused, under popular leaders, and probably nothing less than adult suffrage could have satisfied the lively and egalitarian people. Barbados ultimately followed the precedent set by Jamaica, but not before it had, in spite of a more restricted franchise, elected a sufficiently popular government for itself. There are Barbadians, among others, who continue to think that the privilege of voting should be reserved for citizens who have first acquired some minimum of literacy, and that universal enfranchisement may not be a strictly necessary safeguard. Adult suffrage would certainly seem to be a highly questionable expedient to apply to the far less mature African colonies where, above all in the 'plural societies', the electorate includes highly disparate elements. The day when experiment was to be necessary there too was nearer than those responsible for the new Jamaican constitution realized. Quite suddenly political agitation became a force in many of these untutored and hitherto quiescent societies. 'Go slow' had been the sufficient watchword; now a leading indirect ruler suddenly pronounced in *The Times*: 'The time has come when the tempo must be increased'—as John Gilpin might have said when his horse bolted! Even before the end of the war the Colonial Office was working almost feverishly at the revision of colonial constitutions, great and small. The old principle of buttressing the executive by providing an official majority was generally abandoned, the local executive being left instead to keep on terms with a legislative assembly dominated by unofficial representatives; but all proposals were carefully framed to meet local idiosyncrasies, and always with due sense of the inevitability of gradualness. But very soon the spokesmen of two important African colonies, Nigeria and the Gold Coast, were making it plain that they were not prepared to accept such prefabricated constitutions —determined, rather, to follow ways of their own.

A sudden burst of self-assertion by peoples who had hitherto accepted their dependent status almost without question was the not surprising outcome of the germination of ideas under the stimulus of war. The abnormally active comings and goings of this second war more than ever widened human intercourse—with the disturbing effects Kipling had foreseen a generation earlier. Air fleets circling the world necessitated Allied and especially American air-bases, and these brought garrisons and streams of passers-by to many obscure and lonely colonial stations. Tens of thousands of Africans and others served far afield in Burma. At the same time their people at home were pressed to *produce* more and more—often by experts flying in and out, on impossibly quick missions, to stimulate supplies. A Second World War in the lifetime of one generation further shook the prestige of the western powers—more than ever when an eastern nation joined, triumphantly for a time, in challenging western ascendancy. This time, moreover, a strong body of educated men and women, the 'emergents' aforesaid, were making their own assessments. Modest but dynamic secondary education had taken effect. It had been only in the 1920s that colonial governments began a forward movement, stimulated and guided from London and by the Advisory Committee's review of African education in 1925 when Achimota, the most advanced school in West Africa, was opened. At that time Budo, in Uganda, was almost alone in East and Central parts; even in South Africa, which was considerably more progressive, African spokesmen were for a long time all 'Lovedale boys', trainees of the one outstanding school. The price was now to be paid for the gravest weakness of all earlier colonial policy. Even after the founding of secondary schools little thought was given to the future of their scholars; there seems to have been a hazy notion, left over from the days of *laissez-faire*, that they would put their energies to use and create new forms of wealth and employment for themselves. They, as was more natural, looked at once for the prestige-giving jobs already created, particularly those of government; but indirect rule made it more than ever official policy to govern through local chiefs and to preserve old custom. Originally this often chimed with practical convenience; but in the 1930s the practice left the growing middle class shut out from useful public work for the benefit of their own people, and therefore untrained for responsibility. The colonial system offered them no prizes and they had to find other means of livelihood and expression. One outlet left wide open was to launch into politics on their own account. It was thus that political journalism became the popular pastime in all the new countries.

The new intelligentsia, particularly strong in British West Africa, found little to attract them to share even in the war effort and for the most part stayed at home; but also during the war the number of those finding their way to British and other universities, formerly a trickle, was becoming a steady stream, and there was now a home audience for anything new they learnt. In their former isolation their destiny was almost exclusively bound up with that of their particular European metropolitan; so lately as 1938 Mr. Wallace Johnston, an advanced Creole politician who had already made things hot for himself in the Gold Coast, was rousing Freetown; the talk at a crowded meeting of his I attended one evening at the Wilberforce Hall was in fact pure British Labour Party! In the same year, however, the leadership of the

Jamaican masses devolved on Mr. (now Sir Alexander) Bustamante, a colourful personality who drew for inspiration on an intimate knowledge of the American way of life, and had some acquaintance too with the practice of Spanish dictators. The early war years saw the rise of Dr. Azikiwe, an Ibo, who was American-educated, and broke new ground in Nigeria as the proprietor and editor-manager of a chain of newspapers. The stream of nationalist disapproval that poured out on the British administration caused fully more pain than inconvenience to its officers; they had never before had their good faith and their credentials so violently challenged; in spite of official discountenance the latest number of the leading 'Zik' journal was usually obvious in the *In*-tray of government offices about 1944. Even before the war was over the dissemination of ideas had finally ceased to be a British monopoly. Their common use of the English language at once exposed not only the student class but also the stay-at-homes and their new journalists to the full blast, for example, of Indian Congress propaganda, to American Negro teaching on the baleful influence of race and colour prejudice, and to all the anti-imperialist or anti-colonialist doctrine which presently took the world stage—a highly explosive mixture. Communist influence was probably no more than a ferment; the academic rather than the international variety of this doctrine works potently enough through the intellectual 'fellow traveller' who hates to acknowledge that anyone can be more advanced politically than himself! This class is always a force, above all in the highly cosmopolitan student circles of London—and it was there that the most highly educated Africans now learnt to give shape to the tumult of new ideas breaking in upon them. The physical facts of Africa, the condition and the needs of its masses, counted for very little in an often confused debate. It was towards the end of the war that a London undergraduate gave it out that his first term's studies had been very profitable; he now knew what his grievances were! The student audiences I came to know well took unkindly any suggestion that Africa is on the whole ill served by nature, or that the disabilities of its peoples (who are no landless proletariat) arise in large part from the poverty of its resources. The Eastern spokesmen now provided them with a different and sufficient answer—the imperialism their even poorer people lived under had drained off the profit accruing from the use of cheap labour to exploit their countries' natural resources; colonial governments, even the D.C.s, were imperialist capitalist stooges. It counted for nothing that the D.C.s' functions were still so many and various just because the specialist departments were so inadequate, and even C.D. & W. had done little to train and use the growing educated class to fill the gaps. My friends were, I fear, less seriously concerned about the actual work waiting to be done, than aware of the office of D.C. as something desirable in itself, and even enviable, a post that would be better adorned by one of themselves. The outcome was a series of nationalist movements, set to overthrow the existing power and to bring the colonial governments under nationalist control. For a brave moment one of the much-harassed governments gave a lead. In 1946, taking time by the forelock, Sir Arthur Richards (Lord Milverton) promulgated a liberal (but tailor-made) constitution that was to serve Nigeria for nine years; this so-called Richards Constitution survived barely two. Nigeria being at least three distinct countries, an instrument which took full cognizance of the wants of the conservative Muslim North failed to meet the aspirations of the Christian-cum-pagan East and West. A more satisfying Federal Constitution was still preparing ten years later when the Gold Coast had shot ahead of Nigeria to become independent Ghana.

It was back in 1935 that a bright youth from the Gold Coast, one Kwame Nkrumah, set off to college with high hopes of returning to serve his country. Like Azikiwe he went not to Britain but to U.S.A. Nkrumah had some thought of becoming a Catholic priest, having been educated thus far at a Catholic mission school, but after ten fruitful *wanderjahre* he moved on to register as a candidate for the Ph.D. degree at the London School of Economics. His biographer says no more about the L.S.E.; a ceaseless round of political meetings obviously filled his two years in London. In 1947 he sailed at last for home. There, in 1949, he broke with the then ruling leaders and became the architect of a new and more closely-knit political party known as the C.P.P. (Convention People's Party). It was thus no spontaneous uprising that stirred the Gold Coast; the seed fell from without. The British contribution was the grant, on the new Jamaican model, of universal suffrage. Nkrumah set himself to court the masses, especially of the crowded towns of the Gold Coast Colony—with such success that the men recognized as African leaders when I resided in the Gold Coast at intervals between 1943 and 1945 passed quickly out of the primacy. This select class—men who had 'been to' British or other universities and once ruled the roost—now came to be known with scorn to the enormously increased and very lively local school population as 'been-to's'!—a term certainly not current in 1945. Kwame Nkrumah and his party quickly monopolized the fight—to the simple slogan, 'Self-Government Now' or, for short, 'S.G.N.'.

The moment was propitious. The war was over, but the loosening it effected in stiff political joints remained. In 1945 a general election had put a Labour Government in power in Britain. In 1947 India became independent. The price was partition; only the impartial imperial authority had held acutely divided sections together for so long, but the internal political situation made it impossible for the imperial administration to function. There were those in Britain who were ready to make a virtue of necessity; many even claimed kudos—without necessarily receiving it—for their magnanimity in voluntarily abandoning their Empire; a strong section of the ruling Labour Party always had guilty feelings about imperialism and welcomed the opportunity of practising positive virtue by disposing of an evil inheritance. Other former dependants were very ready to take the lead given them; Burma withdrew even from the Commonwealth. None of the colonies at this stage contemplated the Indian brand of complete independence; most were content for the Governors to retain reserve powers which left them ultimately responsible for law and order, if not also for 'good government'. But colonial leaders too were ready to claim that self-government is better than good government, and some of them—building on Mahatma Gandhi—were dangerously inclined to claim a sacred right even to *mis*govern themselves.

Expectancy thus ran high, especially in Nkrumah's Gold Coast where the prevailing political excitement culminated, early in 1948, in destructive riots in the capital, Accra. The sympathetic and liberal findings of a British Commission of Inquiry led to the appointment of a committee of legislators, all of them Africans, presided over by Mr. Justice (Sir Henley) Coussey, and their well-reasoned report became the basis of a new 'advanced' constitution which was approved by H.M.G. in 1950—but not before several of the leaders, including Nkrumah, had been given terms of imprisonment for 'positive action' in favour of more complete 'S.G.' immediately. At a general election early in 1951 the new mass electorate gave Nkrumah and his C.P.P. a triumphant majority and another die was cast. H.M.G. well knew the risk to good government, and the mere difficulty of finding Africans to staff so many ministries; but there is no doubt its advisers also pointed out that the only alternative to giving the elected representatives their way was to import troops and try to hold the country down by force of arms. The only choice left open was to summon Nkrumah straight from prison to take office as Chief Minister. The Governor, Sir Charles Arden Clarke, saw himself cast for the role of nurse to a bold experiment and showed the utmost patience; the Chief Minister, for his part, gave the sympathetic Governor his close co-operation, and worked steadily with him and like-minded British officers to make a smooth transfer of power and maintain effective administration. The many D.C.s who remained at their posts ceased to be direct representatives of the Crown, becoming instead Government Agents; the civil servant heads of departments became Secretaries to political ministers. Recruitment of administrative officers in Britain ceased forthwith; 'expatriates' were to be replaced and the service wholly 'Africanized' as soon as possible. The new ministers' aim was to keep their party's enthusiasm at top pitch by pressing on towards the goal of 'S.G. Now'! By 1955 the Gold Coast, though still technically a colony, was self-governing, with Nkrumah as its Prime Minister. The stage was set for the next step to full Commonwealth status in 1957.

Self-government may long have been the ultimate (and also 'bipartisan') objective of British colonial policy; but this Gold Coast development was by no means according to plan. It had been tacitly assumed that a more adult political status would follow of itself on social and economic advance. Colonial Office tradition puts it down to the Fabian Secretary of State, Sidney Webb, that for a few years after 1930 each colony's Annual Report purported to be a record of its 'social and economic *progress*'. As late as 1950, in the pronouncement already cited, the doctrine was explicit that political progress must be buttressed by corresponding social and economic development. The new Gold Coast, however, was for taking its political hurdle at once, at any cost. Education, it is true, was looked on even too confidently as the 'Open Sesame' to all the prestige of the West, and got a priority; the 620 government or 'aided' primary schools of 1949 had by 1955 become some 3,900—this last total manifestly including even more than the 2,900 listed in the earlier year as independent or 'bush' schools that had failed to qualify for State aid; English tradition had put quality before quantity.

An ambitious project also took shape for a dam on the Volta River to provide power for processing rich deposits of bauxite; incidentally, it would bring many thousands of acres of good land under irrigation. Work actually began on a harbour at Tema; the nearby capital city, Accra, had hitherto been served only by a rough surf-boat landing and needed something more efficient to handle heavy traffic to and from the Volta, as well as cocoa. It chanced that in the first years of Nkrumah and his ministers high cocoa prices kept Gold Coast revenues more than 'buoyant' without any special effort on their part; they were free, therefore, to indulge such ambitions while concentrating rather on formal constitutional advancement. The slow labour of social reconstruction, the necessity of which C.D. & W. was born, may even have suffered a set-back.

One day, when the Gold Coast was 'in the news', the reigning Secretary of State explained to me, a little regretfully but very decidedly, that his attempts to guide the policy of the emerging colonies must take account of 'the new climate of opinion' abroad in the world. The circumstance that British ideas no longer enjoyed any exclusive influence in British colonies became manifest more particularly when the other states emerging from dependence began to find the Assembly of the new-born United Nations a reverberating sounding-board for their opinions on the rights also of the colonial peoples. The League Covenant of 1920 had recognized degrees of dependence; its mandates were expressly graded; those of the A group, for the succession states of the former Turkish Empire, were temporary; thus Iraq and others were reasonably deemed to have served their apprenticeship under mandate and became full states members of the U.N. before 1950. B mandates applied to the former German colonies, chiefly in Africa, and were expected to be more enduring, if not permanent. The modern school incontinently heap all the more or less dependent peoples together as victims, past or present, of one and the same 'colonialism'. From the deliberations of the Bandung Conference of 1955 in Indonesia there emerged a so-called Afro-Asian *bloc* of states pledged to wage war in the U.N. Assembly against imperialism and colonialism in all its manifestations. The benevolent sympathy and support of the U.S.A. at once made the not in itself very formidable new *bloc* a force to reckon with. In the simple American tradition colonial rule is, by a very partial interpretation of certain historical events, the very antithesis of American democracy. But accumulated feelings of resentment underlie especially the Asian approach, making this not merely anti-colonialist but almost downright anti-Western. The self-assertiveness of many of the members of the family of nations is a measure of weakness, their passionate egalitarianism a measure of unequal attainment—and such things self-government can of itself do little to remedy. These peoples were once too cavalierly classed as 'backward' (a word the cult of equality put out of court). But enhanced political status also puts a stop to any fresh consideration of the facts of backwardness. The more emphatically the aspirations of the specifically colonial peoples were championed, the more their highly distinctive needs passed out of consideration. The colonial question is basically social and economic; it now came to be treated as if it were purely political.

The colonial powers quailed under a barrage and fled the field, making little attempt to defend their position. A leading Liberian once handsomely acknowledged the contribution made by colonial rule to the phenomenal progress of his century-old free republic's neighbour, the Gold Coast, or Ghana. But H.M.G. panicked. The deservedly honoured Colonial Service abruptly became H.M. Overseas Service. Self-government was so much the fashion that, in its name, the westernized Creoles of Freetown were lumped together with otherwise wholly tribal African Sierra Leone, a tiny minority in a self-governing unit. Other Creoles, the descendants of the Bay-men who made Belize, and are essentially West Indians, suffered a variant of the same experience. The colony of British Honduras, for whose existence they alone were the warrant, comprises some 9,000 square miles, richly afforested but poor, and the Creoles are little less than half of its slender 60,000 population. Rather than insist on this attractive but completely non-viable colony joining the Federation of the West Indies, with which alone it has real affinity, H.M.G. allowed its politicians to continue to toy with the idea of standing all alone in self-governing independence.

So much heady anti-colonialism was likely to provoke some reaction and this came, suddenly but not surprisingly, from the force of Afrikaner nationalism, long quiescent (see Chapter 9) but always watchful, and especially sensitive to the rise of a rival all-African national spirit. In 1948, to the discomfiture of General Smuts who had underrated their electoral strength, and certainly also to their own surprise, the Nationalists under Dr. D. F. Malan were returned to power with a clear majority. They turned with zest to a programme in no way modified by their fifteen years in querulous opposition. The direct republican cry, though always first in favour with their own elect, was consistently muted for fear of stirring the emotions of the English-speaking electorate. The country was now too prosperous to be deeply moved again by an appeal to protect 'poor whites'—yet the tacticians knew that their most powerful weapon was the latent fear of the black masses. In next to no time the doctors had re-worded the prescription; they would still 'save white civilization' but, discarding the heavy Latinity of 'segregation', they substituted the word *apartheid* in the homely Afrikaans idiom; this promised a clear and total separation of the races at each and every point of contact. Such a delusively simple answer could be reached only by men with their eyes fixed, not on the complex facts of the present but on the glamorous past, rigid traditionalists for whom history existed only in a received version, textually inspired. All they saw needful in the unbelievably changed South Africa of 1950 was a republic on the model of 1840. The 'proper relations' the *voortrekkers* then demanded are implicit in *apartheid*; they were tersely summed up by Nationalists in the phrase 'white *baas-skap*' (mastership).

Unlike the contemporary Secretary of State, the Nationalists took no account of changing climates of opinion; their unchanging tradition is to stand alone. It was therefore undismayed, though with pain and annoyance, that they at once found themselves doing battle with a strong and vocal world opinion. Attempts to restrict the competition of an Indian minority in Natal had long ago brought the Union into conflict with the youthful Gandhi and, later, with the Government of British India. After 1947 the disabilities laid on Asians were taken up by the free and independent states of India and Pakistan, and made the subject of strong representations to the United Nations. The Union answered with the legally incontrovertible plea that the action complained of was a matter of internal policy and, as such, outside the competence of the U.N.; but the U.N., in the prevailing state of opinion, and to the chagrin of South Africa, was susceptible to complaints of racial discrimination. International relations were now truly international; no concert of great powers any longer made decisions binding on the whole world, and the rights of the underprivileged were of especially lively general concern. A country said to be guilty of making second-class or outcaste citizens of its own subjects was acting contrary to the principles of the Charter to which U.N. states-members subscribed. The sufferers thus were assured of sympathy and the grievances of Asians in South Africa became a hardy annual at meetings of the U.N. Assembly. The debate was exacerbated by the Union's steady refusal to acknowledge any responsibility to the U.N. Trusteeship Council for its administration of the former League of Nations Mandate, South-West Africa, a large but desolate region which the original grant expressly allowed it to rule as an integral part of the Union. Year after year critics insisted that the Union which, in the name of *apartheid*, was now subjecting not only Asians but its own African majority to laws deemed to be racially discriminatory, must render a full account of its dealings with its mandated peoples. Claiming that this too was a matter of internal policy, and finding that, unlike the older Mandates Commission (an expert, specialist body), the newer Trusteeship Council was a cross-section of the U.N. Assembly (overwhelmingly non-colonial and at any rate anti-colonialist), the Union Government was driven to refusing point-blank to recognize the interfering U.N. as the lawful heir to the Allied and associated powers from whom the mandate derived. Mounting criticism of its undoubtedly internal 'native' policy did nothing to divert the Union from its course; but at last, in 1956, South Africa deliberately cut itself adrift and renounced all but a 'token' membership of the U.N. In spite of this the debate carried on in the glaring publicity of New York for ten critical post-war years had long since established the Union Government's domestic doings as front page world news—of itself a startling development.

In the Nationalists' estimation political *apartheid* always came first; one part of their object had already been gained for them—the price Smuts paid for 'fusion' with Hertzog was an Act of 1936 which decreed separate representation for Africans on a communal roll. After 1948, having long ago repudiated General Hertzog's tenderness for civilized coloured folk, they were set to get coloured voters also removed from the common roll. But the 'entrenched' clauses of the Constitution still stood and cost them a long struggle. Only after winning another election, and fighting two test cases, they finally eluded the constitutional obstacle (and the Court of Appeal) by packing the Senate—and that only in 1955. All the more because of enforced delay the party had to show its resolve to keep its promises. Afrikaner leaders lean at any time to the habit of their Teutonic rather than of their more pragmatical Anglo-Saxon cousins, and are happier working to a set theory than at administrative detail; and certainly their simpler rank and file are readily persuaded to accept *apartheid* on the statute book as evidence of *apartheid* well on the way to being achieved. When, therefore, the move against the coloured vote failed to make headway in their first years of office they turned at once to prohibitions and barriers that were at once spectacular and irritating—enforced separation of the races on trains and buses, or even on park seats and railway platforms—pin-pricks that especially hurt the more advanced and respectable 'non-Europeans' of all sorts. On a grander scale, and with an eye to the future, the Government embarked on a stupendous task of 'National Registration'; every potential voter, European, Coloured, Asian or 'Native', must be placed definitively, with full pedigree and photograph, in his appropriate caste. With an extraordinary disregard for personal suffering, a dark-complexioned coloured family whose way of life was wholly Western might be torn from its roots and directed by official *ukase* to join the Native group—or the blow might even fall on one individual member. The marriage of whites with any but whites was made illegal. A Group Areas Act decreed separate districts, both business and residential, even in long established, cosmopolitan urban areas, for each of the racial categories. Asian traders pushed out from their businesses to begin again in the void were the first to suffer; but European interests were also affected and the boards on whom the work devolved made but slow headway in this 'unscrambling' process.

It was next the turn of the African people and here the Nationalists were at any rate logical. Wanting nothing so much for themselves as their old republic back again, they proceeded to make it their business to refurbish the African tribal system they saw with real regret decaying or already decayed. Had economics been their stronger suit—and Nationalist business or industrial interests were still only slight—they must have given prior attention to the reasons for tribal breakdown. Instead, they set out with earnest deliberation to put Humpty-Dumpty together again. It was in 1950 that I met some of their chief advisers studying British practice in Tanganyika with much approval; not long afterwards (belatedly adopting the principles of indirect rule), they were setting out to 'find the Chief', as the basis of new-old 'Bantu' Authorities (as it were N.A.s). The Union, however, in spite of so much virtual 'segregation', had an unusually large number of educated modern men and women; there are in the bigger towns also many thousands utterly detribalized, like the youth who told one too-knowing official that his 'Chief was the Mayor of Johannesburg' and he 'drank water from the tap'! The educated might find themselves (as in the worst British practice) subjected to a tribal or Bantu Authority, or required to accept the official 'ethnic grouping' in towns where they would be bereft of all political rights whatever.

The growing complexity of South African life really had the industrially inexperienced Nationalists in an almost excusable panic; and yet so much mere showmanship was possible at all only because the country still enjoyed unheard-of prosperity. This prosperity is by no means fortuitous. The revenue derived from the traditionally judicious taxation of mining profits has always been well applied to water-conservation, irrigation, first-rate agricultural and veterinary services, and to the fostering of industries, including steel and, latterly, oil from coal. The opening of new mines, together, latterly, with the recovery of uranium as a by-product of gold-mining, helped an economy which was already broadly based on gold, diamonds, base metals and coal, besides a sometimes very profitable wool industry, and secondary industries that struck root in the war years. In the course of a long visit in 1949 I found the disturbing phrase 'poor white' gone clean out of currency; the landless white *bijwoner* (squatter) class whose real misfortunes disturbed us in the hungry '20s was absorbed in industries or in mechanized agriculture. 'Native' labour was now perpetually 'short', so that even the lowest paid workers, black and white, old and young, were earning regular wages.

Even so, two or three years of militant *apartheid* were more shattering to harmonious race relations than anything in past history. In a letter I had late in 1949, within a year of his death, General Smuts wrote sadly:

> 'The worst of course is the change which is coming over our coloured and native peoples. There the damage may perhaps be irretrievable.'

The possessive pronoun reflects the benevolent paternalism which had carried the country over many rough places, but passed with his own last administration in 1948. Smuts himself, a little distantly, respected the full and free Cape tradition, but he was grooming a whole-hearted believer to be his successor; the second J. H. Hofmeyr unhappily died shortly before Smuts himself. On the other hand the Nationalists' luck held. For a moment, towards the end of my 1949 visit, an economic 'recession' threatened. In that same letter General Smuts saw just a little hope that 'harder times' were bringing a change: 'Experience is the best teacher', he concluded sententiously; he reasonably hoped the history of 1933 might be repeated. This time the British devaluation of sterling in September 1949, and the higher sterling price of Rand gold, again restored and increased South Africa's prosperity, but only left her Nationalist rulers free to indulge their fantasies. At a renewed peak of prosperity (for which the Government contrived to take the credit to itself) a still more decisive general election in 1952 entrenched them in office.

For all its luck, the renewed Government found it harder than ever to harmonize theory and practice. Economic prosperity on a nation-wide scale, and the rapid industrial expansion from which it grew, were new, and the consequences not only unfamiliar but embarrassing. The Nationalist rank and file, there is no doubt, thought of *apartheid* nostalgically, as a return to the days when the great African majority was well out of sight—except, always, the irreducible minimum needed to work on the farms. It was all very fine to have National Registration and a long-term Group Areas Act on the statute book, but farmers were the principal sufferers from the new labour shortage; wages in agriculture being steadily lower than in industry, the farms were by-passed by labour drifting townwards. The drift in itself threatened to make nonsense of 'separateness', but it also provided urgent political reason for action. 'Control' now became the watchword: in almost the words of the 1840 model, towns must have as many 'Natives' as found white employment, and no more. I sympathized with an excellent officer in an important town on whose door I saw the notice proclaiming him to be 'Controller of Urban Influx'! Africans were forbidden even to follow the instincts of 'economic man'. The already large agglomerations of African wage-earners needed services and amusements such as other Africans could best supply; but, reckless of the resentment caused by depriving men of this opportunity, the authorities treated these others as virtually prohibited immigrants. To justify themselves they gave a new turn to their own doctrine; with a peculiar addiction to abstractions their theorists now pronounced the only alternative to the ruthless separation of the races to be *integration*. This outcome would seem to be possible only as a very slow, almost imperceptible historical process: but the very word integration was shrewdly calculated to conjure up in the minds of South African *plattelanders* visions of homes and families invaded straightway by hordes of dusky fellow-citizens. This second nightmare made the vision of *apartheid* a real spell-binder! Political pressures were thus carrying Government practice far away from the doctrine approved by their own best teachers. High-minded idealists in or near the Dutch Reformed Church, especially at its old headquarters, the University of Stellenbosch, have from the beginning taught explicitly that *apartheid* demands sacrifice—the sacrifice of the convenience of native labour, the surrender even of sufficient European-owned land to make possible a really viable 'Bantustan'. Racial theory contributed, however, to the absurdities of reconstructed tribalism and 'ethnic grouping', and also marred more promising reforms. A Bantu Education Act bludgeoned through Parliament considerably extended state aid; but its rigid state control also caused the closing down of well-established mission schools, thus depriving the 'Bantu' of their surest hope of a liberal education on traditional lines. Instead of the former steady trickle of westward-looking liberals, the outcome must be a spate of African nationalists. Though an official inquiry had newly pronounced separate universities only 'a second best', if not impracticable, a Universities Bill in 1957 proposed the exclusion of all non-Europeans from existing universities as soon as departmentally managed and controlled separate universities could be brought into existence.

At the same time this *apartheid* Government gets less credit than it deserves for constructive work. The theory is that in 'their own areas' Africans should have free scope for their fullest ambitions, and these half-ruined Reserves have in fact engaged the authorities in some major efforts at well-conceived 'betterment'. Even the harassed urban workers, so far as they are recognized as necessary, are the beneficiaries of social services that are more advanced than anywhere else on the African continent and include old-age pensions; medical care and hospitals are good. The notorious shanty-towns of the Rand are the least significant part of the story of African housing; in wide African travels since the war I have seen no better African housing anywhere than in many state or municipal aided townships in the Union, paid for out of 'white' rates and some of them let at 'sub-economic' rents. It was the 'influx' of wage-earners, the same the Government vainly sought to limit, that for long all but swamped the mere physical labour of building for so many. The apostles of *apartheid* could thus retort triumphantly to the outside criticism they so hotly resented, that Africans from far-away Nyasaland, Tanganyika and Angola, who failed to get places in the quota of voluntary recruits to the mines, were dodging the frontier controls in their eagerness to reach the Union. For them at least the alleged police state was El Dorado—but this, of course, was only because of 'full employment', which alone made this Government's wild experiment financially possible.

In spite and in face of the theory of their idealists it was the Government itself which temporized on the crucial labour issue. Severely practical, it was not prepared to risk the national prosperity by letting mines and industries, still less agriculture, go short of the labour they demanded. The ruinous compromise was that this labour must be explicitly 'migratory', and on no account allowed to dig itself in. Africans, it was decreed, were too 'backward' to be allowed to form trade unions of their own and must, on principle, be excluded from existing 'mixed' unions. So many restraints and restrictions could be enforced only by piling on more restrictive laws and regulations. The Cape tradition being repudiated, these rash administrators ignored the principle that, above all in such a polyglot society, laws must be readily understood and broadly accepted as at once just and equal. On the contrary, a continuous stream of stiffening amendments to basic measures like the Natives (Urban Areas) Act of 1923 points to the inefficiency of its regulations except as a means of stirring up more discontent. Ever changing, almost unknowable prohibitions swelled the grotesquely high proportion of purely technical offenders already overflowing the Union's prisons in consequence of the Pass Laws, which still threaten summary arrest and imprisonment for any passless African worker—one who fails, it may be, to risk a day's wages for time lost in waiting for the renewal of a 'pass' showing him to be lawfully employed. Reckoning to know their Africans, and how little organizing ability they have at any time, the Nationalists judge them little likely to attempt combined resistance. Thanks always to full employment, the workers are unusually well off. The masses are undoubtedly submissive and personal relations in home and factory continue to be good. But resentment (which the critics expect too readily) is growing, especially in the more responsible classes. Some of the urban areas, notably on the Rand, have seen an almost complete collapse of law and order; in the early days of *apartheid* a well-to-do African, who had reason to feel the effects of this breakdown, assured me he would rather suffer the lawlessness of hooligans of his own race than 'gang-up against them' with the police. The guardians of the law tend to be rated as the militant branch of the Nationalist Party. Yet actual unrest, or official fears of unrest, only became the warrant for still tighter 'control'. Ultimately the definitions enshrined in a wide-ranging Suppression of Communism Act vested in the Minister such loose and comprehensive powers that anything resembling anti-Government political campaigning became positively hazardous.

Yet *apartheid*, born of the sheer inexperience that sees the country's social perplexities as a 'problem' calling for a straight solution, remains a dream. A commission of the Union Government's own choosing produced in 1955 the massive (Tomlinson) Report which concluded that an outlay of £105 million might so far recondition the Reserves as to provide a fair subsistence for perhaps 50 per cent of the Bantu by the year 2000. The Government itself, always practical, shied off it, but the Minister directly concerned, Dr. H. F. Verwoerd, went on record as boasting—surely a *reductio ad absurdum*—that it is the virtue of *apartheid* to provide a programme so moderate that it may take '300 years' to work out. Amid the kaleidoscopic changes engulfing this already highly varied society no one can hope to plan ahead even for ten years; but, with sublime assurance, he would lay down the lines to be followed by ten succeeding generations. The essentials of the situation can be simply stated. No longer rival rural communities, as they once were, the 'advanced' people of South Africa and those less advanced are now thrown together, for good or ill, into all the confusion of a rapidly developing modern state. The only possible course for its rulers is, therefore, to keep accurate measure of whatever change is measurable, to have the machinery of administration geared to meet new occasions as and when they arise, and to run as smoothly as may be from one year's end to the next.

South African ministers nevertheless had reason to complain that their U.N. and other critics were often wide of the mark. The political (republican) by-play is an often disregarded distorting influence, but some attempt to regulate the competition of poor blacks with 'poor whites' is still essential. The critics never got beyond citing the blundering attempts that were made as evidence of ruthless white racial discrimination against black. Yet the U.N. majority also seeks to separate the conflicting races; they are for the delusively simple solution of making all 'colonialism' give way to national self-government, as in the Gold Coast. America, warm in support, was happy when weak war-torn Libya was set to become an independent kingdom, or a time-table fixed the 'liberation' of an inchoate Somalia. Some were a little disturbed to find that the newly freed Sudan stood invested with a recognizably 'colonial' problem in its own southern province, and that, about the same time (1953), a self-governing constitution for British Guiana had to be hurriedly suspended when the Guianese were smitten with near-communist prepossessions and refused to let this instrument function. The British Government itself was so much concerned to forestall egalitarian criticism by the Trusteeship Council that its Tanganyika officers were years later still being required to prepare the very diversified peoples of this trust territory for early and united self-government; interrupting more urgent routine work, they had to summon its most primitive tribes to meet in open *baraza* to hear lessons in constitutional law and history! Till thus moved by pressure from the very new force of 'world opinion' British colonial rulers, like South Africans and others in daily contact with the realities of life among backward peoples, were no doubt inclined to underrate their subjects' desire for freedom to go their own way. The advocates of *apartheid* now fly to another extreme, but they also go some of the way with their critics. They accept it that (in their own half-ruined and impoverished areas) the dependent peoples must be free to rise to any heights, provided it is strictly 'on their own lines'; and of course the process must not be hurried—the '300 year' commendation stands! Development must also be under white direction; Dr. Malan and others viewed the sudden emergence of the Gold Coast with pained surprise, even with suspicion, above all because it lacked this guidance. Yet such 'separate development' had been proclaimed to all the world as the only sure way to peace and harmony and Prime Minister Strydom, accordingly, spoke entirely in character when, on more mature consideration of the implications of *apartheid*, he announced, and indeed went on to give practical proof of South Africa's desire for peaceful co-existence and cordial co-operation with such all-African states.

History suggests that there really is reason to be uneasy. Suddenly thrown back on their own resources these inexperienced colonial peoples will not only have to manage their own affairs; they must also establish satisfactory relations with infinitely more complex foreign interests than originally brought upon them the 'colonial' interference now complained of—and if they fail or fall into disorder, the poorest and weakest must suffer most. World communism, too, will now be standing by, ready to take every advantage of unstable conditions—like those arising from the unequal development of the Balkans fringe of the European family of nations which led directly to the war of 1914 and the disruption of a former European order. The dangerous rivalry set up by the existence of so many ill-assorted and disunited states of unequal power threatens the whole world order with what an older generation would have termed 'balkanization'. In this already unstable world order South Africa is a fully sovereign independent state, even if a great majority of its people are virtually excluded from any share in the government. But the U.N. will be unhelpful till it gets beyond condemning South African policy as based on nothing but race and colour prejudice. In the Union, as rarely in the same degree anywhere else, the majority, being not only *unprivileged* but also typically immature, threaten, at once, the livelihood of the weaker of their political masters and the stability of the State as a whole. Yet *apartheid* is impossible because so many Africans, and other non-Europeans, are sufficiently 'advanced' to be already—in a phrase reiterated in the Johannesburg Joint Council by the late R. V. Selope Thema, one of their stoutest early leaders—'part and parcel' of the highly prosperous SouthAfrica that is. The major charge against the Afrikaner theorists is that their separate or (as they sometimes prefer to call it) *parallel* development would have one all-white state lording it over the Tomlinson Report's fourteen or sixteen economically impossible Bantu 'heartlands', and in fact 'balkanize' South Africa itself.

It is thus, between them, that the advocates of *apartheid* and their critics have given *colour* a wholly new prominence. In all the history touched on in this study colour, as such, has never figured; there has been, and is, only too much else to impede the coming together of two utterly distinct and different worlds. As the outward and visible difference, colour was likely to obtrude as soon as members of the weaker peoples should begin to 'emerge' and assert themselves. Since virtually all the people who were still colonially ruled after the Second World War are so-called 'coloured', the emotional disturbance arising from colour-consciousness has all but stopped the sober study of the facts. Thus the leaders of the newer eastern states found it politically convenient to ascribe the ills of their own traditionally unequal and, some of them, caste-ridden societies to 'imperialist exploitation', and it was easy and natural to go on to court allies by identifying the imperialism they professed to know with 'colonialism'. Enlightened Americans needed no convincing of the evils of colonial rule, and were ready also to recognize colour prejudice as a baleful influence nearer home. At least since J. A. Hobson's Boer War classic on *Imperialism* many English intellectuals have been ready to accept the view that the retarded development of the dependent peoples everywhere is the outcome of their dependence—a corollary often pronounces the resulting massive and world-wide problem of race and colour to be wholly European-made. A visiting Nigerian minister clearly betrayed the influences at work; boasting, in a broadcast, of it being the good fortune of his country that no European can lawfully own an acre of its soil, he then slipped into reverse and added in perfect innocence: 'And there is *no* colour bar!'

This obsession with the accident of colour is a peculiarly unfortunate distraction. Even the term Race Relations cannot be accepted as covering the field. In our day, as never before, scientific progress and the speed and relative ease of communications make possible, and indeed demand, a concentrated attack on the inequality that underlies racial divisions. The weaker need the help of the stronger peoples; but these can do their part only if the less well-equipped co-operate, showing themselves no less whole-heartedly ready to receive than the stronger are to give.

Chapter 11

NEW PATTERNS IN EAST AND CENTRAL AFRICA

*

In the years of reconstruction after the Second World War the claims of the emerging Africans of the West Coast, and the counter-claims of long-established Europeans in the south, dominated the international debate. The guidance offered for the conduct of the very intricate and varied domestic affairs of the less forward colonies was highly generalized; a prescription for immediate self-government was no help to those actually struggling to devise workmanlike machinery to fit widely differing circumstances. The new emphasis on colour as the basis of racial tension (a theme on which from opposite standpoints the South Africans and their critics were agreed) was peculiarly inappropriate in the East and Central African territories where both Europeans and Asians had well-established interests, closely linked by sixty years of 'contact' (and for good rather than for ill) with those of the original inhabitants. These newer lands (all of them first put on the map at all only by Livingstone and his successors), were less directly in the international limelight; but their immature and inexperienced peoples could not remain unaffected by the currents of opinion blowing now not only from Accra and Lagos but from Delhi and New York, and very decidedly also from the Afrikaner metropolis, Potchefstroom. The growing race-consciousness evoked by the appeal to race solidarity evoked much passionate feeling in people whose genuine patriotic emotion is generally still reserved for the tribal heritage. Africanism (Lord Hailey's word) rather than nationalism became a revolutionary force. The Mau-Mau outbreak in Kenya was a grim example of long suppressed African consciousness finding terrifying expression in a fantastic barbarism. Africans on the whole undoubtedly wish to share more fully rather than to destroy the material benefits they owe to the West; most have refrained from any such violence, knowing it to be sterile.

The cry of Africa for the Africans was to be expected, but Africans must have more than Africa; for them, certainly, 'a new world must be called in to redress the balance of the old'. Even West Africa, which is already entirely their own, is far from self-sufficient or united; its new African rulers are appealing for capital and other help from outside, and offering all and more than they can afford in return. Only the West Coast peoples had the middle class I spoke of, and therefore ready-made leaders of their own race. These leaders have little outside competition to thwart their ambitions. But they lose at the same time by missing the ever-present object-lesson of skilled productive work by which to set their standards. The absence of immigrant Europeans is not the unmixed advantage it is commonly assumed to be. East and Central Africa may in the long run be better placed; their gravest disadvantage is that they have been called on to face changes that came, when they did, more suddenly and with far greater violence. Almost all in one short lifetime, in the twentieth century, plantations sprang up all over these regions, mining enterprise developed, and European settlers were the means of introducing strange new activities that had their influence far beyond their main centre in Rhodesia and Kenya, the local people being left to adapt themselves to such innovations as best they might.

It was in fact the modest and unsatisfying role of the African population to keep this new activity going by providing unskilled labour; on the whole they did so with cheerfulness and goodwill; the ambitious or venturesome still make great efforts to reach the Rand, the strongest magnet of all. The effect of so much travel on tribal cohesion or social stability of any kind is another matter; for one reason or another most African mine-workers return home from the Rand or the Copper Belt to the Transkei, Tanganyika, Angola, after anything from six months to a year or two; sisal workers similarly return from Tanga to Ussukuma or the Southern Province of Tanganyika, cotton-pickers from Buganda to Ruanda-Urundi, Southern Rhodesian farm-labourers to Nyasaland. Few of these workers take their wives or children with them, and the absence of so many men for very long periods reduces the output of food and plays havoc with the social life of the tribes. It is true that the young men like roving and find little to occupy them in a static and decaying tribal life; more and more of the women, too, see no harm in making what they can out of the cities' demands. Inevitably many of both sexes are lost to their tribes for ever, and tribal order is thus the first victim.

The migrant labourers' prospects of advancement in industry, or in the towns to which they flock hopefully, are restricted in the first place by their lack either of experience or of training. An additional factor (peculiar to East Africa) is that there migrant tribal labourers have to meet the direct competition of Asians. Indian traders established themselves in Zanzibar early in the nineteenth century, supplying the Arab Sultanate with manufactured goods, and often with capital for forays into the interior after slaves or ivory. These early traders, men of wealth and superior manners, were important enough to warrant the setting up of a British consulate in the island (see p. 149). A different class altogether arrived with the building of the Uganda Railway whose contractors called upon the 'coolie' class for unskilled work that the local African population could not or would not take on. Later, when the railway was a going concern, foremen, mechanics and station staff were recruited among the Sikh artisans, and the more educated 'white collar' class in India. Immediately after the completion of the railway there were deliberate 'settlements' of surplus Indian labourers; it was at that time that the Highlands were declared 'white' to bar them from an Asiatic flood. Asians finally found their *métier* as traders and did the country good service by bringing trade to areas it would not otherwise have reached, but at the price of the retail trade of the East African territories becoming virtually an Asian monopoly. The railway's experience, and the presence of Asians ready and able to take their chance, gave them an unshakeable hold on all the ancillary jobs incidental to the growth of towns and industries; Sikh station-masters, Goan clerks, Asian *fundis* of all kinds, made a valuable contribution to the development of East Africa. It is another matter that, far from teaching Africans their trades, the presence of Asians now rather hinders the rise of the middle class of Africans so necessary to any greater African self-sufficiency. The old African order has had less opportunity of adapting itself to the new developments because of this Asian interposition.

The frustration said to beset African efforts in the critical Eastern territories is not to be dissociated entirely from this Asian competition; there are three times as many Asians as Europeans in Kenya and Tanganyika; in Uganda, where African production of cotton and coffee is considerable, Asians have even ousted Europeans from business and outnumber them by ten to one; in Nyasaland they also have an important hold on the local trade. Overall, Asians number nearly 200,000, not including the remnant of an older Arab colony. In this East African context the fashion of equating the colonial question with one of colour is clearly too simple. In a just view the presence of any competent people is a source of strength. The economy must be looked at as a whole, and not as a field in which European, Asian and African interests eternally conflict and must be balanced one against the other. But the point has not yet been met that gave rise to the 'paramountcy' debate of the '20s (Chapter 8); these nationals of Commonwealth countries, India and Pakistan, owe their present favourable economic standing too much to the weakness of the African majority. Most of the Asians began at as low an economic level as any Africans, but they successfully applied superior skill, a greater capacity for work, perhaps a greater desire for this world's goods, and certainly a greater understanding of how they can be acquired and increased. At this stage the Asians' near monopoly of retail trade and of skilled or semi-skilled labour hinders the emergence of Africans more than any European activity. A new technical college in Nairobi which is to train both races to the highest level, and to whose funds Asians have contributed largely, is a recent and a promising development. Asians at any rate are a more advanced people and cannot be absolved from their share of direct responsibility for African advancement.

It is hard for the East and Central African peoples, the latest to arrive on the world stage, that the facts of their situation are so unusually complex. West Africans have long been in touch with the outside world without their own ways being seriously affected; they may well err from over-confidence in their ability to stand alone. The Southern tribes have been brought to their present pass by gradual conquest; they themselves view the state of the Union less tragically than outsiders are wont to do; they are, in spite of all, an essential part of a thriving economy, and well aware that at any rate their economic opportunities are greater than any the tropical territories can yet offer. Unusually long, close contact has taught these southern Africans much that is serviceable, and the knowledge with which they have been armed, like their opportunities, are, they know, a Western contribution. There is reason to think that many of them adopt the philosophy of the old Afrikaans motto: '*Alles sal reg kom!*' ('All must come right.'). The east and central peoples, on the other hand, have special reason to be merely bewildered. Their own earlier conditions were highly insecure; active slave-raiding was finally suppressed only in the 1890s. Very soon they began to get their introduction to new things as a steady stream of 'labour', always 'migrant' labour, flowed to the farms, plantations and mines. But, again very soon, much of the territory was unusually sharply involved first in one, then in a Second World War. By the time even the first was over a fear of 'settler' designs on their land was greatly stimulated by circumstances for which European immigrants were in no way responsible. Many of those 'oases', the fertile mountain slopes, were becoming over-populated; old-fashioned, forceful readjustments among Africans were prevented by the white rulers' insistence on 'law and order'; tribal divisions and poor communications barred migration. The pressure of population was some of it due to the higher survival rate that resulted from health services, so that even the white men's good works counted against them. Settlers, it is true, and industrialists, were too busy struggling to establish themselves to be given to thinking in those days in terms of 'partnership'. The new tide of world opinion that began to flow after the second war broke thus on people who saw 'development', and ever more rapid change, taking place all around them, yet entirely as it were 'over their heads'; it was change in which Africans had no assured part. The educated tended to ascribe this to their colour, and also to see 'development' practised by white men as 'exploitation'. By the early '50s every colony had its own organized African Congress; though each tended to follow a course of its own the uniform name suggests the influence of Indian example; the leaders, a very small group, were in touch with the same advisers, as a rule also with one another, and all spoke substantially the same political language. The party line became more and more clearly to resist making with European groups or interests any working arrangement that might stand in the way of the ultimate goal, a purely African government.

The colonies in this region pay a price for being actually a jump ahead of the West Coast. The more vigorous of their economies are increasingly dependent on the fruits of expanding white enterprise; Europeans on the spot keep this activity going and almost of itself it initiates more. A great proportion of the Europeans, having made their homes in Africa, are in the true sense colonists, an integral part of its population. Not all are directors or landowners; many are, rather, workshop reared, and these fill a gap that may yawn increasingly in the all-African territories; many white youths, among them children of South African Boers, have turned from independent farming to supervisory work in all kinds of construction and maintenance, often in African areas as 'District Assistants'. The whites are thus not only too strongly established to be thrown out but have made themselves indispensable. On the other hand, being so few, they cannot long continue to dream of domination, as more and more of them clearly realize. Economic changes, over which they have little control, leave little place for old-fashioned 'settlers', but settlers' sons are proving adaptable and seizing in these various ways the openings provided by a broadly based and expanding economy. Here, if anywhere, accommodation between

African ambitions and economic necessity should be possible; failure here can only mean disruption and bring ruin on all races—but the African leaders, though fearful or resentful of European methods, and fired also by an ambition to take charge themselves, are no less eager for progress.

A smooth transition to agreed and settled order was not however, to be expected, and at a time of steadily mounting general tension the grievances of the Kikuyu tribe suddenly made Kenya again a storm centre. In 1890 the young Lugard was impressed by this tribe on his journey to Uganda, and distressed to find on his return that the behaviour of some lesser members of his company had given them serious offence. Soon after this the rinderpest epidemic of the '90s virtually broke the power of the Masai and relaxed their pressure on the Kikuyu; but this pest, and the smallpox that followed it, had affected the Kikuyu also and meant that more land than usual lay idle when about 1897 a railway construction camp was planted at the most obvious halting place before the climb to the Rift Wall. This camp, originally on more or less empty debatable land lying between the Kikuyu and the Masai, grew to be the one considerable town in the whole area, Nairobi. It is certain that Nairobi, growing up on the very edge of the land later demarcated as their 'Reserve', afforded the Kikuyu unusual opportunities of observing and learning new things both good and bad; together with the Highland farms planted in its vicinity it also relieved them of any need to look further afield for work or markets. The Kikuyu, in fact, were not given to migration; they proved to be among the most home-staying, the most tenacious of soil and custom of any of the tribes affected by 'contact'. In spite of the opportunities at their door, and though they became the best labourers on white farms, they clung to their own agricultural methods and system of land-holding even when their living standards began rising. The fresh wave of white settlement that followed the 1914–18 war synchronized with rather than caused growing congestion among them and, as their numbers grew, made them ever more consciously land-hungry. It was a growing awareness of Kikuyu discontents that prompted Norman Leys and others to level their criticism at white settlement. The Kikuyu themselves readily accepted it that 'settlement' as such was the all-sufficient cause of their troubles.

So it was that in October 1952 the White Highlands of Kenya became the scene of the worst recorded outbreak of African violence, the Mau Mau atrocities that plunged the whole colony into a state of emergency that was to last for four years. The outbreak had African features that defy analysis, but was evidence also of tensions peculiar to the Kikuyu. The habitual official reliance on coastal Swahili as a lingua franca made for misunderstanding and neglect of the vernaculars; I have several times watched tribal audiences harangued in fluent Swahili that was manifestly less well understood than the speaker supposed. Only two or three government officers, and not very many civilians, spoke Kikuyu. Yet the Kikuyu were as tenacious of their language as of the rest of their heritage; cut off from easy communication they turned in upon themselves. Reforms initiated for their benefit, especially anything like anti-erosion work that affected the land, could easily be misinterpreted to them by leaders speaking their own language, and the Government remain almost totally in the dark as to what was going on. Just before I paid my first visit to the country in 1930 a definite stand by the Scots Mission against the fanatically adhered-to custom of female circumcision raised a storm marked by ugly incidents that were prophetic of Mau Mau. As a result some dissidents broke away and set up an Independent Kikuyu Church and a network of independent schools, all markedly nationalist. It was in those early '30s that Jomo Kenyatta was in London drinking in reassurance from the anthropologists of the value of unspoilt African institutions. The ambitions of this exceptional 'emergent' when he at last returned home would always have been hard to satisfy; but the consequences of the local Government's failure to meet his need by absorbing him in its own service were serious. The Second World War brought activity and prosperity to the Kikuyu along with the rest of Kenya and drove grievances underground; Kenyatta appeared content to withdraw himself and live on the tribute of his people as head of the independent school network. On a visit in 1949 I found the schools flourishing and causing some dismay by the crude nationalism they made their main teaching. At Fort Hall a rueful D.C. told us how women had been organized to lie down in front of tractors making anti-erosion terraces; soil conservation, which was making great headway in Nyanza, for instance, was completely halted in Kikuyuland where it was most needed. 'Jomo Kenyatta', they said, 'is behind it.' The position seemed to be much the same even in August 1952; there was still no overt move. The sullenness and discontent of the Kikuyu had come to be taken for granted and was too lightly discounted. In spite of warning symptoms, seen as such later, both Government and public were taken by surprise when, in October, the storm broke. The method of Mau Mau was an only too thoroughly African appeal, in corrupt and distorted fashion, to the power of old cults; the obscene oaths imposed were intended to set those who took them beyond the normal pale. By far the most of the victims of the bestial murders that followed were fellow tribesmen who either refused to take the oaths or failed to keep them. It is possible that the plans of the leaders in some way miscarried and that what was to have been a general rising degenerated into an outbreak of blind resentment; but its suppression taxed the Government to the limit. The decisive resistance was made by devoted Christian Kikuyu.

The compelling needs of security now overcame even the old reluctance to interfere with established custom. The Kikuyu, who had hitherto lived in scattered individual homesteads, were concentrated for safety in compact villages where they could be at once defended and insulated from terrorists. Here was an unlooked-for opportunity of agrarian reform; progress was made in getting scattered and often tiny patches of land held by one family voluntarily rearranged to form economical farming units; soil conservation went ahead. Outside the Reserves overdue reforms of the farm-labour or 'squatter' system could no longer be put off. All over the country government had been too distant; lest others might be tempted to follow the Kikuyu example, grievances must no longer be allowed to smoulder in dangerous seclusion; closer administration was necessary, and policy must also be better understood and based on general consent.

Africans, in short, even if an only half-formed African opinion was almost impossible to weigh accurately, had to be taken into account, quickly, as a *political* force. Not so long ago indirect rulers were pinning their faith to the idea of building on tribal institutions, but they had discreetly left the relations of N.A.s with any kind of central or territorial government for consideration at some later date. The Kenya Government itself had gone one better and even then had functioning here and there what were not merely *tribal* but comprehensively *local* district councils, still however without having thought out the place of such councils in the national system; and this already included separate or communal representatives of Europeans and Asians. London, for its part, had pronounced in 1922 that in Kenya the interests of the African majority must be 'paramount'. This dictum proved hard to interpret and a new slogan was given currency: as a multi-racial state Kenya must have a multi-racial government, all the races having their equal say. A new constitution promulgated in 1954 (in the secretaryship of Mr. Oliver Lyttleton, Lord Chandos, and known by his name) took the hazardous step of extending the communal system; established precedent suggested that the election of African representatives be put on the same communal basis. This way of meeting the sudden but urgent political necessity of finding the African masses a place in a parliamentary system of government (that to them was almost meaningless) put parliamentary institutions under unwonted strain. The racial theory of colonial politics is once more the culprit; African opinion is no more an undivided whole than European or Asian opinion, unless perhaps when it is thus sharply pitted against such other abstractions. Communal representation at the centre inevitably focused the politics of Kenya more than ever on its racial rivalries. It was left, surprisingly, for the more uniformly 'backward' neighbouring state, Tanganyika, to pioneer a return to the forgotten or neglected Cape practice of registering its electors on a 'common roll'; in 1958 it was preparing to fill a proportion of its parliamentary seats by requiring all candidates to canvass the suffrages of qualified voters of all the races. No other way offers of making them not merely representatives of a section, but at least potential builders of the required multi-racial state.

Tanganyika itself, however, illustrates the difficulty of taking short cuts to self-government in any of these predominantly tribal agglomerations. This trust territory has no natural internal cohesion; something of its great variety, and also of its potential, was impressed upon me by two extensive tours, one in 1930 and another all the more illuminating for being made twenty years later. Ninety per cent of the people are clustered round ten or twelve centres, most of these widely separated by miles of arid 'bush' from any other, and several of them in the state of internal tension induced by the purely local overcrowding already referred to (p. 237). Internal communications are abnormally difficult, even by African standards; the central railway line was designed, after the German manner, to meet strategical rather than economic or administrative needs; any north-south journey by road necessitates some wide detour, and besides, though barely one quarter of the whole vast area has a reliable rainfall, even certain of the main trunk roads are impassable in the rainy season—unusable, that may mean, for half the year. The administrative capital, Dar-es-Salaam, feels and is very remote from any of the provinces; yet, roads and railways being as they are, there is no obviously more suitable alternative. The history of the territory has rather emphasized geographical influences and left it economically and politically backward. Thirty years of German rule introduced sisal (still the greatest revenue producer) and established the coffee industry, but it was a severely military rule; at least one (Maji-Maji) rebellion was ferociously suppressed. From 1914 to 1919 the armies, alternately German and Allied, were in sole control. Since then the *boma*, once truly a fortified post, has become no more than the district station, the sergeant-major having made way for the British D.C.; but the British of the earlier days were, after all, no more forward than the Germans in purposeful works of reconstruction and development. In the years between the wars even British rule was often a little tentative; caution was always induced by the Mandates Commission's questions and criticisms. The unblushingly 'colonialist' claims of the 'unsatisfied' powers, moreover, grew steadily stronger, making actual retrocession of the territory to Germany a possibility that discouraged experiments involving long-term commitments.

In spite of such restraining influences the reorganized or actually new colonial administrative and specialist services (Chapter 10) were able to do something to give Tanganyika a promising fresh start after 1925. In a tribal society where tribal loyalties were so shattered by the rough usage meted out by the Germans, there was much to be said for restoring African self-respect by such indirect rule as was pursued here with energy and enthusiasm under the watchful eye of Sir Donald Cameron. But even Sir Donald was obliged by 'recession' to retrench sorely needed staff, and the 1939 war checked recovery, or at any rate diverted energy needed for reconstruction. Since the war the prodigious groundnuts scheme has been and gone, causing some confusion, but clearing the air of the romantic notion that development can be rushed. C.D. & W., which began in the '40s, continues to make an important contribution, and after 1950 another notable Governor, Sir Edward (Lord) Twining, supplied energy and drive. Mining may grow in importance if, for example, known but inaccessible coal deposits at any time prove workable; but mining revenue rose appreciably only in the '50s when the Williamson mine reached full production. The main assets of this large ill-developed expanse are still sisal from the coast belt, coffee from the mountainsides, and cotton from the lake basins. The weakness remains that the revenues of such a preponderantly agricultural economy are always very short of its capital needs.

The unity of Tanganyika is, of course, artificial—tribes of the far north-west have affinities rather with Uganda, and the Masai of the north are cut off from their own people in Kenya—but its many parts are none the less truly interdependent. In the last resort there is uniformity even in its variety, and the imposed unity has real advantages; no Nairobi, no Copper Belt, dominates its politics; the Europeans, a more cosmopolitan body than their British fellows in Kenya and fewer in number, are a stimulus rather than a complication; being more aware of the needs of the country as a whole than any of the African sections, their influence is helpful in counteracting the pressure of merely parochial affairs at a time when truly common, even national interests are visibly growing. One really new feature stood out above the many material improvements I saw after twenty years. Every *boma* now has more than a handful of educated Africans—teachers, clerks, medical and agricultural assistants, the occasional lawyer or doctor, a growing number of university graduates. There are also a great many mechanics and drivers. These, being by no means always of the local tribe and therefore by the old rules almost expatriate, are essentially *Tanganyikans*. The future depends greatly on these men being successfully absorbed into their new station as Tanganyikans indeed; otherwise they must inevitably become frustrated 'agitators'. The black-coats—clerks and teachers—may be worst placed; as in most of these new countries, they have to maintain their higher standards, pay for books and for their children's education, on salaries that are actually lower than those of mechanics or lorry drivers. But the mechanics class too may be a focus of discontent. It may happen, as here and there in Tanganyika, that the local tribe monopolizes the patronage of an unusually prosperous N.A.; self-assured incomers, not unjustly proud of their modernity, found a base for a time in the groundnuts camps; now they often find themselves ranking again as outsiders.

Late in the day, yet at an earlier stage of their own development than others like the Gold Coast, all these newer colonies are thus producing their own middle classes; even more because they lack the economic strength deriving from a profitable cocoa industry these need to be saved from suffering the disgruntlement that came of the studied official boycott of the emergents of the West Coast. As products of the new age they may be cruelly out of the swim in a country where the old tribal order not only lives on but is, far more than any European influence, still the dominant factor. For example, stronger tribes such as the coffee-growing Wachagga like to go their own way; greatly valuing central government services, they would gladly take more for themselves; but, having little appreciation of the cost of staff and equipment which must serve the whole country, they much resent having to send their boys and girls away from their delectable mountain to training college at Mpwapwa or to high school at a torrid and (so they complain!) lion-infested place like Tabora. Because the parts are so aloof from each other, and so very unequal, it is a far cry to the goal of national self-government. But the emergents are there nevertheless, already a part of the inevitable and necessary new order. They above all can make it or mar it. The authorities, therefore, were putting first things first, and realistically facing the facts of the situation, when they made full political enfranchisement the reward of attainment and set the qualified of all races to vote together on a 'common roll' to choose representatives for a popularly based national assembly.

The isolation suffered by individual emergents almost everywhere goes with evidence from Uganda, the third of this East African group, to suggest that the relations of Africans with other Africans may be at least as hard to order as those with Europeans and Asians. The central kingdom, Buganda, has not its like nearer than the Nigerian emirates. Bananas from well-tilled groves (and of a cooking variety) are the staple diet, and meat from their own cattle, or from next-door Ankole, (though not milk) is plentiful. The export or cash crops of the peasant farmers of this fertile, lake-side country are in the first place cotton and coffee, but also maize and tobacco. Foreigner-directed plantations are fewer than they were, but Indian-owned estates provide most of East Africa's supply of sugar. The Baganda are predominantly Christian (Catholic and Anglican in about equal numbers). Their women are notably graceful (so unlike their Kikuyu sisters) and well dressed. The prosperity of Buganda is such that migrant labour, Banyaruanda and Nilotic, has long flowed freely to serve Baganda employers. The ginning of their abundant cotton was till lately a European or Asian monopoly, and retail trade is still almost wholly Asian, but the solid achievement of the Baganda themselves does credit to them and to their teachers. The colonial administration, too, has had its reward for so early linking Buganda by rail to the outside world (Chapter 7). Peace and a quiet well-being have reigned here and in the neighbouring states or 'kingdoms' which were once vassals or rivals of Buganda but have since been incorporated in the Uganda Protectorate. The Protectorate, however, has its fringe of peoples of other stock who are less well equipped than those of the thriving kingdom of Buganda. Conscious of past dominance (and perhaps because the Protectorate Government functioned within their own territory at Entebbe), the Baganda came insensibly to think of its authority as appertaining to themselves; the traditional dignity of their own Kabaka was unimpaired, and these lesser peoples were ignored as of little account. Equilibrium reigned and Uganda was pointed to as an almost model African colony—till the ferment of ideas in the post-war years, further stimulated here by spectacular economic advance, brought a sudden upset.

The crises in post-war Uganda had a character of their own. In the profoundly peaceful Buganda of 1930 I noted discontents that seemed to portend the birth of politics on Western lines, but no Nkrumah returned from his studies abroad with a revolutionary programme ready made. That revolutionary tensions existed within the Baganda order itself became evident in 1949 when I arrived in Kampala in time to see the smoke still rising from the ruins of houses set on fire by rioters the day before. This outbreak was a protest aimed not directly against the Kabaka but against the traditional Baganda method of appointing his Court. In terms of the Uganda Agreement of 1900 (p. 164) the Kabaka, or a Regent acting in his name, continued to be a personal ruler, holding the power of appointment to all offices of government. The undertaking was to consult with and govern in accordance with the advice of a British Resident, but in practice the lesser chiefs and the members of the *Lukiko* or parliament, as well as the more important dignitaries, were still the Kabaka's nominees. After the war the world 'climate of opinion' inevitably suggested a more democratic form of government. British policy certainly favoured reform, not only, however, in Buganda, but for Uganda as a whole. Buganda, as the most advanced unit, naturally claimed first attention, and the inclusion of an elected element in the *Lukiko* at once strengthened political sentiment, if it were only by giving countenance to the traditional opposition of 'Outs' after the many years in which British recognition had weakened tribal checks on the functioning of the Kabaka as an absolute ruler. The more progressive critics, mostly Baganda, welcomed the idea of self-government, but they have never learnt to think of Buganda as only one part of a larger unit, the Protectorate. Harassed by mounting Protectorate issues, and by unfamiliar pressure on such wider questions from within what had been *his Lukiko*, in 1952 the Kabaka repudiated his responsibility to act on the advice of the British Governor. The Governor, responsible for the Protectorate as a whole and taking a stand on its indivisibility, decreed and quickly effected the Kabaka's exile. This action as quickly ended the dissensions among the Baganda; even those who had come near revolt in the riots of only three years earlier made common cause with those who demanded the return of the Kabaka as the people's acknowledged spiritual head. Three more years of pleading, mourning, and hard bargaining ended happily with the return of the exile—but it was to a new Uganda; the Agreement of 1900 was at last comprehensively revised to allow for a stronger and more broadly-based central government.

These political happenings in Uganda are evidently to be associated with the intense economic development of these crowded years and the social changes that came in its train. A major hydro-electric plant harnessed the Nile waters as they pour from Lake Victoria over the

Owen Falls; cheap power stimulated industry, for example at Tororo, a mineralized site on the eastern border; large-scale copper-mining, on the Ruwenzori range in the west, necessitated a considerable extension of the railway. White-owned plantations were fast disappearing, but industrial expansion brought many managers and technicians in its train, besides a flow of migrant African labour. The new white industrialists were sometimes seen as likely to think of 'settlement'—and events in Kenya had long since made all politically-conscious Africans apprehensive of any such development; or the influx, and the coming of highly capitalized copper mining, might appear as threatening to make Uganda another Rhodesia—when at the height of the crisis in the Kabaka's affairs the plan of federation for Rhodesia and Nyasaland became a political question a furious outcry arose from the exile's friends because, in an after-dinner speech, the ruling Secretary of State mentioned the possibility of a 'Federation' also of East Africa. Sympathy is due to those who honestly feared the effects of rapid industrialization on the essentially African character of Uganda. Some, however, added an ill-thought-out rider to this proposition and saw the situation as calling for African government on the new Gold Coast model. It had its appeal that such a government could only be staffed by men of their own modern outlook; but how far short any aspirants were from having a considered plan for grafting a new order on to the old trunk may partly be judged by the course of events in Uganda itself. The Baganda, at least, by far the most advanced of the component peoples, showed themselves to be disturbed, not so much by the new economic activity as such, as by the threat of its Protectorate-wide distribution to their old practical if unexpressed primacy. Their concern was the greater when the Colonial Office showed its anxiety to keep up with economic development by appointing a progressive Governor, Sir Andrew Cohen, and he for his part set to work enthusiastically initiating a great expansion of education and of community-welfare work throughout the Protectorate. From the British standpoint the high standing of the Baganda necessitated their political advancement; but the authorities, in all innocence, always thought of them as the natural leaders of a united Uganda. The revised Agreement of 1955 clearly contemplated the Baganda playing their full part in a strengthened Protectorate legislature. Yet early in 1957 unofficial but distinctly 'traditionalist' Baganda were canvassing a petition protesting that the barely two-years-old Agreement had been accepted at all only as the means of securing the Kabaka's restoration. They now once more demanded self-government—for the Baganda!

The new Africans, in short, those in Uganda and everywhere else, have not faced the limits set by purely practical considerations to the application of the also quite new principle of self-determination. Uganda, admittedly, like Tanganyika, is an artificial unit; but long use and wont have linked the parts together in wholly beneficial habits of co-operation and made them truly interdependent. Break or even seriously weaken those links and trade and transport must be dislocated, industry languish and revenues decline, to the detriment especially of services needed to promote better standards of living. The European and Asian promoters of economic enterprise look in Uganda to the central Government to ensure stable and orderly conditions throughout the Protectorate, and they cannot function without such. In their zeal for self-government, for themselves, the Baganda were for boycotting the central Legislature. Here as elsewhere, however, the apparent clash of racial interests is in the first place a symptom of disorder rather than its cause. The status of foreigners is readily secured, if need be by diplomacy, when the state in which they operate is in the stable control of its own people. The fundamental difficulty in Africa is that the mass of the population is (to invoke the forbidden word) 'backward'. The pooled resources of the artificial unit, the colony, served to make a beginning of the necessary remedial services but could not adequately expand them. These public services cannot be reduplicated at will, much less splintered, as a separate provision for all the separate claimants would require. It is not as if even the forward-looking people of Buganda could make their country a self-contained, self-sufficient unit. The Baganda proper are a relatively small patrician class; self-government for them, or for their near kinsmen who similarly dominate the adjoining provinces, would leave a considerable class of labourers, Banyaruanda and Nilotics, in an equivocal if not almost rightless position. The advocates of immediate self-government as the way forward are jumping the starter's gun; the sentiment that inspires the Africans among these is justly described as 'Africanism' rather than nationalism. The weak outer provinces would be weak indeed without Buganda; but the interests even of Uganda, including Buganda, are too closely bound up with those of Kenya and even Tanganyika for any of the three to be able to go forward in complete isolation.

It may be, once more, that some in Tanganyika had one part of the answer. In the early '50s the idea was being canvassed that its eight provinces be consolidated into perhaps five more nearly autonomous yet linked 'regions'; the obstacle proved to be the prohibitive cost of even such limited reduplication of services as 'regionalization' seemed to require. Devolution is clearly desirable but cannot serve without co-operation, preferably at something actually above the old 'colonial government' level. There was a time when central direction, if only by a High Commissioner, might have sufficed to foster a habit of co-operation, against the time when improved communications came to make active collaboration easier. Mr. Amery could probably even have 'federated' East Africa in 1929 (p. 181), but the opportunity passed. In 1947 a Labour Government, recognizing the need, went so far as to vest aviation, income tax, customs, posts and telegraphs, railways and harbours and other functional services in the control of a useful but strictly business organization, the East African High Commission, a body consisting of the Governors of Kenya, Tanganyika and Uganda together with officers and a Legislative Assembly. This Commission remained dependent, above all for funds, on the local units. Only a more fully effective higher authority can meet the need; but since 1947 the hope of getting it by agreement has actually receded. The challenge stands to be met by the new Africans. Some have been known to perorate on the coming United States of Africa; but in changed times they must first of all reverse Dr. Philip's rule and turn from such 'generals' to the thorny 'particulars'. By West Indian analogy, there is always a hope that the University College at Makerere (itself a High Commission responsibility) may be the seed-bed of a broadly based East African loyalty.

The same mere incoherence is a mark of the African society of the Rhodesias and Nyasaland, the three southern colonies of this east-central group. Having neither coast belt nor major mountains the southern three have little of the marvellous physical variety of their neighbours, but the conditions and the way of life that left each fragment unrelated to any other are substantially the same. In the middle '50s Africans were still 85 per cent of the total population in Southern Rhodesia, over 90 per cent in the Northern part, and some 99 per cent in Nyasaland. None of the tribes has the wealth and standing of the Baganda; the Matabele were once among the stronger units but their far from enlightened despotism controlled only a limited area; the tribes of Nyasaland, who have perhaps the best situation, were freed from slave-raiding only in the 1890s by the establishment of the *pax Britannica*—which also brought more systematic European immigration. These lands were, after all, spacious, thinly peopled and quite undeveloped; there was room for immigrants and their help was even necessary; they undoubtedly brought the African peoples greater security and some modest advance from their former low level of subsistence. Becoming established, however, the influence of the European minority prevailed in 1952, in face of some active opposition among the Africans (and even more sheer bewilderment), to take a short cut to a formal political unification of the kind that eluded East Africa. The resulting Federation poses in even sharper form the problem that vexed Kenya and Tanganyika—how to consolidate any multi-racial state. Here once again the disequilibrium, the symptom, is to be distinguished from its basic cause, the chaotic disorganization of the original African society.

The Federation itself was no bolt from the blue. Rightly or wrongly the region as a whole came under representatives of the one British Crown after 1890; even Nyasaland was in the Rhodes domain to the extent that in the beginning only Mr. Rhodes's cheques kept Sir Harry Johnston's nominally imperial administration functioning (p. 171). Rhodes himself certainly planned for the whole as a unit, even when the almost impossible difficulty of travel necessitated dividing Rhodesia itself into three separate parts (Southern, North-east and North-west), each with a governor of its own. It kept the connection faintly alive that the North-east (Fort Jameson) could normally be reached only by way of Nyasaland and the Shire River, but the multiplication of 'governments' was wasteful of effort and money: customs barriers were restrictive and made against co-operation; the unproductive North (even after its parts were amalgamated in 1911) had to make do, till the opening of the copper mines, with a total annual revenue averaging less than £1 million, and services for its million Africans, so far from expanding, tended to die of sheer inanition. Only Southern Rhodesia made steady though limited progress: its planters could not hope to make a viable unit of an inland colony with no port of its own, but they alone were politically conscious, and sufficiently informed to be aware always that there was no future for them in isolation. When in 1923 a majority of their electors forswore the destiny that would have made them, as Rhodes intended, not an extension of the Cape but part of a very different Union of South Africa, they chose to become a self-governing colony. But their leaders were almost at once considering an alternative; the moment the copper discoveries began to improve the material prospects of the North, the hunt was on for a unified government that would serve the Rhodes domain as the economic unit it was at last becoming. By this time, however, owing to the Kenya debate, African interests had come to the fore and the initiative of white interests in Southern Rhodesia was brought into question; their power made their self-governing colony a misfit in the *amalgamation* originally proposed, and threatened to extend their alleged 'domination' to two almost wholly African Crown Colonies. It was not till 1938 that the Home Government was moved to appoint a Closer Union Commission. Lord Bledisloe in his Report agreed that the proposed partners had important common interests but considered talk of union premature; they were too unequally matched and the differences in native policy were even dangerously wide. More was to be heard of these views, but war followed immediately, in 1939, and it was only towards its end that action was taken on Lord Bledisloe's one positive recommendation and a Central African Council set up to 'co-ordinate' policy on matters of obvious common interest. On this Council the two colonial governors, who were subject to London, found themselves uncomfortably yoked with the independent Prime Minister of Southern Rhodesia and in 1950 it became in name what it had been in fact, no more than an inter-territorial secretariat. A fourth secretariat in an area which already had three was no way of overcoming economic limitations, and these were increasingly felt. The upsurgence of Afrikaner nationalism after 1947 made settlers of British stock more reluctant than ever to be thrown back on the South African Union. A highly prosperous Northern Rhodesia, on the other hand, was now a more desirable partner, and its smaller body of Europeans, being only rather isolated Rhodesians, were willing to be wooed. The white planters of Nyasaland were few in number, and lukewarm, but they eventually joined what by 1949 was a considered campaign for closer union. At the first big conference, held on the border at the Victoria Falls, the white Rhodesian sponsors of the agitation made the mistake of being rather off-hand about the demand for African participation in their deliberations. By this time the attitude latent in the Hilton Young Majority Report of 1929 (p. 181), and more explicit in Lord Bledisloe's now ten years' old comments on Rhodesia, had become widely accepted: 'native' interests were seen as something separate and distinct from those of the country as a whole. In the political nonage of the great mass of the population their interests are, rightly, the special responsibility of the officers of the colonial power; but the dichotomy which puts white and native interests in inevitable and eternal conflict is a fixation of South African experience and practice originating in the days when the only recognized function of natives was to supply cheap labour. The cult of exclusively Native Affairs conflicts directly with the very possibility of the comprehensive colonial development which is now the aim. So many hold this outmoded view as an article of faith that the Rhodesian movement was suspect from the first for its 'settler' inspiration. The Rhodesian leaders, nevertheless, quickly made one important adaptation: *amalgamation* of the territories was dropped and *federation* became the objective, precisely for the reason that this was better calculated to reassure African doubters, secure local 'interests', and give the proposed unified state a more stable foundation. Succeeding conferences, moreover, did much to clear the issues. Few any longer doubted that the further progress of the three territories must depend on capital investment—and capital would be more readily attracted if natural resources could be pooled under one government. It was seen, too, to be impossible, without general development, to produce sufficient to pay for the schools and health services needed for African advancement. Great teachers like Dr. Robert Laws had laid foundations in Nyasaland and shown the possibilities; he had organized both his station and its work with great thoroughness; his consistent use of English as the teaching medium materially helped to give many Nyasalanders an unusually good start in facing the changes that awaited them. But the work so well begun was halted; world depression froze the grants-in-aid of mission schools from 1932 till 1945. Though Nyasalanders, with no more than primary education, had been in demand even in East Africa, times were changing and secondary education was coming to be expected all over the continent. Yet, left to its own resources, Nyasaland was unable till nearly 1950 to meet the cost of even one regular secondary school.

Such practical considerations weighed so much even with the cautious Labour Government that in 1951 it was moved to call a body of officials to confer in London—a strong team consisting of serving officers from each of the three territories, together with senior representatives of both the Colonial Office and the Commonwealth Relations Office. This professionally impartial body reached unanimous agreement that the interests of the territories were inseparably bound together, and that the differences even in 'native policy' were more apparent than real. To be on the safe side it advised that the 'native affairs' of the two colonies should remain under Colonial Office control, but subjects on an agreed list were to be vested in a federal government—chief among them 'economic and financial affairs', but also immigration, Federal courts, railways and other inter-territorial services. A Federal Assembly of thirty-five members should include fourteen elected Southern Rhodesians, eight and four from Northern Rhodesia and Nyasaland respectively, six elected Africans and three European representatives of African interests. As further safeguards against white 'domination' this Report proposed a statutory African Affairs Board and a Minister of African Affairs with independent status of his own.

A political conference which followed pronounced against the unattached Minister (the 'cuckoo in the nest'!) as infringing the principle of cabinet solidarity and this was dropped. The Labour Government, though hesitant, were half convinced by their official advisers of the value of Federation; and the D.C.s were instructed to put the federation proposals before the people of the two colonial territories in full detail. Yet at the same time, to avoid the appearance of anything like pressure, and to make sure that any change had free African consent, they were strictly enjoined on no account to take sides or appear to be commending the scheme. The D.C.s, never mere watch-dogs, have by almost immemorial practice been the chiefs' and peoples' advisers, the means of introducing new ways and practices by their own show of enthusiasm. They alone were in a position to reconcile Africans to a policy designed to serve the common good of the new national whole of which, in spite of themselves, they had become a part. The hold-back order inevitably aroused suspicion and, indeed, did lasting damage by throwing the generality of Africans into prolonged mental confusion on the whole subject of federation. The small body of vocal Africans protested to the last, being also strenuously backed by sympathizers in Britain and elsewhere. A plan of union emerged nevertheless from the long series of conferences, and this was first approved by a referendum of the electors of Southern Rhodesia, then endorsed by the Assemblies of the two Crown Colonies. The Conservative Government, which had taken over from Labour in November 1951, held its hand awhile but at last, though fully alive to the risks either of proceeding or of further delay, gave its approval; the Federation of the Rhodesias and Nyasaland came into being in 1953.

In spite of its stormy birth the infant state was soon economically thriving. New industries sprang up, and buildings to accommodate the industries, their personnel and the many immigrants who poured in. The prosperity of the copper industry, which made so much possible, served also to supplement the World Bank contribution to the capital cost of a major (Kariba Gorge) hydro-electric project on the Zambezi. Even if the need to harness the Shire, in Nyasaland, came second to Kariba, African interests were not overlooked. The mining industry took the lead in breaching the industrial colour bar; after difficult negotiations white trade unionists were persuaded of the need of African advancement and agreed to the opening of certain grades of more responsible work to qualified Africans. There was progress, too, in other fields. A well-equipped University College opened its doors in 1957 to qualified students of any race, creed or colour. British C. D. &

W. funds contributed to the cost, but this open-door policy was the deliberate choice of the local white sponsors of the university movement.

The Federation was clearly full of life; whether or not it was also to be looked on as a healthy infant depended much on the observer's point of view. The new state could legally be brought into being only by the British Parliament, and by old convention British colonial policy is an expression of the undivided national will; but the Labour leaders divided the Commons on this issue; as they knew, a number of Conservatives shared their own doubts; yet several experienced Labour members believed in federation but abstained from the division. The movement was in fact colonial-sponsored and the major casualty in the clash of opinion was thus the so-called 'bi-partisan' tradition in the home country. The moral surely is that the fate of any colony comes at last to depend not on the colonial power but on its own people. It is the distinctive feature of the Federation that the people concerned are neither all white (as for political purposes they were in the old America), nor all black (as in Ghana), but both white and black; also, by a peculiar inversion of roles, the whites are impatient of remote control and therefore the stronger 'anti-colonialists'. The assumption that the interests of these whites necessarily conflict with those of the African majority is naïve; this premise of racial theorists is contradicted by such facts as moved the conference of devoted 'native affairs' officials to advocate the closer union of the predominantly African colonies with their settler-ruled neighbour. The settlers' record is not unimpeachable; but their positive contribution to the advancement of the indigenous peoples also stands. The assignment to ensure that advancement is evenly shared, and to place the state on a safe and lasting foundation, is local; it certainly cannot be met from London or by the U.N., but only within the borders of the Federation.

The local white community gets less credit than it deserves for the way it has played its part. In the early days of the Federation movement its organizers were not so much disinclined to take African opinion seriously as merely baffled to know how it could express itself. Being independent people the Europeans often differ sharply among themselves, but they are still concerned, with reason, to preserve their civilized inheritance, not merely their own interests. The Home Government had its peculiar responsibility; but as the wind of controversy rose the responsible colonial leaders, Sir Godfrey Huggins, now Lord Malvern, and the present Sir Roy Welensky, also quickly and visibly adapted themselves to the times and took pride in guiding their sometimes apprehensive followers on new and untried paths, one way or another bringing them to the point when the inescapable necessity in the first place of African representation is generally accepted. Though the pattern of this settlement may be that of the old North America, and the later South Africa, the tradition, as critics forget, is different, deriving directly from the Cape of Good Hope of the tolerant days before 1900 (see Chapter 7). From the beginning literate Africans with modest means could register as voters; there are more of these than is supposed; men who were obviously entitled to register were, I discovered, refraining from doing so; it made a resounding African grievance to point to the absurdly small number of enrolled African voters—besides which, any one who was qualified to vote was of course also liable to qualify to pay income tax! On the eve of federation the Government tactlessly chose to increase the property qualification, to match the reduced value of money; but the majority party also expressly rejected a proposal to depart from the established principle of the 'common roll'. The simple solution of universal suffrage, however, will not serve in this divided and unequal society; the essentially democratic need to safeguard minorities calls, rather, for means of gauging not merely the dimensions of opinion but its real *weight*. Seen in this light the first years of the Federation were not so much a prolongation of debate as a period of gestation—a condition, it has been said, that excuses a little indigestion! The Southern Rhodesians always mistrusted the plan of nominating African M.P.s and, preferring that candidates should have to face electors of all races, introduced an element of election in the choice of representatives in their own territory. On tour in 1952 I found the Capricorn Africa Society bent on popularizing the idea of a common, multi-racial African citizenship, and of a colour-blind, if also a 'plural voting' common roll. In 1957 a Southern Rhodesian judicial commission recommended a 'dual' roll; electors would vote together, but the votes of fully qualified voters would have a higher numerical value. The danger of 'communal' elections was at last better understood; the real difficulties of safeguarding civilized standards in the present uneasy transitional state of society were being faced.

Conscious of a long road ahead, the promoters of reconstruction were tempted to challenge *apartheid* by labelling their own programmes 'partnership'. The industrialists are finding that the offer of 'African advancement' perhaps rouses more enthusiasm. At any rate the attempts to adapt the franchise laws to the facts of this complex society still get too exclusive attention. The 'common roll' could and should have spurred more Africans to qualify, but the politically-conscious among them have been taught, and too many of them prefer to teach a barren 'Africanism'; sensitive to personal slights, they rarely betray consciousness otherwise of any but purely political issues. Not even the most intransigent African leaders really want to be rid of the Europeans and of the help they bring. Political agitation persistently used to sway the masses may indeed produce a total breakdown; but the well-being of the African people depends rather on maintaining the stability of the economy, and to this (Central Africans having no appreciable export of their own) their independent contribution is still negligible. It is true that Europeans would be well advised to do more to ease the difficult upward progress of fully 'emerged' Africans. But if they themselves are to continue to put heart and hope into their work they too must see their future secure. Being even now as much a part of the African whole as the organizers of the Boston tea-party were of America two centuries ago, they may be driven to talk rashly about 'independence'. Yet they cannot, and would not if they could, hope to produce ordered stability by force. For this reason, call their present offer 'partnership' or what you will, it deserves to be fully tried. It remains (and this consideration calls for a separate chapter) that a happy issue depends above all on what the African peoples learn to contribute, positively, to the building of a more stable new order.

Chapter 12

THE BLACK MAN'S BURDEN

*

The story of the Colonial Age ends sadly near where it began. The inexperience which originally brought colonial peoples into subjection still prevents them standing squarely on their own feet. The smallest and most isolated even of tribal units already have individual members of respectable educational attainment, but many more who are drawn, as by the compelling force of gravity, into a new world outside the traditional tribal orbit. Thus new experiences breed vague and uneasy aspirations among the masses, and also a new if undefined sense, for example, of African oneness. Such profound and often sudden emotional disturbance requires that those affected should learn from the history of other peoples; but the colonial university colleges seem to have elected to pass over in their prescribed teaching the story of the Celts and Germans, Goths and Franks, Angles, Saxons, Picts, Scots and Normans of whom western Europe was born. Our own Middle Ages became real to me as a teacher of history only when I began to learn more of the people who are now in such violent transition. Castles in ruin, even noble churches still in use, cannot compel students to be constantly matching knowledge with reality as any one must who travels by 'bush' roads to find tribal initiation schools still competing with those of Christian missions, and sees in the better missions —enclaves, as they are, of cultivation, healing, and learning—a live pattern of life in medieval monasteries. As in the earlier Europe, custom still rules; but the local courts wrestle unequally to adapt rules evolved for the control of seasonal, subsistence cultivation on 'shifting' sites (often on open 'strips') to the conditions of a more settled agriculture; they are vexed too by disputed claims to the ownership of more permanent assets—cocoa trees, for example, that may bring in a handsome return not in one season only but for sixty or seventy years. To let the study of history begin for such people with the discoveries that first brought Europeans in upon them does poor service to historical understanding (which the almost forgotten teaching of Lord Acton pronounced to be better than historical learning); seen in their proper setting the discoverers would appear as themselves 'emergents', only one remove from the agrarian subsistence economy whence we all started, rather than as super-men, or even as demigods unjustly favoured by Providence. By way of counter to such teaching many forward-looking Africans understandably seek to re-root themselves by building up a romanticized historical past of their own; thus the emerging Gold Coast linked itself with Ghana, a shadowy empire in the distant Sudan. It became the mission of this new Ghana to find expression once more for the distinctive African ethos, still reflected in common gifts and traits, but almost lifeless on account, it was believed, of the subjection suffered by the African peoples since the overthrow of the old Ghana (in our own early Middle Ages) by foreign conquerors. At least, on this showing, European invaders must be absolved of blame for retrogression that began a full thousand years ago.

For the first three centuries of the Colonial Age the influence of Europeans on the black-skinned peoples was in fact very slight. Their responsibility, at the receiving end, for the African slave trade, and therefore for stimulating the raids of Africans on the weaker of their own people, is not the whole story; it was also the Western conscience that revolted at last and Britain that took the lead for most of a century in the active repression, first of the overseas traffic, then of the activities of slavers in Africa itself. But before any large part of Africa had been brought actually into the colonial sphere, the British tradition of colonial policy had settled to a pattern determined by experience in the overseas settlements and in the West Indies, and this, I have suggested (p. 95), hindered a ready adaptation to the special needs of people so very differently situated. Unlike even the West Indians, the Africans not only had their tribal institutions intact, but usually continued to manage most of their own domestic affairs. Sharp internal divisions, however, and other consequences of their long isolation, facts of history, made them late starters in the race to organize themselves to face a world growing steadily more complex. Even in the 1860s, when West Indian affairs compelled reconsideration (Chapter 3), and still more by the time of the partition of Africa, the standing of what were known as colonies and dependencies respectively was apparently so different that their paths were assumed to diverge completely. South African distractions later had the effect of focusing attention exclusively on race relations, rather than on the need to remedy the fundamental cause of strain, the inadequate equipment of the weaker races for the self-government which was, theoretically, always the natural destiny of every British colony.

Those first called on to wrestle with the hard facts of life in the new Africa had little occasion to think of constitutional government of any kind, or of setting up representative institutions. Individuals, counted in units, began the work. Such men were drawn, like Captain Lugard, by a fascination they could not explain; weak in everything except courage and tenacity, they could exist at all only with such local help as was offered, and they lived too much from hand to mouth to look far ahead. The more regular government officers who followed, being still few and isolated, were constrained to devolve on any of the local chiefs whom they could in some sort hold to their responsibilities. Such slender British rule could in any event make little difference, but the introduction of white-directed productive enterprise followed—with incalculable consequences. The East-Central African (Chapter 11) peoples were more affected than most of the West Coasters, who always had a stronger economic life of their own; white plantations being prohibited by law, and virtually by the still forbidding climate of the West Coast, Africans were left to manage for themselves the production of cocoa and groundnuts and cotton, as well as the forest palm-oil; but though white enterprise added only a relatively small mineral output, the increase in production put tribal institutions under strain even there. If the adaptation of these institutions was never very successful it was at least their own affair. Except on the West Coast, however, once the difficult pioneering stage was past a steady increase in the numbers of white planters, miners, 'settlers', even industrialists, necessarily created a demand for labour, in parts that were on the whole sparsely inhabited. The labour, therefore, was as a rule the 'migratory' labour whose coming and going of itself put the social order under new and unwonted strain.

The government instinct was always to be protective of African interests, but *laissez-faire* ruled in every colony, however slender its resources. The authorities, as a result, were inconsistent and might blow hot and cold; in Kenya they gave their blessing to experiments in white settlement, then stalled over the grant of land titles; but yet again they were moved in the interest of production to give their approval to fiscal and other measures designed to 'encourage' Africans to work on white farms. In the Government view tribal stability required that workers should return home as often as possible; it was taken to be a necessary insurance against sickness and old age that they retain their tribal status since this gave them a hold on land of their own; farm workers, therefore, were condemned to be no more than 'labour tenants', and to live in 'squatteries' rather than in modern villages; they might wish to make new permanent homes, but even leasehold tenure was frowned upon. The same paternal and protective principle determined the official attitude to the socially more revolutionary work on the mine-fields. The official rule was that workers must be discouraged, if they could not be forbidden, to contract for more than two years at a time, and a few mine owners systematically tried to make their hands feel at home by letting them build huts for themselves and find their own food for the very few months they were expected to serve. The stronger mines as systematically made themselves pioneers of welfare and good nutrition. But, even though the Rhodesian copper mines might report a high accident rate among workers returning from their often prolonged holidays, the Government refused to act on the idea that some might want to better their position by staying on to learn their trade. Rhodesia's Belgian neighbours in the Katanga were at once more realist and more venturesome. Acting on a 1928 Report, the first to appreciate the strain of migration on tribal life, they took the calculated risk of turning their mining camps into villages of families, complete with clinics and schools, where workers might stay on to master their trade and the children grow up as members of a new and 'stabilized' society of mining or urban workers. It is the governments' doing that migratory labour became the norm in British Africa. The same tender regard for established African custom has made governments very chary all over the continent of allowing or helping the people to adapt their traditional usages, especially their land systems, to the changes that the transition from subsistence agriculture to the so-called cash economy make unavoidable.

This social revolution might move headlong in the rich cocoa districts of the West, or abruptly but very differently in 'reservoirs' of labour like Nyasaland. More usually the change was gradual, almost imperceptible, and therefore hard to measure. No outside authority could reasonably be expected to control this situation, or even to be consistent. Many British officers wrought tirelessly to check the disruptive effect on native institutions of the new ways the people themselves courted; but the always slender administrative machinery of the white rulers left them powerless to reshape the society, as the times required, in new moulds. 'Law and order' was the one outstanding contribution made by 'colonialism'; the rule of law was universally appreciated and marks one step on a long road. But, so far from being autocrats, colonial officials with intimate knowledge of local needs were always under the necessity of getting the sanction of the distant metropolitan government, and this had the effect of making British colonial administrations perhaps peculiarly undecided.

The very humanity of the colonial tradition in part derived from humanitarian sentiment, and certainly made the authorities watchful to conciliate it. This body of opinion, we know, was at perpetual feud with strong local interests and kept the Colonial Office in an almost continuous ferment of uncertainty. British humanitarianism, besides being traditionally given to denouncing sin, is also subject to a time-lag all its own. Home-staying critics of colonial policy are apt to make the generous emotions aroused in their youth serve them for life, without feeling any urge to keep abreast of developments. As a young man Sydney Olivier was known as an advanced thinker and made a contribution of his own. Just before he became Governor of Jamaica he applied his considerable Caribbean experience in a vigorous little book, *White Capital and Coloured Labour*; starting on a theme vainly preached long ago at the Cape by Dr. John Philip—the stupidity of employers who looked on coloured labour as 'a present convenience', on the workers as producers only, not potential consumers—Olivier looked positively for a perhaps idealized African or West Indian society made up predominantly of free peasant cultivators. When in 1929, nearly a generation later, the veteran Olivier reissued his book, his warnings still had relevance, and his sonorous sentences were at once seized on as a textbook by the critics of white government in Kenya (Chapter 8). Many of our leading editors and publicists, who got their introduction to colonial affairs in their generous youth, round about that year, still make the negative, denunciatory parts of Olivier's teaching their starting point—to them it is still the whole trouble that white capital exploits black labour. But the great catastrophe of our generation, the Second World War, has outmoded the old evocative slogans; 'white exploitation' and 'native rights' are war cries of a battle now won; even South African legislators know very well they are defying the spirit of the age; it is only the way forward that is in doubt. Many of the dependent peoples' new-found friends and advocates, and a few of themselves, would hold that since the coming of Europeans was the disturbing influence Europeans should now remove themselves. Almost in the same breath they call on the metropolitan powers, and America, to supply the capital needed to develop latent resources, technicians to launch industries, and teachers to train the once dependent peoples to take over and manage for themselves.

The alternative is that local men must now be found to man, first of all, the administrative service. In its hey-day the Colonial Service drew at will on men picked year by year from among the honours graduates of all the universities of Britain and the Commonwealth. The field is now restricted in the first instance to the handful who in any one colony have qualified at a university. The abler and more ambitious of these may be tempted away by prizes in the new field of politics. There are local assemblies to be filled, if not federal parliaments as well, besides the chairmanship of cocoa or cotton boards or development commissions—even ministerial portfolios. Yet since governments are now so very decidedly expected to be *doing* things, administrators must be reinforced by an increasing number of scientists, technicians, teachers and others whose services command a seller's market. The new states' resources of trained intellects cannot adequately meet so many new diverse calls. Visitors are bewildered by the Proteus-like reappearance of the same little group of African leaders—in politics and journalism, at meetings of trade unions and of the local African Congress, as boardsmen, bankers, it may be ministers. The Federated West Indies' much more considerable reserve of competent man-power has no match in native Africa, yet even it is being hard taxed to fill so many new posts. Elsewhere secretaries and clerks have been promoted to fill the top posts, leaving a vacuum below them. With state business so much in the hands of novices the quiet efficiency with which the old service went about anything it undertook could become hardly even a memory. The Principal of Khartoum University has quoted an estimate that some 46 per cent of the population of one not untypical unit, the Sudan, are producers, but those available to plan, direct, and manage their activities are only 'one-tenth of one per cent' of that total; he justly notes that these are over-burdened. As for training, an honours degree in Arts is of itself no guarantee of a man's capacity for running the affairs of the state, any more than a paper certificate, even a B.Sc. in engineering, automatically fits its possessor to manage a great mine. Much experience is almost bred in the bone of the more established peoples, but it is only slowly acquired. Recognizing a deficiency in the national equipment, the rulers of Ghana and the Nigerian states retained the services of many ex-colonial civil servants (now become 'expatriates'), and continued to offer generous terms to British and other volunteers from without; yet many of their departments went short of their full establishment.

In spite of this scarcity of trained man-power, or perhaps because of it, the future of the all-African territories seems full of promise; bursts of energy and gay exuberance mark the burgeoning of political freedom or, in Ghana and Nigeria, its actual attainment. They have the stimulus of knowing how much depends on themselves. One bright young woman graduate from Nigeria 'wished she were twenty people', that she could do justice to the work crying out to be done; for her and her like truly

'Bliss was it in that dawn to be alive. . . .'

In the mixed areas, on the other hand, visible tensions fill observers with gloomy forebodings. If history is any guide the ultimate test has yet to come; there can be enduring stability in either region only when the great mass of the people are able to share more fully in new adventure. The prospects of attainment may, therefore, actually be brighter in the troubled 'mixed' territories; their tensions may even be evidence that inevitable growing pains are further advanced. Their not always welcome white colonists are one obvious source of that sorely needed directive man-power; rightly regarded, these could be their great asset; having their roots in the land, local knowledge and experience, and warmly felt local loyalties, they also possess a well-rooted tradition of work for work's sake, and inherited standards of competence. But there is a contribution to be looked for from the African side; help cannot be forced on unwilling recipients. Even teachers and technicians must have the assured and whole-hearted co-operation of those they would help, and even then they cannot themselves do the social rebuilding asked for.

The world-wide attention which first fired the African leaders' ambitions gave them a bad start by making it appear (Chapter 10) as if it only needed the removal of the intruding colonial powers to set all the colonies functioning fully and freely. But it is not only political stability that is impossible on the visibly shaken social foundations of these societies. The champions of colonial freedom perhaps saw as much when, like the promoters of C. D. & W., they made economic self-sufficiency a necessary accompaniment of political reconstruction; but they made too light of the no less devastating effects social conditions must have on their economic programme. Economic development, desirable in itself or even essential, has many enthusiastic African backers but these, with the rest, commonly evade one of its most important implications; the self-sufficiency aimed at for the colonies or ex-colonies cannot be increased without modernizing not only their governmental forms but their people's whole way of life. Once the end is accepted the means are not in doubt; the capital outlay demanded, and the help of technicians and teachers, are indispensable. But the vendors of capital are shy of unstable conditions, and those called on to help cannot be indifferent to the political uncertainties attendant on their life's work. The colonial peoples' old social order had disintegrated before governments or humanitarians had awakened to the need to let their leaders find their own feet. The remedy now proposed—in effect 'industrialization'—is actually more medicine of the same order as has brought this social chaos upon them. Supposing the stronger dose ultimately has the desired effect, there must be some uneasy years of transition before states are truly ready to manage entirely by and for themselves.

When anti-colonialism was strongest in the United Nations, when Ghana was showing the approved way forward, actually too when the Mau-Mau terror was at its height in Kenya, a British East African Royal Commission was preparing a weighty report, published in 1955, which almost for the first time laid bare some of the fundamentals underlying the essentially *social* economic problems of the colonial societies. The malaise of Africa, the report reminds us, is the result of its old world being shattered beyond repair; too many of its men and women drift into a new world in search of the security the old no longer affords them; yet, perhaps inevitably clinging to the ways of the old, they have difficulty in finding lodgement there and drift back again. Their inexperience, their irregular habits and general lack of competence, far more than any barriers put in their way, leave them at a disadvantage in their new occupations. At the same time the breakdown of the old order is hastened by the prolonged absences of so many of its able-bodied members; tribal land rapidly going to ruin, or already ruined by misuse or neglect, is the most painfully familiar sight in modern Africa. Many of those who best know the terrain, especially the geologically old, leached and eroded soils of the tsetse-infested 'bush' of east-central Africa, would make this the most pressing African 'problem'. Year by year, as they see it, the native inhabitants eke out an ever poorer living, but medical services, remedial and preventive, add to the numbers of those who must be fed. Every individual tribesman can no longer hope to get each his own plot or plots of tribal land, much less to win a comfortable subsistence on the overcrowded oases, the hillsides and lake basins, but the open flats remain barren and unfruitful. Only better food production, an improvement both in quantity and variety, can win better standards of living and satisfy awakened human ambitions. In face of this it was, I think, Mrs. Elspeth Huxley who put it that every honest observer must be either a neo-Malthusian or else a neo-Micawber! The Royal Commission itself was set to work originally to the theme couched much in those terms in a dispatch by Governor Sir Philip Mitchell.

The Commission discounted Malthusian anxieties as unwarranted by the evidence, pointing for answer rather to the restrictive influence of tribal custom; in a subsistence economy mere abundance, or expansion of any kind, will never be seen as serving any useful purpose. Going flatly counter to the basic principle of indirect rule, they saw the weakness of the African economy as arising from tribal divisions, and even more immediately from the communal basis of tribal land tenure. As things are there is not even food enough to go round, and production can be increased only when subsistence agriculture gives way to intensive cultivation by farmers trained as specialists in their calling, and freed from tribal interference by the steady introduction of legal protection for the rights of the individual. To ensure the inalienable right of every tribesman to his own lot is no longer practically possible; those crowded out must depend on wage labour in the service either of new-style native farmers or in outside industry. On the model tried in a small way on the Belgian Congo mines the temporary compounds, urban 'locations' and farm 'squatteries' must become the homes of a 'stabilized' community.

So much economic individualism, 'so much Adam Smith' as one critic put it, was hard doctrine. The governments of the territories immediately concerned shied off it as more than tribal opinion could be expected to stomach; but, as Adam Smith did, the report will require the attention of policy makers for many years to come. Most colonies, and not only those favoured by soil and climate like the growers of Ghana cocoa or Chagga coffee, already have numbers of individualist African farmers demonstrating that better methods give a better yield and are profitable—even if one or two progressives I have known have had to be given 'special protection' from interference by a hostile populace and jealous chiefs. Here and there in Rhodesian 'reserves', even in some South African 'betterment areas', notably in Kikuyuland (p. 240), a measure of rationalization has been successfully applied sometimes recognizing individual holdings, and normally separating arable and grazing from residential areas. Pressure in favour of individual holdings may well increase as more wage-earners appear who wish to use their savings in capitalized farming and at any rate to build homes to retire to; but progress must be slow without the more general acquiescence of the absentee labouring class in such an invasion of their communal right to this increasingly unreliable insurance against sickness and old age—it is not only the migratory labour class as such that needs 'stabilizing', but its place in the society. Some of the purely economic questions may be best answered by mining enterprise, as Rhodes saw and the story of the Copper Belt proves; besides giving employment and breaking the old stagnation, the very existence of the Kimberley mines helped almost to streamline the development of the Rand; so again the expertise of the Rand helped the Copper Belt. A mine being always a wasting asset, the powerful copper companies may be relied on to see that any mineral secrets hid in the tsetse bush beyond are fully explored and exploited. But African labour, besides being ill-equipped for the fuller life economic progress should make possible, is still unequal to the work it is called on to do. A most efficient West Indian sugar firm regretfully decided (while the East African Report was preparing) that the unreliable quality of the labour available in populous Nyasaland, besides tribal land rules, barred them from the Shire valley. At least the over-population the pessimists fear is almost entirely local, and some of the alleged rapid growth of numbers the result chiefly of better census-taking. An agricultural officer, bemoaning the obviously poor European agriculture of a good average district of Northern Rhodesia, explained this as being due to the workers being not only inefficient but *too few*. On the other hand the redistribution of the population, which is often desirable, promises to raise very sharply the difficulties attendant on the infiltration of African 'strangers' into territory in possession of other tribal owners. The introduction of mining or any other industry, in short, while answering many of the economic questions, must raise many others of even greater social and political complexity.

Yet the challenge of the East African Report remains to be met. Africans cannot have it both ways, standing pat in their old ways while hoping to take their due place in the larger world. When African society was more malleable many more desirable changes in tribal practice might conceivably have been gently insinuated by their colonial rulers; but the awakening of tribal and national self-consciousness, manifested even in some new racial animosity, now throws it inescapably on their own leaders to take the lead, first of all in arresting the further decay of the old rural life. A general increase in the people's productivity is the only sure way to economic progress and, even then, economic success will be barren unless the changed conditions which it necessitates are genuinely accepted by the people with conviction, and, as the report puts it, increasing 'contentment'. Old fears and prejudice have to be met and overcome; newer phobias, too, have been born, above all of the alienation of land to irrupting Europeans and of the real or alleged consequences. This European irruption, when all is said and done, was only the march of history overtaking Africa, as it was bound to do; the disadvantages it brought are greatly outweighed by the real benefits,

The educated leaders of today are themselves evidence of the benefits, and only they can mediate these to their less enlightened fellows. White attitudes are, I suggested, being sensibly modified; Rhodesian statesmen, for example, have shown awareness of what is needed. The profound psychological disturbance suffered by Africans of all classes may be gradually stilled as they see and come to accept more work of the kind already begun in and for their countries (p. 237) by *white* natives of East Africa.

African leaders, for their part, can draw for guidance on the story of their expatriates in the West Indies, where a long training in representative government is clearly bearing fruit. West Indian opinion is not merely Western; it is essentially that of modern men; English (often, it may be, 'as she is spoke') is the national language, and there is a growing literature of more than merely local significance. The forms and the spirit of parliamentary procedure are common ground, accepted by all. Those most actively participating in the political game are predominantly of a middle class, but such a class is a much larger proportion of the whole than for example in Ghana, and provides the staff for a very competent civil service; its politicians seek popular remedies for social discontents and bid actively for the suffrages of the 'commons'. The white minority, much the same proportion of the whole as in Central Africa, has come to stand aloof from politics, but its essential members are none the less emphatically *West Indians*. In the economic sphere their directive work is backed by the power and drive of outside capital, which imports also a considerable body of 'expatriate' white industrial employees. Even if the separation of political and economic power is on racial lines this society is effectively multi-racial. Painful tensions persist, but for the most part below the surface; politics appear stable. The fundamental weakness is what it has always been—that the economic resources of the islands are unequal to the needs of the ever-growing population of unskilled and largely landless labourers. Some good judges consider in fact that the troubles especially of Central and South Africa present the West Indian picture in reverse. African tensions are rendered more acute by economic prosperity. Opportunities expanding rapidly (and a shortage of labour) make both white and black eager to cash in on them while the going is good; even governments, notably in South Africa, go unrestrained by the caution normally induced when the national exchequer is lean or, as in the West Indies, almost empty. At one extreme white doctrinaires look on the very prosperity of the Union as the unaided achievement of 'white civilization', feeling it more than ever incumbent on them to defend this heritage to the last; at the other the leaders of black Africa are inclined to shout loudly for a share proportionate to the mere numbers rather than to the achievement of the African population.

The restraint called for, and the political art of compromise, are perhaps not to be expected all at once from African leaders. Unlike their 'detribalized' West Indian fellows they have had little practice in choosing representative spokesmen by free election, and almost none in the even more important habit of making the pros and cons of public policy a matter of closely reasoned debate. African custom almost forbids compromise, as I had impressed upon me by a close-up view of a famous recent episode. All the world heard how the Bamangwato heir to the chiefdom, Seretse Khama, was banned from acceding, and put it down, almost *sans phrase*, to his temerity in marrying an English girl; the Government, it was believed, took fright at protests led by the South African Prime Minister, excluded Seretse from his domain and left the tribe lamenting. In October 1950 the tribe was actually all but unanimous in backing the Regent Tshekedi against the marriage. World-wide publicity, however, at once made the issue a test of the soundness of H.M.G.'s attachment to the principle of racial equality, and as such it was hotly taken up in African circles in London and wherever else groups of the educated class were in a position to speak on Africans' behalf. Under pressure from without (and with growing awareness that the alternative to Seretse was the prolongation of the strong but not always popular regency of Tshekedi), by June 1951 the Bamangwato had turned against Tshekedi and demanded the return of Seretse. It has been too little noted that for some time after Tshekedi thus lost the support of the tribal assembly, the *Khotla*, he was in physical danger; neither he nor his handful of faithful followers, far the ablest and most experienced of the sub-chiefs and tribal administrators, dared show face within the tribal boundaries; when I met them in August they were camped at a cattle station safely across the border. At a score of meetings in Bamangwatoland the spokesmen, clearly a tribal second team, spoke with one voice. Actually the tribe was riven by a split which opened the prospect of a prolonged dynastic feud; but the show of unanimity was the significant thing—the tribal instinct for solidarity had come uppermost, the habitual conformity, the intolerance of nonconformists or of anything like an opposition. In any fight waged to remedy a specific grievance, such for instance as a spontaneous bus boycott, this power of standing together is highly effective. But it also makes the inexperienced masses peculiarly good material for leaders of ability and education who choose to play on their emotions,

Tribal habit and tribal ways of dealing are a force to be reckoned with, and they make Africans difficult material for parliamentary government which proceeds on the assumption, so foreign to their tradition, that there are two sides to every question.

Even African students do not seem to share the normal youthful joy in asserting their own independence. At Fort Hare College a year or two before the Bamangwato affair, and in particular during a long evening alone with a mass meeting of students, not one of those who clearly knew when my hecklers were (even outrageously!) wrong dared a word in my support. Again in 1952, at meetings up and down the three Federation territories, groups or small audiences of the intelligentsia, though uniformly good-tempered, conceded never a point, remaining throughout glued to something very like a party line. Try as I might I failed to get them beyond reiterating their strong *feeling* against federation; none would make reasoned criticisms of the detailed proposals of the White Paper then in circulation, or suggest alternative ways of starting and financing the services they expected and demanded. In this case the D.C.s, we know, had been forbidden to express any views for or against. As if following this cue the word had gone round that Africans must refuse all discussion. The Labour politicians who looked for a free expression of African opinion by leaving them to a free debate can only have supposed, with Gilbert, that every little African is born either a little Liberal or else a little Conservative. This was to reckon without the subtle forms of pressure against which even a giant like Tshekedi Khama was helpless. Pressure, indeed, is not always so subtle but may be plain intimidation; the Christians who defied Mau Mau had a faith which armed them against such pressures, but there are not yet many Africans with the high moral courage to take an unpopular stand and defend it on principle through thick and thin.

The plan of Central African Federation as it emerged from the conference of officials in 1951 was clear at any rate on the economic conditions of progress, and on how much must depend on bettering the equipment of the African masses. The East African Commission had not yet reported but Federationists dwelt, perhaps even too exclusively, on the need to provide training and services, and the means of paying their cost. The proposals would excuse some apprehension and even more confusion; but they were sponsored by undoubted champions of African interests as likely to help the people forward, and they deserved to be met with better than blank negation. The Africans I met at that time were unco-operative and unconstructive, but though they were also serious-minded, and obviously troubled, the monotonously uniform sentiment they expressed was by no means all their own spontaneous reaction. Teachers and clerks, most of them, with a sprinkling of farmers and small business men, they were the cream of the local schools, well ahead of most of their own people—the promising nucleus of tomorrow's much larger body of responsible citizens. But they were also appreciably behind a still more select few who, if not themselves of the student class, at least drew their inspiration direct from the political thought issuing from the forcing house that equipped Kwame Nkrumah to organize revolution on the Gold Coast. All over Africa local tactics were coming to be directed thus from without, as by a modern 'bush telegraph' radiating from London and other international centres. The territorial middle class was in no position to compete, and if it could perhaps would not feel much need to give an independent lead of its own; with the result that, as in the Bamangwato *Khotlas*, the emphatically stated, internationally sponsored, fashionable idea of the moment dominated everywhere, percolating even to the workers crowded together in the towns and mining villages. Many of the ultra-modern individuals, Dr. Nkrumah for one, have shown (much helped by universal suffrage) a gift for organizing mass support; the politically immature masses have thus come to be courted, with heady and unsettling effect.

But in the circles where political ideas originate the 'backwardness' of these masses, so far from being acknowledged as the governing factor in the situation, is a forbidden topic; officially approved films of a royal visit to Nigeria and of Ghana independence allowed the world never a glimpse of village conditions. Anything that calls attention to the continuing existence of a more primitive Africa must be embarrassing to political leaders, a small highly privileged minority who habitually put themselves forward as the typical representatives and spokesmen of a repressed people. The isolation of the student class has got the superstructure of the new states they would build detached from the only possible foundations. Few as they are, the war-time increase in their numbers robbed them even of the close individual tuition enjoyed by many of their still fewer predecessors. Being pioneers, the earlier post-war African students certainly missed even the often brutally frank guidance our own undergraduates have to put up with from seniors among their contemporaries. For want, above all, of this very helpful discipline, their politics were untempered by criticism. The most honest disagreement expressed by outsiders was at once suspect as of hostile intent. On matters of African policy they turned rather to the uncritical and imperfectly informed sympathy of such 'progressives' as were ready to meet their most extreme claims, after the over-civilized modern fashion, with mere 'appeasement'. In this awkward stage of development, as if content to be fobbed off with a sort of 'special relationship', these young men come near depriving themselves of one of the highest privileges of the *equality* they demand; those with deeper knowledge and wider experience than ours are able to treat us as equals only if they feel free to give us the benefit (and the honour) of their most candid criticism. The awkward phase will pass. It was heartening to hear a senior Nigerian make his juniors at a university seminar face the real intricacies of Nigerian Federation; they for their part assured me that his political views would 'cut no ice' at home; but the incident held promise of a time coming when mere feeling will be tempered by more serious thinking. The ultimate answer can only be more of the direct responsibility colonial governments were too slow to give; as General Smuts quoted: 'Experience is the best teacher.' But these Africans' ambition to take charge would in truth be more easily satisfied if only they were inspired by a sense of *mission* for the work of relaying the foundations of their own societies.

The two world wars, which so much hastened the end of the Colonial Age, did nothing whatever to change the conditions that were met for a time by bringing these societies under the control and increasingly responsible direction of outside powers. The 'transfer of power' involved in the passing of this 'colonialism' is an operation which tends to leave a vacuum and (even without a contribution from the force of world communism) there is fissionable material enough to be dangerous if the functions fulfilled by the colonial system are merely left aside. The new states will want to preserve the trade and intercourse, made safe and easy where once they were impossible, by the often arbitrary demarcation of colonial boundaries. The mere break-up of an artificial unit like Nigeria might leave a group of succession states with former rivalries become even sharper than before. Improved transport and communications have brought neighbouring states into new relationships which must be ordered by themselves when London no longer serves as the link. This consideration explains, ultimately, the local drive for Central African Federation; and it will not answer for Nyasalanders (become conscious, a few of them, since 1952, that their little state is not after all self-sufficient) to ignore established economic ties and to profess a preference for union with Tanganyika (from which they are sharply cut off by a barrier knot of mountains). The control of European and other foreign adventurers was normally the treaty-made, even the prime responsibility of the protecting power; now the foreign interests have actually become an essential part of the new state.

To meet its internal needs, or to promote its Volta schemes (p. 220), the self-governing ex-colony, become master in its own house, must show itself credit-worthy. The colonial power, though at fault in devolving too little responsibility, was at its best in acting big brother to the unprivileged and uncritical mass of peasants, and it saw at last what was asked of it when it linked development with welfare and itself footed the initial bill. This work was sometimes interrupted by political disturbances which it failed to foresee must be an inevitable result of its own unwonted activity in the social field. At last the most advanced of the new colonial political leaders discovered with something of a shock that the acquisition of independent self-government automatically cut off Colonial Development and Welfare funds, and also the more strictly business operations of the *Colonial* Development Corporation which provided highly valued technical advice, and sometimes stepped in where governments could not and private enterprise would not venture. In the past the spending of C. D. & W. money had to conform to rules laid down by H.M. Treasury; in the new phase the World Bank, American Foreign Aid or U.N. organizations will impose conditions at least as stringent as those of the Treasury; and none of these will be as accessible to pleas, or so easily moved by local pressures, as the 'colonialist' foster-mother. There is even some danger of the inexperienced and needy rulers of these new countries (like some hard-pressed governors before them) making disadvantageous bargains, or becoming subtly dominated by and dependent on some large capital concern. This danger from powerful monopolies was guarded against by the Colonial Office as it came to learn from experience; in the newest phase such experience may go to waste, or have to be rebought. The weakness of colonial rule, we see in retrospect, was that it innovated too little and too slowly. But the new rulers' predecessors set them a high standard of integrity and hard work; the quiet unpretentious devotion of the British Colonial Service to the interests of the most out-of-the-way, the most primitive, or even of some decadently sophisticated peoples, initiated new ways and skills without imposing them. Poor natural resources, imperfectly developed, were one major cause of paralysis. The Governor faced with a demand from a lively chief for a road or school was very likely to protest the claims of less progressive districts, and that he must always spread the butter of money and man-power as far as it would go. The shortages and makeshifts that resulted involved a great deal of overwork; but the high standards demanded were also responsible for the failure to use local talent, and to allow or even to enforce responsibility, or to train successors. These were to be wanted sooner than was ever expected.

The British contribution was the stock-pattern expansion of parliamentary institutions, supplemented at most by some modest five-year plans; this political lead had the natural effect of turning African leaders' thoughts to self-government as an end in itself, without prompting any serious thinking about how such responsibility was to be used. Modernity showed itself in enthusiastic advocacy of large plans like the Volta scheme in Ghana; industrialization was a popular catchword. But even in this field politics dominated, and the sudden popularity of trade unions, even in the more mature West Indies, can tempt their leaders into using industrial pressure for political ends. Certainly great efforts were made in the last days of the Gold Coast to meet a genuinely popular demand for more schools. For the purposes of education several new governments have dared, as their British predecessors never could, to levy substantially increased direct taxation, and this is evidence of how political maturity is fostered by self-government. The weakness remains that the great mass of the people have no real comprehension of the goal set by the country's active leaders.

The full 'Africanist' programme contemplates government by and for Africans everywhere on the Ghana model. But in the mixed colonies a policy imposed by and depending on the mere weight of African numbers, being no different in kind, would merit the dusty answer likely to result from *apartheid* imposed further south by the unchecked power of a European minority. The whites chafe even more than their rivals at 'remote control' from Downing Street. Some Africans would hope to throw it on H.M.G. to 'hold the ring'; but this difficult assignment is to be only till they themselves are ready to take over. On this showing the imposed colonial authority is doomed, whichever side prevails, and the people of all the different races must sooner or later settle their own future. Above all else they should now be seeking agreement among themselves, and—hard saying though it may seem—some clear move in the direction of conciliation is overdue from the African leaders. Just ambitions must not be thwarted, but neither must Africans be misled by the racial teaching of world sympathizers into brandishing the big stick of mere numbers. The conduct of their countries' everyday affairs will affect the interests of Africa's millions, as individuals, as variously as those of its thousands of Europeans. The general principle, that Africans are entitled to their share of influence in the conduct of affairs, is sufficiently accepted for their leaders to turn their attention rather to the troublesome particulars. Africans (Lord Malvern has said, in forthright conversational idiom) would be welcome to the fullest voting power if only they would 'muck in' together with whites, judging every political matter on its own merits for its likely effect on tomorrow's bread and butter. The accidental colour of the voter's skin would then become irrelevant.

The spectacular and revolutionary changes that swept the African colonies in the post-war decade affected, it remains to be said, purely *external* relations. The executive powers of the British Governor and his officers were at first much reduced; latterly they have in many parts actually been cut off and transferred bodily to the elected representatives of the people. In the old practice, since 'native' courts functioned freely and supervised most local affairs, the Government's activities were mainly directed to the ordering of matters of national concern—police and security, a limited range of services and public works, external affairs. This left the tribal authority of chiefs almost intact.

The external changes had been rushed through almost precipitately; the place of local and tribal institutions was never inquired into; they were left untouched to function independently as best they might, or to be fitted into the new order later, as circumstances might dictate.

The new changes came about through strong popular pressure, but this was almost entirely from the towns; tribal chiefs, disinclined to thwart a popular movement, either acquiesced or stood aside, perhaps without much comprehension of how they must be affected at last by the rise of new leaders. Few of these were even members of the old ruling class but, typically on the Gold Coast as it still was, the C.P.P. made all the running and took full charge; any opposition that showed itself was cowed, after the African fashion, by the organized Party, and overwhelmed at the first elections by the votes of the mass electorate. Chiefs and traditionalists, visibly strong in Ashanti and the Muslim Northern Territories, found themselves faced with an abrupt change of rulers; new men, almost all from the Coast, now advised and in effect directed the Governor; the D.C.s they knew as H.M.'s representatives became 'agents' of the new African ministry. Such redefinition was necessary, but it was allowed to appear as an attempt to rivet central control when the real need was to forge some link that might bind the parts together.

The strength of attachment to tribal authority has on occasion (as in the Kabaka dispute) been used by the new leaders for their own ends; its real strength is perhaps not yet fully determined, but so long as the vast majority of the people are peasants who rely for subsistence on their patches of tribal land, communally controlled, their attachment to old custom will determine their general attitude. The new men were by no means necessarily accepted by the masses. To make good their status they found themselves committed to a struggle to hold their gains by establishing effective internal power. Knowing they had something less than nation-wide support, they suddenly found themselves with wide patronage in their gift. When the last British administration had turned away from indirect rule to set up county councils on the English model, special effort had been required to induce the chiefs who dominated the districts to accept an infiltration of men of the new educated class; now the tables were turned, and local councils became a useful source of preferment for staunch party supporters who would at the same time replace aristocratic rivals of the new rulers as the chairmen, whole-time secretaries and staff of the local councils. The already considerable field of patronage was thus enlarged, and the party in office encouraged to use its influence both to buy more power and as a means of keeping it. The exuberance of spirit that marked the beginnings of the new age will be wasted indeed if it gives way to the mere excitement created by the prospect of what our eighteenth century knew as 'places'—and modern jargon terms 'jobs'. Practices that limit the choice of personnel in an already limited field of competent candidates may profit individuals, but must be a loss to the efficiency of services needed to raise the level of the less privileged masses.

It is still 'the condition of the people' question that is neglected. The technical process of making new states is one thing but, for all the modern passion for equality among peoples, the building of nations is another. The old colonial governments were authoritarian and, placed as they were, could hardly otherwise have held their fragmented charges together. The new democratic leaders may find authoritarianism forced upon them by the same unhealed divisions and, interpreting parliamentary democracy in their own way, may lean to the totalitarianism we dislike for ourselves. British colonial rule was at its best with the rural peoples. The good D.C. backed the interests of 'his' people by unremitting championship of their cause at headquarters, and headquarters was at pains to hold a just balance and protect the more backward districts. The D.C. was a lonely figure, but his African successor may well be lonelier still; the new men, predominantly urban, certainly feel the masses as a drag on their progress, and are not readily attracted to work in the 'bush', in technical services or even agriculture; the aristocratic tradition may be temporarily in eclipse and with it the tradition of service. But the political centre of gravity which has already shifted more than once may shift again. The European-trained intellectuals of not very long ago rank now, it will be remembered, as the 'been-tos'. Dr. Nkrumah has claimed to be the supplanter of 'middle class' predecessors. The masses now have votes and are sensitive to an appeal by personalities. That being so, any government has its foundations in shifting sand unless its authority in its rural districts is fortified by intimate knowledge and understanding of the people's needs and moods. Thriving towns are good to see, and the excitements of political debates in the assemblies are stimulating—not least when speakers conjure up visions of the essential Africa finding at last a full expression and making its own distinctive contribution to world thought. Those who speak thus are apt to believe themselves to be the successful leaders of a revolution. But in fact the revolution has hardly yet begun. The foundations of the future Africa must first be laid in each of the separate states that are. The very possibility of a true expression of the African spirit demands, first of all, that those who dream of such a future should make more humble acknowledgement of the Africa that is.

BIBLIOGRAPHY

*

This bibliography makes no attempt to be comprehensive. It is designed to provide a selection of reading matter that bears on the subjects discussed in this book and which may be of interest both to the general reader and the student of colonial and Commonwealth affairs.

I. GENERAL

ANDREWS, C. M. *The Colonial Period of American History*. London 1934–38. 4 volumes. A detailed history. The author approaches the subject 'from the English end. . . . It brings the mother country into the forefront of the picture'.

ANDREWS, C. M. *The Colonial Background of the American Revolution*. New Haven 1924. Revised Edition New Haven, 1948. Four essays —an attempt to explain early history of the U.S.A. in terms of the colonial relationship with Great Britain.

BEER, G. L. *The Old Colonial System*. New York 1912. 2 volumes.

BEER, G. L. *British Colonial Policy 1754–1765*. New York 1927. A portrayal of British policy and an account of the preliminaries of the American Revolution.

BENNETT, G. (ed.) *The Concept of Empire. Burke to Attlee*. London 1953. Select documents.

BILLINGTON, R. A. *Westward Expansion*. New York 1949. A detailed history of the American frontier from 1492 to 1896.

COUPLAND, SIR R. *The Durham Report*. Oxford 1945. An abridged version of the Report with introduction and notes.

CREIGHTON, D. G. *The Commercial Empire of the St. Lawrence 1760–1850*. Toronto 1937. A study in commerce and politics which traces the relations between the commercial system of the St. Lawrence and the political development of Canada.

DE MADARIAGA, S. *The Rise of the Spanish American Empire*. London 1947.

DE MADARIAGA, S. *The Fall of the Spanish American Empire*. London 1947.

FRANKEL, S. HERBERT. *The Economic Impact on Underdeveloped Societies. Essays on International Investment and Social Change.* Oxford 1953.

GALLACHER, J., and ROBINSON, R. 'The Imperialism of Free Trade.' *Economic History Review*. August 1953.

GIPSON, L. H. *The British Empire in the Eighteenth Century—Its Strength and Weakness*. Oxford 1952. An Inaugural Lecture delivered before the University of Oxford.

GOUROU, P. *The Tropical World. Its Social and Economic Conditions and its Future Status*. London 1953.

HACKER, L. M. *England and America. The Ties that Bind.* Oxford. Inaugural Lecture 1948. An historical analysis. The flow of capital is seen as a civilizing and binding force.

HALL, H. DUNCAN. *Mandates, Dependencies and Trusteeship*. London 1948. This volume contains in addition to the text a substantial section of League of Nations and United Nations documents.

HAMILTON, GENESTA. *In the Wake of Da Gama*. London 1951. Introduction by Elspeth Huxley. A graphic survey of the history of Portugal's attempts to colonize the East Coast of Africa between 1497 and 1729.

HANCOCK, W. K. *Argument of Empire*. Penguin Books 1943.

HANCOCK, W. K. *Survey of British Commonwealth Affairs*. Volumes I and II.
Volume III by P. N. S. MANSERGH.
Volume I. Problems of Nationality 1918–1936.
Volume II. Problems of Economic Policy 1918–1939. Parts 1 and 2.
Volume III. Problems of External Policy 1931–1939.

HARING, C. H. *The Spanish Empire in America*. Oxford 1947.

HARLOW, V. *Founding of the Second British Empire 1763–1793*. Volume I. Discovery and Revolution. London 1952.

HARLOW, V. and MADDEN, F. *British Colonial Development 1774–1834*. Oxford 1953. Select documents.

HOBSON, J. A. *Imperialism*. London 1948. (First published in 1902.)

JEFFRIES, SIR C. *The Colonial Office*. London 1956. A volume of the 'New Whitehall Series'. The author began his career in the Colonial Office in 1917.

JENKS, L. H. *The Migration of British Capital to 1875*. London 1938.

KNOWLES, L. C. A. *The Economic Development of the British Overseas Empire*. 3 volumes. London 1924–36.

LENIN, V. I. *Imperialism, the Highest Stage of Capitalism.* 2nd English edition. London 1934.

PARES, RICHARD. 'The Economic Factors in the History of the Empire.' *Economic History Review.* May 1937.

PARKINSON, SIR COSMO. *The Colonial Office from within 1909–1945.* London 1947. A short and personal account of the work and character of the Colonial Office and its civil servants.

PRESTAGE, E. *The Portuguese Pioneers.* London 1933.

ROSE, J. HOLLAND, NEWTON, A. P., BENIANS, E. A. (General Editors.) *The Cambridge History of the British Empire.* Volumes I–VIII. Cambridge 1929.

SCHUYLER, R. L. *The Fall of the Old Colonial System. A Study in British Free Trade 1770–1870.* London 1945. Deals primarily with Colonial commerce and defence.

SMITH, ADAM. *The Wealth of Nations.* Various editions. Note particularly Book IV, Chapter VII 'Of Colonies'.

SUTHERLAND, L. S. *The East India Company in Eighteenth Century Politics.* Oxford 1952.

TURNER, F. J. *The Frontier in Amer can History.* New York 1937. Turner's celebrated 'Frontier' thesis.

VLEKKE, B. H. M. *Nusantara. A History of the East Indian Archipelago.* Harvard 1943. Detailed survey of government and economic policy.

VLEKKE, B. H. M. *The Story of the Dutch East Indies.* Cambridge, Massachusetts 1946. A narrative for the general reader.

WEBB, W. P. *The Great Frontier.* London 1953.

WHEARE, K. C. *The Statute of Westminster and Dominion Status.* London. 1st Edition 1938, 5th Edition 1953.

WHEARE, K. C. *Federal Government.* London. 3rd Edition 1953.

WIGHT, M. *The Development of the Legislative Council 1606–1945.* London 1946.

WIGHT, M. *British Colonial Constitutions 1947.* Oxford 1952.

WILLIAMSON, J. A. *A Short History of British Expansion.* London. The first edition of this history was published in 1922; the fourth edition takes the story up to 1952.

WINT, GUY. *The British in Asia.* London 1954. A new and revised edition.

II. WEST INDIES AND SLAVERY

BURN, W. L. *Emancipation and Apprenticeship in the British West Indies.* London 1937.

BURN, W. L. *The British West Indies.* Hutchinson's University Library. London 1951.

BURNS, SIR ALAN. *History of the West Indies.* London 1954.

BUXTON, C. *Slavery and Freedom in the British West Indies.* London 1860.

BUXTON, C. *Memoirs of Sir Thomas Fowell Buxton.* Everyman edition, London 1925.

Cmd. 6607. *West India Royal Commission Report.* Chairman, Lord Moyne. H.M.S.O. 1945.

COUPLAND, SIR R. *The British Anti-Slavery Movement.* Home University Library, London 1933.

COUPLAND, SIR R. *Wilberforce. A narrative.* Oxford 1923. London 1945 (new edition).

KUCZYNSKI, R. R. *A Demographic Survey of the British Colonial Empire.* London 1948–53.
Volume III. The West Indian and American Territories.

MACMILLAN, MONA. *The Land of Look Behind* (Jamaica) 1957.

MACMILLAN, W. M. *Warning from the West Indies. A Tract for Africa and the Empire.* London 1936. Penguin Books 1938.

MOTTRAM, R. H. *Buxton the Liberator.* London 1946.

OLIVIER, LORD. *Jamaica.* London 1936.

PARES, R. *A West India Fortune.* London 1950. The history of a West Indian sugar plantation in the Island of Nevis and then of a sugar factory business in Bristol based on the family records of the Pinney family.

SIMEY, T. S. *Welfare and Planning in the West Indies.* Oxford 1946.

THORNTON, A. P. *West India Policy Under the Restoration.* Oxford 1956.

'THE TIMES.' 'The British Caribbean.' London 1950. Eight articles and a leading article from *The Times* reprinted as a pamphlet.

WILLIAMS, E. *Documents on British West Indian History 1807–1833.* Port of Spain 1952.

WILLIAMS, E. *Capital and Slavery.* Chapel Hill 1945.

III. AFRICA

ALTRINCHAM, LORD. *Kenya's Opportunity.* London 1955. The autobiography of Sir Edward Grigg, a former governor of Kenya.

APTER, D. *The Gold Coast in Transition.* Princeton 1955. A case study of political institutional transfer.

AWOLOWO, O. *Path to Nigerian Freedom*. London 1947. Foreword by M. Perham. A book 'written in the forthright, almost sledge-hammer, tradition of political pamphleteering'.

BROOKES, E. H. *South Africa in a Changing World*. Cape Town 1953. A short essay portraying South Africa in world perspective by a leading South African who represented the Africans of Natal in the Senate for more than fifteen years.

CAMERON, SIR D. *My Tanganyika Service and Some Nigeria*. London 1939. The autobiography of a distinguished colonial governor who played a leading role in the development of indirect rule.

CAROE, SIR OLAF. 'Land Tenure and the Franchise. A Basis for Partnership in African Plural Societies.' *Journal of African Administration*. October 1954.

CAROTHERS, J. C. *The African Mind in Health and Disease: A Study in Ethnopsychiatry*. Geneva. W.H.O. 1953.

CAROTHERS, J. C. *The Psychology of Mau Mau*. Government Printer. Nairobi 1954.

Cmd. 1922. *Indians in Kenya*. H.M.S.O. 1923.

Cmd. 2387. *Report of the East African Commission*. Chairman, the Hon. W. Ormsby-Gore, M.P. H.M.S.O. 1925.

Cmd. 3234. *Report of the Commission on Closer Union of the Dependencies in Eastern and Central Africa*. Chairman, Sir E. Hilton Young. H.M.S.O. 1929.

Cmd. 4556 of 1934. *Report of the Kenya Land Commission*. Chairman, Sir Morris Carter.

Cmd. 9475. *East Africa Royal Commission Report 1953–55*. Chairman, Sir Hugh Dow. H.M.S.O. 1955.

COUPLAND, SIR R. *Exploitation of East Africa 1856–1890*. London 1939.

COUPLAND, SIR R. *East Africa and its Invaders*. Oxford 1938. Reissued 1956.

DAVIDSON, BASIL. *The African Awakening*. London 1955. A commentary on conditions in the Belgian Congo and Angola.

DE KIEWIET, C. W. *The Imperial Factor in South Africa. A Study in Politics and Economics*.

DE KIEWIET, C. W. *History of South Africa*. Oxford 1941. A graphic outline of the social and economic development of the Union.

DIKE, K. ONWUKA. *Trade and Politics in the Niger Delta 1830–1885*. Oxford 1956.

FRANKEL, S. HERBERT. *Capital Investment in Africa*. London 1938. A companion volume to Lord Hailey's *An African Survey*.

GUNTHER, JOHN. *Inside Africa.* London 1955. A comprehensive survey of the whole African continent by a distinguished American author.

HAILEY, LORD. *Native Administration in the British African Territories.* H.M.S.O. 1950–53. 5 volumes.

HAILEY, LORD. *An African Survey.* London 1938. Revised, 1957. The monumental study of political, social and economic problems of Africa south of the Sahara.

HALPERIN, V. *Lord Milner and the Empire—The Evolution of British Imperialism.* London 1952. A study of the evolution of the Commonwealth in the light of Milner's achievements, of his ideas and of their influence upon others.

HANNA, A. J. *The Beginnings of Nyasaland and North Eastern Rhodesia 1859–95.* Oxford 1956. Traces the early history of missionary and commercial activity in the region of Lakes Nyasa and Tanganyika, and continues with a detailed study of the building up of the Nyasalandadministration during the first four year s of its existence.

HODGKIN, THOMAS. *Nationalism in Colonial Africa.* London 1956. A comparative study of the theory and practice of colonial policies of the main colonial powers in the post-war era and an examination of the anatomy of African nationalism.

HUXLEY, E. *White Man's Country. Lord Delamere and the Making of Kenya.* 2 volumes. New Edition. London 1953.

JOHNSTON, SIR HARRY. *A History of the Colonization of Africa.* Cambridge 1899. This history covers the exploits of the British and the foreign peoples who have participated in the colonization of Africa. The author himself played a leading role in the opening up of Africa.

KUCZYNSKI, R. R. *A Demographic Survey of the British Colonial Empire.* London 1948–53.
Volume I. West Africa.
Volume II. East Africa, etc.

LEWIS, ROY. *Sierra Leone.* A Modern Portrait. London 1954.

LUGARD, LORD. *The Dual Mandate in British Tropical Africa.* London 1922.

MACMILLAN, MONA. *Introducing East Africa.* 2nd Revised Edition. London 1955.

MACMILLAN, W. M. *Complex South Africa. An Economic Footnote to History.* London 1930.

MACMILLAN, W. M. *Cape Colour Question. A Historical Survey.* London 1927.

MACMILLAN, W. M. *Bantu Boer and Briton. The Making of the South African Native Problem.* London 1929.

MACMILLAN, W. M. *Africa Emergent. A Survey of Social, Political and Economic Trends in British Africa.* Pelican Books 1949.

MARAIS, J. S. *The Cape Coloured People 1652–1937.* London 1939. A study of racial relations.

MARQUARD, LEO. *The Peoples and Politics of South Africa.* London 1952.

MARVEL, TOM. *The New Congo.* New York 1948. A general survey of the history and development of the Belgian Congo by an American author.

MILLIN. S. G. *Rhodes.* London 1933. New and Revised Edition London 1952.

OLDHAM, J. H. *New Hope in Africa.* London 1955. The philosophy and aims of the Capricorn Society.

OLIVER, ROLAND. *The Missionary Factor in East Africa.* London 1952.

ONABAMIRO, S. D. *Food and Health.* Penguin Books, West African Series 1953.

PERHAM, M., and CURTIS, L. *The Protectorates of South Africa.* Oxford 1935. The question of their transfer to the Union.

PERHAM, M., and SIMMONS, J. *African Discovery.* London 1942. An anthology from the works of the British explorers of Africa covering the period from 1769 to 1873.

PERHAM, M. *Lord Lugard.* London 1956. Volume I of Lord Lugard's official biography covering the years 1858–98.

PERHAM, M., and HUXLEY, E. *Race and Politics in Kenya.* London. 1st Edition, London 1944. New and Revised Edition 1956. A debate by correspondence. The latest edition contains a reassessment of the position as seen in 1955.

RICHARDS, AUDREY (ed.) *Economic Development and Tribal Change.* A Study of Immigrant Labour in Buganda. Cambridge.

ROSE, J. HOLLAND, NEWTON, A. P., BENIANS, E. A. (General Editors.) *The Cambridge History of the British Empire.* Volume VIII. South Africa, Rhodesia and the Protectorate. Cambridge 1936. A standard work on the economic and political history of Southern Africa.

STEER, G. L. *Judgement on German Africa.* London 1939.

'THE TIMES.' 'South African Realities.' London 1955. Special articles and a leading article from *The Times* reprinted as a pamphlet.

TOWNSEND, MARY E. *The Rise and Fall of Germany's Colonial Empire 1884–1918,* New York 1930.

U.G. 61/1955. *Summary of the Report of the Commission for the Socio-Economic Development of the Bantu Areas within the Union of South Africa.* The 'Tomlinson Report'.

UNITED NATIONS. *Enlargement of the Exchange Economony in Tropical Africa.* 1954. Deals with structural changes taking place within the traditional economies of tropical Africa in response to the widening of the market and the commercialization of production.

WALKER, E. A. *The Great Trek.* 3rd Edition, London 1948.

WALKER, E. A. *History of South Africa.* First published 1928. Revised as *A History of Southern Africa* 1957.

INDEX

*

Aba riots, 203
abolition of slave-trade, 45, 53, 145
Aburi, 165
Accra, 93, 150, 204, 219
Achimota, 216
administration, *see* Law
Admiralty, 31, 46, 129
Africa, continental, 11, 92, 95–6, 139–41, 148, 151, 165, 186, 205, 217, 275; early southern, 10, 85, 125; limited natural resources of, 153 ff., 217; partition of, 154 ff., 171–2; as a 'scramble', 162–4; significance of, 158, 162
African Congress movement, 237, 291
African Lakes Corporation, 151
Afrikaner national sentiment, origins and growth of, 85, 97, 110, 125, 136–9, 192 ff., 222 ff.
Aggrey, Dr. J.K., 181
agriculture; colonial, conditions, development, difficulties of, 12, 19, 28, 56, 166, 190, 194, 213, 256, 263–6; beginning of, Cape, 97 ff., Kenya, 178, Rhodesian, 174; Imperial College of Tropical, 186
Albany, Congress of, 36–7
Algoa Bay, 99, 108
America, British North, 9, 14, 16, 28 ff., 37, 48, 68, 123, 183, and *see* Canada
American expansion and trade, 15, 16, 42, 101, 129, 136, 162; views on colonies, 9, 45–6, 67, 184, 221—Negro influence on, 204, 217; *see also* U.S.A.
Amery, Rt. Hon. L. S., 76, 77, 180–2, 200, 207, 211, 298
'Anti-colonialism', 26, 183, 217, 221 ff., 263; among 'settlers', 253, 272
Antigua, 13, 81
apartheid (and *see* 'segregation'), 222–232
Assemblies, Colonial Legislative, or Parliaments, 32 ff., 63 ff., 83, 86–9, 93–4, 112, 116, 214–5; East Africa, 179–83; High Commission, 248; Central African, 251 ff.; legal standing of, 58, 81, 176; development of, neglected, 204, 272
'Apprenticeship', slave, 58 ff., 65, 81
Arabs, 95–6, 141, 148–53, 158–9; significance of their trade, 162
Architecture, colonial, 56, 99–100
Asians, as immigrants, 82, 224–5; in East Africa, 235 ff. *See also* Indians
Ashanti, 22, 182, 273
Asquith, Rt. Hon. H. H., 187
Augier, Dr. F. R., 89
Australia, 47, 63, 68, 183
authoritarianism in the newer Africa, 274
Azikiwe, Dr., 217–8

'backward' peoples, relations of 'advanced' and, 229–32 *et passim*
'backwardness', 11, 18 ff.; term become 'taboo', 221, 269
Bacon, Francis, 13, 166
Bagamoyo, 153, 159
Baganda (the people), *see* Buganda (the region), and Uganda
Baikie, Dr. W. B., 143, 145
Baker, Sir Samuel, 148, 154
Balfour Declaration, 76
Bamangwato, 147, 163, 169; split among, 267–9
Banks, Sir Joseph, 47, 141–2
Bantu languages, and use of vernacular, 18, 98, 117, 239
Baptist missions, 54, 84
Barbados, 13–14, 56, 81, 208, 215
Barkly, Sir Henry, 87
Barnard, Lady A., 31
Barnato, Barney, 167
Barnes, Mr. Leonard, 61

Index

Barotseland, 172
Barrow, Sir John, 146
Barth, Heinrich, 142–3
Basuto, Basutoland, 117, 127, 130, 135, 139, 193
Bathurst, Earl, 45
Bechuanaland, 115, 127, 139, 146, 152, 154, 168–9; British, 169
Beira, 171, 174
Belize, 222
Benin, 19, 96
Bennett, Gordon, 150
Bentham, Jeremy, 53
Benue, River, 142
Berbice, 46, 84
Berlin Conference, 92, 164, 169; its 'principles', 156
Bethelsdorp, 108, 114
Bible Society, British and Foreign, 54
Bismarck, Prince, 155–6
Bledisloe Report, 250
Boer republics and republicanism, 103, 128, 168, 172–3, 194, 197–9, 226–8
Botany Bay, 47, 64
Botha, Gen. Louis, 187
Bounty, voyage of, 47
Boyd-Orr, Lord, 206
Braddock, General, 37
Brazil, 14
Brazzaville, 155
British Columbia, 72
British Honduras, 222
Broken Hill, 174
Brougham, Lord, 84
Brussels, 155, 161
Budo School, 216
Buganda, 148, 151, 160, 162; Kabaka of, 245–6
Bulawayo, 128, 173, 174
Buller, Charles, 64, 65, 69
Burchell, William, 146, 152
Burke, Edmund, 45, 52
Burns, Sir Alan, 88
Burton, Richard, 148
Bushmen, 18, 97, 100
Bustamante, Sir Alexander, 208, 217
Buxton, (Sir) Thomas Fowell, 52, 53, 55, 57–8, 60–1, 113–14, 120, 124, 131–2, 188
Byron, Capt. John, 46

Calabar, 145
Caledon, Earl of, 108
Cambridge, 42, 52, 147–8, 150
Cameron, Sir Donald, 182, 201, 203–4, 242
Cameroons, 156, 187
Campbell v. *Hall*, 30, 87, 88
Canada, 21, 35, 37, 46, 48, 62, 64, 73–4, 76, 86–7, 136; self government in, development of, 66–71; Maritime Provinces of, 60, 70
Canning, George, 57–8, 83
Cape Coast, 14, 145
Cape of Good Hope, 16, 47–8, 58, 64, Chapter 5 *passim*, 128–9; responsible government at, 70, 96 ff., 131, 133, 137–9; Rhodes as Prime Minister of, 168, 172–3
Cape Coloured People, 75, 98, 190, 198; *see also* Hottentots
Cape Town, 99, 108, 111–13, 131
Capital, new states need of, 260, 271
Capricorn Africa Society, 254
Caprivi Zipfel 157
Carey, William, 54–5
Carlyle, Thomas, 20, 63
Carnarvon, Earl of, 89, 135–6
Castlereagh, Lord, 53
Cathcart, Sir George, 132–3
Cattle, place of, in African economy, 99 ff., 125–6, 129, 130, 137, 174, 178–9, 194
Central Africa, 248–55 and *see* Nyasaland, Rhodesia
Ceylon, 48, 111, 214
Chad, Lake, 142
Chaka, 126; wars of, 126–8
Chamberlain, Joseph, 75–6, 93–4, 168–9, 186–7, 211
Chartered companies, 158, 170–1, 175; British South Africa, 164, 167 ff.; Imperial British East African, 158 ff., 164; Royal Niger, 163–4
Christians, African, 159, 160, 162, 240, 268
Church, Dutch Reformed, 100, 125, 138, 193, 227; *see also* under denominational titles, Missions
Church Missionary Society (C.M.S.), 54, 84, 143, 148, 151, 159
civilization, of India and the East, 11, 19, 27, 73, 90
civilization, Western; 11, 17, 19, 24–7, 56, 83–6, 107, 144, 257; world reaction against, 210 ff., 216; weakened confidence of upholders of, 210, 221–2
Clapham Sect, 51–2, 63

Clarke, Sir Charles Arden, 219
Clarkson, Thomas, 52
Cloete, Col. H., 129
coal, 129, 242
Cobbett, William, 63
cocoa, 165, 188–90, 243, 256, 258
Codrington College, 84
coffee, 178, 235, 242
Cohen, Sir Andrew, 246
Coillard, François, 172
Colesberg, 101
'colonialism'; in theory, 26, 42, 111, 190, 221; in practice, 165
Colonial Office, 24, 39, 45, 73–4, 76; in slavery crisis, 58 ff., 63–5, 79, 81, 83; as builder of Crown Colony system, 88 ff., 92–4; dealings of, with Cape frontier, 122 ff., 133; with tropical Africa, 175 ff.; views on mining, 175–6, 199–200; reorganization of, 199–200; on need of social services, 206–9; backs 'indirect rule' (q.v.), and thinks again, 215; in modern constitution building, 220, 246, 271
Colonial Service, 33–4, 94, 165, 178, 183, 188, 217, 220, 271; expansion of 200; Africans in, 261. *See also* District Commissioners, (D.C.s), Governor, (the Colonial)
colonial *status*, 18, 73–4, 106, 111, 138
colonies; and 'the colonial question', 9–10, 16, 23–4, 29, 45–6, 93–4, 106, 117–8, 123, 143, 183–5, 208–9, 221; unpopularity of, 62 ff., 66, 199; wider issues involved than, Race and Colour, 231–2
colonization; European or Western, 17, 34–5, 80 ff., 95–6, 100–1, 111, 130, 151, 153; some results of, 266–7. *See* Planters, Settlers, etc.
'Colour'; undue modern stress on significance of Race and; 184, 195, 217, 231–2, 235–6, 253
Columbus, Christopher, 82
Congregationalism (or Independency), 28, 54, 114
'commandos', origin of, 100, 120
Commissioners, Eastern, at Cape, 111, 115–16
Commissions; Cave, 175; Hilton Young (*Closer Union*), 181–2, 184, 190, 250; Kenya Land, 183; Ormsby-Gore (East African), 180, 182; Phelps-Stokes, 181; Royal East African, 263–5; South African Native Economic, 194; West Indies Royal, 186, 211; and *see* Durham
Commission; High, East African, 248; South African, 131, 135, 139, 169
Commissions; functioning of royal, 39, 69, 91
Commonwealth, 9, 72–8, 168, 207, 219;
Commonwealth Relations (Dominions) Office, 77, 177
communism, 25, 202, 217, 229, 231, 270
Congo, river, 96, 142, 151
Congo Free State, 155, 172; 'atrocities' in, 163
Congo, Belgian, 187–8, 206; 'stabilized' labour in, 258; and *see* Katanga
constitutions, colonial, early, 34, 36, 67; a new order of, 213 ff.
Cook, Capt., 47–8, 141
copper, 99, 176; and *see* Mining
Copper Belt, Northern Rhodesia, 22, 176, 208, 242, 258
cotton, 188, 190, 235
Coupland (Sir) Reginald, 207
courts, law, reform of Cape, 106, 108–10; incident of 'Black Circuit' due to, 109–12, 125, 137; Supreme, Cape and South African, 110, 111, 131, 133, 224
Coussey, Judge (Sir) H., 219
Creoles, British Honduras, 222; *see also* Freetown
Crown Colony system, 88–95; *also* 10, 33, 65, 74, 163, 176, 211–14, 250
Cumming, R.G. Gordon-, 147
Curtis, Mr. Lionel, 76, 177, 205

Dar-es-Salaam, 180, 241
Dawson, Mr. Geoffrey, 207
de Beers Consolidated, 160, 170, 178
de Kiewiet, Dr. C. W., 90
Delagoa Bay, 47, 172
Delamere, Lord, 177–80
Demerara, 46, 82
de Mist, Commissioner, 107
de Soto, 13
development, colonial, 19, 56, 166–7, 200, 207, 230; conditions of further, 260 ff. *See also* agriculture, education, health, social services
Development and Welfare, Colonial (C.D. and W.); the Acts, 208–9, 211; functioning of, 212–3, 242, 262, 271; Development Corporation (C.D.C.), 211

de Wet, General Christian, 109
Devonshire Declaration (paramountcy), 180
diamonds, 106, 135, 154, 242; *see also* de Beers, Kimberley
Dicey, Prof. A. V., 53
Dingaan, 127–8
Discoveries, geographical, 11, 18, 20; and *see* Geography
discrimination, racial, *see* Laws, discriminatory
District Commissioners, the (D.C.s), 217–8, 220, 242, 252, 268, 273–4. *See also* Colonial Service, indirect rule
Dominica, 89
Dominions; and Dominion status, 9, 73–7, 205; and dependencies, 66, 257
Donkin, Sir Rufane, 114
Drake, Sir Francis, 46
Drakensbergen, 127–8, 166
D'Urban, Sir Benjamin, 120–25
Durban, 129, 130
Durham, Earl of, 39, 64, 69; his Report, 69
Dutch, the, 14, 47, 96, 129; Batavian Republic, 107–8; East Indian Company at Cape, 96–103

East Africa; British Protectorate of, 161; German, 156; in general, 47, 126, 146–65, 187–8, 233–48
Education, colonial; results of, 22–3; of slaves 51; in West Indies, 83 ff.; missionary, of Hottentots, 108; at Freetown, 143; and later in West Africa, 145–6; in Rhodesia, 174; Cape Government helps, 137; Phelps-Stokes Reports on, 181; some difficulties of, 212; in newer age, 216–8, 220, 272; check to, in Nyasaland, 251; effects of, on Africans at universities, 269–72
Egypt, 148, 154, 157
Elgin, Earl of, 70, 71, 87
Eliot, Sir Charles, 177
Ellis, Rev. William, mission secretary, 124
Emin Pasha, 154, 163
Empire, British: First, 30, 45–6; referred to, 48, 72, 75–6, 83, 86, 151, 161, 168, 187, 203, 207; Marketing Board, 205
English language, African use of, 251; and cf. Bantu, Swahili
Ensor, Sir Robert, 166
equality, racial, 270
'Exeter Hall'; origin of term, 55; referred to, 58, 60, 181
Eyre, Governor, 88, 89
evangelicalism, 45, 54–5, 85, 100

Fabrigas v. *Mostyn*, 30, 94
Fairbairn, John, 111, 112, 113
Falkland Islands, 46
Federal idea, the, 72 ff., 133–6, 177, 181–3, 218; necessity of, 247–8
Firth, Dr. R., 205
Fish River, Great, as Cape boundary, 102, 117, 126
Fisher, Sir Warren, 200
Florence, SS., affair of, 91
foreigners and foreign interests, in colonies, standing of, 271
Foreign Office, British, 155, 161
Fort Duquesne, 37
Fort Hall, 239
Fort Jameson, 171, 249
Fox, Charles James, 52, 53
Franchise, electoral; Cape practice *in re*, 117, 137–8, 224, 228, 241; adult, introduction of, 214–5, 218, 272–3; 'common roll' and 'communal', debate on, 240–1, 243–4; in Southern Rhodesia, 254–5
Freetown, 51, 93; Creoles of, 143, 216, 222
French, the, in America, 23, 29, 39, 40, 44, 47; in West Indies, 34; in nineteenth-century Canada, 66–7, 71; in Africa, 149, 155–6, 162
French Evangelicals, 130, 171–2
Friends, Society of (Quakers), 51, 196, 214
'Frontier', American theory of, 15 ff.; applied in colonial context, 23, 25, 28, 36, 40, 42, 44, 100 ff., 117–18, Chapter 6, *passim*, 178
Froude, J. A., 207

Gaitskell, Mr. Arthur, 187
Gambia, 87, 89, 142–3, 145, 157, 164
Gandhi, Mahatma, 26, 219, 223
geographical discovery and influences, 11, 18, 23, 257; in Africa, 141; in South Africa, 99–103; in Rhodesia, 174; in Kenya, 177; in Tanganyika, 241

Index

Germans in Africa, 153, 155–8, 160, 162, 168–9, 187, 241–2
Ghana; beginnings of, 220, 222, 257, 261 ff.; aims and influence of, 272; and *see* Gold Coast
Gilbert, Sir Humphrey, 13
Gilbert, W. S., 268
Gilks, Dr. J. L., 206
gold, 106, 145, 154, 188; Witwatersrand, 136, 172–3, 194–5, 226
Gold Coast, 64, 143, 145, 164, 188–9, 215; constitutional development in, 218–21
Goldie, Sir George Taubman, 158, 164
Gondokoro, 148, 154
Gordon, General Charles, 154–5, 159, 167
Gordon, George W., 88
Government, British; colonial policy of, on slavery, 58 ff.; at Cape, 107, 111, 116, 129, 132 ff.; South African, 139, 169, 187; on West Indian reconstruction, 63, 68, 81 ff., 87, 91 ff.; post-war, 208 ff.; in tropical Africa, 141–4, 149, 160–3, 171, 179–83, 199 ff., 219–20, 230; on Central African Federation, 246, 250–2; adopts Indirect Rule, 204; pronouncement in 1950 on, 208–9; hesitancy of, 154, 199 ff., 258–9
government, colonial, passing of, as 'transfer of power', 270
government, local; in colonies, 81–2, 111–2, 202, 240; relations of, in new states, with central authority, 273–4
Governor, the Colonial, 30–2, 38, 63, 67, 69–70, 74, 87–9, 92–4, 213–14, 219; caution of, 271
Graaff-Reinet, 101, 103
Grahamstown, 103, 111, 121
Grant, Charles, the elder, 52
Grant, Charles, Lord Glenelg, 122–5, 137
Grant, Sir J. P., 90, 211
Grenada, 87
Grenville, George, 40
Grey, Earl (Lord Howick), 70, 71, 80, 82, 87, 138
Grey, Governor Sir George, 72, 133–5, 137, 139
Griqualand Griquas ('Bastards'), 127, 130–1, 154
Grogan, Col. E., 171
Guadeloupe, 48, 50
Guggisberg, Sir Gordon, 189
Guiana, 13
Guiana, British, 50, 56, 59, 79, 82

Hailey, Lord, 205, 207–8, 233
Haiti, 49, 51, 88
Hall, H. Duncan, 14
Hampden, John, 33
Hannington, Bishop, 159
Hartley, Henry, 154
Hastings, Warren, 44
Health conditions in colonies, 19–20, 32, 79, 82–3, 86, 140–2, 145–6, 165, 188, 200–1; new emphasis on, 204, 211; *see also* Medicine, Nutrition
Heber, Bishop, 85
Herschel, district of, 193–4
Hertzog, Gen. J. B. M., 193, 197–8, 224
High Veld, South African, 101, 126–31, 134, 147, 166; Rhodesian, 151, 174
Hinterland (and 'spheres of influence'), 156
Hintza, Chief, 121, 124
History, study of, 10–11, 26–7, 230–2, 256–7
Hobson, J. A., 25, 232
Hofmeyr, J. H. (first), 168, 173, (second) 138, 226
Homer, 19
Horton, Sir R. Wilmot, 64
Hottentots, 97, Chapter 5 *passim*; vagrancy among, 107, 116, 120
Howe, Joseph, 67–9
Hudibras, 32
Huguenots at Cape, 97
Huggins, Sir Godfrey (Lord Malvern), 253, 273
humanitarianism, 38, 144, 153, 162; new phase of, 260; and *see* Philanthrophy
Huskisson, William, 115
Huxley, Mrs. Elspeth, 180, 263

Imperial Conference, 75–7
'Imperial Factor', 37, 168
Imperialism, 25–7, 45, 75 ff., 136, 166, 157, 187, 217, 219, 230; and the 'Imperial Factor', 37, 168
Independency (*see* Congregationalism)
India, 26, 73, 219, 223; British, 9, 26, 73, 75, 149, 180, 223; East, Company, and trade, 44, 57; Dutch, at Cape, 96–102
Indian Civil Service (I.C.S.), 26, 33, 201
Indian Congress, 26, 179–80, 217
Indians, American, 14, 16–17, 20, 28, 35 ff., 40 ff., 45, 136

Indians (and Asians) as immigrants, 156, 179–80, 223
Indies, East, 96, 97, 113
indirect rule, 24, 184–5, 189, 199–205, 215; comparison of, with direct rule, 90–1, 202; passing of, 274. *See also* (Native Administrations)
International African Association, 155
Islam, 19
ivory, 152

Jackson, Sir F. S., 159
Jamaica, 49, 56, 58, 62, 145, 208, 212; constitutional moves in, 63–5, 86–92; 214–5; economic and social conditions in, 79–83 (and *see* West Indies); free peasantry in, 82, 85, 88 ff., 260; Jews in, 80; 'Rebellion', 65, 87–8
Jameson Raid, 172–3
Janssens, General, 107–8
Jebb, Mr. Richard, 74, 75
Jinja, 162
Johannesburg Joint Council of Europeans and Natives, 196–7
Johnson, Sir William, 36, 37
Johnston, Sir Harry, 152, 163–4, 171, 249
Johnston, Mr. Wallace, 216
Jones, Rt. Hon. A. Creech, 92
Jones, Dr. T. Jesse, 181

Kafirs; use of the term, 100; and 'Kafir' Wars, 98 *et seq.*, 119 ff. *See also* Xosa (Ama)
Kaffraria, British, 131
Kalahari, 127, 146–7, 168
Kampala, 159, 160
Karagwe, 18
Kariba Gorge, 252
Karroo, 99, 101
Katanga, 172, 176, 206, 258
Kat River, 119, 121
Kei River, Great, 121
Keiskamma River, 103, 119
Kenya, 14, 177–85, 189, 195–6, 207, 238–41, 258, 262–3; and *see* East Africa, Settlers, Kikuyu, Masai, Wakamba
Kenya Highlands, 12, 151, 159, 177; as 'white', 178–80, 235, 238
Kenyatta, Jomo, 204, 239
Kerr, Philip (Marquess of Lothian), 191
Khama, Chief, 163, 169
Khartoum, 261
Kikuyu, 179, 184, 204, 206, 238–40
Kilimanjaro, 148, 149, 177, 180, 187
Kilwa (Quiloa), 152, 153
Kimberley, 135, 154, 167–8; and *see* de Beers, diamonds, Griqualand
King, the, in government of colonies, 29–32, 36, 37, 43, 44, 67
Kingsley, Miss Mary, 23
King William IV, 123–4
Kipling, Rudyard, 25, 26, 166, 215
Kirk, Sir John, 150
Kitchener, Lord, 156
Knibb, Rev. William, 85
Knysna, 99
Kondoa Irangi, 153
Krapf and Rebmann, missionaries, 148
Kruger, President S. J. P., 172, 198
Kuruman, 127, 167–9

Labour, in the colonies, 14, 22, 49–50, 106, 141, 144, 166, 190, 200; living and working conditions of, 107–9, 115, 173–4, 217, 260, 265; scarcity of trained, 261–2; migrant, 126, 193–4, 227–9, 234–5, 247, 258; transition from slavery, 58–61; supply of, 80–2, 97, 114, 171, 225–6, 234, 258; competition of white and coloured, 191, 194–5. *See also* Hottentots, slavery
Labour Party, British, 216, 219, 248, 268; attitude of, to bi-partisan policy, 253
labour, policy of colonial governments on, 258–60
Lagos, 93, 142, 164, 203, 204
Laird, MacGregor, 143
laissez-faire economics, 33, 43, 83, 94, 211, 216, 258
Land: American Indians' rights on, 17, 36, 38; colonial demand for and use of, 99 ff., 108, 117–8, 124 ff.; in West Indies, 88; conditions on, in modern South Africa, 193–4; in Rhodesia, 174–5; in East Africa, 178, 227–8, 262–4; economic development of, 21, 29, 190; squatting on, 128, 137, 193; individual displacing communal tenure of, 264–5
Lander brothers, 142
landdrost, the, 106
Lavigerie, Cardinal, 151, 157, 161
law; and administration, 10, 28, 30 ff., 38, 43, 64 ff., 124, 128–9, 133, 143–4,

law; and administration—*contd.*
162–5, 175, 183–5, 189, 212 ff., 261; and order, 17, 30, 33, 38, 50–1, 114, 117–8, 133, 152, 157–8; effect on, of transfer of power, 270 ff.; (law) Koranic, 201; Roman, 12, 17; Roman-Dutch, 134; tribal, and custom, 120, 121 (*and see* Indirect Rule); law, the rule of, 30, 134; at the Cape, Chapter 5 *passim*
laws: 'discriminatory', 116, 176, 195, 198–9, 229–32, 252, 258
laws (statutes) particular; Cape Hottentot Code, 108–9; Cape Hottentot Vagrancy Law, 116–7, 121, 125; Cape 49th Ordinance, 126; Cape 50th, 115–7, 125; Cape Masters and Servants Act, 117; South African Natives Land Act, 193; South African Natives Urban Areas Act, 228
Laws, Dr. Robert, 251
League of Nations, 20, 180, 189, 210; Mandates of, 180, 221, 223–4, 242
Lenin, V. I., 25
Leopold II, King, 155
Leopoldville, 185
Lewis, 'Monk', 56, 79
Leys, Dr. Norman, 181, 221, 238
liberalism, Western, 24, 112–14, 137–9, 187, 195: South African Nationalist repudiation of, 197; changing modern trend of, 162, 191, 195, 198–9
Liberal Party, British, 138–9, 187, 199
Liberia, 207–22
Lippert Concession, 170
Livingstone, David, 18, 47, 54, 127, 146–50, 155, 167, 233; on need of commerce and Christianity, 151–2
Lloyd George, D. (Earl), 211
Lobengula, Chief, 169, 170–2
London, City of, 29, 36, 50, 167; County Council (L.C.C.), 214; as African political centre, 267
London Missionary Society (L.M.S.), 54, 107–8, 112, 119, 124, 130, 147
Lovedale mission, 55, 216
Lowe, Robert, 83
Lualaba, river, 172
Luapula, river, 172
Lugard, F. D. (Lord), 160–2, 164, 177, 189–90, 199, 201–3, 238, 258
Lushington, Stephen, 52, 116
Lydenburg, 130
Lyttelton, Oliver (Lord Chandos), 240–1

Macaulay, Lord, 44, 115
Macaulay, Zachary, 51
McCulloch, Dr. W. E., 206
MacDonald, Sir John, 73, 74
MacKay, Alexander, of Uganda, 151, 159
Mackenzie, Bishop, 150
Mackenzie, Rev. J., 85, 169 *and note*
Mackinnon, Sir William, 154, 158–9
Maclean, Capt. George, 144
maize, 12, 99, 129, 174, 206, 242
Makanna, 103
Malan, Dr. D. F., 192, 198, 222, 230
Maji-Maji rebellion, 241
Majuba, 136
malaria, 20, 21, 130, 143, 146, 150, 208
Malaya, 203, 207–8
Malays, Cape, 98
Malinowski, Professor B., 23, 200, 207
Malthus, 64, 263–4
Mansfield, Lord, 30, 51, 195
Maqomo, Chief, 119
Marais, Dr. J. S., 110
marriage customs, West Indian, 80, 85–6
Marx, Karl, 25
Masai, the, 18, 95, 148, 159, 177–9, 206, 238
Mashona, 169, 171, 173
Matabele, 127–8, 134, 169–72, 248
Matopo Hills, 173
Mauch, Carl, 154
Mau-Mau, 233, 238–40, 263
Mauritius, 48
Maynier, H. C., 103, 107, 109
Mbandine, King, 163
Medicine, School of Tropical, 187
mercantilism, 29 ff., 46–8, 97
Metcalfe, Sir Charles (Lord), 70, 87
Methodism, methodists, 45, 54, 84, 145
Mico Charity, 83
middle class, African, 145–6, 204–5, 209, 234, 275; middle-class 'emergent', 21, 23, 27, 209, 216–8, 237–8, 254–5, 265 ff.; in Tanganyika, 243–4; West Indian, compared with, 266–7; early neglect of, 271–2; responsibility resting on, 267 ff.
militia, colonial, 31, 88
millet, 101
Milner, Sir A. (Lord), 167; Milner Kindergarten, 138, 177, 191

Milton, John, 152
mines, mining rights, 170–1, 175–6, 192, 199–200, 225, 234, 242, 265 and *see* copper, diamonds, gold
missionaries; Christian, activities and influence of, 17, 54, 85, 103, 112, 119, 141, 145–7, 158, 167, 174, 256; modern trend in, 181
missionary movement, Protestant foreign, 45, 54 ff., 84 ff.
missions, Anglican, 83, and *see* C.M.S. S.P.G., U.M.C.A.; Scots, 54, 145, 150, 238, 251; 'Free Kirk', 55. Moravian, 54, 84. *See also* Baptists, L.M.S., Roman Catholics
Mitchell, Sir Philip E., 214, 263
Mississippi, 13, 35
Moffat, J. S., 169
Moffat, Robert, 127, 167
Moghul Empire, 26, 44
Montreal, 67
Montserrat, 13, 82
Morant Bay, 87
Moselekatze, 127–8, 169, 170
Moshesh, 127, 130–1
Mozambique, 158
Mpwapwa, 153, 243
Mtesa of Buganda, 151, 154, 158
Murray, Dr. Gilbert, 210
Muscat, 149
Mwanga, 159

Nairobi, 177, 182, 238, 242
Namaqualand, 99
Namier, Sir Lewis, 28, 44
Napoleon I, 48
Natal, 127, 129, 131, 223
nationalism, African, 227, 233–4, 247–8, 254–6, 257, 265; claims of, 266–7
Native Administration (or Authority), 'N.A.', 201–5, 213, 225, 240. *See also* Indirect Rule
'native policy', use of the term, 250
Navigation Acts, *see* trade laws
Navy, Royal, 129, 143
Negroes, American, 28, 42, 106, 181, 217
Nehru, Prime Minister, 26
Nevis, 13, 14, 56, 82
New England, 14, 28, 101
New Orleans, 35
New York, 29, 40
New Zealand, 14, 47, 64–5, 174
Newton, John, 144
Ngami, Lake, 147
Niger, River, 96, 142, 164; expedition of 1841 to, 61
Nigeria, 145, 164, 199; constitutional changes in, 215, 218, 261 ff.; as a unit, 270; Southern, 202–3; indirect rule in Northern, *see* Indirect Rule
Nile River, 148, 154, 162, 245
Nkrumah, Dr. Kwame, 218, 220, 269, 275
Nonconformists, English, 29, 55, 84
Norman, Governor Sir Henry, 90
Nova Scotia, 66 ff.
Nugent, Lady, 56
Nyasa, Lake, 149, 150
Nyasaland, 152–3, 158, 161, 165, 171, 228, 235, 246; as a unit, 270; education in, 251; labour in, 259, 265
Nutrition, Reports on, 205–7; on mines, 258; and *see* Health

Ohio, 35, 37, 40
oil, palm, 143, 258
Oil Rivers, 143, 164
Oldham, Dr. J. H., 181
Olivier, Sydney (Lord), 88, 90, 211; on labour, 260
Ontario, 66–7
Orange Free State (or Sovereignty), 127, 134–5
Orange River, 99, 126, 128, 130–1
Orde-Browne, Sir St. J., 141
Ormsby-Gore, W. (Lord Harlech), 180, 208
Oswell, William, 147
Ottawa Agreements, 205
Oxford, 167; colonial affairs at, 200
Owen, Capt. W. F., 47, 114

Pacific, South, 19, 47
Paine, Thomas, 45
Palmerston, Lord, 132–3
Panama Canal, 21
Pares, Prof. Richard, 14
Park, Mungo, 96, 141–2
Parliamentary government, 32, 45, 52, 81, 89–90, 94; as legacy to colonies, 272
Parliamentary Select Committee on colonies, 66
Pass laws, South African, 108, 228
Peace; of Paris, 35, 39, 46; of Versailles, 49
Peel, Sir Robert, 70
Pennsylvania, 28

Peters, Dr. Karl, 159–60
Philanthropy, 51–3, 83–4, 103, and *see* Humanitarianism
Philip, Dr. John, 47, 54, 113–17, 120, 123–5, 130–2, 137, 138, 169, 179, 248, 260; Philip MSS., 113 *note*, 131
Philip, Mrs. J., 120, 123
Pinneys (of Nevis), 14, 56, 57
Pim, Howard, 196, 197
Pitt, William (Earl of Chatham), 48
Pitt, William, the younger, 44, 48, 49, 52, 53, 56
Placemen, 'places'; 31, 274
Planters, colonial, 14, 35, 165; in West Indies, 55 ff., 81, and *see* Sugar, Settlers
politics, colonial; development of, 93–4, 110 ff., 168, 196, 204–5, 209, 211, 253–4; in Kenya, 183–5; in post-war West Africa, 215–21; in Uganda, 245–7; one-party trend in African territories, 267–9; demagogy in, 269; place of African masses in, 274; exclusion of non-whites in, in South Africa, 225, 228–9. For African background, *see tribal society*
Pondoland, 128, 134
Pontiac's War, 39
population, colonial; statistics of, 20, 35, 86–7, 152; at Cape, 96, 106; in Central Africa, 248; local pressures of, 265–6, in Rhodesia, 174, 176; in Kenya, 178–9; distribution of, in Tanganyika, 241
populations, colonial, class divisions of, 80, 88, 92–4, 98, 126, 156, 224; South African, compared, 191
Portal, Sir George, 160
Port Elizabeth, 111
Portuguese, the, 11, 96, 148–9, 156, 158, 171
Potchefstroom, 233
Press, the colonial, development of, 111, 216–7
Pretoria, 127, 173
Pringle, Thomas, 111
Protectorates, 17, 157, 171; South African High Commission, 165

Quebec, 72; Quebec Act, 44, 66
Queen Adelaide, Province of, 121–3, 125
Queen Victoria, 26, 75, 86, 147
quinine, 12, 143, 145
Quilimane, 147

Race and Colour, American Negro over-emphasis on, 204. *See* Colour
'race relations', 18, 38, 119, 183–5, 191, 228–32, 233; advantages of mixed colonies, 262 ff.; South African Institute of, 196
Raleigh, Sir Walter, 13
Railway, Uganda, 161–2, 179–80, 235; Voi-Taveta branch of, 180, 183
Railways, Rhodesian, 174, Sierra Leone, 186; South African, 172; West African, 186
Rand mines, *see* Gold
Read, Rev. James, 109, 112, 119
'regionalism', desirable, difficulty of, 247
Reitz, Hon. F. W., and Deneys, 134
Retief, Pieter, 128–9
Reservations, Indian, 38; and Reserves; 'Native', 19, 137–8, 192–3, 196, 238, as 'locations', Hottentot and 'Kafir', 108, 121
Revolution, American, 15, 28, 43, 45, 95, 210; Whig, 39
revenues, colonial, *see* taxation
Rhodes, Cecil J., 37, 74, 85, 139, 158, 161, 166–76, 178, 186, 249
Rhodesia, 74, 207, 248–55; mineral rights in, 175–6, 199–200; Northern, 92, 199–200; Southern, 172 ff., self-government in, 177, 'native' policy of, 173–5, progress in, 249 ff.
Rhodesias, Federation of, and Nyasaland, 176, 246, 248 ff.; development of, 252–3; negative African attitude to, 268–9; the local origins of move for, 270
Richards, Sir A., Lord Milverton, 218
Rift Valley, Great, 159, 161, 238
rinderpest, epidemic, 19, 178–9
Rio Cobre irrigation, 90
Rogers, Sir F. (Lord Blachford), 68
Roman Catholic missions, 44, 80, 160, 178, 218; White Fathers', 151, 157
Rosebery, Earl of, 161
Ross, Sir Ronald, 21
Round Table, the, 76, 207
Rousseau, J. J., 51
Rovuma River, 150, 152
Rowntree, Mr. Seebohm, 192
Royal Empire (Commonwealth) Society, 75; Royal Geographical Society (R.G.S.), 146, 148
Ruanda-Urundi, 187
Rudd Concession, 170

rum, 49, 63
Russell, Lord John, 67, 70, 132

St. Domingue, 49
St. Kitts, 13, 81, 208
St. Lawrence River, 72
St. Vincent, 208
Salisbury (Fort), 171, 173, 174, 186
Sand River Convention, 132–3
Schmoller, Gustav, 31
Secretary of State, the, 31, 34, 70, 75, 89, 120, 171, 200, 221; residual power of, over chartered companies, 171; veto power of, 74
Secretary, the Colonial (or Chief), 31–4, 45; his secretariat, 213
'segregation', policy of, 103, 192–9, restarted as *apartheid*, *q.v.*, 222
Select Committee, Joint Lords and Commons, on East Africa, 184; South African, on Hertzog Native Bills, 197–8
self-determination, 153, 221, 247
self-government, responsible, 25, 87; evolution of, 62 ff., 71, 93–4; Cape, 133; modern movement towards, 205, 212–20, 247, 257–8; a lesson from, 272
Selous, F. C., 171
Seretse Khama, 267
Settlers (and *see* Kenya, Rhodesia), 195, 213–4, 234, 258; constitution made by, 237–8; in Tanganyika, 182, 242; Africans nervous of, 236–7, 246; modern attitude and standing of, 184–5, 255, 262
Sharp, Granville, 51
Sheffield, Lord, 42
shipping (and *see* trade, colonial), 29, 48, 51, 52
Shire, River and Highlands, 149, 150, 209, 252, 265
Sierra Leone, 51, 141, 143, 164, 222, and *see* Freetown
sisal, 234, 241
Slagter's Nek Rebellion, 109, 110, 137, 162
slavery, crusade against, 45, 49, 55, 58 ff., 112, 132, 157–8, 161
slaves, living conditions of, 50, 51, 79–82, 152–3; status of, 51, 65, 81
slave trade, 14, 50, 60; in Africa, 144–5, 151 ff., 257
Sloane, Sir Hans, 80
Smith, Adam, 29, 39, 62, 115, 264
Smith, Col. (Sir) Harry, 122, 131–2, 137
Smith, John, of Demerara, 58, 84
Smuts, Rt. Hon. General J. C., 47, 177, 187, 189, 198, 205, 222, 224, 226, 270
social services, 83 ff., 183, 193, 200, 211–2; under Indirect Rule, 204; cost of, 247–8; in South Africa, 228; Congo, 258; and *see* agriculture, education, health
Somerset, Lord Charles, 111, 119
Somersett's case, 51
South (i.e. southern) Africa, 16, 37, 65, 72, 76, 132–40, 190–1, 236; missions in, 54, 107 ff.
South Africa, Union of, 139, 167, 173, 176, 190–9; and Southern Rhodesia, 249; constructive side of, 227–8; Nationalist governments in, policy of, and their critics, 194 ff., 222–32; labour and position of 'poor whites' in, 191–4; rebellion in, 187; *South Africans* and *Afrikaners* in, 131, 197; modern economic and industrial revolution in, 225–6
South West Africa, 156, 168, 187, 223–4
Spanish, the, in America, 12–13, 29, 62–3
S.P.G. (Society for Propagation of the Gospel), 54, 84
Speke and Grant explorations, 148, 158
Spice Islands, 29
Stamp Act, 34, 40
Stanley, H. M., 18, 150–1, 155, 158
Statute of Westminster, 76
Stellenbosch, 99, 227
Stephen, Sir James, 45, 58, 63, 65, 68, 81; the elder, 52
Stockdale, Sir Frank, 57, 206, 211–12
Stockenström, (Sir) Andries, 116, 122
Strÿdom, Prime Minister, 230
Sturge, Joseph, 84
Sudan, 156–7, 230; Gezira scheme in, 187; labour in, 261
sugar, 14, 48, 80, 81, 83, 91; organization of, industry, 49–51, 57 ff., 62–3
Sutherland, Miss L. S., 44
Swahili, use of, as lingua franca, 239
Swaziland, 139, 169; 'freedom' of, 162–3
Swellendam, 100
Sydenham, Lord, 70

Table, Bay, 96; Mountain, 99
Tabora, 153, 158, 243
Tanga, 180

Tanganyika, 148, 172, 182, 187–8, 228–30, 241–4; southern province of, 152; German rule in, 241–2; indirect rule in, 203–4
Tawney, Prof. R. H., 12
Taylor, Sir Henry, 63, 65, 81, 87
taxation and revenue, colonial, 32–3, 40, 43, 74, 82–3, 87, 131, 176, 200; and direct taxation, 202; and expenditure, new phase, 211–12, 220–1, 271–2; West Indian resources limit, 266
tea, 165
technology, modern, 27; and industrialization of colonial societies, 260–3
Temple, Mr. C. L., 190
Tenniel, Sir John, 161
Thackeray, W. M., 28
Thema, Mr. R. V. Selope, 231
Thomas, Rt. Hon. J. H., 180
Thomson, Joseph, 159
Timbuktu, 142
tobacco, 12, 14, 96, 174
Togoland, 156, 187
Tom Cringle's Log, 56
Tomlinson Report, 229
Tongaland, 171
Tororo, 246
Trade, Board of, 30, 38
trade, colonial, 29, 30, 35–6, 38, 45 ff., 71, 143–5, 147, 162–3; depression hits, 205; internal African, 145, 146, 151 ff., 160–1, 175; Uganda, 188; Gold Coast, 188–9
trade laws (Navigation Acts, etc.), 11, 15, 31, 33–4, 40, and *see* Mercentilism
transport, colonial, 18, 25, 29, 49, 98 ff., 107, 129, 141, 146, 174–5, 186–7, 201, 213, 270; by porters, (slaves,) 152; in Tanganyika, 241
Transvaal, 127, 132 ff., 147, 163, 167–9; *Grondwet* of, 133–4, 197
Treasury H.M.'s, 31, 83, 87, 90–1, 93, 161, 187, 200, 212, 271
Treaty states, 122, 130
tribal society, African, 18–19, 23–4, 40, 100–1, 117–8, 140–1, 248–9, 256, 258–60; law and custom in, 130–1, 151, 157–8, 163, 201–2; modern pressure on, 188 ff., 201–4, 262; in South Africa, 192–4; in newest age, Chapter 12 *passim*; persistent conformity of, 267–9
Trek, Great Boer, 125–37, 146, Chapter 6; political significance of, 134, 139
Trinidad, 46, 54, 58, 82, 186, 208
Tripoli, 142
tropics, colonization of, 17, 140–1, 154, 157–8, 178, 188, 208
trusteeship, 44–5, 223, 230
tsetse (trypanosomiasis carrying) flies, 22, 145, 146, 165, 175, 263
Tshekedi Khama, 267–8
Turner, F. J., 15
Twining, Sir Edward (Lord), 242
Tyali, Chief, 120

Uganda, 150–1, 154–5, 158–65, 244–9; Uganda Company, 151, 165; Uganda Agreement, 164, 245–6
Umtali, 171
Uncle Remus, 56
United Empire Loyalists, 66
United Nations, 221, 223–4, 229, 232
United States, 19, 21, 26, 42–3, 71–3, 190, 217–8; Civil War of, 72, 136
University Colleges; Fort Hare, 227, 268; Fourah Bay, 143; Makerere, 248; of Rhodesia and Nyasaland, 252–3; of West Indies, 10, 248; work at, 145, 151
Universities: historical courses and work at, 145, 151, 256–7; Africans at British, 216–18, 261–2, 267 ff.
Universities Mission (U.M.C.A.), 150
uranium, 225
utilitarianism, 45, 53

Vaal River, 128, 131, 172
van der Kemp, Rev. Dr. J., 107, 109
van der Post, Col. L., 19
van Plettenberg, Governor, 101–2
van Riebeeck, Jan, 96–7
Venn, Rev. John, 52
Verwoerd, Dr. H. F., 229
Vienna, Congress of, 53
Victoria Falls, 147, 174, 250
Victoria, Lake, 148, 154–5, 160, 165, 245–6
Virginia, 13, 14, 28–9, 32, 35, 37, 39
Visscher, Sir Hanns, 199, 207
Volta River scheme, 220, 271, 272
von Lettow-Vorbeck, Gen., 187–8

Wachagga, 243
Wakamba, 179
Wakefield, Gibbon, 64 ff., 69
Wallace, A. R., 85

War, course or effects of Seven Years, 35, 48, 50; Napoleonic, 46–7; American Civil, 88, 136; South African, 76, 94, 102, 136, 172–3, 175, 177, 179, 187, 193, 200; First World, 9, 23, 66, 74, 76; in East Africa, 179, 205–6, 211; Second World, 20, 34, 93, 183, 186 ff., 205, 208, 210, 215 ff., 230, 236–7, 239, 260
Warren, Sir C., 169
Washington, George, 28, 37, 40
Watson, Sir Malcolm, 21, 207
Webb, Sidney (Lord Passfield), 32, 33, 157, 181, 183, 207, 220; and Beatrice, 32
Webb, W. P., 16
Welensky, Sir Roy, 253
West Africa (and *see* Gambia, etc.), 24, 48, 84, 141–6, 152, 157, 164, 190, 236; comparison of, with East Africa, 258
West India Committee, 50
West Indies, 10, 13, 29, 46–7, 75, 78, 145, 200, 248; constitutions of, 65; and modern development of, 207–9, 211–2, 214–5; Federated, 261; social conditions in, 55, 56–61, 257; strength and weakness of, 94, 266; trade of, 34, 39, 48 ff.; and *see* individual islands, labour, planters, slavery, sugar
Wilberforce, William, 52, 53, 55, 63, 113–4
Willshire, Fort, 119, 121
Wilson, Sir Samuel, 181–2
Wine-farming, Cape, 100
Wint, Mr. Guy, 90
women, African, position of certain, 203, 234, 239

Xosa, Ama-, 101 ff., 126, 131 ff., 137, and *see* 'Kafirs'

Yao, 152

Zambezi, River, 127, 147, 149–50, 157–8, 170–1, 175, 252
Zanzibar, 47, 149–50, 153, 154, 159
Zulus, 95, 102, 126 ff., 135–6